JOHN TRAIN founded Train Smith Investment Counsel and is chairman of Montrose Advisors. He has written hundreds of columns for the *Wall Street Journal*, the *New York Times*, *Forbes* magazine, *Harvard Magazine*, and the *Financial Times* of London. His best-selling books on investing include *The Craft of Investing*, *The Money Masters*, *The Midas Touch,* and *Preserving Capital and Making It Grow*. He has been appointed to part-time positions by Presidents Reagan, Bush, and Clinton. Married and the father of three daughters, he lives in New York, spends summers in Maine, and travels extensively.

MONEY MASTERS of OUR TIME

John Train

HARPER

NEW YORK • LONDON • TORONTO • SYDNEY

HARPER

HarperCollins books may be purchased for educational, business, or sales promotional use. For information, please e-mail the Special Markets Department at SPsales@harpercollins.com.

First HarperBusiness paperback edition published 2003.

Designed by Elina D. Nudelman

Library of Congress Cataloging-in-Publication Data has been applied for.

ISBN 0–887–30970–4

HB 05.17.2021

Tempora mutantur nos et mutamur in illis.

(Times change and we change in them.)

Contents

Introduction

This book revises and brings up to date the most interesting studies of great investors found in *The Money Masters* and *The New Money Masters,* while adding some remarkable new ones. A few of the masters, including Peter Lynch, George Soros, and John Templeton, have branched off in different directions, so my descriptions emphasize those parts of their careers that illuminate their investment techniques. Two, George Soros and Warren Buffett, have become sufficiently notable so that in addition to describing their investment methods I attempt brief biographical evaluations.

I have always liked to develop relationships with great investment managers. In the 1950s I went to work for and indeed became a client of Imrie de Vegh, whose fund had the best of all performance records in that decade. Some time later, when his firm was still small, I got to know T. Rowe Price and put money under his management, as I did with A. W. Jones and other highly successful investors of that period. Later on my firm invested with Warren Buffett, Mark Lightbown, Julian Robertson, George Soros, Michael Steinhardt, and Ralph Wanger.

In this book I focus on notable portfolio managers, the men whose own decisions to buy and sell have actually made money grow, who are not merely administrators. How do they reason? Where do they get their information? How much do they depend on fact and how much on psychology? What are their stock selection criteria? What stocks are they buying now, and why?

My subjects represent several schools of investing, including "growth," "value," "technology," "emerging markets," "specialty companies," "micro-caps," "turnarounds," "top-down," "bottom-up," and so on.

These schools fall into three main philosophies: futurology—peering into the fog a bit farther than the crowd; lab analysis—studying with a little more care and imagination than others what's under the magnifying glass right now; and opening up a new category in hitherto overlooked areas. Which method you prefer should depend on how you think and *what's not overpopulated at the moment.* Thus, the outstanding investor knows when to change styles. That's the point of my epigraph: "Times change and we change in them."

Although an investor can sometimes strike it rich with a big coup, there's no luck in professional portfolio investing, any more than in master chess. It's a skilled craft, involving many decisions a week. The year-in, year-out manager of a large portfolio can no more pile up a superlative record by luck or accident than one can win a chess tournament by luck or accident. So the techniques that demonstrably do succeed—and those that usually fail—are well worth understanding.

The reader will observe that most of my subjects are older (even retired) men who have followed a definable technique over most of their careers (or perhaps one technique that when appropriate changed into a different one): The longer the record of a particular approach, the more useful it is for purposes of study.

Indeed, the subjects whose investment careers fell in the recent past can be particularly interesting, first, because the passage of time lets us contemplate them with a clearer perspective, and second, because their ideas are no longer regularly accessible in the financial press, even if of great value. For example, T. Rowe Price fell out of favor in 1975, and yet his approach turns out to be particularly applicable to the huge high-tech market boom that continues as I write. I have heard George Gilder—that rare thing, an excellent economist (because he understands transforming technologies)—say that to invest in the information age companies you had to lay aside conventional analysis and make a leap of faith. That is indeed how it had to be done! In Price's lingo, find the leading companies in the "fertile field for growth." Similarly, the smaller companies—now called "micro-caps"—beloved of Philip Carret and Ralph Wanger will surely have their day in the sun once more, as will Robert Wilson's short-side artistry.

The strictly disciplined "value" approach espoused by Benjamin Graham and John Neff and now neglected may well be the appropriate technique in the market cycle that follows the present growth boom.

It's not quite true that there is nothing new under the sun, but the best statements of great principles are often of perennial merit.

In the blowoff phase of a bull market some jazzy operators record marvelous performances for a while, but in the downdraft that follows, many of their favorite holdings go bankrupt and then plunge into the drink like Icarus. Go-go operators regularly lose much more money for their customers than they ever made. Traveling light going up, they drag huge followings down with them when they collapse. This applies to most derivatives speculators and day traders, and to virtually all commodity speculators.*

Anyway, it seems safest to let such practitioners run their course before trying to describe them. There will be some fascinating lessons to be drawn and successful high-tech portfolio managers to study when the present information age stock boom sorts itself out.

Finally, there are always far more ways to lose money than to do well, and all the masters offer valuable admonitions and caveats.

Some chapters of this book were written a while back and then brought up to date. However, in the interest of vividness I have often kept the descriptions in the present tense.

To sum up, I've tried to choose wise masters who illustrate useful methods, and are thus particularly instructive to study. As Bismarck said, even fools profit from their own experiences; how much better to profit from the experience of others!

---

*Commodity speculation is a casino whose purpose is to fleece the customer, not build his capital. It should not be offered to retail investors by reputable securities firms. Why is it illegal to make book on the ponies and legal to solicit bets on sowbellies from ignorant punters?

One

T. ROWE PRICE
MR. GROWTH STOCK

THE GREAT BULL SURGE OF THE 1990S WAS A PERFECT T. Rowe Price market. Everybody got rich, but some people got *really* rich: those who spotted the hot new growth stocks—Microsoft, Intel, Cisco, AOL, and the rest—and rode them to glory. They often made ten times or so on their money—sometimes a hundred times. The investors who failed to tie on to this prodigious opportunity mostly held off because they couldn't properly evaluate the companies and felt they ought to understand anything on which they risked their capital.

So how could one have made the decision to ride this wave on the basis of the imperfect understanding that most of us bring to high technology? This chapter describes the technique.

The one key thing you did have to determine was that computer software, the Internet, biotechnology, telecom, and the rest of the high-technology landscape were *real* and were exploding. Changing the world, in fact. In other words, that here was a great growth opportunity. Not a hard truth to determine! But the difficult part, *how* to participate, is what the Price technique can tell you. So here goes.

Like Benjamin Graham, Price, who died in 1983, gave his name to an entire theory of investment. The "T. Rowe Price approach" was once heard on Wall Street almost as often as "a real Ben Graham situation," the prevailing orthodoxy before Price arrived. Price's growth-oriented thinking gradually pushed aside the "value" style systematized by Graham. Indeed, Price may have popularized the term "growth stock." Price created a large pool of capital: Already substantial while he still headed it, the company he founded, T. Rowe Price Associates, Inc., in

Baltimore, eventually became one of the largest in the country but branched out from its founder's ideas. What follows describes Price's own philosophy, developed during the years when he actually ran his firm.

His thesis, briefly, was that the investor's best hope of doing well is by seeking the "fertile fields for growth" and then holding those stocks for long periods of time. He defined a growth company as one which shows "long-term growth of earnings, *reaching a new high level per share at the peak of each succeeding major business cycle* and which gives *indications of reaching new high earnings at the peak of future business cycles.*" (It may, however, have declining earnings *within* a business cycle.) Coca-Cola (which became by far Warren Buffett's largest holding) was for a very long time exactly such a company, as were Merck, Wal-Mart, and Texas Instruments.

Price held that since industries and corporations both have life cycles, *the most profitable and least risky time to own a share is during the early stages of growth.* After a company reaches maturity, the investor's opportunity diminishes and his risk increases. Successfully working out and applying this approach made him one of the most famous investment practitioners of his day.

A portly man with sad eyes and a dark mustache surmounting a knowing, tired, and somewhat grim smile, Price came from Glyndon, Maryland, then a summer resort for people from Baltimore. His father was a country doctor.

Investing was his life. Like most of the greatest investors—or artists or professionals of any sort—Rowe Price lost himself in the task; his first interest was always in superior performance, not in making a killing for himself. He was thus a good professional: The client came first. "If we do well for the client, we'll be taken care of," he liked to say. He craved immortality in the record books. To help shape his own monument, he kept a close eye on what the press said about him, and later, long after retiring from his firm, started writing articles on his investment ideas to create a new performance record.

In his eighties, Price still got up at 5 A.M. He was exceedingly disciplined and organized, with an agenda for each day, always executing the items in the order listed and never taking up unlisted ones. Similarly, when he bought a stock at 20, he also established that he would sell some at, say, 40 and did even if things had changed for the good. If he had determined to buy more stock at 13, he would even if the news from the company was discouraging.

An associate recalls him as being "amazingly able, irascible, and ego-tistical." He was "Mr. Price" to almost everyone; he wouldn't be aboard the ship at all unless he was the captain. He was able to say, "I make a lot of mistakes . . . I'm not very bright," but all the same, everybody who worked with him always had to do exactly as he specified. Since he hated to delegate responsibility, he would have made a poor industrial manager.

To be a great investor, one must be a contrarian, a loner. But it's vir-tually impossible for loners to create a self-sufficient organization. Typ-ically, the strong-willed loner has weak followers. He thus must either sell his company to outsiders to realize a capital value for his efforts (which leaves his clients prey to the acquisitor) or else, with great trep-idation, sell it to his own followers, as did Price, who was openly con-cerned that his followers were not fit to succeed him. The best hope for the organization is to have a talented successor still in his thirties when the sixty-five-year-old founder is ready to retire. The latter may not be jealous of a much younger man—not his psychological son and rival, but his grandson.

T. Rowe Price Associates had a relatively small volume of assets under management until late in Price's life. In the early 1950s the firm's portfolios totaled only a few hundred million dollars, and in 1966, when Price was in his late sixties, the firm ran approximately $1.5 billion, while a number of investment counsel firms started at the same time were several times larger. Price himself did not believe that his firm could expand further after he retired. When he sold out to his associates, they offered him an arrangement under which he would participate in the company's growth for five years, but he declined, only to see the portfolios under management expand fourfold during that period.

The company had two extraordinary pieces of luck after Price retired. First, smaller growth companies became extremely popular with investors, giving six years of glory to the Growth Stock Fund and even more to the New Horizons Fund, and the exploding market for pension fund management brought the managers of pension funds to the firms with the best recent records. Back then, Charles Shaeffer, who succeeded Price as president, was a supersalesman. As a result, the firm gained an enormous amount of new business, riding that cycle's growth boom all the way up. (Later, it rode the cycle down again.)

There was, one can see in retrospect, a certain conflict of interest between the firm and the clients who gave it their money to manage based on its record. Probably it should have announced—as Price, in retirement, did personally—that the growth mania was being over-done, then switched to a balanced approach, and refused to accept business from investors seeking flat-out growth-oriented management.

Price made available the audited holdings and performance figures of a "model growth stock portfolio" consisting of the common stock-holdings of two family accounts, one started in 1934 and one started in 1937, from inception through 1972.

The amounts involved were modest at the outset, and cash and bonds were omitted. It was, in other words, a demonstration of stock-picking, not of portfolio management. That said, the performance was striking. One thousand dollars invested in stocks in 1934, with divi-dends reinvested, but not including tax, would have become $271,201 by December 31, 1972; the investment would have grown roughly only half as much if one had begun at the end of World War II. The market value, ignoring dividends, grew approximately twenty times from 1950 through 1972, and roughly four times from 1958 through 1972.

Some of the individual stock purchases worked out amazingly. For instance, by the end of 1972, Black & Decker, held for thirty-five years, had risen from 1¼ to 108; Honeywell, held for thirty-four years, had gone from 3¾ to 138; 3M, for thirty-three years, from ½ to 85⅛; Square D, also for thirty-three years, from ¾ to 36⅞; Merck, held for thirty-two years, from ⅞ to 89⅛.

Obviously, a taxpaying investor who finds stocks that he can hold for the better part of a lifetime enjoys a marked advantage over one who buys and sells at shorter intervals, since he postpones capital gains taxes indefinitely and thus has the use of the tax money he would oth-erwise have paid out, besides avoiding brokerage commissions. Because of compounding, his after-tax results will greatly exceed those of an equally skillful investor who must pay capital gains taxes and broker-age commissions as he goes along.

I became very conscious of this difference in the 1950s, when I was associated with the investment counsel firm that ran the best-performing mutual fund for that decade out of the two hundred or so funds then in existence. It also had about the highest portfolio turnover. The runner-up by a narrow margin was T. Rowe Price's Growth Stock Fund. After a while I realized that the Price Fund, which had one of the lowest portfolio turnovers, was doing a better job for most of its shareholders after taxes. Nor did the system need to be operated by a genius. Mr. Price was a sensible, astute, and exceedingly experienced man of iron discipline and a strong will, but did not profess to be a prodigy. On the contrary, one of the merits he claimed for his approach was that a nonprofessional could carry it out successfully.

Considering all this, I concluded that in the real world an investment approach based on searching out the exceptional company with a view to holding it for long periods of time should work out better for an experienced and able but not phenomenally well-equipped investor than would a buy-and-sell approach. He wouldn't have to know as many different things or make as many difficult decisions.

"Even the amateur investor who lacks training and time to devote to managing his investments can be reasonably successful by *selecting the best-managed companies in fertile fields for growth,* buy[ing] their shares and retain[ing] them until it becomes obvious that *they no longer meet the definition of a growth stock,*" said Price.

Criteria

Can the amateur investor really do that? Consider some of Price's requirements for growth companies:

1. *Superior research* to develop products and markets
2. *Lack of cutthroat competition*
3. *Comparative immunity from government regulation*
4. *Low total labor costs,* but *well-paid employees*
5. At least a *10 percent return on invested capital,* sustained *high profit margins,* and a *superior growth of earnings* per share

To select such stocks, he said, the investor needs experience and judgment, and must take into account general social and political influences as well as economic ones. All this, I would judge, does indeed lie within the competence of a diligent, experienced nonprofessional.

Price maintained that there are two aspects of capitalizing on the "fertile fields for growth": identifying an industry that is *still enjoying its growth phase,* and settling on the *most promising company* or companies *within that industry.*

The two best indicators of a growth industry are *unit volume of sales* (not dollar volume) and *net earnings.* Both of these criteria would have pointed you at the computer software and Internet-related stocks in the 1990s, while keeping you out of those with no earnings. Often the way to play such growth areas is not through the service providers, but by owning companies—such as Cisco, Intel, and Microsoft—*that make things that the service companies must in turn buy:* not panning for gold, but selling the pans. *Return on investment* must also be watched carefully. To be attractive, an industry should be improving in *both unit volume* and *net earnings*. Many studies are available on a regular basis showing which industries are experiencing the fastest growth. Investors are usually aware of the most exciting ones, but are often not aware that they are maturing.

Price points out that when an industry finally begins to mature and then go downhill it may do so on "leverage": carrying profits down even faster than unit volume. Early in his career he correctly identified railroads as a maturing industry: Railroad ton-miles had started to decline in the face of improving business, and continued to do so. Since fixed charges did not decline equally, profits fell drastically.

Price had no difficulty in perceiving that with increasing government control, public utility companies were likely to become unsatisfactory investments. Even before World War II he readily identified the superior prospects of aviation, diesel engines, air conditioning, plastics, and television over, for example, the maturing automobile and steel industries.

An old industry that is experiencing new growth, whether because of new products or new uses for old ones, may also become attractive for investment: new growth products have transformed the office equipment, specialty chemicals, and oil drilling industries and given new life to their stocks.

How do you find the best companies within an attractive industry? They must have *demonstrated* their superior qualities, either by showing improving unit growth and profits right through the down phase of a business cycle ("stable growth") or by showing higher earnings from peak to peak and bottom to bottom through several cycles ("cyclical growth"). When one finds such companies one studies where they are going and tries to determine if they will be able to prolong their superiority.

Some of the qualities that may contribute to that are:

1. *Superior management*
2. *Outstanding research*
3. *Patents*

4. *Strong finances*
5. *A favorable location* (where applicable)

Only if these factors should persist can one decide that a company is probably a growth stock.

When growth turns to decadence, it can usually be attributed to the erosion of former advantages. For instance:

1. *Management may change* for the worse.
2. *Markets may become saturated.*
3. *Patents may expire* or new inventions render them less valuable.
4. *Competition may intensify.*
5. *The legislative and legal environment may deteriorate.*
6. *Labor and raw materials costs may rise.*

These adverse changes will be reflected in unfavorable comparisons in *unit sales, profit margins,* and *return on capital.* They warn the growth investor that it's time to move along.

Price *did not believe in specific predictions* of a company's future. "No one can see ahead three years, let alone five or ten," he said. "Competition, new inventions, all kinds of things can change the situation in twelve months." As a result, the "valuation models" that are popular on Wall Street—which project future earnings year by year, apply a discount factor, and give a theoretical price today which one compares with the market price—are highly suspect. According to Price, one should just *stick with the best companies in the highest-growth industries as long as their progress continues.* Do not try for a pinpointed mathematical approach that creates an illusory certainty out of an unknowable future.*

That, then, is the technique that found some of the great supergrowth stocks of the 1990s in software, e-commerce, biogenetics, and telecom. Not spread sheets and projections, just *buying the leaders.*

Price never carried his argument to its logical conclusion by comparing countries as he did industries and companies. For years, while he was active, the Japanese economy offered wonderful investment

---

*I like to demonstrate this by a modest example: What will be the income of a New York taxi driver fifteen years from now? You could try to calculate it predicting inflation, GNP and population growth, gasoline and car prices, and dozens of other factors: all useless. All you can know is that if he works hard, the taxi driver will make a very modest living.

opportunities, both because of the extraordinary productivity of the Japanese themselves and because of foreign investors' neglect of the Japanese market. Some of the greatest companies in the world languished for years at three and four times earnings, even though they were becoming larger and stronger all the time. But Price reasoned that he was doing well enough, and had better stick to what he knew best.

Contemplating an investment, Price liked to ask, *"What is the investor's own return on the money he invests?"* If you buy a stock at a high price-earnings multiple—40, for instance—you are getting an "earnings yield" of only 2.5 percent on *your* money, whatever the company itself may be earning on *its* corporate capital. Further, your dividend yield in such a situation will probably be less than 1 percent. Of course, you hope it will rise, but it will take a long, long time for those dividends to total as much as you would have received from bonds yielding, say, 9 percent.

The low return on a growth stock bought at very high multiples becomes particularly serious in periods when bonds are offering attractive yields as an alternative, as Price pointed out in a pamphlet, *Principles of Growth Stock Valuation.*

Buying Points

Price proposed a specific plan for buying any stock, which one should *write out and then adhere to.* It has two parts: *fixing a price,* and then *buying (and selling) on a scale.*

A. Valuation

As one might expect, Price emphasized the price-earnings multiple approach to equity valuation, rather than the appraising of hard assets (although late in his career he became keenly interested in natural resources).

Several factors help determine the multiple of earnings one should be prepared to pay:

1. Above all, *a record of earnings growth.* But one shouldn't project the rapid increases of the dynamic phase of a growth stock too many years into the future.
2. The best time to buy is when growth stocks, especially those one is interested in, are *out of fashion.*

3. *"Blue chips" with a record of rising dividends are worth a higher multiple than secondary stocks without dividend growth.*

4. *Stable growth stocks are worth more than cyclical stocks* subject to the vagaries of the business cycles, and of course *cyclicals are worth a higher multiple of their recession earnings than of their boom earnings.*

5. *One should pay a lower multiple* of earnings for growth stocks when bonds are available at high yields.

6. Similarly, when the general level of stock prices is low enough so that they are yielding 5 percent or more, one should pay lower price-earnings multiples for growth stocks than when stocks in general are high enough to bring yields down to, say, 2 or 3 percent or less. Put differently, *the "total return" of growth stocks has to compete with that available from bonds or stocks* in general.

In practice, Price seemed to fix the appropriate price-earnings ratio for a desirable growth stock by noting the high and low P/Es of the last few market cycles and establishing a target P/E at something like *one-third over the lowest P/E the stock touched during the period.*

B. Scale Buying

Price's examples indicate that *as a stock fell to his target buying range he started buying quite vigorously,* without "bottom-fishing," which he clearly felt did not pay. If a stock went a lot below the initial price he paid, he would have done some buying near the lows, but most of his buying averaged out not too far below his initial target price.

Selling

Price emphasized that one has to be able to tell when a company's earnings growth is coming to an end. He didn't say how to do it, except to warn against some changes and pitfalls:

1. *Beware of a decline in the return on invested capital.* That's often a warning of the onset of a company's maturity.

2. *Business recessions create a confusing background* against which to study the performance of a particular company. Its earnings may decline because though its growth is still intact it is being dragged down by general conditions, or on the contrary its growth may really have peaked, which one may overlook in the general business decline.

3. *Some industries,* such as real estate and fire and casualty insurance, *have their own cycles* that are separate from the business cycle, confusing things further.

Scale Selling

When he did decide to sell or cut back on a stock in a bull market, *Price waited until it had risen 30 percent over its then upper buying price limit.* At that point he sold 10 percent of the position, and thereafter an additional 10 percent each time it advanced another 10 percent.

However, he would sell out at the market a stock scheduled for scaled elimination *if the bull market peaked out,* or *if the stock itself seemed to be collapsing, or if there was bad news from the company.*

Price Changes Tack

By 1965, Price had spent thirty years as a growth stock advocate. Originally he had been almost alone in recognizing the investment merits of companies whose earnings rose from one business cycle to the next. Little by little he had attracted such a following and built such a large organization that not only was this method called the "T. Rowe Price approach" but many of his favorite holdings—Black & Decker, Emory Air Freight, Avon Products, Rollins, and Fleetwood, for example—became known as "T. Rowe Price stocks." But then in some instances they got much too high—fifty to seventy times earnings.

So Price finally announced that the time had come to change, and over several years published a series of reports that he summed up in a pamphlet, *The New Era for Investors.* It created a great stir in the investment community, not so much among those who read it, since its reasoning is most persuasive, as among those who merely heard about it. T. Rowe Price advising against the "T. Rowe Price stocks"! What next?

Price had just decided that there weren't many bargains left in the kind of stock he wanted to buy. His goal was that a stock should double its income and market value over ten years (or less if inflation is high), but that's far from easy if it's already at forty or fifty times earnings. What happens if something goes wrong? And what hope is there that such multiples will still be applied to those stocks at the end of the period?

Price had decided that in the excitement over growth that might never happen, investors were neglecting natural resources assets. He therefore formulated what he called his "new era" approach, which meant, in addition to growth stocks, buying assets that should be inflation-resistant: real estate, natural resources, gold and silver.

He cut back on his growth stock investments and put a substantial part of his family assets, including what he got from the sale of his firm, about equally into bonds and stocks, the stocks being mostly in his "new era" selections, particularly gold stocks.

Ten years later these holdings were at a substantial profit, unlike the rest of the market, and particularly unlike the growth stocks.

Price v. Price

To Price's intense dismay his successors in his firm went right on playing the old game, putting the funds that came in to them for management into the same sort of stock, apparently almost indifferent to how much they were paying for a dollar of earnings or dividends. (I remember, in fact, an enthusiast close to the company telling me that it was if anything *better* to buy the stocks with the highest price-earnings ratios, because then when the earnings advanced—as they surely would, since that was why you'd bought in—those stocks were the most certain to rise, since they enjoyed the highest degree of institutional acceptance. Also, of course, the impact of a dollar's rise in earnings is higher if the market capitalizes those earnings at a multiple of fifty rather than a multiple of ten.)

We now recognize all this as the usual silly rationalization of the herd instinct, but that's how it happened.

By 1974 what Price feared had come about. Growth stocks became a disaster, with many falling 75 to 80 percent from their old highs. A share of Price's pride and joy, his New Horizons Fund, lost 42 percent of its asset value per share in 1973 and then 39 percent more in 1974. The whole fund fell in size from $511 million to $203 million over the two years, as redemptions followed the market decline.

It could almost be said that the Price organization had been fated to ride the 1974 bear market right over the waterfall. Price's successors would have needed the courage to quit a winning game in its most successful period. It was profoundly gratifying for the firm to have important clients beseeching it to manage their money. Turning them away would scarcely have been in the nature of things, and would have involved a repudiation of what the firm stood for—including selling many of its holdings, which would have risked breaking their prices once the word got around. It would also have involved restructuring the firm's research department, which was dedicated to growth stock analysis—about like shutting down a highly successful French restaurant and reopening it as a sushi bar: theoretically possible, but most unlikely. Finally, everybody was just too busy booking new business to worry about what lay ahead. Stocks like Avon were rising by 1 and 2 percent a month. Price Associates bought them, and Morgan Guaranty picked them up. The price rose further. U.S. Trust and other banks and mutual funds piled aboard. That put the price up still more. Private Swiss banks serviced by the same brokers got on the bandwagon. Other funds and hedge fund managers came in. This made the original purchase look very smart, so Price Associates bought more. The cycle continued. Even more delightful, the rising prices created wonderful performance figures, meaning more clients and higher fees.

When growth stocks fell from favor in 1974, the very name "growth stock" became virtually taboo on Wall Street. The same institutions that had rapturously bought Avon in 1973 as a "one-decision" holding at $130, or fifty-five times earnings, dumped it in 1974 at $25, or thirteen times earnings, until by late 1974 the wringing-out process had gone so far that Price himself decided it was safe to begin buying growth stocks once more, though not necessarily the same ones. While their market prices had collapsed, many of them had moved that much further along their life cycle toward maturity, and thus offered less potential.

So in his personal portfolios, Price changed tack still again. He divided his interests into three categories of stocks: "growth stocks of the future"—companies that he felt were still at an early point in their life cycle; older, seasoned growth companies with less dynamic prospects but whose price had declined below what he felt they were worth; and a mixed grill of companies, notably natural resources—gold, silver, and others—that had fallen to what he called "receivership prices."

By late 1977, Price had grown so disturbed by the confusion in the public's mind between his personal investment philosophy, which although growth-oriented was keyed to buying only real values, and that of his old firm, which he felt had gotten locked into a simplification of his ideas, that he gave a number of interviews and statements to make clear that "Price Associates and Rowe Price are as different as day and night."*

---

*The firm itself did not suffer as much as its clients. The pension funds that remained as clients added new cash, and the firm created fixed-income funds that were very popular. And in later years it stabilized and grew immensely.

There's a certain melancholy humor in this spectacle of indignant older gentlemen excoriating their successors. One is somehow reminded of another eminent Southerner, Colonel "Kentucky Fried Chicken" Sanders, denouncing the "goddamn slop" that his specialty became after he sold the company.

Anyway, Price was right. His company had so much money under management when the growth stock balloon collapsed in 1973–74 that very possibly the firm (not Price himself) lost more dollars for its clients than it had previously made for them, since in its earlier great period it was so much smaller. With hindsight it's hard to conceive of all those intelligent, trained, experienced money managers, not only in Price Associates but also in the Morgan Guaranty, the United States Trust Company, and many other distinguished establishments, happily holding on to and indeed buying more of the high-flying growth fad stocks at prices that could not possibly be justified even if the companies achieved all that one could dream they might and still more. Even sadder, some of Price's followers who bought his stocks near the top sold out in desperation after they had dropped by three-quarters, abandoning the growth idea just when it was about to pay off all over again. It isn't hard to understand why Price wanted to stand apart from all this.

How could Price have avoided the catastrophe? Only in two ways, that I can see. Having worked out his growth doctrine he could have imbued his firm with a basically flexible and pragmatic approach, always insisting on common sense, realism, and flexibility as the highest investing virtues. Perhaps, as the prices in the growth sector reached catastrophic levels, the team would have cut back. Or he could have found and cultivated a worthy successor, another master investor to grow up at his side and eventually inherit his authority—someone with the wisdom and strength to alter course drastically when it became necessary. But that, since Price's makeup didn't permit it, was not in the cards.

The great bull market of the 1990s was a perfect Price environment. As I write, though, in 2000, parts of the market exhibit extreme exaggerations that remind those who lived through it of the 1973 period: Price understood then that the values that had once seemed compellingly attractive had become much less so, and took action. Would he do the same today? I think so.

TWO

WARREN BUFFETT
A SHARE IN A BUSINESS

IN RECENT DECADES, WARREN BUFFETT, ONCE LITTLE KNOWN even in his hometown, has become "the sage of Omaha," one of the country's most successful investors and richest men. His ups and downs—mostly ups—and even casual utterances make news in the business press. Since of these there is an increasing flow, he has become the more convenient to study.

Buffett started out as a disciple of Benjamin Graham, the most eminent theoretician of the "value" (as distinct from "growth") technique of investing. He has edited Graham's *The Intelligent Investor,* an outstanding exposition of that technique. But when a disciple becomes in turn a master himself, or when times change, he rises above the previous orthodoxy and breaks new ground. As we will see, Buffett is no exception.

If you had put $10,000 in his original investing partnership at its inception in 1956, you would have collected about $267,691 by the time he dissolved it at the end of 1969. He had never suffered a down year, even in the severe bear markets of 1957, 1962, 1966, and 1969. (He had a bad one in 1999.) When the partnership was wound up, you could have elected to stay with Buffett as a shareholder of Berkshire Hathaway, Inc., which was spun off from the partnership and became Buffett's investing vehicle. In that event, your $10,000 would recently have been around $50 million. (This prodigious performance depended in part on deploying insurance company reserves to buy equities instead of the usual bonds, and on using one company to buy another, and thus is not comparable to mutual fund performance.)

For all his wealth, Buffett's manner has been called corn-fed; it is straightforward and genial. Professionally, he is in the vulture business, but he is a cheerful sort of vulture. A round face with a wide mouth is bracketed by deep smile-wrinkles. His quizzical eyes peer from behind large horn-rimmed glasses. From a high hairline, surmounted by a somewhat unruly thatch, run heavy vertical frown lines. Buffett's clothes are rumpled Middle West. Of a chunky build, he loves junk food, including hamburgers, French fries, fudge, and cherry-flavored Pepsi. He has been known to decline a proffered glass of wine at dinner, saying, "No, thanks, I'll take the money." In short, Warren Buffett doesn't live magnificently. There's no palace in town or country villa, no yacht or breeding establishment, no art collection or the wide benefactions of the old-time tycoon.

Alas, from the conspicuously rich everybody *wants* something. Buffett's wife, Susan, once a nightclub singer, moved to San Francisco, in part to escape the unending demands of worthy causes in Omaha. The two remain on amicable terms, but Buffett then took up with housekeeper-companion Astrid Menks, a former hostess at the same French Café in Omaha that Susan once sang in.

Buffett has created modest trusts for each of his children, but does not want to give them more for fear of corrupting them. He says: "My kids are going to carve out their own place in this world, and they know I'm for them whatever they do." But he refuses to bequeath them "a lifetime supply of food stamps just because they came out of the right womb." His offspring are not necessarily delighted by this solicitude. Daughter Susan says, "It's sort of strange when you know most parents want to buy things for their kids and all you need is a small sum of money. . . . He won't give it to us on principle. All my life my father has been teaching us. Well, I feel I've learned the lesson. At a certain point you can stop."

He finds that happiness comes from small improvements, not by getting somewhere once and for all.* Being able to add on one room to your house is what makes you happy, not living in a palace. He believes in "a meritocracy based on equality of opportunity." Inherited wealth, with a life supply of food stamps presented upon birth based only on

---

*An idea shared by Robert Wilson (see Chapter 16). Objectively, after a certain level one does not improve one's situation by getting rich, and one is well advised to try to modify one's point of view to reflect that.

proper selection of parents, is "socially unjust."* Consistent with that philosophy, he is leaving the bulk of his fortune to a foundation, which some day may be one of the largest in the world.

The Insurmountable Moat

The essence of Buffett's investment thinking is that *the business world is divided into a tiny number of wonderful businesses—well worth investing in—and a huge number of bad or mediocre businesses that are not attractive as long-term holdings.* Most businesses are usually not worth what they are selling for, but on rare occasions the wonderful businesses are almost given away, based on current gloomy economic and stock market forecasts. When that happens, buy boldly! Buffett likes to sit with half a dozen or so core holdings plus a dozen or so held for possible resale. He characterizes traditional diversification as the "Noah's Ark approach: You buy two of everything in sight and end up with a zoo instead of a portfolio." (Extreme concentration is his own preference, not a general truth for everybody. I discuss this later on.)

For Buffett, the key to a good business is its business franchise—the extent to which it is surrounded by a moat, so that another company can't muscle in to squeeze its prices and profits. The competitiveness built into the American economic system inhibits the creation of great franchises. Parts of U.S. industry make so little money, in fact, that they have trouble attracting the investment capital needed to produce goods and services required by society. When they can't, the government enters, and does the job badly. Witness the fantastic wastefulness of the public housing that the government puts up after rent control wipes out the small, efficient landlord.

Asked about the concept of business franchise, Buffett explained:

> The test of a franchise is what a smart guy with a lot of money could do to it if he tried. If you gave me a billion dollars, and first draft pick of fifty business managers throughout the United States, I could absolutely cream both the business world and the journalistic world. If you said, "Go take the *Wall Street Journal* apart," I would hand you back the billion dollars. Reluctantly, but I

---

*For that matter, some say that bestowing vast sums on clever stock market operators, as distinct from real producers, is also socially unjust. Buffett, a long-term investor, has suggested a 100 percent tax on *short*-term profits. Most people think that it's right and proper for whatever *they* are to have advantages.

would hand it back to you. The real test of a business is how much damage a competitor can do, even if he is stupid about returns. The trick is to find the ones that haven't been identified by someone else.

The businesses that Buffett thinks *are* worth owning—those with powerful franchises—sometimes fall into the category he calls "gross profits royalty" companies, perhaps better called "gross revenues royalty" companies. These have included TV stations, newspapers, international advertising agencies, and the largest insurance brokerage companies. Benefiting from the heavy investments of the companies they serve, they require little working capital of their own to operate and, in fact, pour off cash to their owners. The unfortunate capital-intensive producer—General Motors, let us say—ordinarily brings its wares to its customers' notice by passing through the tollgate of the "royalty" holder: J. Walter Thompson, the *Wall Street Journal*, the local TV station, or all three.

Other valid franchises Buffett has liked include insurance and reinsurance, financial companies such as Wells Fargo Bank and "Freddie Mac," some specialized situations such as Sperry & Hutchinson Green Stamps, furniture and jewelry retailing, and candy manufacturing, but there aren't many that enjoy both a substantial and a well-secured niche. In recent decades he has branched out of Graham-style value situations in favor of huge multinational consumer companies, such as Coca-Cola and Gillette, both surrounded by very deep and wide moats indeed.

I went to visit Buffett for a few days in Omaha. His office is on a high floor of a modern building. The office was clean and anonymous, with framed documents on the walls and a box of fudge on a table, to which Buffett helped himself from time to time. It's delicious—made by See's, a Berkshire holding. A bookshelf on the wall held, with other financial volumes, several editions of Graham and Dodd's *Security Analysis*.

Buffett, looking genial and ruddy, with an inquisitive expression, put his feet on the desk, poured himself a Pepsi-Cola, and, in the somewhat toneless manner characteristic of Midwesterners, cheerfully began to babble about what was on his mind:

When I was a kid at Woodrow Wilson High School in Washington [business of refilling glass of Pepsi; pours cherry syrup into Pepsi, then pours more], another kid and I started the Wilson Coin-

Operated Machine Company. I was fifteen years old. We put reconditioned pinball machines in barbershops. In Washington you were supposed to buy a tax stamp to be in the pinball machine business. I got the impression we were the only people who ever bought one. The first day we bought an old machine for $25 and put it out in a shop. When we came back that night it had $4 in it! I figured I had discovered the wheel. [Finishes glass of Pepsi, pours another, and adds cherry syrup.] Eventually we were making $50 a week. I hadn't dreamed life could be so good. Before I got out of high school I bought myself an unimproved forty-acre farm in northeast Nebraska for $1,200.

Buffett's father, a hyperconservative of messianic zeal who was revered by his children, served four terms as a Republican congressman and then became a stockbroker. A man of great personal integrity, he had little interest in money: When congressmen's salaries were increased from $10,000 to $12,500, he returned his raise to the Treasury. He was merely amused by Warren's moneymaking activities, and hoped his son would become a clergyman.

At twelve, Warren became fond of handicapping horse races and compiled and sold a tip sheet called *Stable Boy Selections*. He persuaded his father to ask the Library of Congress for all the books they had on horse-race handicapping and betting, and today wonders what the library made of Congressman Buffett's request.

Later, we find him in the business of retrieving and reselling golf balls and running several paper routes for the *Washington Post*.* Delivery of papers accounted for most of his original stake of $9,000, with which he paid for college.

He was also fascinated by stock market technical analysis, and developed his own market timing signals. It all made no real sense to him, however, and he discarded that approach in 1949, after reading *The Intelligent Investor* by Benjamin Graham while at the University of Nebraska. The following year he went to Columbia University because both Graham and Dodd (of *Security Analysis*) were teaching there.

---

*Newsboy Makes Good. A substantial component of Buffett's wealth today is his holdings in newspapers. He is the largest outside shareholder of the *Washington Post*, the *Boston Globe*, and the *Buffalo Evening News*. One of his newspaper investments, the *Omaha Sun*, didn't pay off financially, though it won a Pulitzer Prize for exposing how Boys Town had become a fund-raising machine.

Buffett noticed in *Who's Who* that Ben Graham was a director of Government Employees Insurance Company (GEICO), which sold automobile insurance directly by mail, bypassing the brokers. He went down to the company's office on a Saturday and pounded on the door. Eventually a janitor opened up, and Buffett asked if there was anybody around he could talk to about the company. The janitor took him upstairs, where one man was in his office, L. A. Davidson, later chief executive officer. Buffett questioned him for five hours, then went away excited about the company and its stock.

Upon graduating, he offered to work for Graham for nothing. Graham declined, so he went back to Omaha and entered his father's stockbroking firm. He pushed GEICO energetically but found it extremely hard to place. Indeed, some insurance agents put pressure on Buffett's father to stop Warren from promoting an agentless underwriter.

After a while Warren had another idea, that one ought to be able to get the people who understand a company to buy stock in it. Kansas City Life, for instance, was trading for three times its statutory earnings, or a 33 percent "earnings yield," while selling insurance whose policyholders' benefits grew at only 2.5 percent per annum compounded. Buffett thought that the general agent, who sold policies daily and mailed the checks to Kansas City, would have to know that Kansas City Life really did exist—people never were quite sure about GEICO—and would be a natural candidate to buy the stock. Quite the contrary. The agent was buying life insurance for himself and his family, content with the 2.5 percent compounding in his policy, while rejecting the 33 percent compounding in the stock! Buffett never could interest him in buying shares in his own company.

In 1952, aged twenty-one, and for a number of years thereafter, he put an ad in the paper offering a class in investing, hoping to attract customers. He paid $100 for a Dale Carnegie course on addressing an audience. Some of the "students" did invest and became multimillionaires as a result, even centimillionaires.

Buffett and Graham

Buffett kept in touch with Graham, sending him ideas in the hope of receiving stock exchange business. Graham, in turn, was generous with his time and thoughts, and in 1954 he suggested that Buffett come to New York to see him. Buffett went, and was hired to work for Graham-Newman Corporation, where he spent two instructive years. Today he finds it hard to describe what he did there, but it must have included analyzing hundreds of companies to see if they met Graham's investment criteria.

Ben Graham didn't worry about moats or tollgates. He never would have bought American Express during the salad oil scandal, or Disney, two of Buffett's early coups, let alone Executive Jet Transportation or Coca-Cola. He did not believe in "qualitative" analysis—studying a company's products, how it operates, and its apparent future outlook. He never talked to managements. He believed in doing all his work by exhaustively studying the figures generally available: "quantitative" analysis. He didn't want to make use of any information that would not be available to his readers. This technique was highly profitable while it lasted, but does not really satisfy Buffett, who finds such mechanical investing all too similar to "filling out an application for group life insurance." Also, it can only work for a relatively small amount of capital.

I asked Buffett how he thought one might do by holding the bargain issues listed in financial publications from time to time. Not too brilliantly, he felt. *If you buy and hold on, you will do only about as well as the companies themselves do. Since they have a low return on capital, that means not outstandingly. To grow fast you need a high return on capital. So, you must be sure to sell a "Graham" investment at the right time, whereas you can hold on to a higher-growth company for as long as it goes on developing rapidly.*

After his two years as a journeyman in the workshop of the master, Buffett was glad to set forth into the great world as a master himself. For the second time he returned to Omaha, where he bought a roomy house, to which he has added sporadically, and started on his own.

In retrospect, one is not too surprised that, given such mental equipment, such fascination with the subject, and such a thorough academic and practical preparation, Buffett should have done exceedingly well. Nobody, however, could have foreseen his prodigious record.

When it comes to money matters, Buffett enjoys the immense advantage of coming from Omaha rather than Boston, say, or Florence. I say advantage because everything in Omaha, as in many other American towns, seems focused on business. No nonsense about solemn temples or gorgeous palaces, no quaint bookstores, no loggias or inviting arcades, no riverside benches for lovers, no museums or great collections. Instead, office buildings, the terminus of the Union Pacific, car rental agencies, farm equipment wholesalers, machine tool companies.

I doubt if there exists in Omaha an important building or business with whose economic history Warren Buffett is unfamiliar. You can walk around the downtown area with him and hear him rattle off the financial characteristics of every structure and business he passes.

Just as an old family doctor often can recognize anemia before a patient has taken a seat in his office, Buffett, glancing at an annual report, will start pointing eagerly here and there in the text, showing why there's too much inventory or not enough return on plant. Of all the investors in this book, Buffett is the one who most perfectly understands the companies he owns stock in as businesses: living organisms, with hearts, lungs, bones, arteries, and nervous systems. It is madness, he would say, for an investor buying a stock to have anything else in mind than the operating realities of the underlying business: its management, the condition of its plant, its customer and labor relations, its cash position, the amount of capital tied up in it—the animal reality of the enterprise. Buffett believes that those on Wall Street who talk of the stock trend or institutional sponsorship are ridiculous, combining laziness with ignorance, and he compares them with astronomers setting aside their telescopes to consult the astrology page.

He thinks of a stock only as a fractional interest in a business and always begins by asking himself, "How much would I pay for all of this company? And on that basis, what will I pay for 1 percent or 10 percent of it?" There are very few companies he considers interesting enough to buy at all, and even those he will look at only when they are very unpopular. Then, if one knows for certain what the values really are, one can have the confidence to buy in the teeth of general gloom.

In 1956, at the age of twenty-five, Buffett started a family partnership with $100,000 in it, after a while adding all his own money. As manager he received 25 percent of the profits above a 6 percent annual return on capital.

Every year Buffett wrote his co-investors:

> I cannot promise results to partners, but I can and do promise this:
> a. Our investments will be chosen on the basis of value, not popularity.
> b. Our patterns of operations will attempt to reduce permanent capital loss (not short-term quotational loss) to a minimum.

His stated goal was not absolute but relative: to beat the Dow Jones by an average of 10 percentage points per year. In general, he bought undervalued listed stocks, which he found much better values than whole companies. He was also frequently involved in merger and arbitrage situations. Occasionally he bought a controlling interest in a public company or an entire private business on a negotiated basis. He refused to tell his investors what he was doing. He points out that if, for instance, he had reported to his partners that 40 percent of their money was in American Express, or that he was heavily long silver futures, they would have been concerned, asked questions, mailed him things to read. At best, he would have wasted a lot of time; at worst, he would have been influenced by their reactions. He says it would have been like a surgeon carrying on a running conversation with the patient during a major operation.

Thus, in 1961 he became chairman of Dempster Mill Manufacturing Company of Beatrice, Nebraska, which made farm implements and was the biggest employer in town. In 1963 he decided to form a group to buy it. In 1965 he took over Berkshire Hathaway in New Bedford, Massachusetts, a textile manufacturer with a long record of unprofitable operations. It was selling for $7 a share, behind which was $10 of working capital—a typical Ben Graham situation. While it became his vehicle for other acquisitions, the actual manufacturing operation never did get straightened out, and was eventually closed down. His experiences in the textile business contributed to his firm conviction never to attempt another "turnaround."

One Berkshire annual report (whose style is often attributed to *Fortune* writer Carol Loomis) cites Samuel Johnson, "A horse that can count to ten is a remarkable horse—not a remarkable mathematician," and adds that "a textile company that allocates capital brilliantly within its industry is a remarkable textile company—not a remarkable business." (This is true, but an un-Grahamish sentiment.)

Through Berkshire, Buffett duly bought a number of entire companies: a candymaker (See's), a trading stamp company (Blue Chip Stamps), several insurance companies and banks, another textile company, a savings and loan association, one daily and one weekly newspaper, and a steel service center. Negotiated purchases, he used to say, can't ordinarily be made on the bargain basis sometimes possible in common stock investment. A sole owner is unlikely to become as crazy as the market sometimes is, so the most one should hope for in a private purchase is a reasonable deal, not a great one. (However, as Berkshire has gotten to be a large affair, it has had to buy entire companies and has frequently done very well indeed.)

Buffett brought off a spectacular transaction in 1964 when American Express collapsed in the market during the Tino de Angelis salad oil scandal. Studying the company carefully, he determined that the danger from those losses would be limited, while its basic strengths, the credit card operation and the traveler's checks, would be unaffected. He put a major part of his then assets into the company, and saw the stock quintuple in the next five years.

In 1969, the stock market was booming, even junk stocks were selling at premium prices, and Buffett couldn't find bargains anymore. He sent another letter to his partners:

> I am out of step with present conditions. When the game is no longer played your way, it is only human to say the new approach is all wrong, bound to lead to trouble, and so on. On one point, however, I am clear. I will not abandon a previous approach whose logic I understand (although I find it difficult to apply) even though it may mean forgoing large, and apparently easy, profits to embrace an approach which I don't fully understand, have not practiced successfully, and which possibly could lead to substantial permanent loss of capital.

Buffett had an additional problem: he had become fond of some of his principal holdings, such as Berkshire Hathaway, and no longer wanted to sell them at all. That, obviously, put him in potential conflict with his investors, whose interest might have been to sell.

So after thirteen years, he decided to fold up the partnership. It had gained thirtyfold in its value per share, and through the addition of more than ninety new members and the success of its investments had grown to over $100 million. Buffett's profit participation as investor-manager, plus the compounding of his own capital, had made him worth some $25 million. Investors were given back their money and their proportional interest in Berkshire Hathaway, of which he became chairman. Some were guided to other advisers, some into municipal bonds. Buffett sent his partners a useful discussion of municipals (see Appendix I).

Three years after the partnership was liquidated, the market plunged into the collapse of 1973–74. Buffett was now able to buy big pieces of some of his favorite "gross profits royalty" companies at give-away prices: 8 percent of Ogilvy & Mather, 16 percent of Interpublic, 11 percent of the *Washington Post,* and large percentages of the *Boston Globe,* Capital Cities (an independent chain of television stations which also owned newspapers), Knight-Ridder Newspapers, Lee Enterprises, Media General, Pinkerton's. Most increased enormously in market value. He said he was indulging his acquisitive instinct by "playing several different games," in newspapers, insurance, and other areas.

Media Businesses

In 1977, through Blue Chip Stamp Company, Buffett paid nearly $35 million to the estate of Mrs. Edward H. Butler, Jr., for the entire Buffalo Evening News Company. At the time, the city had two newspapers. The other was the *Courier-Express,* owned by the Conners family. The *News* had a weekly circulation of about 280,000 and a Saturday circulation of 295,000. The *Courier* sold 125,000 copies during the week and 270,000 on Sunday. Buffett has always felt that a daily paper without a Sunday edition could not succeed, and so he sank additional money into the *News* to start one, which began with the free distribution of three sample Sunday papers. The *Courier* brought suit, claiming that the give-away program "could possibly be the catalyst to put us out of business."

Buffett testified that if the *News* became a monopoly newspaper, it would be worth three times what he had paid for it, but he claimed that the possibility of killing off the *Courier-Express* was not in his mind when he resolved to publish a Sunday edition. Maybe. The *Courier-Express* went under, all right.

As to the "franchise" of a newspaper, Buffett observed then:

> The economics of a dominant newspaper are excellent, among the very best in the business world. . . . While first-class newspapers make excellent profits, the profits of third-rate papers are as good or better—as long as either class of paper is dominant within its community. . . . Even a poor newspaper is a bargain to most citizens simply because of its "bulletin board" value.

Broadcasting companies have enjoyed superb growth and provide cascades of cash. As a result they have maintained strong values in purchases by private buyers.

Television stations are not entirely without risk as investments. In theory, the government can fail to renew a license, although in practice that almost never happens. Regulation and new technology could change the economics of broadcasting. But otherwise the arithmetic of television stations is astonishing: they often net 50 percent on sales, require no working capital, have only minor fixed assets, and have no inventories except for a supply of movies, which can be bought on credit.

Beating Bobby Fischer

An enormous advantage the independent investor enjoys, says Buffett, is that he can stand at the plate and wait forever for the perfect pitch. If he wants it to come in exactly two inches above his navel and nowhere else, he can stand there indefinitely until an easy one is served up. Stock market investment is the only business of which that is true. You can wait not only for the bargain, but for the particular one that you understand and *know* to be a bargain, the one that "screams at you."

I have a little riddle I offer to clients when I'm trying to explain this point, and tried it on Buffett: "How can you beat Bobby Fischer?"

Buffett finally gave up.

"Get him to play you any game except chess."

In other words, stick to what you know for sure. Buffett often observes that you might improve your investment performance by having a quota, a limit to the number of investment ideas you could try out in your whole life: one a year, for instance . . . or even fewer. You only have to do a very few things right in your life, he says, so long as you don't do too many things wrong. You should therefore resolve ahead of time to make only a few big investment moves.

Many times, though, the investment manager lets his advantage be turned into a disadvantage. Feeling obliged to remain active, he swings at far too many pitches, instead of holding off until he has an absolute conviction. He seems to hear the clients howling, "Swing, you bum!"*

---

*This is also a central Benjamin Graham idea. It has a psychological side not mentioned by Graham: Action, including trading, manifests power, a deep human desire.

What It Takes

Buffett thinks that to succeed as an investor you must have six qualities:

1. *You must be animated by controlled greed, and fascinated by the investment process.* You must not, however, let greed take possession of you so that you become in a hurry. If you are too interested in money, you will kill yourself; if not interested enough, you won't go to the office. And you must enjoy the game.

2. *You must have patience.* Buffett often repeats that you should never buy a stock unless you would be happy with it if the stock exchange closed down for the next ten years.

3. *You must think independently.* Jot down your reasons for buying: "**XYZ** is undervalued by the market at $500 million because . . ." When you have them all down, make your decision and leave it at that, without feeling the need to consult other people: no committees. Buffett reasons that if you don't know enough to make your own decisions, you should get out of decision-making. He likes to quote Ben Graham's dictum: "The fact that other people agree or disagree with you makes you neither right nor wrong. You will be right if your facts and reasoning are correct."

4. *You must have the security and self-confidence that comes from knowledge, without being rash or headstrong.* If you lack confidence, fear will drive you out at the bottom. As an example of the folly of being too market-conscious, Buffett cites nervous investors who don't know the facts and thus make a habit of selling stocks when they go down. Crazy, he says. It's as though you bought a house for $1 million and immediately told the broker that you would sell it again if you got a bid of $800,000.

5. *Accept it when you don't know something.*

6. *Be flexible as to the types of businesses you buy, but never pay more than the business is worth.* Calculate what the business is worth now, and what it will be worth in due course. Then ask yourself, "How sure am I?" Nine times out of ten you can't be. Sometimes, though, the bell rings and you can almost hear the cash register. However, *nobody is clever enough to buy stocks he doesn't really want and resell them to someone else at a profit.* The bigger fool in the "bigger fool theory"—accepting a bad buy to sell it to someone dumber than you are—*is usually the original buyer,* not his intended victim.

As we talked out this list, I added four requirements that Buffett, but not many others, can fulfill:

7. Have ten or fifteen years of intensive theoretical and practical training—including a number of years under the greatest investors—before you start in yourself.
8. Be a genius of sorts.
9. Possess a high degree of intellectual honesty.
10. Avoid any significant distractions.

Wonderful Businesses

What are the characteristics of the few wonderful businesses?

1. *They have a good return on capital* without accounting gimmicks or lots of leverage.
2. *They are understandable.* One should be able to grasp what motivates the people working in them, and why they appeal to their customers. Even IBM, which looks straightforward, has changed character several times, such as when it went from punch cards to magnetic tape, and again when it introduced the 360, betting the future of the whole company on the success of one system.
3. *They see their profits in cash.*
4. *They have strong franchises and thus freedom to raise prices.* The number of truly protected areas in our economy is minute. Their very rarity is the greatness of capitalism. Start a Japanese restaurant and, if it works, the neighborhood soon has two, four, eight, then sixteen Japanese restaurants. Their profitability declines until the owners just have a job, not an exploitation.

American Express, for instance, has had two perfect natural business franchises. The first is its billions of dollars of cash "float" from the traveler's check business. Essentially the company is always borrowing without interest from the purchasers of these checks and relending the money at high interest. The second has been the American Express credit card. When Buffett saw the cost of the cards gradually increase from $3 a year to $20, with no loss of acceptance even during the salad oil scandal, he knew that here was something unique.

5. *They don't take a genius to run.*

6. *Their earnings are predictable.*

7. *They are not natural targets of regulation.*

8. *They have low inventories and high turnover.* In other words, they require little continuing capital investment. There are many high-growth businesses that require large infusions of capital as they grow and have done little or nothing for their owners—a lesson investors periodically relearn.

9. *The management is owner-oriented.* Buffett observes that one can sense quickly when management thinks of itself first and the shareholder second. In such a case the investor should stay away. He considers it an atrocity when controlling shareholders go public at high prices in a bubbling market, then fail to perform, and eventually force the public investors out at 50 cents on the dollar.* He insists on managements who regard stockholders as partners, not adversaries. This attitude is of course the opposite of that of certain economists who consider shareholder distributions just another cost of doing business. An interesting theory, but no way to attract capital!

10. *There is a high rate of return on the total of inventories plus plant.* (Receivables usually offset payables.) This test, applicable only in certain industries, exposes many bad businesses that seem to have high earnings but in fact are wormy—some of the conglomerates, for example. Stock promoters during frothy markets crudely but successfully dress up ordinary companies to fit the current fashion of the investment world, but return on capital is hard to fake. *This is an extremely important way in which Buffett's approach differs from standard brokerage house analysis.*

11. *The best business is a royalty on the growth of others, requiring little capital itself.*

---

*Benjamin Graham deals harshly with this maneuver in Chapter 15 of *The Intelligent Investor*, 4th rev. ed. (New York: Harper & Row, 1973): "Financial authorities have given little attention to the questions about fair treatment that arise in such repurchases; the stockholders themselves have not thought about it at all. It is time that a basic principle was adopted here—the principle that a corporation should deal fairly with *all* its owners, and that it should pay a fair price to those who are selling their interest back to it."

I once asked Buffett about buying companies that were showing increasing profit margins and rising earnings, or were gaining institutional acceptance, or had just skipped dividends, or other formulas. Buffett replied then that Benjamin Graham had examined any number of such techniques and found that nothing bettered the approach of buying a company at a substantial discount from its working capital and selling it when it was valued in the market at close to 100 percent of its working capital. (Later, to be sure, Buffett branched out from the Graham approach.)

Buffet believes almost no one should ever go short, but if one does, *it is best to go short the entire market*—a representative list—rather than stocks one considers overpriced. Ben Graham tried going short overpriced stocks. Three out of four times it worked, but the fourth time he would get murdered, as an already overpriced stock was run up to the skies by public enthusiasm. Buffett himself has no interest in shorting.

I described visiting Tambrands when the stock was in the dumps, and being told by the financial vice president that a couple of years before, with the stock selling four times higher on lower earnings, he had been inundated by analysts, whereas I was the only one held seen in weeks. Buffett replied that it's always like that: One of the surest signs that you are on safe ground in buying a stock is that there is no mention of it in any recent index of the *Wall Street Transcript*, which reprints a great many brokerage house write-ups.

Of all Buffett's ideas perhaps the simplest and most important for a nonprofessional to grasp is just this: *Value will in time always be reflected in market price.* It's just a question of time, and not always very much time. Most investors don't have the profound feeling professionals acquire that market anomalies are perforce ephemeral. If a bond is selling out of line with other bonds of similar tenor and quality, it *will* move to its correct value. If a stock that really does represent $1 worth of solid assets is selling for 60 cents, it *will*, sooner or later, go to $1 and, indeed, quite likely to more than $1 since prices of stocks, and of the market as a whole, eventually reflect not only fair value but excessive valuation.

"Are You a Fanatic?"

In discussing qualifications for business managers, Buffett grinned and recommended a one-line employment form: "Are you a fanatic?" A manager must care intensely about running a first-class operation; if his golf game is what he thinks about while shaving, the business will show it. A good manager should be a demon on costs. He need not have fancy data processing equipment, or even a budget: He should *know* his costs, down to how many stamps he uses. Buffett mentioned Peter Kiewit, then regarded as the leading businessman in Omaha, whose company was perhaps the most successful construction firm in the world. There were no carpets in the executive offices, no consultants, and the bosses were there on Saturday. Buffett doesn't mind having managers who are over seventy years old. Gene Abegg, for example, from whom he bought Illinois National Bank, ran it until he died in 1980 at eighty-one, and other companies Buffett controls are run by elderly men and one nonagenarian woman. Buffett treats them with the utmost skill: No operating manager quit in thirty-four years.

The manager should feel and act as though he were the owner of his business. Buffett hates managers who exploit their position to the disadvantage of the owners—for instance, those who tell stockholders a tender offer at 40 is grossly inadequate, while selling part of the company to themselves through liberal stock options at 25; or who sell stock at less than intrinsic value to finance an acquisition at more than intrinsic value; or who fail to buy in their own stock in the market when it is far underpriced because they want to expand, not contract, their own domain, even though the shareholders' interests would be served by a repurchase program.*

Bad Business

Buffett likes to say, "When a management with a reputation for brilliance tackles a business with a reputation for poor fundamental economics, it is the reputation of the business that remains intact."

1. Some of Buffet's least happy early investments were in *retailing* (including trading stamps). He used to say then that he did not understand the retail field. In addition to investment losses on several retailing securities, his negotiated purchase of Hochschild Kohn, a Baltimore department store, also proved a dud. Figures and close observation don't suffice. You need a special flair to under-

---

*As Benjamin Graham says, management "almost always wants as much capital from the owners as it possibly can get, in order to minimize its own financial problems. Thus the typical management will operate with more capital than is necessary if the stockholders permit it—which they often do." *Intelligent Investor,* Chapter 4.

stand what's going on in that field. A store can report good figures year after year and then, as Buffett learned the hard way, suddenly go bankrupt. Later, though, he made some extremely successful investments in furniture and jewelry retailing.

2. *"You bet your company" situations*, such as aircraft manufacturers. Periodically, they have to put the whole company on the line just to stay in business.

Other businesses to avoid include:

3. *Farm-related enterprises.* They have a very long inventory cycle (a whole crop year), and you have to finance the farmer, who has no cash until the harvest (which may fail) is in the barn.* You may show a bookkeeping profit, pay taxes on it, and still end up with receivables that you have trouble collecting.

4. *Businesses heavily dependent on research.* Ben Graham always disagreed with the Wall Street belief that a company with an overwhelming advantage in research and development tends to maintain its lead over its competitors. Graham felt that if the company had to spend so much to stay ahead it was a sign of weakness, not strength.

Buffett counters that in Graham's day there were lots of businesses with inherently privileged positions, which didn't need to spend massively on R&D to hold their lead; today there are very few, so Graham's antipathy to R&D companies is no longer applicable. Buffett nevertheless can't understand the high-technology companies, and for that reason won't touch them.

To that I in turn would reply that the ordinary investor isn't going to understand a large and complex business anyway, so the historical excellence in research of a Merck, say, probably should give him a better indication of its future prospects than could be gained from an attempt

---

*I told Buffett the story of the two farmers in Georgia who were guests on a radio talk show. "What would you do, Jim," the MC asked the first farmer, "if a rich uncle left you a couple of million dollars?"

Jim was thrilled. "Why, ah'd pay off the mortgage, get mahself a new tractor, send the kids to college, and put in a new kitchen. Then ah'd take Minnie round the world like we've always wanted to do."

"And what'd you do with your million, Josh?" the MC asked the other farmer.

Josh wasn't so sure. He rubbed his chin and thought. Finally he said, "Well, ah guess ah'd jest go on farming till it was all gone."

to really understand 3M. Philip Fisher, as we will see, also disagrees with Graham, believing that a successful commitment to innovation is an essential quality in a company that is going to build value for its owners. Outstanding research can keep you ahead.

5. *Debt-burdened companies.* A house with no mortgage obviously is worth more than one that is burdened with one.
6. *Chain-letter businesses*—those with geometric growth requiring more and more cash.
7. *Managements that don't tell the truth.* If they don't, then Buffett doesn't want to be in business with them. Many annual reports are a disgrace, he says. If grave mistakes are made or adversity threatens, the annual report should say so frankly, in the way that one partner would talk to another. Instead, these reports are all too often exercises in optimism and flackery—sales pitches rather than honest expositions.
8. *Long-term service contracts.* Discussing casualty insurance, Buffett observed that it can be fatal to owe an obligation to provide something in the distant future without knowing what it will cost. If you write workmen's compensation and a policyholder is disabled, you are short doctors' fees and hospital costs for twenty years against dollars received today. (Insurance, nevertheless, is Buffett's largest direct business interest. *Assuming first-class management,* other characteristics of the insurance business, notably limiting the dollar value of future obligations, enable it to cope with inflation.)

An easy way to evaluate a life insurance company is to look at its intrinsic worth ten years ago, for instance, and then today: in almost all cases the rate of compounding is unexciting.

"Long-tail reinsurance is a terrifying business," Buffett once told me. "You can have an obligation pop up at you twenty years later with a huge price tag that you never anticipated." (Delayed asbestosis and other such liabilities essentially ruined Lloyd's.)* "Reinsurance rarely turns out to be what it's sold as. Some of the slick fellows who sell it look as conservative and modest as you could possibly want—straight from Central Cast-

---

*Many in England believe that the huge scramble to bring in new "names"—often American—to expand Lloyd's was partly in expectation of vast impending losses.

ing. But they'll stick you all the same." As we will see, though, Buffett later in effect turned Berkshire into a reinsurance company.

Beware Smokestack Industries

One of Buffett's most important messages is his recurring admonition to steer clear of the standard big American heavy industries requiring continuous massive investment. Many of them are in trouble. The cause is competition, overregulation, rising labor costs, and the like. The symptom is that just to stay in business many of these big industries need more money than they can retain out of reported earnings after paying reasonable dividends. To stay in the same place they require endless infusions of net new cash, like many countries in Africa. To be sure, there are dividends on the new stock and interest on the new bonds that they constantly issue, but basically these dividends and interest payments are a loss leader to induce the investor to buy the new securities being issued. He has only an outside chance of ever seeing his principal again in real terms. "Jam tomorrow and jam yesterday, but never jam today."

I observed that this was in a way the subtlety of American capitalism. The owners are coaxed along into putting more and more money (or reinvesting more and more profits) into plant, but are not able to take out net cash that they can take home to spend. It's like fishing with cormorants: They have bands around their necks, so they can have the satisfaction of diving for the fish and filling their gullets, but cannot actually swallow the fish, which are taken away by the boss—in the case of American corporations, by the government and everyone else except the shareholders.

All the Money for Half the Company

Venture capital propositions interest Buffett scarcely at all. Typically, the promoter invites you to put up all the money in a speculative undertaking in exchange for half to three-quarters of the company. Most new ventures soon fail, however.

In a market washout, on the other hand, you can buy a flawless company for a quarter of what it it's worth right then and there, without having to pay off the promoter or take the risk that his dream will never be realized.

For example, when Buffett bought into Disney in early 1966, the stock was at its low, selling for a quarter of what it was worth to a private buyer, with the admirable creative management already in place. The market was placing no value on its huge inventory of former hits, which can be reissued every few years forever, it seems.

The Fortune 500 Syndrome

If you could put a chief executive under sodium pentothal, says Buffett, and dig into the rationale behind his acquisitions, you'd often find he was inspired by his yearning to move up a few places in the *Fortune* list of the five hundred largest companies, not by concern for the value per share of his own company. Many companies, including banks, are run into the ground because the president is concerned with size rather than quality; he becomes hypnotized by his company's rank within the industry.

The Crocker Bank in San Francisco, Buffett observed, paid a premium of approximately $90 million over book value (about twice book, in fact) to buy a troubled bank one-sixth its size, U.S. National of San Diego. Crocker then sold its own stock well below book to pay a large part of the cost of this purchase. The CEO (now retired) did not take the attitude of an owner but of an empire builder. The banker became more important, and the stockholders became poorer. Buffett quotes Morris Shapiro: "There are more banks than bankers."

It's usually better for company not to have a formal acquisitions department, Buffett feels; it results in a pressure, usually misguided, to buy for the sake of buying. Too often the members of the department merely regurgitate what they know to be the inner desires of management.

Using Cash to Buy More Cash

One of Buffett's favorite techniques is to buy a company, such as one in the insurance business, that possesses free cash he can use to buy the next company possessing free cash, and so on. For instance, when Buffett began buying Blue Chip Stamps in 1968, the company had a "float" of over $60 million in outstanding unredeemed stamps. With $25 million of this money Berkshire bought See's Candies, whose annual sales were then $35 million. See's annual sales volume is now multiples of that, and its pretax earnings greatly surpass Buffett's purchase price.

Similarly, Buffett made his purchase of 100 percent of the *Buffalo Evening News* through Blue Chip Stamps.* Blue Chip also bought 80.1 percent of Wesco Financial Corporation, which was then able to buy 100 percent of Precision Steel and Mutual Savings & Loan. Wesco, an

---

*Lord Thomson, the late Canadian magnate who owned fifty-seven American newspapers, had the same idea. He once said, "I buy newspapers to make money to buy more newspapers to make more money. As for editorial content, that's the stuff you separate the ads with."

extremely successful investment, bought 2 percent of Fireman's Fund; Berkshire bought another 5 percent at the same time.

Also, Berkshire makes use of the "float"—premiums held until losses need to be paid out—in its insurance business to buy stocks: essentially a margin account. In addition, it is investing cash reserved to pay deferred taxes. These two sources of low-cost leverage amount to tens of billions. Investing them in stocks or lower-grade preferreds increases risk over what it would be if they were bonds.

To help understand the leverage in this process, which might be called the cash multiplier effect, think of the growth of an empire. Prussia, once a small state, added the military and economic strength of dozens of neighboring principalities to its own and created Greater Germany, with its formidable military apparatus. This larger entity next looked around for further prey. In due course the Wehrmacht gobbled up Austria, the former Czechoslovakia, Poland, Holland, Belgium, and France. Napoleon did exactly the same thing. In these examples, soldiers acquire more soldiers and the gold to pay them with. Those soldiers acquire still more soldiers and gold, until the empire becomes unstuck.

A long discussion in the June 5, 1998, *Grant's* calculated that "in the period from 1991 to 1997 the compound annual growth rate of Berkshire's leverage adjusted pretax returns beat the comparable S&P 500 rate of return by just more than 3 percentage points."

In other words, on a strictly like-for-like basis Buffett's stock-picking (as distinct from business) skill is less remarkable than it appears.

Banking

Buffett points out that banking is one of the few industries in which *there is no advantage to being number one.* What counts is how you manage your assets, liabilities, and costs. And in those respects, size means practically nothing.

He considers banking a splendid business if you don't go crazy. Unfortunately, there is a real risk of precisely that. How do you control lots of eager young men who can manufacture immediate earnings by incurring risks that are not apparent until much later? Often, as Barings and many others discovered, you can't.

In discussing the contrast between a good, tough, businesslike bank manager and a romantic and unbusinesslike one, Buffett commented with amusement that David Rockefeller periodically used to announce that the only thing wrong with Chase, as year after year it lost ground to Citibank, was a few of his top subordinates.

Buffett noted that the Freedom National Bank in New York, an ethnic bank advised by several larger ones, including Chase, lost money in 1975 *before* loan losses, and that it bought more New York municipal paper than its own net worth, even though it had a huge tax loss, so that buying tax-exempts was utterly irrational. Buffett said that *socially oriented business activities still have to make sense:* "Doing business in a half-assed way is no favor to anybody."

Commodities

Buffett agrees with me that *it's scandalous for Wall Street houses to encourage their customers to dabble in commodities.* He says that one can sometimes analyze the long-term price outlook for a nonagricultural commodity, notably a metal. If the price gets way below production cost for an indispensable metal, it must eventually recover, but the prices of agricultural commodities are subject to weather and other vagaries of nature; investing in them becomes a matter of flair. Since he depends on analysis for success, Buffett never will invest in an agricultural commodity.

Still, over time, he has engaged in a few commodities transactions. Two were in silver futures. The first was in the Johnson administration, before the price was freed by the government. Every time the President announced that the price of silver would never rise, Buffett went out and bought more. I describe later another flyer in the late 1990s. But he would never buy more than he could afford to take delivery of in cash: If you buy a metal on margin, even though it reaches your target eventually, it may first go down, wiping you out en route.

Buffett finds ownership of actual metal far safer than ownership of a mining company, which spends $1 billion to extract copper, let's say. Then it reinvests much of its profits in more and more development and facilities. Eventually "the consumers have gotten the copper and the company is left with the hole."

When Bonds Are Better Than Stocks

For high-bracket individuals, tax-exempt bond income is often more attractive than the expectable after-tax return from stocks. Looking ahead, in 1999 Buffett thought that growth of the equities in general might return 6 percent, minus inflation, and about 1 percent of investment transaction fees.

From time to time you can get a similar return from good-quality municipals, such as industrial revenue bonds, without the risks of stock ownership. At such a time, municipals are preferable to stocks. In 1999, he observed that only if you thought that interest rates would fall drastically could you justify present stock prices, but in that event you would be better off buying long bond options.

Liquidity in bonds is not very important, any more than it is in stocks. If one can sell in a week, or even a month, that's good enough—and far better than one expects in real estate. How long does it take to sell a farm? Indeed, *the more one is a true investor. the less one need be concerned about liquidity.*

Accounting, the Language of Business

The first step in training yourself to be a first-class investor is to learn basic accounting. Like a chess master, the investor is playing a competitive game. By the nature of any competitive game, the number of top players must be limited. So if you lack a crucial skill that the best players possess, you greatly diminish your chances.

Without an adequate knowledge of accounting, the investor cannot even understand the subject being discussed, let alone determine where the truth lies. Without it, the investor is at the same disadvantage as an aspiring orchestra conductor who cannot read music. Musical notation is the language of music and figures the language of business. Great musicians may have existed who couldn't read music, and there may be some skillful investors who are baffled by accounting, but they are very, very few.

The investor must spot changes in the accounting system of a company he is interested in and be able to interpret the significance of that change. Why has management switched from LIFO to FIFO? Is it in order to manufacture inventory profits to offset a lack of operating profits? Why, in the investment portfolio of a conglomerate's insurance subsidiary, were capital gains being realized and recognized as ordinary income at the parent company level? Were operating earnings faltering elsewhere in the system? Questions of this sort emerge from a careful study of the figures.

Thanks to the SEC, most public companies divulge an extraordinary amount of information, not only in annual reports, proxy statements, and quarterly earnings reports, but also in the 10K, which is a treasure house of insight into a company's affairs. The skillful investor as a matter of course works his way through all the figures in each of these reports. He uses them as a starting point for more detailed inquiries, which he conducts directly with the company, its competition, and other sources.

What if the figures don't give the whole story, as in today's vogue of Internet stocks? In that situation, Buffett won't play. At his 1998 annual meeting he said that if he were teaching a business school course, "for the final exam, I would take an Internet company and say, 'How much is this worth?' And anybody that gave me an answer would flunk."

Buffett has never seen a stockbroker's report on a company that discussed a business the way its manager would discuss it with an individual owner he was reporting to, and in general he does not find it worth reading them. He tells the story, which he said reminds him of Wall Street, of a fisherman who goes into a sporting supply store. The salesman offers him a fantastic lure for bass: painted eyes, half a dozen hooks, imitation bugs—a whole junk shop. The fisherman asks the salesman incredulously, "Do fish really like this thing?"

The salesman replies coldly, "I don't sell to fish."

Stock Options

When an enterprise is controlled by its executives, and these executives are not overly scrupulous, they will often reward themselves with lush option plans based on the performance of the company's common stock. However, says Buffett, the stock may rise even though the executive has *not* done a good job. He notes that in Berkshire Hathaway some executives stand to make as much as $2 million a year in performance bonuses, but only on the results of their division, not on the performance of the stock of the parent company.

Some other injustices of the option technique of rewarding managers, he observes, are these:

1. By the simple compounding of retained profits, a share of stock in a mediocre business where management makes little contribution can enormously increase in value over the years, rewarding the manager in a princely fashion for doing very little.

2. It is often said that giving the manager an option on the stock puts him and the other shareholders in the same boat. In fact, however, the shareholders participate in all the risks, whereas the option holder participates only in profits . . . not a fair deal!

Coca-Cola

After his Capital Cities/ABC purchase in 1985, Buffett did not buy a significant stock position for three years. But on March 15, 1989, Berkshire announced that it had become the largest shareholder of the Coca-Cola Company, with 6.3 percent of the stock. It had paid just over $1 billion, at an average price of $10.96 a share. Eventually it would increase the holding to 7.8 percent.

Perhaps Buffett was giving a coy signal when he mentioned in Berkshire's 1985 annual report that he was switching from Pepsi to cherry Coke. While the quality of Coke's products was obviously a key factor—it makes four of the top five carbonated drinks in the world—Buffett's enthusiasm was also based on the strength of the brand name and the virtual certainty of continued overseas expansion. That happens more easily than in standard manufacturing, since Coke syrup can be exported without necessarily building additional bottling capacity. It is a typical Buffett company: simple and understandable, not high-tech. It exemplifies his maxim "Stick to what you know." The product is cheap, and he drinks it incessantly every day. Every bottle or can renders a penny of profit to the company. For the world it is a symbol of America. (De Gaulle used to rail against *Cocacolonization*.) "Fundamentally, this is the best large business in the world," said Buffett. "It's universally liked—the per capita consumption goes up almost every year in almost every country." In the temperate zone, average daily consumption of fluids is about sixty-four ounces, of which in the United States a quarter or so is soft drinks, over 40 percent Coca-Cola. Soft drink consumption as a proportion of fluid intake seems to rise continually. He added that even with $100 billion he could not take away Coke's world leadership in soft drinks.

Unlike some of his other big acquisitions, such as GEICO and the *Washington Post*, Coca-Cola did not appear conspicuously cheap when Buffett bought it. In late 1988 it was selling for thirteen times expected 1989 earnings, or some 15 percent above the market. The long-term future was what seemed so attractive. Buffett—like everyone else—was highly impressed by then CEO Roberto C. Goizueta, who was using excess cash flow to retire stock and had developed a system of grading managers according to their return on capital, just as Buffett recommends.

In the event, Buffett did not have that long to wait. Within three years his stake was worth $3.75 billion, almost the previous total value of Berkshire. By mid-1999 its value was $13.4 billion—ten times his cost. The market recognized what he had detected earlier, that the position of the brand—its goodwill—was unique.

In buying Coca-Cola, Buffett shifted from the traditional Graham "cigar butts" approach in favor of the technique sometimes called GARP—"growth at a reasonable price." He said recently that before buying he closes his eyes and tries to visualize how the company will look ten years hence. An excellent idea! . . . but not Graham. As his investing style has evolved from Grahamite bargain-hunting for "cigar butts"—value investing—to buying prime growth stocks, Buffett has started dismissing that distinction, saying that both techniques involve analyzing the present value of the future cash flow you expect to receive. That is, of course, partly true, although also a rationalization. The time horizon is quite different: Graham made tactical moves and wanted enough hard assets and cash to provide his margin of safety then and there, even in bankruptcy.

The Salomon Imbroglio

In 1987, Buffett received a call from his friend John Gutfreund, head of Salomon Brothers. Gutfreund told Buffett that Ronald O. Perelman, head of Revlon, was thinking of buying the Oppenheimer family's large holding of Salomon. Perelman was advised by Bruce Wasserstein, who was probably angling for Gutfreund's own job: for Gutfreund a distressing conception. On September 28, Buffett agreed to invest $700 million in a specially created 9 percent preferred stock issue, convertible into common. With this money Salomon could buy back the Oppenheimer stock. Since the preferred paid 9 percent, far more than the common, and enjoyed a senior position, plus convertibility, Gutfreund was giving Buffett a gross advantage over existing shareholders. Unkind commentators suggested that Gutfreund was in effect paying Buffett several hundred million dollars of his shareholders' money for a lifetime employment contract. The fair arrangement would have been for Buffett to buy the Oppenheimer common stock directly.

On August 9, 1991, Salomon disclosed that it had found "irregularities and rule violations in connection with its bids at a number of Treasury securities auctions." It had attempted to partially corner the Treasury note market by making excessive bids—including bids on behalf of customers who didn't know about them. The scandal soon engulfed Gutfreund and other higher-ups, who for months had failed, as was required, to disclose the information to the Treasury, and only did so when investigators were closing in.

Buffett had to become interim chairman. He forced the resignations of Gutfreund and two other top executives, fired two bond traders, and appointed Deryck C. Maughan, chairman of Salomon in Japan, to take over.

Considering management's failure to report the violations, the Treasury decided to ban Salomon from future T-bill auctions. This would have sunk the firm. The decision was reversed after Buffett appealed to the Secretary of the Treasury.

Buffett cut $110 million from the funds set aside for bonuses in 1991. He also sold some $40 billion of Salomon's securities to reduce its market exposure.

Finally, Salomon was fined $220 million, a stunning penalty. Between November 1993 and May 1994, Buffett bought more Salomon stock. Then, on September 24, 1997, Travelers Group acquired Salomon for $9 billion. So in the end the investment worked out well, but at great pain.

Salomon offered Gutfreund a comfortable golden handshake and immunity from lawsuits. He wanted more, and demanded arbitration. In that proceeding his golden handshake was eliminated completely and his immunity to litigation lifted, opening him up to a blizzard of extremely costly suits.

Here is how Michael Lewis summed up the transaction in a *New Republic* cover article (which, however, contained a number of inaccuracies):

> For $700 million and a job guarantee for Gutfreund, Buffett was given a security that combined the juicy bits of a stock and a bond. It guaranteed him a return of 9 percent a year, established him as the controlling shareholder of Salomon Brothers, and left him with about the same opportunity for huge gain as the ordinary shareholder—without the risks. Auctioned on the open market, the $700 million convertible preferred would have fetched anywhere from $850 million to $1.2 billion. His windfall came out of the shareholders' pockets, since his cheap option diluted the value of the existing shares.

Recent Investments

As the market began recovering briskly, Buffett bought Gillette, USAir, and Champion International. All three had been targets of possible takeovers. In each instance, management offered Buffett a new convertible preferred stock. He would receive a fixed coupon—9 percent, on average—and an option to convert to common stock if the shares rose. However, Berkshire undertook not to sell each holding for a decade. The business press was critical. "Mr. Buffett is getting 'whitemail' to stick around and hold management's hand," said the *Wall Street Journal.*

Buffett's $600 million investment in Gillette resembled his Coca-Cola purchase: The company made one main product extremely well, and had a huge and growing overseas operation. (Later it bought Duracell, which now contributes over a quarter of its profits.) It had a long history (dating from 1901, in fact) and a respected chairman, Harvard Business School graduate Colman C. Mokler, Jr., who had been running it since 1975. With the launch of the new Sensor razor in July 1990, Gillette stock began rising dramatically. In April 1991, Berkshire converted its stake into 11 percent of the company's stock. After a two-for-one split, this resulted in 24 million shares worth $1.5 billion; in mid-1999 this figure was $4.6 billion.

USAir and Champion were more curious moves. Both were tough, capital-intensive businesses. For USAir, labor costs, competition, and accidents were all potential problems. Berkshire made its $358 million investment just two days after USAir merged with Piedmont. The following year, six of the nation's top twelve airlines filed for bankruptcy protection. Still, if Buffett lost his gamble, he would nevertheless earn 9 percent interest. If he won, he would have a major stake in a powerful airline. However, USAir lost almost $500 million in the year after Buffett's purchase, and thereafter the stock went right on down. Buffett characterized his decision to buy USAir as "superficial and wrong."

Berkshire's $300 million investment in Champion, a producer of pulp and paper, came in December 1989. That year, though earnings were poor, CEO Andrew Sigler paid himself over $1.2 million, plus stock options. Champion continued to make heavy capital investments over the years and to receive poor earnings in return.

Buffett fared better with his 1990 decision to buy stock in Wells Fargo, a major San Francisco bank. He had again selected a company with a successful image and history, dating back to 1852. But 1990 was a horrible time for banks, and Buffett seemed mad to buy, even though the price-earnings ratio was down to 3.7. But the bank had, in fact, been profitable in every year of its existence, even during the Great

Depression. It also had a stake in the booming California economy, and in the growth of the Pacific Rim.

Buffet bought his shares at about book value, which was $58 at the time—five times earnings. That was down from a recent high of $84. For five million shares (almost 10 percent of the common stock) he paid $289 million.

Wells Fargo was run by Carl Reichardt, a friend of Buffett's. Reichardt was a cost-cutter. He had sold the company jet and frozen salaries of top executives during an earlier rough period. He had also recognized early on the problem of bad third-world loans and had the lowest exposure to foreign loans of any big bank in the country. When Reichardt found out that one of his executives wanted to buy a Christmas tree for the office, Reichardt told him to buy it with his own money. "When we heard that we bought more stock," Charlie Munger, Berkshire's vice chairman, said at the annual meeting in 1991.

As a leading real estate lender, Wells Fargo was thought to be vulnerable to overbuilding on the West Coast. Indeed, that was a prime reason the stock fell almost 50 percent in a few months in early 1990. However, Buffett felt real estate would rebound in the long term.

A year after Buffett bought Wells Fargo it was up 25 percent. He continued buying shares in 1992 at prices ranging from $66 to $69 per share. On January 19, Wells Fargo reported better than expected results, and the stock rose to $99. The real estate market did indeed rebound, and by December 1997, Buffett's 6,690,218 shares were valued at $2.27 billion.

In 1988, Berkshire's Wesco unit bought a major stake in Federal Home Loan Mortgage Co., often known as Freddie Mac. The company had a solid record, a low price-earnings ratio, and a central position in American life. Freddie Mac helps Americans to buy homes; its only direct competitor is Fannie Mae. But immediately after Buffett bought it, the stock dropped by two-thirds. As it recovered, Buffett upped his holding, which by 1999 had multiplied some twenty times.

Buffett was back in the headlines with an announcement on February 3, 1998, that he had amassed 129.7 million ounces of silver, one-fifth of the world's stock. This was more than the Hunt brothers had owned in 1980. He had started buying in July 1997 at $4.22 an ounce. By the first week of February 1998, the price had soared to a ten-year high of $7.20, making Buffett's stake worth over $900 million. He managed to sell off some 30 percent of his holdings that month. The

London bullion market could not handle the volume and temporarily extended its five-day delivery rule to fifteen days. After a month, the regular schedule was resumed. Buffett explained his purchase by pointing out that in recent years the demand for silver from the jewelry and photography industries had exceeded the supply from recycling and mine production.

In the same period he also put $2 billion into twenty-to-thirty-year zero-coupon bonds with a collective face value of $10 billion, later sold at a good profit.

In 1998, Berkshire paid $730 million for Executive Jet, leader in the fractional-ownership market of private jets.

Super-Cat

For a number of years Berkshire has made use of its high net worth to reinsure insurance policies against very large catastrophes—"super-cat." In mid-1985 it invited commercial customers to propose policies for any type of risk with premiums of $1 million a year or more. To avoid protracted negotiation, a prospective customer had to propose his own deal: Berkshire would refuse any offer it found unsatisfactory, with no second chance. This system netted over $100 million in premiums. In November 1996, Buffett agreed to sell the California state-run insurance agency $1.5 billion of reinsurance against the risk of the "big one"—a devastating earthquake—striking before March 31, 2001. Berkshire gets $160 million a year in premiums for four years, or $640 million in all. Actuaries place the odds of the company's losing this gamble at twenty to one, so in fact the bet is very attractive indeed.

General Re

On June 19, 1998, Berkshire Hathaway acquired General Re, a holding company for global reinsurance and related risk management operations, paying in stock. It owns General Reinsurance Corporation and National Reinsurance Corporation, the largest professional property/casualty reinsurance group in the United States, and also holds a controlling interest in a major international reinsurer. The cost of the deal was $22 billion. It created a $56 billion entity. General Re brings over $20 billion in low-cost to no-cost "float," or funds from premiums that have been paid by clients but not yet paid out by the company in claims. It also brought down the percentage of its portfolio that Berkshire had in equity without incurring capital gains taxes, since Buffett had General Re sell its equities before the consolidation.

Buffett explained the move in a press release:

> First, this transaction removes constraints on earnings volatility that have caused General Re, in the past, to lay off substantial amounts of the business that it does write. . . . As part of Berkshire, this constraint will disappear, which will enhance both General Re's long-term profitability and its ability to write more business.
>
> Second, General Re has substantial opportunities to develop its global reinsurance franchise. As part of Berkshire, General Re will be able to make investments to grow into international business as quickly as it sees fit. . . .
>
> Finally, Berkshire's insurance subsidiaries never need to worry about having abundant capital. Therefore, they can follow whatever asset strategy makes the most sense, unconstrained by the effect on the capital of the Company of a sharp market decline. Periodically, this flexibility has proven of enormous advantage to Berkshire's insurance subsidiaries.

Since the whole of Berkshire's capital is thus in a way backing General Re, its CEO is the one person Buffett talks to every day.

GEICO and now the General Re transaction have changed the look of Berkshire from a holding company with a huge embedded capital gains liability to an insurance operating company. However, there is an overcapacity problem in the reinsurance market. And General Re has so far taken a $275 million loss on its share of a workers' compensation fiasco called Unicover, in which its Cologne Re subsidiary and two other companies accepted a $2.8 billion future payout liability in return for a $700 million premium. When he bought General Re, Buffett seems not to have been aware of the problem, which demonstrates the truth of his strictures against long-tail underwriting.

Succession

Warren Buffett was sixty-nine years old in 2000. What will happen when he is no longer there to run Berkshire? For a long time his immediate successor was expected to be Charles T. Munger, Buffett's curmudgeonly colleague and straight man since 1959, who had nudged him away from bargain-hunting and toward buying growth companies. But Munger, seventy-six years old in 2000, is a billionaire himself, and he has drifted out of the picture. Buffett says he didn't even consult him on the General Re acquisition, which transformed Berkshire. So another name is heard: Louis Simpson, head of GEICO, the auto insurance company based in Washington, D.C., which Berkshire owns. Simpson has shown superior stock-picking skills. From the beginning of his tenure in 1980 through 1996, GEICO had a 24.66 percent annual return on its investments, compared to 26.77 percent for Berkshire and 17.25 percent for the S&P 500. Buffett has intimated that the succession may be split, with one man handling operations and another investments.

Buffett has become a financial celebrity, and his annual shareholders' meetings an extravaganza. He is likely to speak for only a few moments before opening the floor to questions, which continue for as long as three hours. The meetings have grown so huge as to require a stadium. Buffett refers to them as "a capitalist's version of Woodstock," with exhibits mounted by the companies Berkshire controls. This is a departure from the spirit of the company's annual report, in whose austerity Buffett takes pride, and from which even photographs are banned. Sooner or later, standouts in almost any field succumb to the temptation of publicity.

Buffett has begun to hobnob with movie stars and other celebrities. He walked on the Great Wall of China with his friend Bill Gates, and he makes soap opera appearances playing himself—one in 1991 and one in 1993 on ABC's *All My Children.* Flattering biographies have begun appearing, and a book of aphorisms—*Warren Buffett Speaks*—offering such quips as "It's only when the tide goes out that you learn who's been swimming naked."[*] Some material in those biographies can be quite instructive,[†] although Buffett's techniques should not all be imitated by less skillful practitioners. One book extolls the "Focus Investment Strategy"—holding very few stocks, like Berkshire. Well, fine: That's like saying that since tennis champions serve with prodigious force, all players should serve as hard as they possibly can. Actually, for most players that just means that their serves go out. Indeed, the new Prudent Investor Rule,[‡] now the law in most states, *requires* that trustees diversify.

---

[*] Actually, though, swimmers are unaffected by a falling tide.
[†] Particularly that material in Andrew Kilpatrick's *Of Permanent Value: The Story of Warren Buffet* (McGraw Hill, 1999).
[‡] See my book *Investing and Managing Trusts Under the New Prudent Investor Rule* (Harper-Collins, 1999).

A website called Buffett Watch can be very interesting for those wishing to follow Berkshire and Buffett's transactions. A sample is included in Appendix II.

Munger's Principles

Charlie Munger, an eminent investor in his own right, expressed several Buffettesque investment principles in a speech of which John Templeton sent me a summary. Here they are, slightly edited:

1. *Specialization in the business world often produces very good business economics.*

2. *Advantages of scale are important.* When Jack Welch says he's either going to be number one or number two in a business or out, he is not crazy, just tough. Too many incompetent CEOs do not understand this. But bigger is *not* better if it creates bureaucracy, e.g., the federal government or AT&T.

3. *Technology can either help you or kill you.* The difference is whether the customer gets all the savings or if some of the savings go to the shareholders.

4. *Investors should figure out where they have an edge and stay there. Stay in your circle of competence.* Remember the John Train question: "How do you beat Bobby Fischer?" Reply: "Get him to play you any game except chess."

5. *Winners bet big when they have the odds—otherwise, never.* Those who make a few well-calculated bets have a much greater chance. Very few investors or investment funds operate this way. So, *load up on a good idea; it is hard to find a good business at a great discount.*

6. *A significant discount means more upside and a greater margin of safety.* Buy shares of a good business at a significant discount to what a private buyer would pay.

7. *Buy quality businesses even if you have to pay up.* Warren Buffett claims this is the most important thing he ever learned from Charlie Munger.

8. *Low turnover reduces taxes and increases your return.* Two investors earn the same compound annual return of 15 percent for thirty years. If the first pays a 35 percent tax at the end of the thirty years and the second pays a 35 percent tax each year, the first investor will have over two and a half times as much money as the second.

Philanthropy

Buffett is a miser, and finds it painful to part with money, even, as we have seen, to give it to his children. He did establish the Buffett Foundation in 1979 to begin making some charitable contributions. That year, when Buffett had a net worth of $150 million, the foundation's gifts amounted to $38,453. By 1990, the figure grew to $2.3 million, and by 1997 to $10 million.

Buffett allows the stockholders of Berkshire Hathaway to designate their pro rata share of the company's charitable gifts. That sounds generous, but isn't. Ordinarily, a large company would make donations to dozens or hundreds of charities, often local. A few would be the CEO's pets. But since Buffett owns almost half the company, he designates not merely a handful of charities—5 percent of the total gift, let's say—but just under half, which goes to his own foundation. It, in turn, gives away very little indeed.

The foundation has two main concerns. The first is the prevention of nuclear war. He has paid $200,000 toward "risk reduction centers" in Moscow and Washington, equipped with faxes and phones, where one could communicate in the event of a crisis. To be sure, the two governments already have this capability, as do media and other companies.

Another focus is population control. More than $8 million of the modest $10 million the Buffett Foundation disbursed in 1997 went to family planning, sex education, birth control centers, and the like. The foundation gave $2 million between 1995 and 1996 for research on the "RU-486" abortion pill. However, birth rates are stabilizing worldwide, except for the moment in some countries such as India, and indeed have fallen to 1.3 children per couple or so in many countries, such as Japan, European Russia, Germany, Spain, and Italy. Several of them will in the near future be losing 30 percent of their population per generation. South America is on the same curve. AIDS may offset high natality in Africa. Even the U.S. population is kept stable only by immigration.

Roger Lowenstein in *Buffett: The Making of an American Capitalist* observes:

> It is striking that both of Buffett's "causes" were aimed at alleviating or preventing *future* sources of grief, such as a future war or a future oversupply of people. Virtually none of his immense resources went to help people who were already born—people who were here and now poor, sick, living in urban blight, illiterate; or

people raising money for here-and-now concert halls, museums, universities, and hospitals (save for endowments of abortion or family planning programs). Buffett's almost exclusive focus on such macro-economic, futuristic issues gave his philanthropy a detached—almost dehumanized—quality.

Summary

How is one to evaluate the stock of Berkshire Hathaway? An extremely difficult task, since one needs to calculate factors that are far from obvious to the traditional analyst. For many years, Buffett himself often announced that he did not expect to be able to put his increasingly unwieldy capital to work at his historic rate of return. This would have been true if he had stuck to the Graham approach, but he found it well within his powers to switch to a growth strategy—not necessarily T. Rowe Price's very high growth, but GARP, growth at a reasonable price. Also, as discussed above, he deploys insurance company cash for leverage. However, there is a "Buffett premium" built into Berkshire's stock price which amounts to an actuarial calculation: How long will he retain his faculties? In 1999 one of the large stockholders closest to the company said that this premium amounts to about a ten-year longevity assumption. Is that a good bet? Who knows? The company might get so big that his traditional maneuvers become very difficult, or Buffett might lose his grip, or, like Munger, he might decide he does not want to keep up this activity forever.

In a larger sense than just business, Buffett is a supremely rational player of a personally irrational game. Think of a pinball player who works the machine month after month and year after year until he has run up a trillion points that he can only exchange for more free games. Buffett is—as he rightly says a great success must be—a fanatic, obsessed with his score. His charities are tiny, given his circumstances, and the purposes of the huge foundation he will leave behind him are little considered, unlike Andrew Carnegie, whose libraries stand all over America.

To get richer and richer vastly beyond what can be spent resembles practicing body-building until you become the size of a gorilla, then a horse, and finally an elephant. Objectively, it does you no good. In "quality of life," or cultural or philosophical terms, Buffett is unremarkable. As he says himself, he does not live better than other people, he just *travels* better than other people—jetting, however, not for enjoyment but from one corporate concern to another.

Of late a new aspect has appeared, Buffett as a cult figure, holding the annual "Woodstock" in Omaha for his followers. One gets a boost from being cheered by admirers, and since perforce the Berkshire shareholders who make the trek to Omaha are fans, it's heady stuff. (There is no counter-convention of those who regret that they *sold* their Coca-Cola to Berkshire.) But the quiet operator often does better than the publicity seeker.* Managing your public image takes away time and attention from what justified it.

Buffett has done well to maintain his easygoing corn-fed persona even though the reality is that of a driven accumulator. (One recent visitor reported that he had gnawed his fingernails down to the quick.) Bill Gates, in contrast, is a prodigious benefactor of society, but is nevertheless broadly unpopular because of his nerdy manner.

An important point deserves emphasis, namely that Buffett is a scrupulously ethical operator by business standards. One cannot be enthusiastic about the "whitemail," to use the *Wall Street Journal* characterization, in the Gillette, USAir, and Champion transactions, but it was legal. The Salomon investment, to be sure, was unsavory, as discussed previously, since it took advantage of the existing shareholders and provoked shareholder suits, but it was legal. And the people in the wholly owned Berkshire subsidiaries seem well content with their lot: They're still doing what they liked doing before (except for John Gutfreund), and under highly stable auspices.

Where does Buffett stand in merit with other public figures? Essentially, he has succeeded in transferring a large sum from the pockets of less skillful investors to those of himself and his followers. His part will someday be turned over to his estranged wife, for this purpose an unknown quantity, and then to trustees to manage for objectives of uncertain importance. But will the whole exercise have been productive? That's not Buffett's concern. He is running up a prodigious score, not building Jerusalem.

The Outlook

Twenty years back, Buffett told *Forbes* unequivocally: "Stocks now sell at levels that should produce long-term returns far superior to bonds." So true! Since then, through November 1999, the S&P 500

---

*"I have observed," said Nick the Greek, "that newspaper publicity is usually followed by a jail sentence."

returned 17.2 percent a year, as compared with about 9.79 percent for bonds.

Recently, however, Buffett has several times issued a somber warning. Equities, he says, will disappoint investors with less than five years' experience, who, according to recent polls, foresee ten-year annual returns of about 23 percent, while even the most experienced investors anticipate about 13 percent.

What about the information age companies? Buffett compares them with the automobile and the airplane. All but three of the hundreds of early car makers expired, and all the aircraft manufacturers in the aggregate made no money net for their investors up to 1992. Just so, argues Buffett, the Internet may change the world, but the stocks are seriously overpriced. The search for *individual companies with a moat around them* is the correct orientation for the investor.

Three

JOHN TEMPLETON
SEARCH MANY MARKETS

DURING THE DEPRESSION, WHILE JOHN TEMPLETON WAS IN his second year at Yale, his father told him that he couldn't give him any more money for his education. So Templeton worked his way through college with the aid of scholarships. After that he won a Rhodes scholarship and went to Oxford for two years, seeing Europe during his vacations. Then he came home to Tennessee, and thereafter migrated to New York, first as a trainee at Merrill Lynch, and after that in a seismic exploration company.

When World War II began, Templeton became convinced that the ten-year slump in stock prices was over and everything would boom—especially the Cinderellas that nobody considered suitable investments. So one day he called his broker and told him to buy one hundred shares of every single listed stock that was selling at less than $1. He got 104 corporate dogs for about $10,000. Four years later he sold the whole kennel for about $40,000—around $1 million in today's money.

Motto: *Never sell on war news.* War is bearish for money, and thus bullish for things, including things represented by stocks.

That extraordinary transaction set the pattern for Templeton's later ones. He *insisted on buying only what was being thrown away.* Also, he had held the stocks he had bought for an average of four years, which usually gives a bargain enough time to be recognized, and a stock to move to a higher multiple of higher earnings—the "double play," as I call it. (Of course, you completely miss the ten- or twenty-year run of the great growth stock in its prime, which for most investors is their best hope of stock market profits.)

Anyway, Templeton took the money and bought a tiny investment counsel firm, which he built up to a medium-sized one and sold to Piedmont Management, except for a small Canadian fund Piedmont didn't want to buy.

At fifty-six, John Templeton started all over again. He resolved, first, that he would never let himself get so busy that he ran out of time—time not only to think about investments but also to reflect on the larger world, particularly the various approaches to religion. He moved to Nassau, and on the grounds of the Lyford Cay Club built a white house in the Southern style, with columns on all four sides. There he assembled his securities files and started giving his attention to managing his one tiny remaining fund, of which he and some of his old clients owned most of the shares. The record of this fund in the next years proved that John Templeton is one of the great investors. Over the twenty years ending December 31, 1978, a $1,000 investment in his fund, with distributions reinvested, became worth about $20,000—making it the top performer of all funds then in existence. About that time, noticing his name year after year in the performance records, I telephoned him from New York, and then went to visit him in Nassau.

The small size of Templeton Growth Fund obviously permitted a flexibility not enjoyed by the managers of a hundred times as much money. A $100,000 commitment in the stock of a small company can substantially affect a fund's performance if it doubles. Also, at that size Templeton could sell stocks and raise cash when he got edgy, which the largest funds almost never do. He sometimes moved 50 percent into reserves, although he says he has little ability to recognize tops and bottoms in the market—a trait he shares with most of the top stock-pickers.

His investment selections range over many markets. He is quite as much at home in the Japanese and Canadian exchanges as in ours, and knows those of most other countries.

Perhaps most important of all, he did not need to stick to large, familiar names—what trust companies call "quality." An established small specialty company with fat profit margins selling for a low price-earnings ratio is often a safer investment—if you are sure you have the facts right—than a huge, mediocre, heavily unionized and regulated standard industrial that sells at a high price because everybody knows about it. Templeton would buy into dozens of little companies his clients had never heard of, and was prepared to take almost all the stock available. Managers of large portfolios avoid smaller companies. They fear—rightly, on the whole—that they can't efficiently learn enough about them. If they are dealing in big numbers, taking the time to master small situations doesn't pay.

Incidentally, the willingness to invest in many countries ties in with a willingness to buy "junior" stocks. Quite often the smaller, cheaper, faster-growing company is outside the United States. For instance, while Safeway was selling at about eight times earnings, with some hope of a 15 percent growth rate in the future, Ito Yokado, the best-managed and second-largest supermarket chain in Japan, was at ten times earnings, growing at more than 30 percent. Templeton felt that in Japan, supermarkets, which are a direct bridge between the producer and the consumer, were still in their infancy, and had decades to grow before they became as common as they are in the United States.

Real estate provides another example. Templeton considers it a field of perennial interest, particularly in an inflationary era. Having looked at real estate companies in Japan and England—where they enjoy great favor with investors—he discovered that the Canadian market offered better bargains than either. Once he had decided to invest in Canadian real estate, he chose a package of companies that almost no American investor—even a professional—would have heard of: Abbey Glen Property, Daon Development, S. B. McLaughlin Associates, and Nu-West Development, all bought at between two and four times cash flow per share; also Allarco, at five times (which, however, he expected to triple). A willingness to invest in smaller companies further implies great diversification among stocks. The fund's portfolio in those days contained over two hundred different issues.

Still, the advantages of internationalism, small size, and diversification into secondary names only set the stage for superior performance. They don't bring it about.

So, what is Templeton's technique? How does he do it?

Flexibility

Templeton's basic philosophy can be stated in one sentence: *Search among many markets for the companies selling for the smallest fraction of their true worth.*

He is not content to buy a bargain. It must be the *best* bargain. Of course, many seeming bargains are nothing of the sort. So when he finds one, he studies and it restudies it, and only buys the stock when he is convinced the values are authentic. Even then, he ruefully admits, he makes constant mistakes. They are inevitable. But because he is heavily diversified, the damage is limited.

The best bargains will be in stocks that are completely neglected, that other investors are not even studying. That, of course, explains the proliferation of unfamiliar names in his portfolio. "Look it over," he said to me, with his usual bland smile. "I'll bet you don't know more than a third of them." I did a bit better, but not much. And a number of the companies I was familiar with were on his list for reasons I didn't immediately think of.

At some time almost anything is likely to become a bargain, if you're in a position to evaluate the neglected factor that will change things for the better. To perceive this factor you have to wear different glasses from those worn by others who don't like what they see. Templeton thinks that more than any other skill, the investor needs this ability to recognize unfamiliar values. He calls it flexibility. *A flexible viewpoint is the professional investor's greatest need, and will be increasingly so in the future.*

Templeton is always attentive to the tendency toward direct or disguised expropriation in a given country—not only outright takeovers, but price controls* and other constraints that inhibit business and destroy the investor's incentive. *Always ask yourself whether a company is in an industry that's a natural candidate for government control.* The answer should be sought on a worldwide basis. For instance, in almost all countries, banks are a natural target of government intervention. So are mining companies.

Templeton offered women's hats as a perfect regulation-proof industry. I replied that through the years the Romans and others tried to regulate the excesses of women's clothes through sumptuary laws—generally without success. Templeton was entertained by my observation that Tampax seemed an unlikely subject of regulation. One could scarcely conceive of Teddy Kennedy rising on the Senate floor to excoriate the profiteers behind this humble accoutrement: "I have here in my hand . . ." (Even Tampax was in fact the subject of an attempt at price regulation in Britain.)

Templeton cited Josten's, Inc., as a company that should not be a natural target of regulation. It is America's leading maker of high

---

* He agrees with "Train's Law"—*Price controls increase prices* (by reducing production). How slow mankind has been to learn this simple truth, and how expensive it has been. Rent control has wrecked large sections of some of our major cities.

school class rings and has a strong position in academic diplomas, caps and gowns, and yearbooks, with steadily rising earnings for decades. He pointed out that hotel-room prices are less subject to control than residential rents. Newspaper chains, I observed, some of which are money machines and ideal monopolies, are regulation-resistant. Freedom of the press!

The other perennial problem is inflation (although not in America, just now). A company must be able to cope with inflation to be a sound investment. Advertising agencies have this ability, Templeton observes: Their income is a percentage of the customers' gross advertising outlay, so as prices go up their income rises accordingly. He believes that eventually most countries should switch to inflation accounting, which shows what a company is doing in real terms, not just in nominal dollars; when that happens, the earnings of companies with high debt loads will at least double as they are seen to be repaying their bondholders with depreciating currency.

Debt-ridden real estate companies are, on the contrary, excellent speculations during inflation. They are thoroughly unpopular—despised, in fact, except in England and Japan.

Another inflation hedge that Templeton likes is shopping centers. Often the leases between the landlord and the operator are specifically drawn to offset inflation and provide for escalation of payments according to a formula linked to turnover. If the supermarket's volume rises, so does the rent it pays to the owner of the center.

While Templeton has tried venture capital investing, his experiences have been unsatisfactory; he was giving far more time to his stable of new ventures than their place in his portfolio justified. A particularly acute example was Investors Overseas Services, Bernie Cornfeld's fund management company, much of whose activity was fraudulent.

Perspective

Listening to Templeton emphasize the importance of trying to see the values that the public is overlooking, I was reminded of Hemingway's advice that at the moment of climactic action a writer should take his attention from the main event—the torero going in over the horns, or the boxer flooring his opponent—and study the crowd, lost in its own emotion, unconscious of itself. Theodor Reik talks of the importance of listening with the "third ear": behind the self-centered babble of the patient there emerges a quite different, simpler pattern—the real message, the essential truth of the situation, of which the speaker is unaware, and for which the therapist should always be listening. But how does the investor escape from the unending static of "news" and opinion, the surge and ebb of the passions of the crowd?

One answer is experience. After thirty years of getting a bloody nose every time he jumps on a bandwagon, even the most enthusiastic investor attains some measure of detachment from the crowd's enthusiasms and desperations.

Templeton has gone a lot further, though, to make it as easy as possible for him to keep his perspective. The distance from his large, cool, porticoed white house on its little hill overlooking the grounds of the Lyford Cay to the roar and shouting of the floor of the stock exchange is measured in psychological light-years. The house itself and everything in it are a silent reproach to excitement and hyperactivity.

Templeton himself—a spare, neat man, even in that warm climate carefully dressed in pale lime-colored trousers and a striped lemon-colored jacket with a neat striped tie—would be, one knows at once, the last man in creation to fall victim to some ephemeral enthusiasm. As he drives slowly in his blue Rolls from his house to the club to have a light lunch with a Canadian banker, is his soul full of passionate yearnings to catch a one-week move in some over-the-counter speculation? Scarcely.

Does he spend feverish days on the telephone, getting the latest gossip from the brokers, the latest news, and the jokes going round the floor? Scarcely. The brokers send him in writing what they think he'd like to see; they do not telephone. The whole mise-en-scène helps Templeton do his job.

The Lyford Cay Club floats in space, financially speaking. Its members are drawn from dozens of countries, and the tone is far more English than American. One has no predisposition to think automatically in terms of American stocks, as a portfolio manager in Minneapolis would, or of European stocks, as would one in Hamburg. The investment scene as viewed from Nassau resembles a coral reef perceived through a glass-bottom boat: You float by and study what seems interesting, without being anchored to one spot or another. Templeton's remoteness certainly helps him reflect judiciously on the risks and rewards in the various countries he is prepared to invest in.

Another advantage to Lyford Cay, surprisingly enough, is Templeton's access to firsthand information. A portfolio manager in New York is likely to have contacts with other portfolio managers and with stock-brokers, who themselves have limited information and are always try-ing to sell him things. The population of Lyford Cay, on the other hand, is made up of successful industrialists and financiers from many parts of the world—they have to be, to pay the dues—and their guests. They have come to enjoy the sun on vacation and enjoy themselves. One can exchange opinions with them easily in that attractive ambience, much more easily than would be likely in an office visit on a tight schedule.

Good Countries

How does Templeton decide which are the countries to invest in and which are not?

Obviously, the ones to avoid are those that have conditions that make investment difficult or impossible: socialism and inflation. The two go together. Either stifles growth.

For years Templeton favored Japan, and historically perhaps the most striking thing about his fund, after its interest in small "special situations," was its concentration of investment in that country, which reached a peak of 60 percent in 1970, and was later cut drastically.

In 1962, when Templeton first got interested in Japan, one could buy the leading companies at two or three times real earnings, with the benefit of extensive hidden assets that didn't appear on the balance sheet. American and European investors just couldn't believe their eyes, so the bargains persisted year after year: pharmaceutical compa-nies growing 30 percent per year and selling for a third of the multiples of the comparable U.S. companies.

By the 1980s, the growth rates were slowing down in Japan, but more important for the investor, the values had been recognized, so the prices ceased to be the bargains that they once were.

Templeton points out that when he first invested in Japan in the 1960s, Japanese investors liked the big names because they had heard of them, and so would pay more for a stranded whale—the Japanese equivalent of a General Motors or U.S. Gypsum—than for a specialty growth company in its dynamic phase. They also gave more weight to the six-month earnings outlook than to the six-year prospects. Then things reversed, and the smaller companies came to sell at a premium over the giants.

Besides Japan, the United States, and Canada, Templeton considers only a few areas suitable for investment: Germany, Switzerland, the northern European countries, Spain, Australia, and New Zealand (the last two of which have at least for the moment shaken off the socialist virus), Hong Kong, Singapore, and South Korea. He finds Brazil of great potential interest.

Technique

Templeton has a few outstanding sources of information for non-Japanese foreign securities, but since the true facts are not publicly available he depends on industry scuttlebutt, insiders' tips, and bankers' indiscretions. "I follow a number of them carefully to see what they've been able to think up," he told me.

Early in his career, Templeton made hundreds of personal visits to companies, going through the plants and sizing everything up. In recent years, however, he has rarely found this necessary. He has a standard list of questions he likes to ask management. One of the first is *"Do you have a long-range plan?"* Then, *"What will be your average annual growth rate?"* If the target growth rate is higher than the historical one, he asks, *"Why should the future be different from the past? What are your problems?"* And then, a key point, *"Who is your ablest competitor?"* and the essential *"Why?"*

Finally, a question that Templeton finds particularly enlightening: *"If you couldn't own stock in your company, which of your competitors would you want to invest in . . . and why?"*

As you find out fast enough in security analysis, contact with a single company can mislead nearly as much as it informs. Management is obviously going to blow its own trumpet. If you visit most of the companies in an industry over a period of many years, you eventually develop an informed concept of the entire group. You learn which sources are reliable, which managements achieve their objectives, which company officers tend to make exaggerated claims. Particularly, even a few minutes with a company's chief competitor or a major supplier may be vastly instructive. Your informant can tell what he knows about a competitor, while he is not permitted to divulge inside information about his own company. Even if he does, you as an investor can be punished for using it. Also, of course, your informant will probably speak more impartially about the outside company.

Templeton also makes extensive use of secondary sources, and indeed relies much more on the figures than on firsthand impressions. Perhaps his most important source is the great panorama of facts in *The Value*

Line Investment Survey (not the opinions, which are half-baked). By working one's way through the fifteen-or-so-year history of such elements as sales, profit margins, depreciation, working capital, and all the rest, one can grasp most of what is essential about the life of an enterprise.

Templeton also finds the *Wall Street Transcript*—which reproduces dozens of brokers reports on companies each week—a valuable aid. To maintain his files in former days he kept an office in a tiny shopping center just outside the gates of the Lyford Cay Club. He used to need a librarian. Then he discovered that he could find the answers to most questions by looking up the company in the index of the *Transcript*.

He makes wide use of brokers, but only for establishing facts, paying no attention to their buy and sell recommendations. Almost no brokers—fewer than 1 percent, he judges—think in his terms. (Similarly, at the time I talked to him he doubted that even one Swiss banker was considering the variations of real estate values between England and Canada that he found so interesting.) Over the years Templeton has learned what brokerage sources are likely to be useful to him for collecting facts. He instantly discards everything else.

A paradox of collecting for profit—whether stocks, works of art, real estate, or anything else—is that the best buy can never be what the dealer or gallery is pushing at the time. A notable book collector, Philip Hofer of the Houghton Library at Harvard, once told me that one of his most successful approaches in visiting a dealer is to ask, "What do you have that you can't sell?" That volume will usually be covered with dust in the cellar, and if of real quality is likely to be a far better buy than the "special" in the window, which will perforce be marked up to what a dealer thinks a passerby will pay for it.

Similarly, if a stock is so out of favor that there are virtually no buyers—that is, if it practically can't be sold—a broker who has to pay a lot of overhead and support his salesmen can't afford to get involved with it; least of all a stock with a small float. Thus the bargain-hunting investor will always tend to be on his own, unable to rely on others for ideas, as distinct from facts.

Templeton's portfolio represents what he thinks are the best buys in marketable securities anywhere in the world—giving full consideration to the safety of the countries where they are found.

Once a stock has moved up and no longer is a bargain, then if he finds a much better buy, out goes the first one. That is, he always uses this comparison-shopping approach to investments.

I asked him if he made any effort to buy stocks just as they emerge from the wilderness, as investment interest picks up. He replied that *if one of two otherwise similar stocks is just starting to attract interest and the other is still in eclipse, then he gives preference to the one that is starting to move.*

In his analytical approach, Templeton starts by trying to determine the intrinsic value of a company. In the mid-1940s his investment counsel firm did as much as any to apply Graham's original, full-scale technique systematically—the analysis of companies through careful study of their significant financial ratios in the hope of establishing true values. The drudgery that this entailed has now been much alleviated by such services as *Value Line.* For a few hundred dollars a year you have easily available most of the information that an office full of analysts assembled for you in the old days less promptly and less accurately. (It has become even easier since the Internet.)

Templeton says that there are a hundred or so factors that can well be considered in making an appraisal, although not all are appropriate to any given enterprise. Thus, in studying a natural resources company you might omit perhaps a quarter of the possible factors; for a manufacturing company, a different quarter.

About four factors are crucial and universally applicable to every situation:

1. *The price-earnings ratio*
2. *Operating profit margins*
3. *Liquidating value*
4. *The growth rate,* particularly the *consistency* of earnings growth

If a company's growth falters for one year, that may be all right. If it misses two years, then it is suspect. However, one should be suspicious of extremely rapid growth. *Ordinarily it is unsustainable.*

I asked Templeton about T. Rowe Price's theory that the investor should seek out the "fertile fields for growth" in the economy—those destined to expand and flourish in the years ahead—and buy the leading companies in them. Templeton replied that at one time or another he had probably owned most of the stocks in the T. Rowe Price Growth Stock Fund, but such companies usually also have high price-earnings ratios. Quite often the specialty company is less expensive, because less understood. It takes neither training nor experience to go out and buy a highly visible premier growth stock without regard to price.

Everything has its season, which does not last forever. The David Babson organization in Boston, which favored top growth stocks, had a six-year span during which its fund almost always ran near the front of the pack. According to Templeton, by the end of that time it *should have been eagerly looking for any good excuse to change its entire approach.* And Morgan Guaranty, which produced such handsome results in the late sixties and early seventies by bidding its Avons, International Flavors, and the like to almost infinite prices: How much happier might they have been if their Mr. Samuel R. Calloway had retired and had sold the lot in 1973 rather than in 1975, after a 50 percent decline.

The cardinal rule is flexibility. You must get ready to change when everything seems to be working particularly well. When the cycle is perfectly in gear with your expectations, prepare to jump.

Don't trust rules and formulas. Thirty years ago, Templeton knew an officer in the trust department of the Chemical Bank who finally, after the market had puzzled so many people for countless generations, got it all together. All the numbers, all the cycles, all the psychological, financial, and fundamental data since the beginning of markets, now trumpeted the same message: The Dow Jones Average was going straight down for three years. He put his clients into cash. Alas! The first year, the market went up. The second, it went up more. And the third year, it went up more than ever.

Templeton has always had prodigious ability, not generally realized, to *discern the central two or three factors required to make a buying decision, and leave the rest in limbo.* This capability of seizing the totality of a situation without fussing about the details often characterizes very powerful thinkers.

Templeton's sometime partner Vance used to enjoy lecturing about investments. Part of his kit was a huge chart plotted on a roll of wrapping paper. It was so big that during his lectures he would have to get a volunteer from the audience to help him unroll it and put it on the wall. This chart plotted the market for the previous twenty years. Then there were different squiggly lines representing the various factors that influenced it—industrial production, money supply, and so on. One squiggly line was best of all. It worked perfectly. Year after year if you had followed it you could have known where the market was headed and made a killing. When the audience, fascinated, demanded to know what it represented, Mr. Vance told them. It was the rate his hens were laying, in the chicken coop in back of his house!

Templeton has endowed a prize for progress in religion which is awarded annually in London. Its value, now about $1 million, has enabled it to attract the interest of eminent persons, notably Prince Philip. Templeton describes it as larger than the Nobel prize, but this means larger than any one of the Nobel prizes, of which there are many. Templeton hopes that the award will help focus attention on the life and work of the recipients, who have included Mother Teresa of Calcutta and Aleksandr Solzhenitsyn.* He has also endowed a business school in Oxford and a building at Princeton Theological Seminary. These munificences, since he has adopted British citizenship, gained him a knighthood.

He compares spiritual growth to gardening. "If you find a weed," he says, "you go out and get rid of it. The same for a bad thought or bad emotion."† I asked him about good works and how nonattachment to material things figures in spiritual development. "Works *come* from spiritual development," he said. "If you *start* with the works you move to humanism, a very different thing." As to nonattachment, he doesn't believe in it at all. He is attached to many things, including the stock market.

The Outlook

In early 2000, Templeton for the first time in his career of almost half a century concluded that all markets in every country were over-priced. He therefore recommended placing 75 percent of one's invest-ment portfolio in bonds, particularly the U.S. Treasury issue indexed for inflation. A disadvantage of that issue is that it is denominated in dollars, a currency he expects to be weaker than those of some other countries, notably Singapore, South Korea, and Australia. So he would diversify among all four.

For the 25 percent equity portion of one's portfolio, he continues to favor health care, and within that sector, a closed-end fund called H&Q Life Sciences Investors, selling at a substantial discount below its net asset value.

---

*To declare an interest, I suggested Solzhenitsyn to Templeton, and since Solzheni-tsyn spoke only Russian, delivered the English version of his acceptance speech in Buckingham Palace.
†I tried on him the Buddhist paradox "The mind of Buddha is steeped in corruption and sin." The point is that to God no created thing is alien; our weed may be God's orchid. Jung makes a similar point: To be complete, we should accept the evil (and the opposite gender) in our nature. Anyway, Templeton seemed unimpressed.

Templeton disagrees with the prevailing wisdom that Europe is an attractive place to invest. Labor unions are too strong and taxes too high, discouraging entrepreneurship, the engine of growth. Only a few countries there, notably England, Ireland, Poland, and Hungary, seem to be resisting the tendency toward government controls and high taxes. Templeton thinks quite highly of China, and believes that the best way to invest there is through a closed-end fund selling at a discount.

In general, however, while very cautious as to the short term, he remains extremely optimistic about prospects for the twenty-first century.

Four

RICHARD RAINWATER
RING THE CHANGES

Richard Rainwater's investing technique resembles no one else's in this book. First, he peers into the future to discern a promising area and tries to visualize an enterprise that would succeed in it. Then, he makes a few concentrated investments in the sector. (So far, like many others.) Then, however, he does not necessarily sit back and wait patiently, but is willing to climb aboard the companies he has invested in, forcefully molding them, hiring and firing, refinancing, merging, until the resulting enterprise approaches his original vision.

So while most investors look for outstanding *management* and then ride with it, taking a passive attitude, Rainwater begins with an investment conception and then acts as an investor/consultant/merchant banker. (Strangely, though, his *passive* investments, on which he's just gone along for the ride like other investors, have had at least as good a return as his active ones.)

Another Rainwater singularity is that his partner is considered one of the toughest cookies in the financial arena, rough field though it is. And not only that, the name of the partner is Mrs. Rainwater—he married her. (He had earlier married his high school sweetheart, by whom during thirty-five years of marriage he had three children, now grown up and in Fort Worth. Like so many of the offspring of the wealthy, they have been described as being somewhat adrift.)

In his career investing on his own, Richard Rainwater enjoyed a net compound annual rate of return of 26 percent through the end of 1998. The figure is dented by a disastrous performance that year, only the second bad one. (For his first five years as a private investor,

Rainwater claimed annual returns of over 70 percent.) Before he went private, his great early success was managing the fortune of the famous Bass family of Fort Worth, Texas; during those years their assets grew a hundredfold, from $50 million to several billion. Since leaving the Basses and becoming independent, Rainwater has focused mostly on three industries: oil and gas, real estate, and health care. In doing so, he has accumulated a net worth that as of early 1999 was estimated at somewhat over $1 billion.

With his dark Mediterranean complexion, air of healthy prosperity, and self-confident smile, Rainwater (who is "Dick" only to those who don't know him) looks well in photographs. He leans to a preppy turnout: polo shirts, loafers or tennis shoes, and perhaps blue jeans. He exercises regularly to Motown music in his Fort Worth office gym, and when in New York plays golf most afternoons with other prosperous financial folk. He likes the challenge of golf: "It takes lots of time, it's difficult, there's a great deal to learn, and the relationship with the other people is fun." He wrestled his weight down to 185 from 225 in 1998, reasonable for a man of six feet two. He exudes a somewhat playful vitality, and speaks animatedly about business or stock car racing. After a business coup, he is likely to trot out a sports phrase: "I just hit a 250-yard drive. Don't tell me to hit 300 yards this time." When analyzing deals with his assistants, he writes on his white office walls with erasable Magic Markers.

When we are talking, he gets a telephone call every now and again about golf. One man proposed an "emergency nine." I asked Rainwater about that expression. "Some people, after eighteen holes, play another nine holes if there's time. It makes you feel better," he said.

He enjoys telling of his days as a high school drag-racing champion. For seven months his souped-up Buick was undefeated at the local raceway. He still occasionally competes. His modified red '57 Chevy goes from zero to sixty in a few seconds, he says. Terrifying! At the American Achievement Awards in 1992, he was asked what sea animal he would like to be. "A dolphin," he replied, "an arrogant mammal in the sea just having a good time." Rainwater always knew he wanted to be active in something substantive: not golf, not (nodding toward me, a tennis player) tennis. He wanted to be involved, engaged.

Rainwater describes himself as an observer, a person of great curiosity. "I was a relatively smart kid. I liked to compete in the classroom. So, even after I had my pot of gold, I didn't stop analyzing. I would go back and understand the elements behind the chaos that I had profited from."

I asked him about his interesting name. He opined that it was of Dutch origin. I pointed out that in that case it should be spelled differently. "Yes, yes," Rainwater replied, "it's German.* My immigrant ancestors went down to Tennessee." His mother's father, named Dieb, was a Lebanese who married another Lebanese in America. He bought a trunk full of notions and traveled through the South selling them. The business became established in Fort Worth and eventually passed to Rainwater's father.

Rainwater has consorted with such Hollywood moguls as David Geffen, Michael Eisner, "superagent" Michael Ovitz, and director George Lucas. Also Warren Buffett, George Bush, Jr., and Roger Staubach, the former Dallas Cowboys quarterback who metamorphosed into a real estate developer.

Rainwater maintains offices in Fort Worth. He shares a pleasant Upper East Side Manhattan condo with his partner-wife, Darla Dee Moore; its elegant furniture reflects her taste, not his. They also have houses in South Carolina and Arizona. Rainwater has no children with Darla, who says she can't spare the time.

He is neat and fastidious; Darla says if he visits "he'll come into your kitchen and start straightening things out and wiping the counters." He loves to play with children and dogs. He is not interested in spending money, collecting, or similar pursuits, and would welcome a modest lifestyle. Darla thinks that he would most like to live in a hotel without possessions and rent whatever he required. "He's young in the way he acts, even in a way childlike. He likes simplicity."

Darla Dee is notable in her own right. A tall, slim, handsome woman, she made her name at Chemical Bank in the 1980s, where she was known as "Queen of DIP"—that is, of debtor in possession financing, a technique of lending to companies in bankruptcy. She grew up in the modest agglomeration of Lake City, South Carolina (pop. c. 9,000), where her mother, a strict disciplinarian, had a job at the Methodist church. Her father, a star athlete, made her do sprints in front of the house, checked her basketball performance, and timed her swimming. His methods are reminiscent of Father Joe's flogging the Kennedy brothers.

---

*Goldwater—a name imposed on that distinguished family by the Germanic authorities—refers to urine.

She knew early that business would be the path onward and upward. After receiving an M.B.A. from George Washington University in 1981 she entered Chemical Bank's training program. Eventually she was earning more than $1 million a year, and may have been the highest-paid woman in commercial banking. She was an exceedingly harsh negotiator, once entering a meeting with the cheerful words "Put on your rubber underwear, boys!" *Fortune* titled a story on Darla "The Toughest Babe in Business." Her big chance came when Rainwater needed someone to take control of Rainwater, Inc., the vehicle that ran his then $700 million in personal assets. In her first three and a half years—working with her husband—she ran its net worth up to $1.5 billion. She also took over Rainwater's seat on the board of Columbia/ HCA, then a $15 billion company.

Darla collects rare books, while not bothering about the scholarly aspects. Originally she preferred those bearing on the birth of capitalism, such as works by Locke, Hume, and other philosophers, and the great French encyclopedia produced by Diderot *et al.* in the eighteenth century. Now she has moved to collecting works relating to her native state, South Carolina. (The family dog, although a husky, answers to Dixie Rae.)

She met Rainwater, ten years older than she, during a business trip to Texas in 1990. They hit it off immediately and were married within a year, canceling a big planned bash in favor of a quiet event on Friday, the thirteenth of December, 1991. "I think of you like an equity investment," he avowed—practical, if not the language of Romeo.

Darla can be kittenish or exceedingly harsh. *Fortune* once described her as "a cross between the Terminator and Kim Basinger, with a wicked South Carolina drawl." She bullies her coworkers. "It causes me problems. In the early days, it got to the point where no one would work for me. The entire group quit on me." Her friends include Martha Stewart and Ogilvy & Mather CEO Charlotte Beers.

Early Years

While still a child, Rainwater manifested capitalistic instincts. At thirteen he secured a paper route and paid other children to actually deliver the papers; they got 80 percent of the fees for doing all the work, while he took 20 percent as the impresario. One up on Warren Buffett, who actually delivered the papers himself!

As an outstanding mathematics and physics student at the University of Texas, Rainwater gained a scholarship to Stanford Business

School. By his graduation in 1968 he had resolved to make a fortune. He materialized one day without an appointment at Goldman Sachs in New York, announcing, "I've done well in school. Gotten essentially all A's. For me, working for Goldman Sachs could be the next step in living the American Dream." Rainwater was eventually hired to sell securities in Dallas. In their first year, he and a partner generated $1.2 million in commissions, of which their share was 16 percent.

Before long the Stanford connection paid off. He had taken several classes with young Sid Bass, the eldest son of Perry Bass, whose uncle had amassed a vast fortune drilling wildcat oil wells. Sid needed someone to help invest the family money, and Rainwater was available.

The beginning was difficult. They sank some $20 million into various propositions and briskly dropped $3 million of it. All the early deals lost money. Rainwater realized that he needed to develop a clear strategy and a systematic methodology. So at age twenty-six, he went on a walkabout, calling on Charles Allen, Warren Buffett, and Philip Fisher. He was looking for a style that was consistently rewarding, rather than being inconsistent and hard to operate, and one "appropriate to [my] skill set," as he says, "which is that I am able to learn."

One of his most important conclusions was that *to succeed you must specialize.* You should *identify, and then be around, areas where practically everybody is successful,* over and over again. He encountered not a few where investors *seemed* successful, but where nobody in the field was really prospering massively.

One person he unearthed was David Dunn of J. H. Whitney & Co., who was consistently successful and had helped make his firm hundreds of millions of dollars from a fairly small capital base. He was extraordinarily disciplined. To the usual venture capitalist mistake of spreading one's bets too thin, he applied the expression "They piss on every deal that comes by"—that is, take a small piece of whatever turns up, a losing strategy.

Dunn himself focused on computers, not just manufacturing but also retailing and wholesaling. He participated in the start of some great companies, including Storage Technology and Prime Computers, among others. A question that Dunn liked to ask about an industry was "Are there some rich people doing this?"—meaning between three and ten, a significant but not excessive number of able fellow participants.

At the end of his quest, Rainwater concluded that there were a number of attractive sectors that he should propose to the Basses, including real estate, arbitrage, and hedge funds, but that above all, they should narrow their focus, stick close to their knitting. Having accepted these ideas and established a winning technique, he says, "they made a magnificent fortune out of a relatively modest initial capital."

This is the usual experience of venturers. Few indeed can sit at a desk and sign checks for a mixed grill of deals coming over the transom. The seller almost always understands the proposition better than you do. Eventually, a successful venture capitalist comes to understand a few areas deeply enough to tilt the odds in his favor.

Developing a Strategy

During his years with the Basses, Rainwater developed the strategy he followed for the rest of his investment career. It has six key parts:

1. *Target a major industry in disrepute that's due for a change.* His aim is to find *opportunity* and *value*. Rainwater feels no particular need to be an expert himself on an industry before buying into it. He thinks on a grand scale: "I'm interested in large industries and in companies that offer products the whole world needs," he says.

2. *Find a particularly attractive company or a sector within the industry.* Rainwater calls this "the opportunity within the opportunity." (What I call the double play.) With oil prices depressed, Rainwater looked for drilling companies; in the health care industry, he focused on hospitals whose occupancy rate could be increased and whose doctors would have a share in ownership; his real estate holdings center almost entirely on a few areas of the Southwest.

3. He also used a different strategy—what in Wall Street lingo might be called a "filter"—that became extremely successful: *Find a company with a long-term, sustainable competitive advantage,* or what some call an impregnable *business franchise.* Disney fell into this category because it has unique assets—its theme parks and cartoon characters.

4. *Find a "world-class player" to run the show.* Rather than try to become an expert in each industry, Rainwater consults experts to find the right manager (or managers) to revive the company. He will then "call a good man and say, 'You take it.'" Sometimes, however, he will do it himself, to try to "put meat on the bones" of his idea.

5. *Never enter an investment alone.* For every private investment Rainwater sets up a partnership, usually including trusted colleagues he has

worked with in the past, and probably experts in the chosen industry. Generally, one of the group runs the operation. This is an
unusual attitude. Most venture capitalists want to be able to impose
hard decisions when necessary, without much consultation.

6. *Improve the risk-reward ratio through financial engineering.* Rainwater
    bought the forty-story office tower where he works in Texas from
    Ray Hunt, of the Hunt family. Hunt had spent between $140 million
    and $160 million on it; Rainwater scooped it up for just $64 million,
    using a $55 million floating-rate loan that cost him less than 6 per-
    cent.

Early Successes

With the Basses in the 1980s, Rainwater had already identified several opportunities in industries undergoing a transformation. The first
was to identify undervalued energy stocks. He bought substantial
stakes in Marathon Oil and Texaco. In 1984, his 9.9 percent investment in Texaco, which was preparing to buy Getty, ended in a hugely
profitable sale back to the company. (Some cried greenmail at the
time, since the Basses had been pressuring Texaco management to
repurchase Texaco's own stock rather than buy Getty.)

That same year, Rainwater entered the turbulent Walt Disney situation. In 1982 the company's earnings had fallen by nearly 19 percent;
the following year they fell another 7 percent. The Epcot center in
Florida was facing huge cost overruns. That was the downside; on the
bright side, the company had relatively low debt, a precious film
library, the Disney characters, and theme parks that generated $1 bil-
lion a year. These assets seemed much more valuable than the company's $2 billion market capitalization—especially considering that
some of them could not be duplicated.

Raider Saul Steinberg was the first to jump in, acquiring almost 10
percent of the company and making a bid in June to buy the rest. Disney paid greenmail to Steinberg on June 9, 1984, taking back his shares
at $7.50 above the market price and earning him almost $32 million on
a three-month investment.

Then Rainwater made an offer to swap Arvida, a Florida land development firm he had gotten into, named for Arthur Vining Davis, for a
$200 million 10 percent stake in the beleaguered Disney. He had
bought Arvida the year before for $20 million cash plus assumption of
$270 million in debt. Disney accepted. Rainwater then set out to help

round up better management. He sought advice from director George Lucas and others, and eventually was instrumental in bringing Michael Eisner, former president of Paramount Pictures, into Disney as CEO.

Eisner's 1998 book *Work in Progress* sheds light on Rainwater's ability to assess a situation briskly. At a key meeting to discuss the future of Disney, Rainwater and Sid Bass, along with several associates, listened to Eisner make his pitch about such issues as the profits to be made from theme park rights to successful films. Eisner describes the scene:

> After about half an hour, Richard stood up to take a phone call and Sid left the room with him. We didn't know it at the time, but as soon as they walked out the door, Sid turned to his partner.
>
> "I like what I'm hearing," he said.
>
> "I'm with you," Rainwater replied.
>
> "Let's go back and tell them we're in for the next five years," Sid said.
>
> Sid later told me that was the sum total of their conversation. In less than half an hour, Sid and Richard had concluded that they stood to earn more by keeping their money in Disney while we sought to turn it around than they would by allowing it to be sold off in parts.

Shortly thereafter, the Basses bumped up their share in the company to 25 percent. By the time Rainwater left the Basses in 1986, that stake was worth nearly $2 billion, representing an $850 million gain. "Disney was an easy fix," he says. "All I had to do was change the CEO."

He became briefly involved with financier Michael Milken in 1984. Eager to test his strategy of using creative financing to increase value, he persuaded Milken to join in a fund to which the Basses and others also contributed. The Bass Investment Limited Partnership started with total capital of $1.2 billion, with $540 million subscribed by Equitable Life. Both Rainwater and Milken contributed investment ideas. The partnership would borrow at 9 percent and put its idle cash into junk bonds earning 15 percent. The first operation was in restructuring the Mattel toy company. They eventually did a whole series of deals, including MCI Telecommunications, McCaw Cellular Communications, MetroMedia, and Intermedics. When Rainwater cashed out in 1989, the fund had averaged 30 percent annually to Equitable and about 100 percent to the general partners.

Rainwater later commented on the wisdom of the Basses in looking outside their own family for financial assistance. "What has always struck me as odd is that if you look at corporations, even corporations that began as family businesses, the way they promote people is based on skill, not bloodlines. But most families continue to make the decisions on who will manage the fortune based on bloodlines. That didn't make sense to me or the Basses."

Flying Solo

In his sixteen years with the Bass family, Rainwater, while multiplying their fortune enormously, had also built up a $100 million nest egg for himself.

When he became independent, the first area he turned to was oil and gas. He was convinced that the depressed oil market had hit bottom, and that as a result several beleaguered Texas outfits were ripe for the picking. The government was "all over the oil and gas drilling industry," says Rainwater, with excess profits taxes, old oil and new oil price ceilings, and so forth. The reason was that the government had developed policies based on the thesis that the United States had to be assured of a regular supply of hydrocarbons without the risk of being compelled to resort to foreign sources. He started with a Houston driller, Blocker Energy. The company had thrived in the 1970s, but by the time Rainwater appeared it consisted mostly of aging equipment and $100 million in bank debt.

Rainwater assumed the loans for $12 million, and quickly went to work rebuilding the company. He persuaded Carl Thorne, the respected head of an offshore drilling firm, to run the operation. They issued $55 million in new stock in April 1987 and renamed the company Energy Service Co., or Ensco. They gave up two million shares of stock to bring in a number of partners, including Hollywood executive David Geffen, who had met Rainwater through the Disney deal.

His funding group for the natural gas area, Natural Gas Partners, took advantage of an opportunity created, as so often, by government intervention. In order to get financing, pipelines had to negotiate long-term contracts to purchase from producers at specified prices and sell to municipalities. However, when the gas business was deregulated in the 1980s, prices fell sharply. Pipelines went to other producers to buy cheap deregulated gas, ignoring their existing contracts. The producers with long-term contracts at higher prices then sued the pipeline companies, which got government relief. Many producers, however, were left holding the bag and went under, as did some pipelines. The resulting extensive litigation and industry chaos created an investment opportunity. To run Natural Gas Partners Rainwater found "a delightful securities analyst called Gamble Baldwin. *Institutional Investor* magazine had said that if it could have, it would have named him number one, number two, *and* number three among all oil and gas analysts."

Rainwater persuaded Baldwin to set up a natural gas operation and went back to his Equitable friends for a $97.5 million investment. The newly formed group was called Natural Gas Partners, which since inception has raised not quite $1 billion from institutions. Ensco and NGP worked in tandem to find and develop projects.

Rainwater continued to build Ensco by adding other troubled companies. In 1989 he saw an opportunity at Penrod Drilling Co., an eighty-four-rig affair once owned by the Hunt brothers. Penrod's major creditor banks had forced the Hunts to give up control in a restructuring. Rainwater, Natural Gas Partners, and Ensco began buying debt from two of the banks at 60 cents on the dollar and up, in order to take over the company's high-quality rigs. "For $430 million [the Rainwater partnership] is getting rigs valued at more than twice that amount," reported *Business Week* in June 1990. Rainwater later merged Penrod with Ensco. By November 1998, Ensco International was one of the largest oil drilling firms in the world. Rainwater's 6 percent stake, even after a drop in 1998, was worth over $100 million. "Once there were five hundred mutual funds and five thousand drilling rigs," says Rainwater. "Now it's the reverse." (He dropped $30 million in Wolverine Exploration, though.)

Some years later, Rainwater found a lucrative opportunity in the troubled empire of yet another Texan, feared raider T. Boone Pickens. In 1996 the stock of Mesa, the oil company Pickens had founded decades before, had sunk from $48 to under $3. Rainwater had been trying to get a piece of it since 1992. Faced with angry shareholders—not to mention $1.1 billion in debt—Pickens flew to Tucson, Arizona, where Rainwater was regrouping at Canyon Ranch, a spa. The two worked out the terms of a deal on the golf course. By investing $133 million for 32 percent of Mesa, while refinancing its debt, Rainwater was able to get the company off the floor.

But there would be another harsh condition: Before the deal was concluded, Pickens was summoned to California. There he was confronted by the fearsome Darla, who told him that he would have to step down because his reputation had become a problem. "I tried to be as tactful as I could," she told *Fortune* in September 1997, "but tact doesn't come easily to me." Anyway, within a year, after arranging a merger with another company to form Pioneer Natural Resources, Rainwater and Moore had a $161 million stake in a major independent oil and gas company.

Honeywell, formerly Minneapolis Honeywell, was a great company, the best in the world in a few lines of business, but weak in a few others in which it lost a great deal of money. The old CEO, Ed Spenser, had been too stubborn to get out of the laggards. Finally Rainwater mounted a proxy fight to get management's attention. It required a lot of work on his part to change things, but finally the company dumped its losers and profits exploded.

At about the same time that he saw opportunities in the energy sector, Rainwater turned his sights to an industry that was so poorly managed it seemed ideal for restructuring: health care.

American hospitals ordinarily ran at about 45 percent of capacity, *and yet everybody stayed in the business.* They were in terrible trouble, because government intervention had encouraged a tremendous overcapacity. He knew that increasing cost-consciousness was putting pressure on hospitals. Why shouldn't they try to achieve the same efficiency standards as other businesses? He recognized that an HMO preferred to patronize a large, centralized hospital company with many hospitals in a given area, offering a wide menu of services. Combing through his contacts in search of the appropriate "world-class player," Rainwater identified Richard Scott, a Dallas lawyer who represented hospital companies in acquisitions. With Scott on board, Rainwater formed Columbia Hospital Corp. Columbia was founded with two cardinal principles. First, the hospitals in his chain had to be run efficiently at high levels of capacity, up from little over half of that. And, second, "Everybody had to be induced to respond to the changes that inevitably were coming about" by letting doctors invest and by giving staff appropriate incentives. Richard Scott and Rainwater each contributed $125,000, combined with $61 million in loans. That was enough to buy two hospitals in El Paso, Texas, and begin acquiring more at a time when there were very few buyers.

Columbia Hospital Corp. was launched on October 19, 1987—the very day of the stock market crash. During that drop, Rainwater took positions totaling $45 million in forty stocks, including Polaroid, Control Data, Gould, and Fireman's Fund. In his thirty-two instances as a passive investor he earned a compound return rate of 66 percent for the few years he held the stocks. The companies in which he took an active role earned him a 43 percent rate.

Rainwater forced rapid expansion of his acquisition by a familiar technique: Create a high-priced stock, then use it as a currency to buy properties. With Columbia's stock selling at eight times cash flow, Rainwater and Scott could buy hospitals selling for five times cash flow and end up ahead immediately. They bought with furious speed, seeking market consolidation by acquiring several hospitals in a given region, notably the Southeast, then closing down some locations and referring patients to the others. They also slashed costs. Within four months of buying a four-hospital chain in San Jose, California, in 1996 they cut or reduced the hours of 890 out of 4,500 jobs. Based on their centralized purchasing power, they sought and received huge discounts on equipment and supplies.

By 1997, after merging with four other companies, including Hospital Corp. of America, in which Rainwater was also an investor, the two-unit start-up had grown to a 347-hospital chain. Rainwater's investment had ballooned to $300 million. Then the company had to cope with government accusations that its hospitals were overcharging for some services. CEO Rick Scott was replaced, and the investment fell under a cloud. In 2000 Columbia was hit with an immense fine.

The government had also brought chaos to the real estate business by trying to do a favor to the savings and loan associations. They had been granted federal guarantees of $100,000 in deposits per customer. This produced a wide diffusion of $100,000 CDs through money brokers, resulting in an immense amount of excess capital coming into the thrift industry. The government's intent was that the money should go into solid investments, particularly real estate projects, but in fact a lot went into crazy ventures. The result was extreme speculation in property followed by widespread bankruptcies.

Rainwater observes that many cases of industry chaos can be traced back to such well-intended but unsound government intervention.

Anyway, by the late 1980s, everyone was selling off real estate in the Texas sunbelt as fast as possible. By then, Rainwater was in a position to snap up many hotel, property, and land development assets at 30 to 35 cents on the dollar. His reasoning was that although many Texas developers had gone belly up, along with the savings and loans that had lent to them, the buildings had in fact been built, the depositors repaid, and the thrifts sold and reopened. With no corporate or personal income taxes, Texas was a prime location.

His first bargain was the forty-story dark-green glass Continental Plaza he bought from the Hunts in 1990. Within two years he raised occupancy from 77 percent to almost 90 percent—partly by occupying the building with tenants from his own ventures, such as Columbia.

Rainwater also uncovered a company that he felt fit his theory of comparative advantage: the Dallas-based commercial real estate firm run by revered former Dallas Cowboys quarterback Roger Staubach, who had a look at almost all good ideas. (This is called in Wall Street the advantage of "deal flow.")

In 1994, Rainwater moved into high gear, forming a REIT called Crescent Real Estate Equities. He raised $350 million in an IPO and went public at $25 a share. His reputation was such that he could take Crescent public mainly on his promise to build the company. Crescent was essentially a "blind pool." An investor was quoted in *Business Week* as saying, "We didn't buy it for what's in the portfolio. We bought it because it's Richard Rainwater." He invested $35 million of his own and "sweat equity" in what became fourteen million shares of Crescent, which started with five office properties, a retail project, and stakes in three residential developments. Within three years, it bought almost $4 billion in properties, most of them at large discounts: eighty-nine office buildings and seven retail properties, plus stakes in ninety-seven cold storage warehouses, ninety psychiatric hospitals, seven hotels, two spas, and five residential developments. Over the same time its funds from operations rose 370 percent and its share price 215 percent. Most of Crescent's cash flow comes from office and retail properties, two-thirds of which are in the Dallas/Fort Worth area. Rainwater succeeded in Crescent by buying high-quality office buildings located in the energy belt at low prices. He foresaw that local conditions would improve, despite falling oil prices, and that he could raise rents. By September 1997, his holding in Crescent was worth $426 million.

Recent Troubles

By 1997, Rainwater foresaw hard times. He expected lower oil prices, and moved to protect the 40 percent of his net worth that was not tied up in the six large companies he owned. He withdrew $70 million from several hedge funds, sold 11 percent of the Texas Rangers baseball team for $25 million, and sold half of Crescent's flagship Hotel Crescent Court in Dallas for another $25 million. By mid-1998 he had assembled a cash hoard of $300 million.

Nevertheless, his personal portfolio dropped $500 million in market value during 1998—a 29 percent decline. Crescent Real Estate Equities fell 42 percent; Pioneer Natural Resources, amid a 40 percent drop in the S&P Midcap Oil and Gas Index, fell 65 percent; Ensco fell 73 percent. Even so, Rainwater sturdily proclaimed in early 1999 that he was still worth over $1 billion. *Forbes* put the figure at $1.1 billion.

Despite these severe setbacks, the only one of Rainwater's six major investments—Crescent, an offshoot of Crescent called Crescent Operating Co., Pioneer, Ensco, Columbia, and Magellan Health Services—that had sunk below its purchase price was Magellan, a psychiatric-care company. Rainwater hopes that it will expand internationally as mental health care develops abroad. As for his oil and gas investments and the real estate investments tied to the fortunes of the Southern energy belt, Rainwater has always maintained that his strategy will pay off when the time comes. "The world will be chasing hydrocarbons for the next ten or twenty years," he said in 1995. He had 20 percent of his fortune in the oil and gas sector at the end of 1998, believing that oil prices would recover to over $20 a barrel within two to five years. (In fact, the price reached $30 by 2000.)

Still, it may be that he is feeling burned out, and will be content to sit with what he has. He admitted as much to *Business Week* in November 1998. "There's no telling how much money I could make going out and doing deals right now," he said. "I've never had so much liquidity at such a time of great opportunity—and had so little interest. I just don't feel the obsession or the passion to go out and do another deal or create another company . . . after thirty years, I'm out of the deal business."

Instead, he is pursuing charitable activities. He plans to give away his fortune once he has taken care of his own family and put aside $120 million in trust for Stanford and the University of South Carolina, his wife's alma mater. He is currently funding some one hundred charity programs, including the Fort Worth Save Our Children Learning Center. "Doing this," he said, "I could live the rest of my life getting up in the morning and saying, 'Boy, I've really got something worthwhile to do today.'"

The Rainwaters have given $45 million to the University of South Carolina Business School, which Darla would like to see brought into

the top rank of such schools nationally. She is concerned about education in South Carolina generally, and is very active in that area. As a
result, she is being invited to consider possible state political activities.

Conclusions

Rainwater says he did what he did because "it was fun, because I
could do it, and it was interesting and satisfying uses of my gift of being
able to do and to think. To succeed, though, you have be obsessed. You
need to be *engaged:* to talk boards into things, to hire the right people,
to convince your backers."

"To be a leader," I said.

"It's not always easy," Rainwater continued. "Sometimes people
aren't convinced. I always felt I was doing the right thing, but they
didn't, necessarily. I would sit there looking at these industries and
realize that other people were seeing the same thing, but that they
were *frozen*. People with the same level of knowledge and used to the
industry, with chaos raining down on them, being crushed or frozen.
After they had spent years being wrecked, they became despondent
and didn't want to leave the office. I would arrive with an idea and
sometimes they didn't want to do it or sometimes they would oppose it.
But once I've determined what to do, I go forward. I fight despair with
facts, and overcome greed by being generous."

"Capitalism works in spite of ideology," Rainwater says. "You can
have an intrusive government, like Singapore, or else a laissez-faire
government, like Hong Kong. It shouldn't make a difference. If the
entrepreneurs do their work, the whole economy will prosper."

Airlines, the telephone company, banks, real estate, were all regulated and then deregulated. In the course of deregulation, the government usually turns the wrong knob and things go awry for a while.
Bringing order to a business that is in chaos, whether a company or a
whole industry, is a working strategy. "Sometimes chaos can be fatal,"
he says, "but sometimes it is just a temporary disruption. I thought
perhaps that I could be the phoenix that would help a business rise
from the ashes. I was trained as a physicist, and so I was able to analyze
thoroughly."

Rainwater describes his objective as "rejuvenating, resurrecting, or
putting a company back on its feet." Five to twenty years is the usual
span of a government intervention cycle. Once the government has
realized that it has made a mess of things, it leaves them alone for a

while. Our government has become much more realistic, having
learned from many horrible experiences.

He believes that we are getting ready to have a golden age in the oil
and gas business, starting late in 1999 or 2000. Then, in due course, the
government will doubtless re-intervene and create some new kind of
chaos.

If he were starting today, he would take an interest in the Internet
and telecommunications. "I'd get four or five really smart guys, take an
office in Palo Alto, and be funding companies in those industries." In
fact, though, he is largely out of business, has few intellectual interests,
and is perplexed about what to do with the rest of his life.

Five

PAUL CABOT
ALL THE DAMN FACTS

THE DEAN OF INSTITUTIONAL INVESTORS IN BOSTON FOR MANY decades was Paul Cabot. He straddled the transformation of stock investment from an essentially impressionistic affair to an opportunistic but at least fact-based craft. He died some years ago, but since almost everything about our talks is as valid now as then, I have left things as written, in the present tense. He ran Harvard's endowment for seventeen years, during which time the money grew from $200 million to $1 billion, not including capital additions. He also founded and for more than fifty years was a partner of State Street Management and Research, which runs a stable of mutual funds, endowments, and private portfolios. The most important is State Street, one of the first American mutual funds. If you had bought $10,000 worth of stock at its inception, the value when I talked to Cabot would have been about $1 million about 56 years later, including dividends and reinvested capital gains distributions: a hundredfold gain.

Cabot ranked in his day as one of the great characters of the Boston business scene. While still a young man, he was elected to the board of J. P. Morgan & Co., both the most powerful and the stuffiest of American banking firms. (Mr. Morgan's desk stood in the middle of the street floor at 23 Wall Street, but he did not require a receptionist or secretary to keep people from approaching him. Nobody dared.) At one directors' meeting, Cabot, a small, wiry man, appeared sporting a big purple shiner and a cut on his forehead. A fellow director commiserated respectfully on his wound—a fall while fox hunting, presumably?

"Christ, no!" bellowed Cabot across the boardroom. "Haven't any of you bastards ever been drunk?"*

At another Morgan board of directors meeting, he was sitting next to Alfred P. Sloan, creator of the modern General Motors and developer of many of the concepts behind today's largest enterprises: decentralized operating management within centralized financial control, return on capital as a cardinal responsibility and test of managers, and the systematic positioning of different makes of GM cars at key points in the market's price spectrum. To this sage, with his tall, stiff collar, grave manner, and incalculable responsibilities, the young Cabot addressed the cheerful question "How's it going?"

Sloan courteously started to describe the point that he and his finance committee had reached in developing corporate policy on the relationship between the wholly owned suppliers, such as Fisher, and the different divisions, such as Buick and Chevrolet.

"No, no!" Cabot interrupted after a while. "The hell with that! What I want to know is, when is it going to make some *real dough?*"

If you ask them in Boston how Paul Cabot got this way, if he's showing off or trying to sound like a sailor or had troubles with his mother, they all say the same thing: "I don't know. He's just always been like that."

One of Cabot's finest hours came in 1972. For several years, McGeorge Bundy of the Ford Foundation had been calling on American colleges to invest their endowments aggressively so they would grow faster, and then to live dangerously not just on the income but also on the market appreciation—including what the market appreciation *ought* to be in a bull market. Heady times! In those days American companies paid out a much higher proportion of their income in dividends than they did later on, when income was deployed for stock repurchases and corporate acquisitions. And of course the capital value of bonds was continuously eroded by inflation. So actual income was the most you could prudently spend.

The Ford Foundation is the chief private source of largesse for American universities, and sounds awfully money-wise to a board of trustees in Savannah, Georgia. When its call came there were many who felt they had better string along. The Ford Foundation's pronunciamento came in the euphoria of a bull market, and it lured a significant num-

---

*In these pages I have considerably purified Cabot's language. He probably suffered from a mild case of Tourette's syndrome, whose sufferers are impelled to use profanity.

ber of American institutions of learning onto the rocks. Yale succumbed; Harvard, yea, even Harvard, was tempted. The president and fellows started wondering if there might not be something to it.

Across the Charles River, over in Boston, Paul Cabot blew his stack. No longer Harvard's treasurer, he fulminated an open letter to the president of the university that promptly attained circulation among the governing bodies, the faculty, and the alumni. It is still vividly remembered both in educational and in investment circles.

Here is the text (minus some statistics and examples):

Dear President Bok:

I have heard that you and other members of the Harvard Corporation are considering the use of capital for current expenses (specifically part of capital gains) in addition to your present policy of using *all* of income on the endowment funds of the University.

The purpose of this letter is to dissuade you from adopting this dangerous, unfair, unwise, and possibly disastrous policy.

Ever since Harvard was founded in 1636, we have had (other than for short periods) higher prices and a declining value for the dollar, i.e., inflation. I guess that you and the other members of the Corporation would agree with me that this will continue in the future, regardless of rather futile attempts which, at best, may only slightly slow the present rather rapid *rate* of inflation.

Unless Harvard and other institutions and individuals recognize this and prepare for it as Harvard has done in the past, the results in the future can indeed be disastrous. If one spends capital, obviously, there will be less in the future to earn money on. It really amounts to robbing the future to take care of the present. Of course, this procedure is tempting to any present incumbent. He'll probably be dead or out of the picture long before the inevitable fallacy of such a policy comes home to roost.

Your two predecessors as President of Harvard, with whom I served, always backed me one hundred percent in refusal to spend capital. Indeed, the income we "availed" ourselves of was, in fact, less by a few million every year than the income earned.

As of June 30, 1948, the market value of Harvard's General and Special Investments exceeded Yale's by approximately $100 million. At the end of fiscal 1971, the approximate market value of these funds were: Harvard, $1.3 billion, and Yale, $547 million. Harvard's investments were three-quarters of a billion larger than Yale's! What caused this? Capital gifts to Harvard were bigger during this period but not enough so as to account for this wide difference. Investment policy had most to do with it, but very important was the fact that Harvard saved money *every* year whereas, in many years, Yale dipped into principal. Yale now has a *policy* of doing so regularly. This unfortunate policy is disguised and made unclear by a formula of mathematical hieroglyphics. The simple fact is: it is Yale's policy to spend principal. . . .

There are other important reasons not to rob the future to make life easier now. The effect on donors and bequests could be very bad. Most givers of endowment funds assume and expect (and indeed sometimes legally specify) that the principal they give shall be maintained, not dissipated. . . .

Finally, I beg you and the other members of Harvard's governing boards not to be a party to the slow strangulation of Harvard's goose that has laid so many golden eggs over past years.

I am giving this letter as much publicity as I can in the hope that it will induce alumni and friends of Harvard and Yale to beg the former not to go down this dangerous and probably disastrous road and the latter to return from it.

Sincerely,
Paul C. Cabot

Cabot won that battle.* Common sense and tough experience again prevailed. The Harvard–Boston tradition has not only won out over the Yale–New York tradition, but has assured its superiority for generations. That means better-endowed chairs for Harvard, more scholarships, bigger libraries, a brighter collection of talent, more useful impact on America and the world. But beware complacency, Harvard!

When the market crashed, many colleges discovered that they had geared up their budgets to an expectation of capital gains that, far from rising as hoped, collapsed. Many endowments, including that of

---

*Although today's practice accepts the idea of constructing a reasonable level of expenditure from a portfolio not necessarily based on actual income alone, but taking account of underlying earnings, since in recent years so much corporate cash flow has been reinvested for growth rather than paid out in dividends.

the Ford Foundation itself, which believed its own propaganda, suffered crippling losses during this period.

> [McGeorge] Bundy urged the same policy on his own trustees and the Foundation's finance committee, of which he was a member, with the same results. Between 1966 and 1974, shocking losses were suffered. At the time of his arrival, its portfolio had a value of some $3.7 billion. By 1970 that had slumped to $2.8 billion and then fell further to $1.7 billion in 1974. . . . Ford has dissipated almost three fourths of the real value of its assets over the past fifteen years, a loss of something on the order of $6 billion of philanthropic resources measured in current dollars. No disaster of comparable magnitude has ever been recorded.*

What, then, is the cardinal point of Paul Cabot's approach?

As often as one asks him the question one always gets the same answer in a different way: realism and care; care and realism. And when you ask old-timers in the Boston investment community for the essence of Paul Cabot's investment technique you usually get the same answer: "He's so careful," they say. "He's so fantastically *thorough.*"

"First, you've got to get *all* the facts," he says, "and then you've got to *face* the facts." Characteristically, he goes on to mutter, "Not pipe dreams."† He always observes that there's no way to *be* a realist unless you've experienced the many facets of reality, which means having attained a certain age. With age, he's become more cautious.

Young people, says Cabot, are optimistic. They come up with fantastic earnings estimates and are sure everything's going to be rosy. The younger you are the more chances you'll take. The older you get the more you've had a chance to see how often there's a slip between the cup and the lip. "I've only got confidence in older men, who've been through depressions, recessions, wars, and all the rest of it."

Paul Cabot spent his career at State Street Management, now housed in light, modern offices near the top of a Boston skyscraper. A

---

*Waldemar Nielsen, *The Golden Donors* (New York: E. P. Dutton, 1984).
†This corresponds to one of my own observations about life, including sociology, international affairs, and many other things: Most people extrapolate comfortably from the recent past, instead of intently studying the present. The future is around us now, but we don't see it.

handsome receptionist inters one's coat in a recessed closet. Everything suggests glossy efficiency.

Mr. Cabot's own office, however, is another story. Suddenly I was back in my Harvard tutor's study when I was an undergraduate. There's an old pencil sharpener screwed to the inside of the door, a covey of simple wooden chairs, a wooden coat rack supporting one gray coat and one Boston hat (Boston hats seem to be seasoned for several years inside tennis court rollers before being inaugurated), a glass-fronted bookcase containing business volumes, and, behind a large plain desk, Mr. Cabot himself, a compact, rubicund man. He wears the New England uniform of grayish tweedy suit with vest.

I asked him how well he had really done with the Harvard portfolio. Did the performance fully take account of capital additions and withdrawals?

"Well," said Cabot, "I took over in . . ." He hesitated, and leaned across his desk to inspect a huge gold-embossed red leather box, apparently the usual retirement token. "Nineteen forty-eight. About all the goddamn thing's good for," he muttered, nodding at the box. "Can't remember dates. When I left in 1965 it had grown 500 percent. Harvard writes off a building in the year it's finished, which is right, because financially they're a liability. It just happens that gifts worked out to about as much as the construction came to, so five times is about how much the endowment really grew. Of course, those were damn good times."

I asked him about his even earlier days. What was it like in the twenties and thirties?

Cabot described some of his earliest transactions with wry amusement.

"One of our first big buys was Kraft—you know, cheese. Old man Kraft had started the whole thing at home, in Chicago. He used to go around in a horse and buggy selling the stuff. Later they found a way of pasteurizing the cheese . . . it ruins it. Makes it taste like some sort of goddamn toothpaste. I like natural cheese myself. Anyway, when we bought the stock it had sales of two or three million. Now it's two billion! We didn't like to go on the board of a company at that time. Now we do. So we asked a friend of ours called Jim Trimble to go on the board of Kraftco to represent us. He was a hell of a hard-boiled character.

"Mr. Kraft was a pious Baptist—never smoked or drank. One time we'd gone out to Chicago and were all in a room in the Drake Hotel. Jim Trimble was on the bed with his feet up. We were all drinking bourbon and smoking cigars. Then Mr. Kraft came in. He told us he'd just borrowed two million from Halsey, Stuart. Trimble popped up like a jackknife coming together. 'Those sons of bitches?' he said. But that wasn't the worst of it. Mr. Kraft explained that Halsey, Stuart had gotten options on half the company as part of the deal. Trimble and I told him he was crazy as a coot. We figured Halsey, Stuart would sell the bonds they got for the $2 million and keep the options, which would have given them half the company. Not so. They gave half the options to whoever bought the bonds. So in a few weeks the bonds went up to 160 percent of par! We really got fed up with Kraft. He was a good merchant but didn't know a goddamn thing about financial management.

"That was how it was in those days. Years later, as a matter of fact, I went on the board myself. By that time they were selling two-thirds of all the cheese in the United States! Anyway, I found myself sitting next to Mr. Kraft at the board table.

"'What does Mr. Trimble think of me now? Am I still crazy as a coot?' the old man asked me.

"'I don't think he's changed his opinion, Mr. Kraft,' I told him.

"When I started out in this business nobody believed in common stocks, you know. People thought they were risky and exotic, unsuitable for a conservative investor. Bonds were the thing. The first serious discussion I ever heard of that presented stocks as a desirable holding was by a guy called Edgar Laurence Smith. It was called *Common Stocks as a Long-Term Investment*. That was the very first. Strangely enough, Edgar Laurence Smith never did it for himself. He died busted."

What were to his mind the characteristics of a very desirable stock?

"The most important quality is management that's able and *honest*. A hell of an easy way to get taken to the cleaners is by some goddamn crook like Ivar Kreuger."*

"Then, you want an industry that's prosperous and that's really needed."

I asked Cabot about insurance, America's largest industry in sales volume, pointing out the remarkable persistence of insurance premium income and the increasing computerization of this type of business. The computer doesn't ask for a raise—in fact, it gets cheaper.

---

*The "Swedish Match King." He floated immense amounts of ultimately worthless paper through Boston's Lee, Higginson.

"I've never understood one goddamn thing about insurance," he said, "except that I don't want to have any for myself.

"Now, a stock I like a lot is Hewlett-Packard. My partner George Bennett knows Hewlett himself. He thinks Hewlett's the best goddamn businessman he ever met. We've got a lot of it. It's okay."

Since Hewlett and Packard were approaching retirement, I brought up the problem of succession; you never know if someone can be replaced.

"A businessman who's that good worries about his successor along with everything else," said Cabot. "Anyway, they've got a lot of stock themselves. They're very interested in the successor management."

"About $1 billion worth at present market," I said. "Still, all of history tells us never to take a successor on faith. Not much grows in the shadow of an oak. Let's hope for the best."

As an example of an industry he liked, Cabot cited pharmaceuticals. SmithKline was his company's largest drug holding. They'd bought it recently and had had a double in it. I observed that they must have a good drug analyst to have caught the turnaround. "We do," said Cabot. "There was a change in the company's management, and we thought we could bet on the new guys."

He mentioned that State Street had doubled its money in ABC. "It's a hell of a well-run outfit. The whole goddamn thing's based on Nielsen. There's this big pot of money for TV advertising, and it's split between CBS, NBC, and ABC, depending on the ratings. ABC's been getting a lot less per unit of time—it's two minutes, or something—than the others. But NBC's dropped to a poor third, and ABC's number one. So we figure ABC's got to get more per unit."

What was the greatest danger to investments?

"Inflation. It's the biggest problem in the world. I don't think we can do a goddamn thing about it. Look at all these government budget deficits—frightening! I remember when I was treasurer of Harvard we had a bookkeeper who'd got the same salary for twenty years. He was doing the same work. He didn't *expect* a raise. You got *promoted*, sure; but not just a raise on general principles. After all, if you have a raise every year and the cost of living goes up the same amount you aren't *really* getting a raise. But you've sure built inflation into the system. How are you going to change that?"

I answered that it seemed to take a fearful shock to change people's point of view, such as losing a war, or a social upheaval. What sort of shock would do that here? The bankruptcy of the Social Security system, I suggested. It's actuarially bankrupt now, and sooner or later the pyramid has to collapse.

"The majority of the people are so goddamn dumb they won't wake up until they starve to death," said Cabot.

What could one do to offset inflation?

In the future, Cabot said, the investor probably won't be able to preserve his capital in real terms, after inflation. I told him that one of the Rothschilds had declared that if he could be sure of transmitting one-quarter of his fortune in real terms to his posterity he'd take it as a bargain.

"How do you invest for yourself?"

"I have a big slug of good-grade municipals. Not New York . . . smaller towns, with a sense of responsibility. Needham [Massachusetts], where I live . . . Newton [Massachusetts]. I keep short and roll them over."

I pointed out that when inflation runs ahead of the return on municipals, that means living off one's capital in real terms.

"Sure, but that's true of a lot of stock dividends too." I agreed: Some dividends are essentially declared out of capital, to get the investor to buy the stock. To that extent, dividends are a taxable return of capital.

What about investing in art, an idea of that time? "I don't know one goddamn picture from another," said Cabot. I noted that contrary to general belief, most works of art decline steadily in real terms from the time they were first sold. Looking around with hindsight at some works of art that have risen faster than inflation is like looking around an old folks' home and seeing a few people that live to be a hundred—what's called survivorship bias. It doesn't follow that most people do.

I asked him which were his favorites from the State Street list. The ones with a small labor component, he answered. "But I don't know. The way I see it, there'll be a bust. And you know what they say, when the cops raid a whorehouse they take away *all* the girls. You can't believe a panic until you've lived through it. In the Depression, for instance, Deere went from 142 to 7. My partner Paine wanted to sell at 7 because he said it was going to go out of business. I tried to dissuade him but I couldn't, so he sold out. And do you know what happened? He changed his mind overnight, but the goddamn thing opened way up, and he repurchased the position the next morning at 10! There aren't many investors who'd be that flexible."

I asked Cabot if State Street tried to catch market swings—to buy low and sell high.

"No," he said. "It's luck. If you're lucky, you win. If you aren't, you lose. What the hell good is that? I'll tell you a story, though," he added. "In 1929 the stock market reached its peak. Then there was a hell of a bust. Then the market made quite a good recovery. During the rise we were about 60 percent cash and 40 percent stocks. Then all of a sudden the U.S. quit the gold standard. I was down in Florida. They called me up. I said, 'Buy all you can.' Paine agreed. So in one day we went from 40 percent in stocks to 90 percent in stocks. The market doubled in the next two or three months. It took us almost a year, though, to figure out exactly what we had bought in that one day."

I asked him about the moral aspect of investment management. "I don't think morals have a goddamn thing to do with it. One time we owned some of the liquor stocks: Schenley, National Distillers, and so on. Sometimes we got letters from shareholders objecting to them. We used to answer that State Street was in business to make money for our shareholders in a legal way, and that liquor was a legal business. If a shareholder wanted to assert a moral principle beyond the legal one, then all he had to do was sell his State Street stock. Only one ever did: an old lady in Vermont with a hundred shares or so."

I asked if as treasurer of Harvard he had been influenced by the sociological overtones of investment. "Not in the least," he replied. "I remember when I was treasurer some editor of the *Crimson* called me up at night. He asked me if Harvard owned Middle South Utilities or Mississippi Power and Light. I told him we did. He said that they wanted me to sell them, that they were unfair to Negroes. I told him that he was a goddamn little squirt. I had a partner on the board and happened to know that they'd been better than almost anybody else down there. 'Go jump in the lake . . . to hell with you,' I said."

I asked Cabot what his point of view would be if a company he had stock in did have a poor record on minority employment, or whatever. "It would be bad business for them. We'd try to persuade them to mend their ways." He thought for a while. "On the whole, business is pretty goddamn moral."

I observed that business seemed to me to be at least as moral as government, and more intellectually honest. "It's a hell of a lot more moral than government," said Cabot, emphatically.

It was the end of the day. Cabot got up from his plain desk, went over to the coatrack, and put on his gray coat and his gray Boston hat. We left his Harvard tutor's study with the pencil sharpener screwed to the inside of the door and entered the long, airy corridor of State Street's modern offices. A group of handsome, intelligent-looking executives saluted him as we passed.

"G'night, boys," said Cabot.

Six

PHILIP FISHER
THE CUTTING EDGE

PHILIP FISHER FRST HUNG OUT HIS SHINGLE AS AN INVESTMENT counselor on March 1, 1931. After a year at Stanford Business School he had gone to work in the security analysis department (then called the statistical department) of a San Francisco bank. Banks sold securities then, and needed some analytical capability, but it was next to worthless. Shortly after Hoover's announcement that prosperity was just around the corner, Fisher switched to a stock exchange firm. Unfortunately, the firm could not wait for Hoover's prediction to come true, and Fisher found himself once again on the street. He later came to consider this one of the most fortunate events in his business life. For some time he had thought that he would like to be independent and so seized the occasion to start his own business, in a tiny office with no outside windows.

He found two unexpected advantages in starting when he did. First, to do his work he needed to talk to company executives, and since they often had little to do, they were delighted to chat. One executive he called on said he had finished the sports page but didn't want to go home yet, and so had said to himself, "Why don't I just let this monkey in to see me?" He became a longtime client, and later confided that a year later he couldn't have seen Fisher: He'd become too busy.

The other advantage of starting in 1931 was that almost every potential client was dissatisfied with his existing adviser—if he had any capital left at all.

In one of his Stanford courses, Fisher had made weekly trips with his professor to visit companies in the Bay Area whose executives were willing to talk seriously about their operations. This professor had helped correct operating weaknesses in a number of companies. Fisher offered to drive, since he had a car and his professor didn't. Driving home, they talked about each company. That hour each week, Fisher says, was the most useful training he ever received.

Among the companies they looked at were one that made fruit-canning machinery and another that made pumps to spray pesticides for orchards and farms. Fisher told his professor that to him those two seemed to have the best prospects of any they had seen. In 1928 the two merged with a third, a manufacturer of vegetable-canning machinery, to become Food Machinery Corporation (FMC). The stock ran up in the 1929 boom, but in the Depression collapsed along with everything else.

When that brand-new investment adviser, Philip Fisher, started calling on potential clients in 1931 he took the opportunity to tell them of his enthusiasm for FMC. For several years the stock afforded him and them no satisfaction whatever, and indeed it performed less well than the market as a whole. By the end of 1934, however, it had caught fire again, and it became one of the darlings of the bull market that peaked in 1937. As it started to become a market leader, the people he had talked to about it became impressed, and bit by bit they began to give him more and more money to handle.

He spent decades in the same office building. During that time neither he nor his office changed much. His reputation as an original, profound, and remorselessly thorough investment thinker continued to grow, as did the value of the portfolios he managed. The common thread of his holdings has always been strength in technology. San Francisco is an excellent place to keep up with the high-tech world.

Philip Fisher became the dean of investment counselors in San Francisco, and remained so for decades, although he always kept the number of his clients to a minimum. "Oh yes, *Common Stocks and Uncommon Profits,*" people would say, referring to his first book. The most he had under management was probably $500 million, the equivalent of $2 billion or so in today's money. His experience and thoroughness gave him the confidence to be original and, above all, patient. He was rightly recognized as a great investor. If you tell a Wall Street professional that Fisher took a major position for his accounts in the original private placement of Texas Instruments and kept the stock ever since, he will be impressed.

Fisher is a friendly man with an easy, courteous manner. Of medium height, he is tall, sparely built, and slightly stooped. His thin, scholarly face, with dark brown eyes behind rimless glasses, is topped with a high forehead and receding hairline. He has a humorous mouth and large, pointed ears. He looks much younger than his years, and at fifteen, when he entered college, he must have looked far too youthful to belong there.

When I visited him, his small, unmarked office contained the simplest steel and plastic furniture. On his plain, worn desk was a white leatherette pen and pencil holder—nothing else. A beige wall-to-wall carpet was underfoot. The walls were embellished by a watercolor of Chinatown painted by a friend, another of a bright red pagoda, and a pseudo-mosaic depicting a bonsai tree and a Japanese lantern assembled by his wife. No equipment could be seen except a telephone and a digital clock (set seven minutes fast)—no files, no calculator, no in and out boxes, no photographs, memorabilia, or knickknacks. By having a handful of clients, few holdings, and very low turnover, he essentially eliminated administration.

Fisher doesn't like expensive things. For years he wore an overcoat from decades earlier and drove an ancient Oldsmobile Six without a radio or frills. He just didn't see the need for a newer car.

Fisher's life revolves around home and office: his work, his wife, his children and grandchildren. (Fisher's son, Ken, has followed his father into the investment counsel profession, but has his own firm. He finds his father as puzzlingly original as others do.) He gets up at six in the morning, has his daily soup, starts telephoning when the New York Stock Exchange opens, then heads for the office.

He enjoys holding forth on almost any subject, and is sensitive and responsive. He has commonsense views on politics, as on most matters. Though he sometimes supports candidates who promise to reduce waste in government he's usually disappointed by their subsequent performance.

Fisher spent World War II in the Army Air Corps within the United States. During his slack periods he had a chance to think about what he would do after the war ended, and he resolved that when he went back to his professional practice his first order of business would be to identify the best chemical company in the United States. So after he was discharged he spent nine months looking them all over, finally winnowing the list down to three. In the end he decided that Dow Chemical was the pick of the lot, and he bought stock in 1946.

In the spring of 1947 he was introduced to the company itself through one of its important customers. After meeting with the management he decided that they were among the most remarkable he'd ever encountered, and, he says, he has never had occasion to change his view. For about seven years in the 1950s the company did not perform outstandingly, but Fisher did not lose confidence or patience, or sell any stock. Its success was legendary, and it long remained one of Fisher's important holdings.

Stephen Horton, a field analyst for Standard & Poor's, first mentioned Texas Instruments to Fisher in 1954, after which Fisher talked to many people about the company, becoming increasingly interested in it. One day he was talking to Emmett Solomon, later president of San Francisco's Crocker National Bank and at that time manager of the Provident Securities Company, a Crocker family holding company. He told Solomon that while he didn't know enough about this small Dallas company to invest in it, still, what he had learned so far was very exciting. Solomon was struck by this, since he and his wife had just met Erik Jonsson, the head of the company, on a cruise to Hawaii, where they'd occupied nearby cabins. Solomon had been intrigued enough to resolve to visit Jonsson's company, and invited Fisher to go with him.

Morgan Stanley had just advised the four founders of Texas Instruments to sell a small amount of their stock for estate planning purposes. After Solomon and Fisher's visit, Provident Securities and Fisher's clients became two of the three purchasers of that placement. With additions bought near the bottom of three market breaks, it became one of Fisher's largest holdings.

Not Ranked at All

Fisher discovered Motorola in a similar way. An investment man passing through San Francisco mentioned to him that Motorola seemed to be a most remarkable company. Fisher visited the company, representing both himself and friends in Fireman's Fund Insurance. Very much impressed, Fisher and Fireman's Fund both bought Motorola stock. A year or so later, Fireman's Fund told Fisher that it had hired a New York bank to go over its portfolio. The bank ranked all their holdings as "very attractive," "attractive," or "unattractive"—all except Motorola, which was not ranked at all, since, claimed the bank, it was not the kind of company worth spending time on. Later still, however, Fireman's Fund told Fisher that Motorola had been its best-acting stock.

These stocks—FMC, Dow, Texas Instruments, and Motorola— became core holdings in Fisher's portfolios, which declined about as fast as the averages in bear markets, but did far better in static or rising markets.

"I don't want a lot of good investments; *I want a few outstanding ones,*" he says. He focuses his attention on a narrow range of enterprises and is unwilling even to consider most companies. He wants above all not to try to be a jack-of-all-trades and master of none. You can't know more than a certain amount, so to know enough you need to focus.

Fisher's general feeling about investments that are of interest to him is that the company in question should combine outstanding *business management* with a strong *technological lead* in most of what it does. He won't invest in companies that depend on the taste of the mass consumer, influenced by advertising, which he does not feel he understands, since his tastes quite frequently differ from the public's. He has found that when he and his wife particularly enjoy some TV series, it is likely to be discontinued by the network because of its lack of popularity. When I heard that, I observed that it seemed to me in the nature of things that a notable investor should disagree with popular thinking. The whole point is to differ from the mass: to be right when the crowd is wrong—if possible, to be the *only* one who is right. I told him a melancholy little maxim I had formulated as editor of the *Harvard Lampoon:* "If we like it, the subscribers won't."

He avoids insurance and other financial companies for two reasons. First, there is enough "cross-linking" between some technological areas and others so that his contacts in one technology company help in appraising another in a different but related area; he enjoys no such advantage in financial enterprises. Second, he understands manufacturing. He feels the areas he covers differ enough in the economic factors that influence them so that he can achieve diversification without venturing into lines of business he feels less sure about.

I asked him how he was able to assess technology in spite of not being a technician. He said that as in any other field, sources and knowledge slowly build up; one piece of technological information leads to another.

Fisher's key idea is that *you can make a lot of money by investing in an outstanding enterprise and holding it for years and years as it becomes bigger and better.* At the end your share in the enterprise is worth a great deal more than at the beginning. *Almost certainly the market price of your share will rise to reflect its higher intrinsic worth.* And certainly *you should concentrate on growth in intrinsic worth:* without that there's no reason for the stock to go up at all.

He ridicules short-term thinking. (In his whole life, he says, he's only known one in-and-out trader who made money consistently.) Pursuing short-term goals Fisher regards as also the worst possible mistake for a company. He therefore insists that *management must first and foremost be working to build the company over the long term.* Growth happens because management is profoundly dedicated to bringing it about and directs all its activities to that objective, and as long as it does this successfully, the investor can stay on board.

Fisher reiterates that the investor who attempts the impossible abandons his only hope of doing well.

Above all, he excoriates the "performance game" hustlers who pretend that one can build capital by guessing what is going to happen in the market a year—or indeed a few months—from now. "I remember my sense of shock some half-dozen years ago when I read a recommendation from the sizable trust department of a theretofore highly conservative bank. The recommendation was to sell the shares of a company which was a customer of that bank and one about which the bank should have had considerable knowledge. However, the recommendation was not based on any long-term fundamentals. Rather, it was that *over the next six months* the funds could be employed more profitably elsewhere. Indoctrinated in the customs of an older and perhaps saner era, I remember my amazement at this pronouncement. Was a trust department either entitled or equipped to act as a short-term trader with funds it was attempting to manage?"

Almost Never

One of Fisher's most notable utterances is on this subject: *"If the job has been correctly done when a common stock is purchased, the time to sell it is—almost never."*

He gives two exceptions: first, if it turns out that *you made a mistake* in your original appraisal; second, if the company *ceases to qualify under the same appraisal method.* The old management may lose its drive or newer management may not be as able. Alternatively, a company may get so big in its own market that it cannot do much better than its industry, or indeed than the economy as a whole. (On the other hand, Fisher, unlike T. Rowe Price, has no objection to holding a mature company that remains the low-cost producer in its industry, continues to innovate, and keeps cutting costs.)

A third exception, which Fisher considers rarely valid, is that *you discover a particularly attractive new opportunity*—such as a company with great promise of a sustained 20 percent annual earnings gain—and, to buy it, you decide to cut back on a holding with lesser growth prospects. However, *you probably know less about the new company than the old one,* about which you have been learning more and more for years, so there is a risk of making a mistake. You cannot, after all, know almost everything that could be important about more than a few companies. *Those years of progressively greater familiarity,* Fisher urges, *should not be thrown away.*

He also argues that *you should not sell because you think that a stock is too high-priced*—has "gotten ahead of itself"—*or because the whole market is due for a slide.*

Selling for either reason implies that you are clever enough to buy the stock back more cheaply later. But in practice, you almost always miss the stock when it recovers. And in addition you have the capital gains tax to pay. After all, if you have chosen the company properly in the first place, with a reasonable prospect that in ten years, say, the stock will have tripled or quadrupled, is it so important that it's 35 percent overpriced today? And there's always *the possibility that the stock price reflects good news you don't know about yet.*

Silliest of all, says Fisher, *is selling out just because a stock has gone up a lot.* The truly great company—the only kind he is interested in buying—will grow indefinitely, and its stock likewise. *That it has advanced substantially since purchase only means that everything is going just as it should.*

"Conservative"

Fisher redefines the word "conservative" around this concept. To him, a conservative investor is one who makes his capital grow in a practical, realizable way, not in a way that can't succeed. People often describe large, well-known companies as conservative investments. But for Fisher, old and famous companies that have passed their prime and are losing ground in the jungle of international business are by no means conservative holdings. Rather, the conservative investor is one who owns winners: dynamic, well-managed enterprises that because they are well situated and do almost everything right continue to prosper, grow, and build value year after year.

The owners of such companies don't have to worry about market fluctuations, since the underlying assets are building: Things are going the right way. Market recognition will follow.

Scuttlebutt

Somewhat surprisingly, Fisher's first substantive (as against introductory) chapter in *Common Stocks and Uncommon Profits* dwells on the importance of scuttlebutt—which he also calls "the business grapevine"—in investing. The theme recurs throughout his writing. In fact, Fisher suggests no other source of information for a number of the points he says a prudent investor must consider, such as management integrity, long-range planning, cost controls, and the effectiveness of a company's research program, all of which are hard to determine from the published figures.

He notes, "It is surprising what the 'scuttlebutt' method will produce. Until the average investor tries it, he probably will not believe how complete a picture will emerge if he asks intelligent questions about a company's research activities of a diversified group of research people. . . ."

And of the quality of the sales organization he says, "Because sales effort does not lend itself to financial ratios many investors fail to appraise it at all in spite of its basic importance in determining real investment worth. Again, the way out of this dilemma is the use of the 'scuttlebutt' technique. . . . Both competitors and customers know the answers. Equally important, they are seldom hesitant to express their views. The time spent by the careful investor . . . is usually richly rewarded."

Fisher is essentially talking about a corporate background check. "The business grapevine," he writes, "is a remarkable thing. . . . Most people, particularly if they feel sure there is no danger of their being quoted, like to talk about the field of work in which they are engaged, and will talk rather freely about their competition. Go to five companies in an industry, ask each of them intelligent questions about the points of strength and weakness of the other four, and nine times out of ten a surprisingly detailed and accurate picture of all five will emerge."

One of the richest sources of scuttlebutt is easy to reach and would not be thought of by most investors: *trade shows*. Their charm for the information-seeker is that many potential sources are assembled in one place, and everyone is there to talk, and indeed to contradict each

other. They, not you, have made the appointment and paid their air-
fare. Far from interrupting the salesman or executive, you are why he's
there. Further, the salesmen pushing their companies' products are
bound to explain how they differ from the competition.

Industry association executives are a valuable source. For the price of a
lunch you can learn wonderful things. Here, of course, you must swear
eternal secrecy, like a newspaperman, or your informant could get into
hot water. The same is true of university and government researchers.
People or companies who buy a company's products will also tell you a
lot, as will the company's suppliers and purchasers, if you can get hold
of them. And former employees will often give you an earful—not
always unbiased.*

Fisher mentions in passing that getting introductions to all these
sources can take as much time as one spends actually talking to them;
for the ordinary small investor it may not be possible. Further. the professional investor enjoys another advantage over the layman: He can
exchange facts and ideas—or stories—with the interviewee, so that the
conversation becomes a two-way street; as the French say, he sends
back the elevator.

Outstanding Companies

In his first book, Fisher describes fifteen characteristics of an outstanding company, and in his second he touches on several more. I
think one can discern about twenty in all, depending on what is considered a separate category.

Though not presented consistently in Fisher's two books, his criteria
can be grouped under two main categories: qualities of management
and characteristics of the business itself.

Characteristics of an attractive *business* include *growth* from existing
products and from new ones; a high *profit margin* and *return on capital*,†
together with favorable trends for both; effective *research;* a superior

---

*A source Fisher doesn't mention but that I like for consumer durables because it's
factual and easy to reach is *repairmen*. Any master mechanic or electrician will give
you his ideas on which cars or appliances last longer and have the vulnerable parts
placed where they are easy—or almost impossible—to get at. *Consumer Reports* often
gives this information in a systematic way. Another source is Internet message
boards, which are often surprisingly frank.
†One must take note of the age of the plant. There may be an apparently high return
on fully depreciated equipment. Warren Buffett's suggestion that you consider the
return on *equity plus inventory* makes excellent sense.

sales organization; a *leading industry position* giving advantages of scale; and a valid *"franchise"*—proprietary products or services.

Management characteristics include *integrity,* implying *conservative accounting; accessibility;* an orientation toward *long-range* results, if necessary at the expense of this quarter's bottom line, without equity dilution; a *recognition of the pervasiveness of change;* excellent *financial controls; multidisciplinary skills* where appropriate; the *special skills* associated with particular industries; and good *personnel policies,* including continuing management training.

Fisher's discussion of personnel policy is particularly illuminating. He insists that a company must consciously and continuously try to make itself a better place to work, from the executive level to union relations, and to be so perceived by its employees. He cites IBM's extraordinary training programs, under which a third of a salesman's entire career is spent in IBM schools; Motorola's Executive Institute, which readies promising executives for higher responsibilities; and the Texas Instruments policy of letting worker teams assign their own goals and communicate directly with top management, sharing in profits according to their performance.

In discussing profit margins, Fisher makes a point that investors sometimes forget: Exceptionally high profit margins can be a honeypot to attract hungry competitors. The safest position may be to have only a small edge on the competition in profit margins, plus a higher turnover, because that leaves little incentive for new competition to move in on you. Fisher ridicules the notion, sometimes put forward by brokerage reports, that a statistically cheaper number two company may be a more attractive investment because it has greater possibilities. A fully installed dominant company—a GE or Merck—is exceedingly hard to displace, as long as management remains alert.

Fisher insists on integrity in management. Insiders have any number of opportunities to benefit themselves at their shareholders' expense, both in material terms and by deceiving them about the prospects for the company. *A greedy management's most common abuse is issuing itself overly generous stock options* when the company's stock happens to be at a low point—selling below book value, say. Time passes, the stock returns to a normal level, and through no merit of its own, management has extracted millions of dollars of value from the shareholders.

Another unsound practice follows in a way from the shareholders' own laziness, when *management is allowed to pursue short-range goals while talking long-term language.* As an example, Fisher observes that *many companies that suffer from poor labor relations describe themselves as "people-oriented."* Sometimes when a company uses "creative accounting" it is deceiving the shareholders into thinking things are better than they are, and is probably borrowing from the future for short-range results. However, the shareholders, particularly financial institutions, are usually aware of this practice. So really *all a company that uses imaginative accounting can expect to achieve is a possible temporary boost for its stock, together with a long-term cap on it arising from the investment community's suspicions about management's integrity.* Investment managers who buy the stock of such companies with their clients' money reveal a lot about themselves as well. The prudent investor belongs elsewhere.

In passing, Fisher laments the Fourth of July tone of so many annual reports. which, he says, may "reflect little more than the skill of the company's public relations department in creating an impression about the company in the public mind. . . . *They seldom present balanced and complete discussions of the real problems and difficulties of the business.* Usually they are too optimistic.

"If a vice president reported to the president the way the president reported to the owners, that vice president would last exactly ten minutes. *The officers of a company often seem to feel that they should treat annual reports as a form of advertising. That's completely wrong."*

Not in his books but in conversation, Fisher makes another point: *Management must have a continuous and effective program of cost-cutting.* There must be a plan, it must be clearly articulated, it must be understood, and it must work.

If a company enjoys a favorable situation and is well run, the shareholders are best served when it reinvests most of today's profits for tomorrow's growth. Companies with a substantial technology component are doing this automatically when they put their cash flow into research and development. This assumes, of course, that the return on this reinvestment is greater than that which the shareholders would be able to earn on higher dividends. If not, the company should give the money back to its shareholders as dividends or through stock repurchases.

If a company can successfully put its profits back to work to build the business for bigger profits later, then its earnings and book value per share will in due course rise, dividends can be increased, the investment community will perceive that both are likely to go on rising, and the stock price will surely advance, although one cannot know exactly when. "It's a good deal easier to know *what's* going to happen than *when* it's going to happen," says Fisher. To use my language rather than his, Fisher is always looking for the "double play": a company's earnings rise; the market gives a higher price-earnings multiple to those higher earnings; the stock soars.

Fisher's Technique

Most readers of this book would have great difficulty investing the way Fisher does. The first question to settle would be whether in the time you have available you could hope to develop a business grapevine or scuttlebutt machine like the one he draws on so heavily: good company contacts in many industries, informants in government and industry associations, investing confreres who will exchange opinions. If not, you may have trouble with his method, since it depends heavily on qualitative factors that—unlike the figures needed in Benjamin Graham's approach—you can never hope to elicit solely from the publicly available material. In this event, says Fisher, you should use a professional adviser, either directly or by putting your money in a well-run fund.

Fisher proposes three successive phases in analyzing a company properly: absorbing the available printed material, triangulating through business sources, and finally visits to management.

1. *The printed material.* This includes the annual and interim reports, a recent prospectus, any proxy material, and the 10-K: the supplementary material filed with the SEC and available to the public. From these you should try to establish the characteristics of the company's accounting, how much is being spent on research and development and what the company means by those terms, management background and compensation, and profit margin trends.

   You should review the available Wall Street literature, primarily for the investment community's perception of the company, since the difference between that perception and reality is what creates the investment opportunity.

2. *Additional information from business sources.* This is where good scuttlebutt is indispensable; the very point where the nonprofessional investor may be shaken off the scent.

You can gather more than facts about a company from secondary sources. You can also learn the key questions to ask of management. If a formerly excellent top executive is showing signs of alcoholism, the company will scarcely volunteer the fact; you can at least try to find out tactfully what is being done about the problem. Again, advance appraisals of the company officers you are going to see will give you some allowance for such traits as overoptimism.

3.   *Company visits.* Fisher hopes to evaluate three things through calls on management: stated business policies, whether those policies are actually being carried out, and the men themselves.

Policies to investigate are the balance between long-term and short-term objectives, sales force training programs, where the research is headed, what the company is doing to build employee loyalty, and what sort of permanent cost-cutting program it has. Since talk is easy, the interviewer should then look for hard evidence that the company's policies are being achieved. Finally, an able and experienced person can often form a true impression of the company's officers by meeting them. You can try to size up whether the person you are talking to is honest and intelligent, sees things in a rounded way, and can make the hard decisions to persist in a policy or pull back when circumstances change.

Buying Points

Fisher offers three wonderful suggestions for timing stock purchases.

First, *buy when the start-up period of a substantial new plant*—which sometimes lasts for months and includes a special sales effort for the new product involved—*has depressed earnings and discouraged investors.*

Often the news of a successful pilot plant and the decision to go to full commercial-scale operations will attract weak buyers, uninformed speculators who will drop out if the stock doesn't rise promptly. Fisher reminds us of an old saying that compares a pilot plant to driving at ten miles an hour over a poor road, and a commercial plant to tearing along at one hundred miles an hour. The public may forget that difference and let itself be shaken out of the stock as month after month the engineers can't get the bugs eliminated. As the stock sags, brokers will hint at more serious problems. This, says Fisher, may give rise to a great buying opportunity, since after the first plant is on stream the company may be able to launch a second, third, fourth, and fifth much more easily.

The second time to buy is on *bad corporate news:* a strike, a marketing error, or some other temporary misfortune.

A third opportunity to buy on favorable terms arises in a capital-intensive industry, such as chemicals, where *an unusually large investment in plant is required.* Sometimes after a product has been in production for a while engineers figure out how to *increase their output substantially by spending a relatively modest amount* of additional capital. This may produce a significant improvement in the company's profits. Until the stock advances to reflect this prospect there should be a buying opportunity.

Fisher also mentions that one should not hesitate to *buy on a war scare.* During this century, almost every time American forces have become engaged somewhere in the world, or there has been a serious danger that they would, the stock market has fallen, and every time it has recovered.

The reason to buy is not that war is good for business and therefore for stocks. It isn't. The reason is that governments plunge into debt to pay for a war, debasing the currency. So the prices of things go up, including stocks, which represent ownership of physical assets. To sell stocks on a war scare in exchange for depreciating cash is lunacy. *"War is always bearish on money,"* Fisher observes.

Fisher argues that the usual way investors buy is silly. They sift through masses of economic data, conclude that the business outlook is favorable, and invest. Almost all investment letters from banks and brokers start out this way, telling the reader that the economic outlook is good (or bad), so one should buy stocks (or hold off "until the outlook clarifies"). While this may sound persuasive in theory, it's impossible to apply in practice. *Economic forecasting is not yet far enough advanced to permit long-range predictions.* Fisher compares it to chemistry during the days of alchemy: "In chemistry then, as in business forecasting now, basic principles were just beginning to emerge from a mysterious mass of mumbo-jumbo. However, chemistry had not reached a point where such principles could be safely used as a basis for choosing a course of action."

Fisher wistfully speculates on how much might be accomplished if the investment community, unlike the alchemists and theologians in the Middle Ages, could apply all the time spent turning out contradictory economic forecasts to something useful.

I would go one step further than Fisher: Not only are the forecasts fatuous in themselves, but they usually echo each other and produce a consensus. The investor who holds off until there's a wave of optimism among the prophets is buying with the crowd and thus paying higher prices. Further, bull markets end and *bear markets begin in good times,* when everybody's optimistic. *The bottom comes in bad times,* when everybody's desperate. The Crash, after all, started amid universal euphoria in 1929, and the greatest buying point in history was when the banks closed in 1932: the market doubled in two months.

Often the investor is safest doing the opposite of what any Wall Street consensus indicates: Far from waiting to invest until the bank's "long-term economic overview" has turned favorable, he should try to hold off until a full-scale recession is in progress and the banks and economists say that all is lost. Then he can get solid assets at a discount and outstanding growth stocks at prices that do not reflect their prospects.

The investor must therefore be aware of both the facts and the perceptions. If the facts are more favorable than the perceptions, sooner or later the investment community will catch on, the perception will change, and the stock will rise.

Income

Fisher holds that a company can best serve its investors by following a consistent, predictable dividend policy; in fact, it is a primary obligation of management to do so. He himself will be looking for long-term growth, which implies lots of reinvestment of profits at a high rate of return to build the business, and consequently a low dividend. Another investor may prefer to have a high dividend, which should in any event be the policy followed by a company without attractive opportunities to reinvest its profits internally. Management should not reinvest shareholders' money at a lower return than they could get for themselves.

Fisher produces an admirable analogy to illustrate his thesis about the need for consistency in dividend policy. Suppose you started a restaurant. A good operator can hope to build up a steady clientele with any of a number of different approaches: low prices and good value; expensive luxury; Chinese or Italian cooking. There are customers for any of these at a fair price. The word will spread and a following will develop. What couldn't possibly work would be a policy that shifted unpredictably: high-quality French one day, cafeteria-style Chinese the next. People wouldn't know what they could expect and would stay away. The same holds for dividend policy.

In passing, Fisher refutes a pervasive Wall Street myth about dividends—that a high dividend can improve one's safety by providing a cushion for the stock in bear markets. Not so, he says. *"Every study seen on this subject indicates that far more of those stocks giving a bad performance price-wise have come from the high-dividend-paying rather than the low-dividend-paying group.* An otherwise good management that increases dividends and thereby sacrifices worthwhile opportunities for reinvesting increased earnings in the business is like the manager of a farm who rushes his magnificent livestock to market the minute he can sell them rather than raising them to the point where he can get the maximum price above his costs. He has produced a little more cash right now but at a frightful cost."

All this follows from Fisher's basic belief that the attractive holding grows and grows and grows, almost always from advantageously reinvested profits. So high dividends mean lower reinvestment, and lower the long-term-growth buildup of value that investment is all about.

Seven

Benjamin Graham
Quantify, Quantify

Benjamin Graham, the greatest investment theorist of his day, loved mathematics, and his approach to investment is mathematical, quantitative. In fact, he may well have been concerned with security analysis primarily as a branch of mathematics. Certainly no earlier investment thinker approached the subject solely through figures, without concern for the quality of the business or the character of management.

Graham's magnum opus is his *Security Analysis*. More useful for almost all readers, however, is *The Intelligent Investor*. Almost every investor should read its three hundred pages. Graham can give a feeling for investment reality. Most of what you hear in Wall Street is blather; Graham helps you see it all in perspective and sense where to look for objective truth.

Benjamin Graham came to New York from England with his parents in 1895 when he was a year old. His father represented the family chinaware firm, Grossbaum & Sons. (The family name was changed to Graham during World War I.) He grew up in Manhattan and Brooklyn, the youngest of three boys. After the death of his father, when Ben was nine, the family was greatly reduced in circumstances. His mother never adjusted to the change, and her anxieties undoubtedly contributed to Ben's subsequent preoccupation with achieving financial security.

He was an industrious student, and almost too good a boy. In his high school years, during which he took jobs to help support the family, he studied Greek and Latin, which became a lasting joy. After graduating from Columbia in the class of 1914, Ben was offered teaching fellow-ships in English and mathematics; instead he went to work as a mes-senger in Wall Street for Newburger, Henderson & Loeb. He soon progressed to doing write-ups and analyses, and during this period he married the first of his three wives. By 1917 he was earning respect as an analyst and had started publishing in financial magazines. He became a partner of the firm in 1920.

Graham was a small, stocky man who became thinner as he aged. He had an odd round face, with heavy lips and light blue eyes. A complex person of boundless energy, he loved literature—Proust, Virgil, Chateaubriand, Victor Hugo, the German poets—and was a fountain of apposite quotations.

By Wall Street standards he had unusually wide interests: the Greek and Latin classics, philosophy, languages. He translated a book from the Portuguese, wrote several books himself, admired Marcus Aurelius, and identified himself with Tennyson's Ulysses, a wily and thoughtful adventurer.

Once at a family gathering for his birthday he delivered this remark-able and revealing piece of self-analysis:

> One of the great heroes of my childhood reading was Ulysses. . . . The *Odyssey* has fascinated me from the beginning, nor has that fas-cination diminished through the years. The wiliness and the courage, the sufferings and the triumphs, of its protagonist carried an appeal which I never could quite understand. At first I thought it was the attraction of opposites—Ulysses enthralled me because both his character and his fate were so different from my own. Only after I had long passed my maturity did I begin to realize that there was quite a bit of the typically Odyssean faults and virtues in my own makeup.
>
> As a youngster I rejoiced to think that Ulysses' wanderings and trials had ended in his triumphant reunion with Penelope, and they both were now to "live happily forever after." But a few years later Tennyson's great poem was to introduce me to the real Ulysses, for whom his island home and his wife's bed could never be more than a port of call. . . .
>
> Then, much later again, I made the acquaintance of Dante's ver-sion of the dauntless expedition and the stormy death of Odysseus, as he is made to recount it in that brief and unforgettable passage

in the *Inferno*.* And, finally, I now hold in my hands a tremendous
epic on the same theme, newly written by the modern Kazantzakis.
Perhaps Ulysses is about my own age as again he leaves his wife
and his now married son. Perhaps he is ageless, as at times I feel
myself. In any case, in his mind of many turns (*polytropon*),† in the
restless heart, in the dauntless body, all under his peaked sailor
cap, I sense an iconoclastic ideal which has attracted me like an
unseen magnetic pole throughout my life. . . .

Graham liked women, but not marriage. His second wife was a secretary, and his third, Estelle, an employee. The French mistress with
whom he spent his final years he took over from one of his own sons. He
developed a passion for dancing and signed up for thousands of dollars'
worth of lessons, eventually abandoning the effort and offering the
unused time to his brother, Victor.

His interest in his own children only really started when they
became concerned with ideas; then he became their walking encyclopedia. A born teacher, he liked to invent stories for them and answer their
questions on any subject.

Generous and kind (he endowed a black church in New Haven), he
was liked by the people he came in contact with, but had few intimate
friends. In a self-description he quoted Estelle's judgment that he was
"humane, but not human." Although an agnostic, he was interested in
religious philosophy. He became a skier when that was an unusual skill,
and a keen tennis player. As a friend says, he had no *minor* faults: he
didn't smoke or drink, and ate sparingly. He was absentminded and did
not like to drive a car. He lived modestly but comfortably, and after he
achieved financial security he was little concerned with money. Late in
life he moved from New York to La Jolla, California, and at the end of
his life to the south of France.

In 1926 he formed a pool, the Benjamin Graham Joint Account,
which he managed in return for a share of the profits. During the first
year he was joined by Jerome Newman, with whom he remained associated throughout his business career.

---

*Canto XXVI. Dante (who like Tennyson had read Virgil and Ovid but not Homer)
consigns Odysseus to the eighth circle of hell for abandoning wife, father, and son.
†Homer also calls him *ptoliponthos*, "plunderer of cities," and *polumetis*, "of many
schemes." Odysseus was both a wily deceiver and a heroic voyager and warrior who
slew his foes on the field and then slew his wife's suitors . . . not quite a security analyst's résumé.

About this time, Graham encountered Bernard Baruch, whom he helped make a number of investments. A person close to the situation adds, "Baruch was lavish with praise privately, but that was all; the relationship was all take and no give on the part of Baruch." Baruch is believed to have offered Graham a profit-sharing association, but not on a basis that Graham found attractive.

The market collapse of 1929 and 1930 hit the Joint Account hard; from 1929 to 1932 it declined 70 percent, compared to 74 percent for the Dow Jones Industrials and 64 percent for the Standard & Poor's 500. But since the Joint Account had been using substantial margin, as investors often did in those days, Graham's actual stock-picking was better than this indicates. Nevertheless, he was personally wiped out in the Crash. Having ducked the 1929 cataclysm, he was enticed back into the market before the final bottom.

From 1928 to 1956, Graham taught a popular evening course at Columbia Business School. In 1934, with Professor David L. Dodd, he published the monumental *Security Analysis,* a basic text for serious students of investing. (As an indication of Graham's skill, the value of the list of undervalued special situations in the 1940 edition advanced over 250 percent in the next eight years, compared to a one-third increase in the Standard & Poor's Industrials.)

In 1944, Graham published *Storage and Stability,* offering a plan to stabilize food surpluses, world commodities, and world currencies. *The Interpretation of Financial Statements,* an excellent book, appeared in 1947, and in 1949 *The Intelligent Investor,* his most useful book for the nonspecialist.

Caution

Graham's greatness as an investor may well have consisted in knowing how to say no. One of his assistants in Graham-Newman has described to me ruefully what it was like proposing a list of carefully selected and researched opportunities for Graham's consideration, only to have him find something substantive to object to in every one. He felt no need to invest at all unless everything was in his favor.

When he finally did buy he was sure of what he was doing. His idea of a good, safe investment was simply buying a dollar for fifty cents over and over again. In any specific case, something may go wrong, but if you do it dozens of times the procedure is virtually infallible. Diversification—a multiplicity of transactions—is thus a key to the method, just as in insurance.

And as he bought, Graham always kept one foot out the door, ready to run if his calculations went awry. This intrinsic caution robbed him of the flair necessary to catch major market moves. Besides reentering the market too soon in the thirties and getting cleaned out, he missed the grand bull cycle that began in 1950, even advising one of his protégés not to go to work in Wall Street in 1951 because the market was so high.

However, in the 1973 edition of *The Intelligent Investor* he was right: "We think the investor must be prepared for difficult times ahead— perhaps in the form of a fairly quick replay of the 1969–70 decline, or perhaps in the form of another bull market fling, to be followed by a more catastrophic collapse." And indeed, the 1973–74 collapse was the most severe since the great crash of 1929–32—at its bottom offering the best buying opportunity since that time.

"Just Show Me the Balance Sheet"

All his professional life, Graham sought explainable, specific techniques that he could teach to others to enable them to select safe and profitable investments. He wanted a method that was entirely *quantitative,* that did not depend on things one couldn't be sure about, such as social trends, a company's future success in bringing out new products, or quality of management. In other words, the antithesis of T. Rowe Price's futurology approach.

He also wanted a method that could be used by anybody, and that therefore depended entirely on readily available published material, particularly the company's own reports.

He and his associates, after working for years, finally, in that prodigious compendium *Security Analysis,* did give the investor the tools he needed. However, the methodology employed was so elaborate that although in theory the book offered the ordinary investor, as well as the professional, the keys to investment success, few nonprofessionals have used it.

Analyzing a number of industries, one after another, Graham explains the financial characteristics of each and shows how, by comparing key operating and financial ratios, the analyst can determine which of a group of similar companies are successful and which unsuccessful, which financially sound and which weak, which overpriced and which bargains. He also discusses bonds and other securities. The analyst who has really mastered *Security Analysis* understands a lot.

Eventually, however, Graham did develop a simple investment touch-stone that can be used by everybody: his definition of the Bargain Issue. It's not a general theory, like "growth" or "management" or "innovation" or "lowest-cost producer," just a measure of undervaluation. And toward the end of his career he developed two additional criteria of a bargain stock. He finally concluded that the availability of these three tools rendered his elaborate earlier technique less necessary.

Investment and Speculation

Graham constantly underlines the distinction between investment and speculation. Investment must be based upon *thorough analysis* and must promise *safety of principal* and a *satisfactory return*. A holding may fail to be an investment, and thus be a mere speculation, because the analysis, the safety, or the return is lacking.

The first pitfall, risk-taking without adequate study, is mere guessing, and constitutes most of what passes for investment in the stock market. By his willingness to bet at the wrong odds the speculator gives the investor his opportunities. In this brief summary of Graham's ideas it is not possible to set forth in detail the analytic methods he proposes one use to establish safety of principal and adequacy of return: They take up hundreds of pages of his *Security Analysis*. He does not, of course, claim that every security can be so analyzed. The outlook for many companies is indeterminable, and he does say that if you buy such companies you are not truly investing but rather gambling, and all too possibly buying at a price set by insiders who know more than you do.

One of Graham's principles takes on cardinal importance every few years when the speculative pot again starts to boil over and enthusiasts make the customary two ghastly blunders in examining a company's earnings record: comparing a year's earnings with those of the previous year retroactively adjusted downward, which gives a delusive impression of endless improvement; and accepting reported earnings without determining whether the company's position really has improved by that amount.

Graham's simple rule is that *real earnings consist of dividends paid plus the increase (or minus the decrease) in the net assets per share—which usually appears as the change in earned surplus, including voluntary reserves.* As a grim example of fake earnings he takes the reported earnings of Dynamics Corporation of America for the ten years ending in 1960, which were

$13,502,000, or 50 cents a share. According to Graham's rule, real earnings were only $6,846,000, or 25 cents a share. There proved to be $6,655,000 of charges against earned surplus, almost all of which should have been charged instead against earnings. Graham ruefully points out that the market pays no attention whatever to reality during periods of speculative enthusiasm.

We see this as I write, in 2000. Coca-Cola and many other outstanding companies are booking nonrecurring sales of subsidiary companies as ordinary income, and some companies are constantly adjusting past earnings downward to inflate their growth.

In 1998, for example, General Motors announced that the previous year's earnings were the highest in its history. Very nice! Then it announced a $4 billion *after-tax* "restructuring" change! Oh, dear! And over the seven previous years GM had taken a total of $7 billion in charges, a third of earnings. Were these really "one-time"?

Cigar Butts

Graham loved the Standard & Poor's *Stock Guide,* which appears monthly and gives the basic financial facts on thousands of stocks, including every stock listed on any major U.S. exchange.

He describes with enthusiasm the pleasures an investment man can know by burrowing into this extraordinary "class album" of all the principal companies in America, companies that have multiplied their market values hundreds or indeed thousands of times, companies with century-long dividend records nestling by a company selling for two times latest earnings, or a stock that went from ⅛ to 68 and back to 3 (of which in a footnote he demurely admits to having at one time been an officer).

He then sets forth a series of criteria that he applied, using information available in the *Stock Guide,* to a number of companies to find out which stocks were likely to advance over a period of years. These criteria include net current assets and debt-equity ratios, earnings stability, dividend record, earnings growth, price in relation to net tangible assets, and quality ranking.

One further criterion, the relationship of price to book value, cannot be derived from using information in the *Stock Guide.*

Graham describes testing these criteria, singly or in combination, and finding in the end that the best by far is simply buying what he calls Bargain Issues, companies selling in the market for less than their net current asset value. He called them "cigar butts"—abandoned by the market, but with some value—a few puffs remaining for whoever wanted to salvage them.

"It always seemed, and still seems, ridiculously simple to say that if one can acquire a diversified group of common stocks at a price less than the applicable net current assets alone—after deducting all prior claims, and counting as *zero* the fixed and other assets—the results should be quite satisfactory. They were so, in our experience, for more than thirty years."

As for these issues, you can make money without serious risk "*if* you can find enough of them to make a diversified group, and *if* you don't lose patience if they fail to advance soon after you buy them. Sometimes the patience needed may appear quite considerable." The 1964 edition of *The Intelligent Investor* had observed that Burton-Dixie was selling at 20, with net current assets of 30 and a book value of 50. It took until August 1967 before all the shareholders were offered 53¾, approximately book value, for their stock. Graham sounds almost apologetic over this three-and-a-half-year wait until his readers got a profit of 165 percent.

One of the by-products of Graham's simplified Bargain Issue approach is that it provides the easiest of thermometers for the overall temperature of the market. If a great many companies are selling in the market for less than their net current assets, then the market is depressed. If there are hundreds and hundreds of them, it's time to plunge heavily.

Graham's technique suggests a high degree of diversification among different issues, in a banking or insurance spirit. At a time when you can invest with safety—that is, when good companies are being sold below their intrinsic worth—you can usually find bargains in many different industries. We all make mistakes: The only way to be safe is to spread your bets around widely enough to let the law of averages operate. Obviously, you must in theory work a bit harder to find several good opportunities instead of one, but in reality, as any practicing security analyst knows, in times of general gloom you always have many opportunities.

Growth Stocks

Many of the older trained securities analysts practicing in America today had the early editions of Graham's *Security Analysis* as their textbook. It will surprise some of them who remember his intense and

correct suspicion of the growth stock slogans of the late twenties—"No
price is too high to pay for Radio"—to learn that in the later edition he
changed his tune strikingly.

He begins by pointing out the extreme difficulty of establishing that
a growth stock really is what it seems. On this subject analysts are usually wrong, and further, when they are right they do not have the confidence to take advantage of it. The great time to own IBM was in the
early fifties, when it was already a firmly established company and yet
had the next twenty-five years of prodigious growth ahead of it. In
1952, however, 118 funds studied by the SEC averaged only one-half of
1 percent of their holdings in IBM! Only later did it become the largest
holding in most mutual funds, when its growth was slowing.

Graham gives several examples to illustrate the difficulty of being
right in predicting the future action of a supposed growth stock. He
cites Wiesenberger's *Investment Companies 1961*. There, the mean ten-
year performance results of all growth funds, assuming reinvestment
of distributions, was 289 percent, significantly less than the similar figure for the S&P 500-stock average, 322 percent. Graham concludes
that one should distrust elaborate calculations of growth stock values.

I must confess, however, that from the same data I conclude simply
that many growth funds don't do their job well, not that none does.
After all, most value funds don't, either. Many growth funds buy *official*
growth stocks whose price is high but whose growth is slowing, or speculative ones whose growth never happens. Some stocks do have rising
earnings for many years, and their market prices rise accordingly;
funds that invest in those stocks have outstanding long-term records.

Everyone is looking for stocks whose earnings should rise over many
years; thus such stocks, if widely recognized, sell for too much. So to
make money at this game one must both correctly identify them and
have enough confidence to buy them *before* they are generally recognized. Particularly, one must not pay high prices for mere speculations.
The safe time to buy quality growth stocks is when their price-earnings
ratios are little more than those of the market.

Curiously enough, Graham, for all his deprecation of overpaying for
growth, considered higher prices more justifiable than those often prevailing in the market. Based on a number of different lines of reasoning, he suggests that a price-earnings multiple of over 30 is reasonable
for a stock with an expected sustainable growth rate of 14.3 percent.
(See the following table.)

Expected % Growth	10	14.3	20
Multipliers by:			
Molodowsky's method	23	31.2	46.9
Tatham's table	25	—	—
"8.6T + 2.1" formula	24.4	36.5	55.3
"8.5 + 2G" formula	28.5	37.1	48.5
"Our preferred method"			
(7-year projection)	23.5	31	41.5

From Graham, Dodd, Cottle, and Tatham, *Security Analysis*, 4th ed. (New York: McGraw Hill, 1962), p. 538.

Technology Stocks

In an appendix to *The Intelligent Investor,* Graham offers a pleasant statistic. The Standard & Poor's *Stock Guide* for December 1968 listed forty-five companies with names starting with Compu-, Data-, Elector-, Scient-, or Techno-. Examining the September 1971 *Stock Guide* he found that two of the forty-five companies had advanced in price, thirty-one had declined (twenty-three of them by more than half), and twelve had been dropped entirely from the guide.*

"It is virtually certain," observes Graham, "that the many technological companies not included in the *Guide* in 1968 had a poorer subsequent record than those that were included.... The phenomenal success of IBM and a few other companies was bound to produce a spate of public offerings of new issues in their fields, for which large losses were virtually guaranteed." (Schumpeter refers to the swarming of the entrepreneurs—conspicuous in high-tech as I write.)

Graham also disapproves of certain types of issues intrinsically. For instance, he finds that new stock issues—IPOs—of companies that previously were privately held are rarely suitable for the true investor. Such new issues tend to be brought to market when the speculative pot is boiling, and are typically priced over any reasonable valuation.

---

*I am prepared to carry this subject slightly further by offering the following three rules on names:

1. A company that changes its name to reflect a current stock market fad will probably decline. Today, of course, the dangerous handle is ".com".
2. A stock group that is attracting such name changes will probably decline.
3. An industry should do well in the market that companies are changing their names *away* from: e.g., the cigarette companies when they became Reynolds *Industries,* and the like.

Graham is also suspicious of exotic securities, including convertible issues and warrants. His reasons for avoiding convertibles are interesting and well reasoned, and rather than recapitulate them in detail, I refer the reader to the chapter on "Privileged Issues" in *Security Analysis*. Convertibles turn out to be mathematically attractive far less often than one would expect, just as one can rarely get mathematically fair odds at a racetrack. Their speculative appeal results in consistent market overpricing.

Privileged issues—notably convertibles—are to Graham "fair-weather investments." In good times they do well, but not as well as common stocks, and in bad times they do worse. Part of the problem is that like new stock issues of unseasoned companies they are often brought to market during times of market enthusiasm, just before significant declines in stock prices. Preferred stocks issued at par are usually bastard issues, offering neither the security of a bond nor the growth potential of a stock.

About the only approach to buying convertibles that he finds reasonable is as a better way of buying a common stock that one wants to own anyway, when the convertible is selling close to parity. Elsewhere he reaffirms the Wall Street maxim "Never convert a convertible."

Obviously, what creates undervaluation and overvaluation is the passion of the crowd. Graham, like a doctor working over a patient who has fallen to the ground in a riot, rarely lifts his head to contemplate the madness around him, but in his books you can always hear that madness howling in the background. What a fantastic commentary on human nature, for example, is the table below, adapted from *The Intelligent Investor.*

Bankers Securities was an investment trust floated in 1928, the last great age of miracles before the hedge fund–conglomerate madness of the 1960s. At the time it was sold, a rapturous public invented fantastic reasons to think that for $1 of value it should pay more than $3; some years later the inevitable hangover was so severe that for the same $1 the same public, now convinced that the world was coming to an end, would pay only 30 cents.

Bankers Securities Corporation

	YEAR-END ASSET VALUE OF COMMON STOCK	PRICE DURING YEAR
1928	$65	$218
1932	424	140

"Mr. Market"

Obviously, companies sell cheaply only when investors are worried about them—often for good reason, be sure. In Graham's own words, someone using his methods would ordinarily buy "when the current situation is unfavorable, the near-term prospects are poor, and the low price fully reflects the current pessimism." Graham at one point produces an admirable parable of the true investor's attitude toward a fluctuating market. Let us imagine that we own an interest in a business in which we have a genially insane partner called Mr. Market. Every day Mr. Market, depending on which side of the bed he got out of and the dreams or fears that possess him at the moment, announces a price at which he will either buy our interest or sell us some more of his. Most of the time we need pay no attention. Only if our sober study of the facts—of which we know as much as Mr. Market—convinces us that his price is absurdly high or low need we take notice of his offer. We need never act except to make an advantageous trade. "At other times," says Graham, the true investor "will do better if he forgets about the stock market and pays attention to his dividend returns and to the operating results of his companies."

Graham adds that one should never buy a stock because it has gone up or sell it because it has declined. Quite to the contrary, he suggests this motto: "Never buy a stock immediately after a substantial rise or sell one immediately after a substantial drop."

In *The Intelligent Investor,* Graham examines and rejects many approaches to market forecasting—buying or selling stocks in general according to a formula, whether the Dow Theory, his own "central value theory" propounded in *Security Analysis,* or any other.

He demonstrates that such formulas lose their utility just when a "playback" shows them to have worked well retrospectively. For instance, "the quality of the results shown by the Dow Theory changed radically after 1938—a few years after the theory had begun to be taken seriously in Wall Street. . . . For nearly thirty years thereafter one would have done appreciably better by just buying and holding the DJIA."

Graham in Practice

The success of Graham-Newman Corporation can be gauged by its average annual distribution. Roughly speaking, if one invested $10,000 in 1936, one received an average of $2,100 a year for the next twenty years, and recovered one's original $10,000 at the end.

The company simultaneously employed six different investment techniques:

1. Buying stocks for two-thirds or less of their net current assets—usually more than a hundred different issues at a time.
2. Buying companies in liquidation, where there seems an 80 percent or better chance of making at least a 20 percent annual return.
3. Risk arbitrage: buying the stock of one company and simultaneously selling the stock of another that it is merging with.
4. The "convertible hedge": buying a convertible bond or preferred stock, and at the same time selling short the common it converts into. The convertible should be bought close to conversion parity, so that if the position is closed out by converting little is lost. The farther the common and the convertible pull apart, the more the profit.
5. Buying control of a company selling for less than it is worth, to force realization of the assets.
6. "Hedged" investing: being long one security and short another—balancing out, so to speak. If one chooses rightly, the issues one has bought will improve and those one has sold short will decline, so one prospers from their relative movement without regard to the general market.

By 1939, Graham-Newman had established that only the first five techniques worked out well enough to justify being continued.

Since then, the second, third, fourth, and fifth techniques—participating in takeovers and liquidations, the convertible hedge, and buying control of entire companies—have become so professionalized as to be out of the question for most investors. So we are left with the first—buying Bargain Issues at less than their net current asset value—as that part of the Graham-Newman technique that is particularly appropriate for most investors today, along with two further ones Graham developed later.

Graham's coup in Northern Pipeline illustrates his methods. Going through the Interstate Commerce Commission forms that pipeline companies had to file, Graham noticed that Northern Pipeline held $95 per share of quick assets, although it was selling at only $65, at which price it yielded 9 percent. Graham's partnership bought a substantial interest in the company, with the thought of encouraging it to distribute the unneeded assets to its shareholders. At the 1928 annual meeting he arrived with proxies for 38 percent of the shares and went on the board of directors. In due course he was instrumental in persuading the company to pay out $50 per share. What was left was still worth more than $50 a share, bringing the total value to $100, or a substantial profit over his cost of $65. This transaction typifies Graham's approach. He didn't care what the company did or if management was capable; he was only interested in undervalued assets. For Graham's game it's actually better if the company can't make a go of things and has to sell out or liquidate, thus giving the investor his reward sooner rather than later.

In 1948, Graham-Newman Corporation and Newman & Graham, a companion partnership, put $720,000, a quarter of their assets, into buying a half interest in Government Employees Insurance Company. GEICO sold automobile insurance to government employees, but always directly, by mail. It has no agency force. It can offer unusually attractive rates, since its costs are low, and experience shows that this class of driver has relatively few accidents.

The value of the GEICO stock held by Graham's group eventually reached $500 million! GEICO then fell on very hard times, and at the dead low in 1977 had lost 95 percent of its peak value, before making a splendid recovery since.

Excluding the GEICO stock received by his investors, Graham was never managing more than $20 million at any one time, a few hundred million in today's money—not a large sum by today's institutional investment standards. By distributing to his shareholders the cash received from holdings that were liquidated, he kept his company from growing. That was because he was not confident of being able to discover more than $20 million of grossly undervalued situations at a time. If he had allowed the money to build up in the company, it would have grown to a very considerable sum—perhaps $2.5 billion in our money—and the results might have been affected.

Graham's explicit followers have always managed a limited amount of money. With the availability of computerized data services and screening tools, the game has become much easier to play, and thus more competitive and less profitable.

Like most great investors, Graham was able to change his philosophy when necessary.

His *Security Analysis* gave any investor of reasonably studious bent an instrument for digging out the values. It contains extensive tables and formulas for such key elements as inventory turnover, working capital ratios, the ratio of sales to plant, operating margins, and the like, set forth industry by industry. It created a system, where before, except for industry specialists and operating management, investors had tended to rely on impressions.

After forty years of this process, however, Ben Graham's truth became everybody's truth, and there was little hope of outsmarting the pack with his techniques. Investment resembles another competitive game, war. From time to time a new technique appears—the mounted warrior, the machine gun, the tank, radar—and sweeps the field. Then the other side adopts it and parity returns. Similarly, Graham's techniques had been generally adopted by the investment industry by the early 1970s, and to enjoy superiority a different weapon was needed.

In a 1976 seminar (published posthumously), Graham reversed his position:

> I am no longer an advocate of elaborate techniques of security analysis in order to find superior value opportunities. This was a rewarding activity, say, forty years ago, when our textbook "Graham and Dodd" was first published; but the situation has changed a good deal since then. In the old days any well-trained security analyst could do a good professional job of selecting undervalued issues through detailed studies; but in the light of the enormous amount of research now being carried on, I doubt whether in most cases such extensive efforts will generate sufficiently superior selections to justify their cost.

He then suggested a highly simplified approach, based on two criteria, to identify bargain issues:

> My first, more limited, technique confines itself to the purchase of common stocks at less than their working-capital value, or net-current-asset value, giving no weight to the plant and other fixed assets, and deducting all liabilities in full from the current assets. We used this approach extensively in managing investment funds, and over a thirty-odd-year period, we must have earned an average of some 20 percent per year from this source. For a while, however, after the mid-1950s, this brand of buying opportunity became very scarce because of the pervasive bull market. But it has returned in

quantity since the 1973–1974 decline. In January 1976 we counted over 100 such issues in the Standard & Poor's *Stock Guide*—about 10 percent of the total. I consider it a foolproof method of systematic investment—once again, not on the basis of individual results but in terms of the expectable group outcome.

His second approach was, he said, similar to the first in its underlying philosophy.

It consists of buying groups of stocks at less than their current or intrinsic value as indicated by one or more simple criteria. The criterion I prefer is seven times the reported earnings for the past twelve months. You can use others—such as a current dividend return above 7 percent, or book value more than 120 percent of price, etc. We are just finishing a performance study of these approaches over the past half-century—1925–75. They consistently show results of 15 percent or better per annum, or twice the record of the DJIA for this long period. I have every confidence in the threefold merit of this general method based on (a) sound logic, (b) simplicity of application, and (c) an excellent supporting record. At bottom it is a technique by which true investors can exploit the recurrent excessive optimism and excessive apprehension of the speculative public.

In 1976, Graham and his collaborators finished calculating the application of his simplified criteria of a bargain stock over the fifty years since 1925. They established that besides his traditional criterion:

Criterion #1

A stock should be bought for less than two-thirds of its net current assets giving no weight to fixed assets and deducting all liabilities in full, and sold at 100 percent of net current assets.

either of the following gave excellent results:

Criterion #2

2a. *The company should owe less than it is worth.* That is, the debt-to-tangible-equity ratio should be less than 1, counting preferred stock as debt;
and

2b. The *"earnings yield"* (that is, the reciprocal of the price-earnings ratio) *should be twice the prevailing AAA bond yield.* Thus, if a stock sells for ten times earnings it has a 10 percent earnings yield, if it sells for five times it has a 20 percent earnings yield, and so on. So if AAA bonds yield 5 percent you can afford to buy a stock at a 10 percent earnings yield (or ten times earnings). If AAA bonds yield 10 percent, a stock must have an earnings yield of twice that, 20 percent, or no more than five times earnings.

Criterion #3

3a. *The company should owe less than it is worth;*
and
3b. *The dividend yield should be no less than two-thirds of the AAA bond yield.* Thus, if AAA bonds yield 6 percent, then a stock should yield at least 4 percent. If AAA bonds yield 9 percent, then the stock should yield at least 6 percent.

Graham and his associates established that stocks conforming to the first two of these three criteria had provided an average annual appreciation rate of about 19 percent over the fifty-year period, excluding dividends and commissions, as compared to 3.5 percent for the Dow (7.5 percent including dividends).

Combining the second and third criteria gave much the same result: 18.5 percent compounded.

Graham had spent his life establishing his basic criterion (#1) and knew its validity, so the appreciation rate was not recalculated in his 1975–76 work.

The rules for selling were simplified:

1. *Sell after your stock has gone up 50 percent;*
2. *If criterion #1 has not yet been met, sell after two years.*
3. *Sell if the dividend is omitted.*
4. *Sell when earnings decline so far that the current market price is 50 percent over the new target buying price.* (In other words, selling rule #1 applied to a hypothetical new purchase.)

The buying criteria assume that *all* qualifying stocks listed in Moody's and Standard & Poor's guides are bought. An investor today using Graham's simplified principles would want to buy several dozen issues at least—the more the better, even if this means buying odd lots. One's own preferences and subjective considerations must not enter into this sort of operation. It would do no harm and would probably even be for the best if except for the figures, the investor knew nothing about the companies he bought—if he put the company's head in a bag, so to speak, assuming he had enough diversification so that occasional blunders would not be disastrous.

To the end of his life, Graham continued to experiment with new approaches to investing, further simplifications of his original ideas. He would test, retrospectively, how these techniques would have worked out.

In the 1980 edition of *The Money Masters,* I observed:

> Some of his former collaborators are now managing money using formulas based on this work. I am, however, somewhat skeptical of their prospects. One can at any time, using computer playbacks, derive formulas that with hindsight would have enabled one to manage money with great success until yesterday. But such methods need not work for the future. Any formula is likely to be rendered obsolete by events. Its own success will eventually be its undoing, as more and more imitators plunge in and muddy the waters.
>
> It would not surprise me if this turnabout occurred sooner than most neo-Grahamites now expect. There are few sure things in the world. A simple, mechanical, and safe way of making money using information available as of the moment—without the "leap of faith" required in most investing, which involves guessing what the future may bring—is bound to find adherents in due course. At that point the Grahamites will have to compromise their methods: Instead of buying at two-thirds of net quick they will, as the opportunities dry up, have to be content with 80 percent of net quick; instead of seven times earnings, eight; and so on. Then all the obvious opportunities will be snapped up—a limited "efficient market" will have been created. Then the old-style laborious analyst, trained, for instance, on that formidable work *Security Analysis,* will come into his own again, aided by the computer. Such an analyst will be able to find values that the neo-Grahamites with their much cruder methods cannot perceive, as a mariner with

radar can venture forth when the one without is held in port. Within the Graham school the full-scale old-fashioned orthodox Graham analyst will have an advantage over the simplistic neo-Grahamites, and within the market the "value" approach will be overdone, so that growth will be where opportunity lies.

The wheel will have come full circle.

As I write in 2000, the wheel has indeed come full circle with a vengeance! Growth stock investing is back in the same ascendancy it was in 1972. One must thus assume, though, that the next cycle will offer opportunities to the old-fashioned value analyst.

Eight

MARK LIGHTBOWN
FIRSTHAND KNOWLEDGE

MARK LIGHTBOWN, WHO RUNS LONDON'S GENESIS CHILE Fund, has intermittently held the title of being the world's most successful emerging market investment manager, among those operating in the classical style. Jim Rogers has had remarkable results using his particular technique, that of being the very first in line when a country's markets open for business to foreigners; still, for him the technique is the winner, not the stock selection, since, if he likes the country, Rogers often buys every stock that's for sale, whereas Lightbown is highly selective.

All great investors are exotics, even if they try to appear otherwise. Lightbown makes no such attempt. He has, with good reason, a high degree of cultural security, and at all times acts himself: a tall, shy, pink-faced, reddish-haired, extremely well-mannered Englishman with a highly cultivated voice. He is thin and slightly awkward. He eats lightly, usually drinks water with meals, has a cup of coffee about once every two weeks. He can walk forever. He is one of the few persons I have known—another having been Professor C. Northcote Parkinson—whose spoken words could be transcribed and printed without alteration. When explaining a complicated point, he assumes a dreamy expression; then the perfectly constructed phrases, complete with figures, pour forth. When he's thinking hard, he closes his eyes and becomes immobile, sometimes smiling faintly.

Lightbown was born in 1963 in London, son of an art scholar, and attended Christ Church, Oxford, where he studied French and German. Thereafter he relinquished the world of scholarship and art in favor of a career in investments, holding positions at Morgan Grenfell and Templeton in London, whence he was recruited by the Genesis family of emerging markets funds.

He goes regularly to Ireland, where his family has a house in the country. I asked him how that arrangement had arisen, and he replied that he had a bit of Irish blood on his father's side, but that basically the reason was that in the 1960s his father had bought a house there to contain his library—several thousand volumes. His father, a former Keeper (curator) of Metalwork at the Victoria and Albert Museum, has written a beautiful book on Piero della Francesca, and is writing another on Crivelli. The house is surrounded by fields, since neighboring proprietors believe in uprooting trees when they can. "Ireland has the least forest cover as a percentage of its surface of any country in Europe—in the single digits," says Lightbown. "I'm sometimes tempted"—this with a little smile—"to write an account of 'Seamus O'Dendrophobe.'"

Chile

Lightbown and I were already acquainted, so when he moved over to Genesis, I had occasion to talk to him about Chile. It's a blessed country, with an intelligent homogeneous mestizo population, nestled like a vertical banana against the lower west coast of South America. The middle class is energetic and entrepreneurial. The country is richly endowed with copper, agriculture, fishing, and timber. No point is distant from the Pacific, making for easy movement of products to ports. Like very few other countries on the globe—the United States being another—it has essentially no risk of invasion by another country. A desert shields it in the north and the Andes to the east, while to the south lies Cape Horn. And it looks across the Pacific to Asia, where the coming century should bring the highest growth of any large region on the globe.

The Allende-Pinochet catastrophe never should have happened. Allende had no mandate to turn the country into another Cuba. He brought in many thousands of armed Cuban revolutionaries and started to take over the government and large businesses by methods like those used to consolidate Communist power in Eastern Europe. Just as in Argentina, the military government that emerged in reaction to the attempted Marxist takeover was exceedingly tough. Soldiers are trained to kill violently, not, like policemen, to control civilians with delicacy. Many radicals disappeared. During the Pinochet period, few

Americans wanted to invest in Chile. During Allende's rule, almost none had dared. By the end of the process, however, when Pinochet was ready to step down, he had brought the country back out of proto-Marxism into free enterprise, guided by Professor Milton Friedman, Arnold Harberger (less well known, but equally important), and the "Chicago boys." The country's economy lifted off. I had known Chile before and during Allende, although I stayed away under Pinochet, and had little doubt that once Pinochet stepped down, politics would return to normal, foreign investment would accelerate, and things would thrive.

So when I was asked to become a director of the Genesis Chile Fund, provided the Chilean government would grant it satisfactory conditions, I accepted. Lightbown moved to Santiago and on behalf of the infant fund conducted a long and eventually successful negotiation with the authorities.

Profiting from the lead they gained by shaking off the socialist stranglehold—often an excuse for corruption—years before their neighbors, the Chilean companies have learned not only to prosper at home but how to assemble capital and know-how to make successful investments in neighboring Peru, Argentina, and even Brazil. So in a way, Chile is becoming a development bank for Mercosur—an early common market of the southern cone countries of South America.

Lightbown prefers to travel, not only to Chile but all over the world, without what conventional travelers would call luggage. His effects when he is under way are principally contained in a large, strong paper or plastic shopping bag: Harrods by choice, although from time to time he has shifted his custom (employing their bags, that is) to other reputable establishments. The whole business is light as a feather. An airline cannot ask him to check such a thing, and so he never has the problem of arriving with his kit gone astray. The price of this arrangement is that he has often seemed the least dress-conscious representative of any major house in London, appearing in scuffed rubber-soled shoes, khakis, and a frayed shirt. Soon enough, however, the people he talks to don't notice. His record and his firm's capital speak more eloquently than spiffy haberdashery. (Some years ago the rumor—untrue—that he had sold some stock knocked down the Santiago Stock Exchange.) And in locations off the beaten path, such as backwoods Sri Lanka, the Mexican jungle, or Cambodia, his turnout seems about right.

Good Companies

For Mark Lightbown the first step in the analysis of any company is to calculate its value based on its present stock market capitalization, both including its debt and without. Then you compare these totals with the similarly calculated capitalization of other such enterprises, and with your own appraisal of the company's intrinsic (not market) value. In other words, how much is an enterprise selling in the market for, compared to its true worth? Then, if you like the conclusion, you set an attractive price range to conduct your own buying.

To calculate that true worth, Lightbown uses several tools. *First, determine the free cash flow* generated by the enterprise. There are two ways to do this. The first is to add net profits plus depreciation and amortization—the conventional definition of cash flow—*and then subtract the expenditures required for the company to stay in business* (not necessarily to grow fast).

The second and, in Lightbown's opinion, better way to calculate free cash flow is to take the *operating profit plus depreciation and amortization and then subtract the amounts required in plant and equipment and additional working capital to maintain the expected growth rate.* This calculation should reveal whether the enterprise will still spin off cash in hand to its owners, or instead demand fresh equity to support growth. It shows also the rate of return on incremental cash reinvested.

Mark Lightbown's third tool derives from his contention that *the aim of every business is to create economic goodwill.* This he defines as the amount above and beyond what you have invested that you could sell the business for. So, in a word, if you put in $1, can you make it worth $1.50 or $2 or $3?

His fourth step is to *determine at what stage of the business that added value arises.* From which activity, which decisions, what market is it generated? This, he reasons, gives one an idea of the *sustainability of the company's profit margins* and the durability of whichever element in the company maintains them.

Lightbown's ideal is a *business requiring almost no incremental cash to grow,* and indeed one that returns cash to the owners for expansion elsewhere.

Alternatively, he looks for *a management particularly adept at creating high rates of return on incremental invested capital.*

Lightbown says he seeks a management that, as it were, does not see itself as being in the shipping business, but in the transportation business. (I pointed out that this is a sensitive subject, since in the middle of the last century my own forebears, under the name White Diamond

Line, ran clippers and packets out of Boston. Alas, White Diamond did not make the transition to steam, let alone embrace the airplane when the time came.) We considered such instances as Lazard Frères and Kidder, Peabody, trading companies that turned into important investment banks, called in England merchant banks. (Almost all merchant banks started as merchants. Like General Electric, now to a considerable extent a bank, they followed opportunity where it led.)

Asked for an example of a company that had successfully adapted itself to changing times, Lightbown cites Swire, a long-established Far Eastern trading and shipping house, which bought Cathay Pacific Airways and then redeveloped its old industrial operations' sites into apartments on a vast scale, and went into other service businesses.

A company that does not visualize its future evolution into other related lines of business *is all too likely to stagnate* where it is, as the world moves on. Putting this idea differently, *one must look at how a company develops its capacity to compete by recognizing changes in its market and adapting to those changes.*

One must gauge the intellectual integrity of management: One must be sure the managers are not deceiving themselves, and are trying to see things as they are, rather than as they hope them to be. They should have no illusions about how markets—or their competitors— are changing. *If they do not see things clearly, they will not respond to change effectively.*

Good Countries

1. *Good companies are the foundation of investment,* but in evaluating a promising country, Lightbown likes to check that *the president and the congress are in alignment.* For instance, when Menem, newly elected as president of Argentina, resolved to free the economy from the controls and restrictive practices of his Peronist predecessors, he had control over a congress that was prepared for these steps. Good ideas about structural economic reform are not enough: the individuals advancing them must have consistent political backing.

2. *A country with abundant natural resources may well have trouble developing consistently,* since it may focus its attention on extracting and redistributing what is already there, rather than on creating new wealth.

This is a most interesting reversal of the usual attitude toward natural resources. I asked about Chile itself, which is extremely rich in resources: copper, of course, but also forest products, fishing, and agriculture. Lightbown replied that the fastest component of the country's development in recent years has been *outside* the natural resources area. My own footnote to this conception is that a company is more likely to succeed if it plays to its country's comparative advantage, which quite often is simply its people. Japan has no natural resources, and Southeast India is booming because of its software programming industry. Cuba, on the contrary, concentrating on sugarcane . . .

Visiting the ancient desert trading center of Palmyra, in what is now Syria, with its magnificent temples and monuments, Lightbown reflected that *trade, even more than production*—particularly agricultural production—is often the route to wealth.

3. The agent of change in a country must *come from within an existing political grouping, but be quite different from that grouping's traditional policies*. This is a striking insight. One can turn to Argentina or Russia: Menem was an old Peronist, and Gorbachev and Yeltsin were Communists; each recognized the bankruptcy of those doctrines.

Menem's election was almost farcical. The free enterprise candidate proclaimed that Argentina had to join the modern world, balance the public accounts, get the government out of business, and deregulate and privatize. Menem, the candidate of Peron's party, which had been responsible for all these regressive measures, just said, in effect, "Vote for me!" Once elected, he did everything his opponent had been calling for.

4. The people in a good country must want to *save and reinvest,* rather than spend money on more Mercedeses. Lightbown cites the example of Chile in the 1980s: The country enjoyed *a large trade surplus, which, he observes, is really a form of national savings.*

5. *The educational level in a good country must be high.* People must be confident that better ways of doing things can be found, be confident enough to want to act on them, and have a sufficient supply of educated people to do so. Not having sharply different ethnic groups is a considerable advantage. A relatively homogeneous population is more likely to advance together toward common goals, rather than quarrel internally.

6. "One requires *mechanisms for stimulating and channeling domestic savings,* so as to avoid being reliant on the kindness of strangers in order to

finance growth," says Lightbown. A developing country needs a high savings and investment rate to install the highways, metro systems, airfields, plumbing, and power plants that we, since previous generations paid for them, take for granted.

7. *A system to permit capital movement should already be in place,* however primitive it may be, rather than having to be created. For instance, *there must be a banking system that at least knows how to take deposits and possesses credit analysis skills,* however crude. A legal system that one can live with should have been created.

I asked Lightbown about the great success that some investors had achieved buying vouchers in Eastern Europe, and for a while in Russia, before any of these things were quite true. Vouchers, Lightbown observed, in a system as primitive as Russia's was then, are really more an entitlement to a place in the queue of claims on the company's gross profits, since it was not yet clear who would be the eventual owner of these enterprises, in the Western sense of ownership, meaning control of cash flows.*

The arrival of a stock exchange is another step that must occur before one can reasonably hope for investment success. As much as a specific legal system, Lightbown observes, one is looking for a *culture,* one that recognizes that the provider of capital is entitled to a return on it, and should be considered a partner in an enterprise even if his role is less creative than some others. *This culture should accept entrepreneurship as a complex creative effort in which all concerned are going to share.*

8. In a propitious country for investment, *the government must keep its hands off business.* It should not run enterprises directly, or impose price controls, or dictate how businesses acquire capital or recruit labor. All these practices militate against the principle that *things should be done better in the future* than they are being done already, which is how productivity rises and new wealth is created.

9. Another criterion Lightbown seeks is that *a country should have low, stable tax rates.* They should give *the incentives needed to retain profits for reinvestment,* without skewing the location of plants or development of industry by providing incentives for irrational investment. Low

---

* Boris Berezovsky calls his vast looting of Russian companies "privatizing the profits."

tax rates, he believes, may be more appropriate for a rapidly growing than for a mature economy, in which very low tax rates may be
an incentive to misallocate capital.

10. *Labor must be deregulated,* since this makes it possible to pay workers
according to their productivity, rather than according to legal privi-
leges that they have acquired but that may not help the company or
the economy.

11. All of these criteria are a way of saying that one must *wait for a person
with the right ideas to come to power, who must then also be able to implement
those ideas.* The measures taken should produce an improvement in
people's living standards within three years, say, so that the leader's
reforms will really take root. The leader concerned with achieving
such policy changes should have the political skills to explain their
benefits, so as to resist the complaints of the unions or special-
interest groups that may lose as a result of them. What the type of
government is that does these things is not important as long as
they are done well, but the government must be likely to maintain
continuity in policy for a decade or so.

Lightbown believes that satisfactory economic development in Africa
will take a long time. "One is expecting people to move from a basic
level of existence to modern life, with the hurdle being raised steadily.
Many countries in Africa are essentially run as family or tribal businesses. This militates against the creation of a stable infrastructure
and against capital accumulation."

I pointed out the paradox of the family in economic development. In
some countries, such as Greece, the sense of family is exceedingly
strong. That's a fine thing, since the family is the basic building block
of society. If it's weak, children won't be brought up properly. However,
in countries like Greece it is extremely difficult to construct large companies. People there are reluctant to say, "I'm an IBM man." Instead,
they are members of their family, and their loyalty will be foremost to
that family, rather than to the large unit by which they are employed.

"Societies that prosper are the ones that see the advantages of coop-
eration," he replied. "They must be able to abandon the peasant attitude of grab and hold tight. *People who don't trust each other won't enter into
ventures together, and under such circumstances the creative side of entrepreneurship
is strangled.* Latin America has generally not learned the Anglo-Saxon
trick of compromise, and as a result lapses too frequently into drastic

measures, even revolution. Both sides will think they are 100 percent right, not just 90 percent right."

Other societies have attitudes that are equally puzzling to investors. In Burma, for example, signs along the road advertise clairvoyant ser- vices.* Lightbown observes that the people there seem to feel that life is predetermined, rather than being something they can influence. This is characteristic of Buddhism and, to some extent, Hinduism. "If the general approach to problems is to resort to intolerant religion or drink—palliatives at the individual level—rather than trying to work together, an investor's prospects are limited," he says.

We discussed the Jim Rogers technique of trying to be at the head of the queue when a country opens for foreign investment. Lightbown goes frequently to Peru, and describes the memory there of Rogers putt-putting up on his motorcycle to the stock exchange one day and asking if there was a broker who spoke English. A seventy-five-year-old English-speaking former member of the Peruvian Olympic basketball team was summoned, and operations went forward. (That broker, inci- dentally, remembers the track victories of Jesse Owens at the 1936 Olympics. He was struck by the look of horrified rage on Hitler's face at seeing a non-Aryan victorious.)

See the World by Bus

Many investors who cannot do a thorough company analysis, says Lightbown, *prefer to engage in political speculation,* which is easy . . . much too easy. Usually they ask questions to which no answers can be found, and thus spend an inordinate amount of time examining the tea leaves swirling about the cup without being able to establish a pattern.

As an example of how you need to see things with your own eyes, Lightbown cites an experience in Venezuela. "One time I was visiting a company that made control valves. This is a satisfactory business, because in the oil industry you need to replace the valve before it breaks down. The company adhered to a good standard of quality, but the product was not inordinately complicated. I traveled several hun- dred miles east of Caracas to visit the man who had built up the com- pany and was now selling it. Four hundred yards away from the plant,

---

* The Burmese currency, the *kyat,* pronounced "khat," is printed in multiples of fif- teen, which is considered more auspicious than multiples of ten.

we encountered a fine new building in an industrial development. In due course it emerged that my host was setting up a competitive valve factory next door to the one he was selling! It was no surprise that under these circumstances the old plant failed to prosper as one would have hoped."

"To get a feeling for how things really happen," he says, *"you should travel extensively by public transport around a country that you are interested in.* Three days in an expensive hotel in the capital city talking to stockbrokers provide you few valid insights. On the contrary, sniffing around the countryside and provincial cities is far more instructive than worrying about the latest opinion polls. It helps you build a mental model of how the different components of the country interact."

Lightbown describes a most uncomfortable night in a Chinese bus on the Burma Road out of Kunming. "The driver's reactions going over bumps were geared to the front of the vehicle, rather than to its entirety, producing very strange effects in the stern, where I was trying to sleep. The next morning we drove up into a valley of small temples in groves of pines. I was welcomed by a monk who insisted on making conversation and sharing his lunch. That might have been satisfactory, except that it consisted entirely of a boiled potato. He felt that there was something wildly comic about the investment business."

Still, he enjoys travel, and doesn't fret about conditions. "You have to take every place on its own terms and look for the good side and the creative people there," he says. "There's no point in going to Africa and complaining that it isn't like London. There are less easy places, though," such as Bolivia and Kazakhstan.

I observed that the process as Lightbown described it resembles wartime intelligence: Analysts, studying a target country's freight schedules and soccer game scores, piece together a much larger picture.

"Yes. For instance, many outside the country say that Argentina is so expensive that it will have to devalue. This, however, only applies to Buenos Aires, not to the provincial cities, where prices are between a third and a half lower than in the capital. Knowing that, one gains a different impression of the competitiveness of the economy. Buenos Aires is to Argentina what Hong Kong is to China: a toll bridge to the hinterland, through which goods are carried in or out. In Asunción at one time the huge billboards that had previously held Marlboro advertisements suddenly sprouted slogans like 'Abandon Bribery!' and

'Denounce Corruption!' From the number of large stone houses with fences and German shepherds, one could only conclude that these exhortations are not to be taken too seriously. The variety of traffic on Indian roads—from camels and bullock carts to modern cars—suggests that India is not really about the much-puffed '200 million strong' middle class. The politicians are likely to respond to a different voter group. The entrepreneur in Bombay may support a project, but that is unlikely to influence national policy. And within the country, development is likely to be uneven and unevenly distributed. This truth contrasts with the simplified images that visitors take back after a visit to New Delhi and talks with several stockbrokers."

Politicians

"One should go and watch a country's political leader make speeches, and take the measure of the man," Lightbown says. "Quite quickly you can develop a valid opinion of the depth of his convictions, his responsiveness in answering questions." I described General Lebed's gloomy reaction to being offered a small glass of port by a French air force general whom we both visited. "Cognac?" Lebed asked hopefully. A bottle and a tumbler being produced, he tossed off a huge slug. "Better! Better! That is difference: Air force fly over, drop bomb, go home. I come down in parachute, TAK-TAK-TAK-TAK-TAK, keel *everybody!* Ha, ha, ha!" He would make a disquieting neighbor.

One must determine whether a country's political leaders are truly convinced that the same things you believe in are important for business, and what their prejudices are likely to be, since that will give an impression of how they may react to an external shock or change of circumstances. By way of agreeing, I mentioned listening to "Lula," the perennial Brazilian leftist presidential candidate, and noticing that he had lost a finger, presumably in an industrial accident. Nobody on Wall Street who held forth on these matters was aware of that. He struck me as a typical absolutely convinced trade union leader, an important category, but another matter from being a statesman, or a friend of foreign investment. "Some analysts operate at what might be called the sophisticated social end of the market—the dinner-party end," said Lightbown. "They may know everybody of importance, and what they said to each other last night, but they are unable to draw broad conclusions with the information that they gain in this way. *They can be too engrossed with transient concerns to master fully the business environment against which expectations must be assessed."*

Distance Lends Enchantment to the View

If you want to reform a country, you have an easier time if it is of manageable size, Lightbown observes: South Korea rather than China, Hungary rather than Russia, Argentina rather than Brazil. Investors are readily seduced by the prospects of a vast country, but fail to adjust for the complications of reforming such an enormous mass of people and the political competition between power centers within the country. State governors may not be willing to follow the center's wishes.

Lightbown points out that one should examine whether public infrastructure has kept up with economic development: the width of the roads, how airports have been expanded. For instance, in the late 1980s, some regional airports in Chile had received no public expenditure since the 1950s or 1960s.

Good Companies

"It is, of course, essential for an investor to talk to company managements. *Most executives tell the truth most of the time, if a question is phrased to be neutral.* One needs to be a good listener. Also, though, *one should ask the backers of the company, or bankers and brokers, about the reputation of the owners and managers. 'Are these people straight or not?'* To learn about a business or a sector, talk to people in the private equity or deal business, since they know about a company and its competition—listed and unlisted—in a way that mere financial agents usually don't. To understand a specific company, one must go up and down it: *Talk to the owners, the managers, and workers in the plant. Central to the process is casting a wide net* to gather many pieces of information. Much of the investment craft is assembling all these fragments into a more complete picture—often over time."

In the emerging markets generally, some lines of business often have higher margins than most, and the investor is well advised to look most closely at those areas. For instance, retail banking is often an attractive field, unless management is inept. Technical publishing is a good business as long as the government pays its bills. A regional airport can be a lucrative toll bridge. Manufacturing branded pharmaceuticals is usually a good business, as are beer brewing and soft drink bottling. Pension fund management is often an excellent business.

Consistently difficult businesses include steel, whose fixed costs are so high that to prosper the plant needs to run at full capacity—which price pressure makes difficult. And steel plants absorb huge amounts of capital. Farming, including poultry, is an extremely difficult life. The farmer cannot control either his yields or his prices. Often governments support marginal producers, distorting the price structure. In textiles and shoemaking there always seems to be someone—often in the Far East—who can make the product more cheaply.

The investor *should be aware of a company's "market control,"* resulting in pricing power. The dominant producers can build and guide the market to their own advantage. For instance, a soft drink bottler with 70 percent of the market, say, can introduce new flavors or formats, and having access to a sizable customer base will capture the new market.

Information Sources

I asked what secondary sources Lightbown found useful: Was it helpful to talk to a company's competitors? "No," he replied. *"I've always found it difficult to extract useful information on a company from its competition."*

How about asking salesmen the key question: Who would you like to work for if you didn't work here? "That's a good question to ask," he replied. "Still, *I find it most helpful to get to know the owner-capitalist of a company,* as well as the managers. *The owner-capitalist has the same problem as the other investors: How does he measure the performance of the business and, indeed, the performance of the management?*

"Then, one should look carefully at how a company launches its products in a country. *If one finds them in out-of-the-way places, one can conclude that they have thought effectively about distribution.* For example, when Quilmes came to Chile, I saw their beer in remote corners of the country. That was an impressive example of brand penetration."

I reminded him of an example from our joint experience. We had been traveling with some other directors of his Chile Fund, and in a seaside town visited a supermarket company that we were interested in. We went all through its store, and the store of a rival supermarket across the road. When we had climbed back in our coach, I asked the group if they had noticed any product that had no competition in either store. It was Duracell: the only make of battery offered in either place.

We visited the Philip Morris company in Buenos Aires, whose plant was visibly worth much more than its market capitalization, so that you were being given its goodwill, market share, and brand strength for less than nothing. Its share price later rose by twenty-five times.

"It is a very good idea to read several newspapers from the places you are interested in. They often reflect the assumptions a society makes about itself. And it can be almost as informative to find what they do *not* include as what they *do* include. You learn from the advertisements which companies are trying to sell what products. It gives one an impression of the sophistication of the market and of the social, economic, and political ideas circulating locally. I try to read two or three papers in each country that I cover." I asked him for some examples. Lightbown smiled. "That well-known compendium *The Island* of Sri Lanka, the *Hindu* and the *Times of India,* the *Buenos Aires Herald, El Comercio* in Peru."

Lightbown Buys a Stock

When he first settled down to buy stocks of outstanding companies in Chile, Lightbown was struck by the number of trucks delivering Coca-Cola around Santiago to restaurants and even office buildings. Clank, clank, crash, crash! He knew that soft drinks sell faster when a country prospers. He studied the distribution of bottles on the tables of diners of all types and ages around Santiago. He concluded that Coke consumption was widespread, and that as the economy grew and wages improved, sales would rise. He asked if the local Coke bottler, Andina, was a public company. It was indeed—listed on the Santiago stock exchange. He read the annual report and scheduled a visit. He visited the general manager, Eulogio Perez Cotapos, in his simple, functional office on the ground floor of the bottling plant. The manager was pleased that an outside investor was taking an interest in his company. He spoke fully about what the company was trying to do and how the business should develop. He expected sales volumes to grow at about 10 percent a year, and the profit margin to improve even more as increased production passed through the plant. Prices could probably be increased somewhat at the same time. The 10 percent expected growth in number of bottles sold should thus translate into a 20 percent annual growth of profits.

Andina stock was selling for 19 pesos a share, equal to four times net profits, twice cash flow. One could thus look ahead three or four years to the day when the company would be selling for ten times higher profits, unless, of course, something horrible happened. But how could it? Pepsi was already on the scene, but had only been able to struggle up to 12 percent or so of the market. A division of the monopoly brewer, CCU, held a quarter of the soft-drink market. (These figures have slowly shrunk since then.) But by far the dominant company was Andina, with over 60 percent (now over 70 percent).

Lightbown's first purchases were at 19 pesos. His local broker tried to discourage him, never having experienced the explosion of soft-drink consumption that follows when a country prospers. Also, Coke and Pepsi were in the middle of an advertising battle, and that alarmed him. But Lightbown *had* experienced this growth in other countries. He concluded that there were only three facts about the situation that one needed to know: Volume would grow, margins should improve, and the price was right. So he bought with confidence. He acquired $1 million worth of stock—about 5 percent of the company.

It all worked out—and how! Bit by bit, Andina increased sales, not only of Coke, but also by introducing new drinks—notably fruit juices—and new sizes. The company listed its shares on the New York Stock Exchange, and bought Refrescos, whose market is the city of Rio de Janeiro. The fruit juice business grew even faster than soft drinks. As I write, Lightbown's $1 million—none of which he ever sold—is worth $70 million, and still going strong.

Lightbown describes his successful investment in Quilmes, an Argentine beer-brewing company. The brewery had detached itself from a motley conglomerate, employing a prospectus written in French, since it sought a listing in Luxembourg. It used no underwriter or other fanfare. Lightbown was impressed by a company that chose not to make a fuss about itself. A substantial proportion of its market price when it went public represented cash. Sales volumes were growing rapidly, profit margins were rising, and beer prices had just been decontrolled. The company was capitalized in the marketplace at a third of its own annual sales. The stock started trading at $.80 a share, adjusted for splits. In due course it advanced fifteenfold to $11 a share, when it was capitalized at about 1.3 times its own sales.

While studying some companies in Santa Cruz, eastern Bolivia, over near the border with Brazil, Lightbown was struck by the general look of his fellow guests in the local hotel, which incidentally charged foreigners about twice as much as locals. Most of the Bolivian group wore dark glasses indoors and gold bangles around their necks. He was also puzzled by what he called consistent inconsistencies in the reported figures of the companies he was examining. Things simply didn't add up. Finally he realized that the export trade of the companies was only to a modest degree conducted through legitimate channels. Most of the goods were smuggled out by the dark-glasses-gold-bangles fraternity, who paid the customs officials a modest *douceur* not to snoop unnecessarily. The companies thus had *three* sets of books: the usual two—one for tax purposes and one for the shareholders—plus the real set showing the clandestine movements of the output.

"One needs to contrast continually the mental model that one has built with new evidence, to see if it needs adjustment," he says. I observed that this is like the scientific method: You develop a hypothesis and then you test it. You improve it accordingly, and test again. "The model is never complete," Lightbown replied. "You are dealing with something that is evolving, so you need to be alert to indications that the ingredients of your model may be rearranging themselves. Then, there is a problem of sources. Very few people think in the same terms as the foreign investor. Someone with his own local fund may think in a similar way, but stockbrokers and bankers have different concerns, and another orientation."

Advice

The *ultimate prize* in emerging market investing, Lightbown emphasizes, *is the medium-sized company* with a solid position in its economy *that is on the way to becoming a big company,* and eventually a regional or world-class company through a combination of organized growth and intelligent allocation of free cash flow. Find that—another Andina, say—stay with it, and you'll make a huge killing: a hundred for one, even. *Don't spend too much time looking for minor opportunities.*

One must examine the barriers to entry in the particular arena a company is operating in and appraise how these are likely to persist. That should lead to the question: *Why* is a company doing well? Is it in the right place at the right time? Is it doing something so well that others can't keep up? This applies particularly in emerging markets. One often encounters a company with a large market share in an attractive sector. One must then determine whether this is due to its acumen and energy, or just because powerful competition—from strong multinationals, for instance—hasn't arrived yet. What will happen to profit margins when it does?

Patience is a central trait of the good investor. Don't worry if the stock hasn't gone up yet, as long as the business continues to thrive. This attitude explains a singular feature of Lightbown's portfolio management: His turnover is only about 15 percent a year—as low as it gets.

In early 2000, Lightbown pointed out that the great multinationals that were able to borrow at 4 percent, say, in the Euro market could be satisfied with a 9 percent rate of return from a company they might acquire in an emerging market. That's far less than the return required by local shareholders in the same market. So *if you buy a good company that is a valid takeover candidate, you're sitting there when a big multinational makes an offer . . . doubling or tripling your money.*

Nine

JOHN NEFF
SYSTEMATIC BARGAIN HUNTER

WHICH MONEY MANAGER WOULD FINANCIAL PROFESSIONALS choose to manage their own money?

Over the years a frequent answer has been one whose name most nonprofessionals wouldn't recognize: John Neff, of Berwyn, Pennsylvania. He is little known outside the investment community because he is modest, gray, and unspectacular. He looks and acts not at all the Wall Street hotshot, but the Midwestern executive: nice house a little way out of town; wife of over thirty years; simple, unfashionable, and slightly messy clothes; no magnificent paneled office, just the disorderly, paper-strewn den one expects of a college department head. He doesn't get into the newspapers, least of all the gossip columns. Main Line society has never heard of him. And yet, he is one of the most eminent financial figures in the country. He is the longest-running participant in the *Barron's* Roundtable: twenty-five years.* Indeed, in several polls he was, as I say, the choice of money managers to manage their own money.

For thirty-one years John Neff ran the Vanguard Windsor Fund, from June 30, 1964, through December 31, 1995. When he retired, the fund

---

*However, researchers in 1995 at Tulane examined 1,599 common stocks recommended by participants in the Roundtable since its inception in 1968. The study found that the advice was no help. If you had bought the panel's buy recommendations one trading day after the issue's publication date and held them for a year, you made .21 percent more than a sample control group of stocks—basically the same result. If you held the recommendations for two to three years, the results were not as good as for the control group. The panelists may be consoled to learn that a similar study conducted by *Market Logic* in 1993 examined two thousand stocks recommended on *Wall Street Week:* The results were virtually identical.

had an annual compound return of 14.8 percent. During that period, $10,000 invested in the S&P 500 would have returned $248,000; the same investment in Windsor would have returned over twice as much—$587,000. Year in, year out, Neff was likely to be among the top 5 percent in performance of all funds. So it's no accident.

A Grahamite

Neff is a "value" man: *He only buys when a stock is too cheap and acting badly at that moment in the market; and he infallibly sells when, by his criteria, it is too expensive,* again always when it is *acting strongly* in the market. He buys stocks that are dull, or to use his own terms, "misunderstood and woebegone," and sells when the market has gotten the point and has bid them up to fair value, or over fair value. In this he is *a classic contrarian,* and an authentic neo-Grahamite.

Where Neff differs from his peers is in his *insistence on income.* Neff claims that *the market usually overpays for the prospect of growth,* but growth stocks have two drawbacks: First, they suffer from high mortality— that is, often the growth doesn't continue long enough after it has been recognized—and second, *you can often get a better total return from a slower-growth company that is paying a high dividend right now.*

He argues the case this way. Suppose you begin on January 1 with a stock whose earnings and thus, eventually, stock price will grow 15 percent a year, but which has to reinvest essentially all its free cash to finance that growth. So you get almost no income. On December 31 you hope to be 15 percent richer through capital gain. Now suppose on the contrary you have a stock with a much more modest growth rate, such as 10 percent, but which, because it does not have to finance high growth, can afford to pay a comfortable dividend—5 percent, say. Here again, at the end of the year you are 15 percent richer: partly because the stock is 10 percent more valuable through earnings growth, and partly because you have put 5 percent in your pocket from dividends.

But which of these strategies is the best? *Neff is convinced that it's the latter, because it's more certain.*

Part of the reason for the weight given by managers to growth, in addition to the tax considerations, may be that until recently individuals measured their progress by capital appreciation only. Only after the domination of the market by institutional investors did total return become the standard measurement. Also, in looking at his own portfolio appraisals, an investor enjoys the sight of huge capital gains and is less aware of the amount of income that he may not have collected, while an institution is intensely conscious of that lost income.

The future dean of the "growth and income" school was born in Wauseon, Ohio, outside Toledo, in the Depression year 1931. His parents were divorced in 1934. His mother then remarried to an oil entrepreneur, who moved the family all over Michigan and eventually to Texas. Neff attended high school in Corpus Christi. He held outside jobs all the way through school and, having little interest in his classes, received indifferent grades. He was not popular with his fellow students. After graduating he took a variety of factory jobs, including one in a company that made jukeboxes. Meanwhile, his own father had prospered in the industrial-equipment supply business and persuaded Neff to join him. Neff found that experience extremely instructive. His father, he says, taught him the importance of paying great attention to the price you pay. "Merchandise well bought is well sold," his father liked to say.

Neff then spent two years in the Navy, where he learned to be an aviation electronics technician. On receiving his discharge, he resolved to finish his education, and so enrolled at the University of Toledo, studying industrial marketing. His interest was fully aroused, and he graduated *summa cum laude.* Two of his courses were corporate finance and investment, and he realized that he had found his métier, having previously thought that finance was a world reserved for Ivy Leaguers. While still at the University of Toledo he married Lilli Tulac, a native Toledoan. The head of Toledo's department of finance at that time was Sidney Robbins, an extremely able student of investments, who in fact was given the important job of updating Graham and Dodd's famous *Security Analysis.* So from the first Neff was exposed to the value theory of investment, which is much easier to quantify, and thus to teach, than the growth, or qualitative, approach. Later he attended night school at Case Western Reserve to earn a master's degree in banking and finance.

Neff then became a securities analyst with Cleveland's National City Bank, where he stayed for eight and a half years, becoming head of research for the bank's trust department. However, as a Graham and Dodd disciple he believed that *the best investments were the least understood,* and thus often found himself at odds with the trust committee, which preferred big-name stocks that would reassure the customers, even though they might not make as much money.* His mentor, Art Boanas, was a dyed-in-the-wool fundamentalist who insisted that the key to investment success was simply digging deeper than the next fellow and constantly testing your figures. When you make up your mind, he said, *stick to your conclusion;* and above all, *be patient.* This style of investing became Neff's own, and has served him well.

After Cleveland, in 1963, Neff joined Wellington Management in Philadelphia. (That name was chosen because the founders thought that the Iron Duke sounded solid.) A year later, in 1964, he was offered the job of portfolio manager for Wellington's Windsor Fund (a hyper-Anglophile title), which had been founded six years earlier.

At Windsor, Neff led a staff of four. Of course, he had access to the parent company's analytical staff of eighteen, located in Boston. His compensation was "in the good seven figures." Part of his employment package was an incentive fee. Still, in his private life he operates with the same philosophy that he applies to buying stocks. His house has few frills except for a tennis court, on which he plays a ferocious game on Saturdays. He likes to describe how cheaply he has bought equipment or clothing, shopping for his footgear at Lou's Shoe Bazaar and his jackets at Sym's, a discounter. In his office he sits in a rocking chair and often ends a phone conversation with a homespun "Okey-doke!" He says that he loves to read history, particularly European, and to travel.

Neff has an earnest, broad, humorous face, with a large chin and a wide, up-curling mouth that reveals a sequence of expressions. His high forehead is surmounted by silver hair, and he wears metal eyeglasses perched on a small nose. He speaks with a gravelly Midwestern voice. A pen is stuck in the pocket of his white shirt. He wears argyle socks.

Sometimes his frugal ways lead to investment opportunities. He was analyzing a company called Burlington Coat Factory Warehouse Corp., and by way of fieldwork sent his wife and daughter to sample the wares of one of the chain's discount stores. They came back with three coats and a strong buy recommendation, which Neff accepted, acquiring half a million shares.

In a somewhat similar way, when Ford brought out its Taurus model Neff became enthusiastic about both the car and the company.

---

*The best practice, if the customer can be brought to understand it, is to buy little-known excellent companies.

Explaining the investment merit of Ford, Neff pointed out that the company had little debt and $9 billion in cash. The difference between Ford's management and GM's, he says, is night and day. GM is arrogant, while the men who run Ford are "home folks" who know how to hold down costs and avoid delusions of grandeur. The president eats with the men from the assembly line, so he knows what they are thinking. A Ford assembly-line worker makes several thousand dollars a year in bonuses, while a GM worker gets next to none. Neff began buying Ford heavily in early 1984, when popular disillusionment with the automobile manufacturers had driven the stock down to $12 a share, two and a half times earnings! Within a year he had accumulated 12.3 million shares at an average price of under $14. Three years later the stock had reached $50 a share and had brought Windsor a profit of almost $500 million.

Neff points out that securities analysts discussing the automobile industry begin by guessing the number of automobiles that will be sold in the following year. Every few months they alter their forecasts to reflect current thinking. They almost never talk about trucks. *And yet both Ford and Chrysler derive more of their profit from trucks, minivans, and sports utility vehicles than they do from cars!* Neff believes that two-thirds of Ford trucks are sold to individuals, not businesses. Young people, particularly in the Southwest, buy pickup trucks. The U.S. manufacturers have about 85 percent of the domestic market in trucks; the Japanese have trouble competing, since in Japan itself trucks are not nearly as popular as here, so they do not have a big home market from which to develop their export lines.

In 1980 the University of Pennsylvania asked Neff to run its endowment. Its performance over the previous decade had been the worst of ninety-four college endowments. Neff reconstructed the portfolio along his usual lines of gray, uninspiring, unpopular, but cheap companies. A few of the trustees objected to this approach, urging him to buy the stocks that were exciting investors at the time. That predilection was, of course, a reason why the performance had been poor previously. Neff, however, resisted these urgings, and over the next decade the performance of the University of Pennsylvania endowment advanced to the top 5 percent of all such funds.

Neff shares two characteristics with most other great investors: He was poor as a boy, and he is a compulsive worker now. His stepfather could never seem to do well, and so the family always had to struggle. He says that he resolved early that he would handle money astutely when the time came. He works sixty to seventy hours a week, including fifteen hours each weekend. In the office he concentrates virtually without interruption and drives his staff extremely hard. He is tough and harsh when he feels that a job has not been properly done. On the other hand, he invites staff participation in his decisions, which they like.

Not surprisingly, given his conservative techniques, Neff's performance tended to rise more slowly than the market in good times, but also to decline less in a weak market.

He points out the importance of skillful executive work in running large portfolios: *The good manager moves faster, particularly in selling on adverse news.* In a bank, when something goes sour in a holding, the managers responsible hate to crawl back before the trust committee and say that they were wrong. (Also, you risk trouble with the beneficiaries if you sell a stock at a loss.) Neff has no such committees to deal with, and also, since he is rarely looking for the same developments as other investors, the change in his opinion is unlikely to coincide with a wholesale exit from a stock. He can slip out of a stock almost as inconspicuously as he entered it.

He tolerates a very high concentration in a few industry groups. For instance, in the Vanguard Windsor Fund 1988 annual report the automotive group reached 22.2 percent of the entire portfolio, banks were 16 percent, and insurance had risen to 13.8 percent in the teeth of gloomy predictions for the underwriting outlook. The leading area, including savings and loans, represented 20.8 percent of Neff's portfolio. Adding insurance, the whole financial sector came to 37 percent. Airlines reached 7.2 percent of the portfolio in 1987, during a period of grim industry news.

In other words, while Neff has relatively few ideas, he backs them heavily. Indeed, in his 1988 report the ten largest positions represented over half the assets of the $5.9 billion fund. Thus, we see a third of a billion dollars in Citicorp, which many investors shunned for fear it was going broke, over half a billion in Ford, and about three-quarters of a billion in just three insurance companies. That's real self-confidence!

One justification for these high concentrations is that he isn't taking far-out gambles: Since he buys only the very cheapest merchandise, should something go wrong, it hasn't far to fall.

Bargain-Hunting

Neff is considered an outstanding securities analyst. Although in recent years he has not himself ordinarily made company visits, he talks to companies at length. He had a team of analysts working for him, but when a new stock comes into view, he will *lead the charge, or, in his own language, "gang tackle" the problem.* By the time he and the team are finished, they should have accumulated the information they require. In his thirty-five years of experience in his profession, Neff had already bought or studied a high proportion of the companies that he may be considering for purchase at any time. In other words, it is often a question of updating his knowledge rather than starting from scratch.

He constantly looks at industry groups that are *unpopular* in the market. He confines his research to stocks with *particularly low price-earnings ratios,* and, ordinarily, *unusually high yields.* And, in fact, over the many years that Neff ran Windsor Fund, *the average price-earnings ratio of this portfolio has been around a third below that of the general market, while it has on average yielded 2 percent more.*

Neff has described himself as a "low-P/E shooter." However, unlike Benjamin Graham, he is concerned with the underlying nature of the company. He wants a *good* company at a low price. Some of the criteria he insists on are:

1. A sound balance sheet
2. Satisfactory cash flow
3. An above-average return on equity
4. Able management
5. The prospect of continued growth
6. An attractive product or an attractive service
7. A strong market in which to operate

Neff claims that investors tend to pay too much for companies with high growth rates, while no growth means that there is something wrong with the company itself. So the bargains where he does most of his buying often run at about an 8 percent growth rate.

The Neff Formula

Neff has an interesting way of comparing stocks, or groups of stocks, with other stocks and with the overall market. At a time when Windsor's portfolio overall had an estimated 9.5 percent capital growth rate together with a 4.9 percent yield, or 14.4 percent in total, the average price-earnings ratio of the stocks in the fund was 6. So he divides the 14.4 percent total return by 6, giving 2.3 as what he calls the *"what you get for what you pay for it"* or *"terminal relationship" figure.*

In early 1989 the overall market had a growth rate of 8.5 percent and a yield of 3.7 percent, for a total return of 12.2 percent. Dividing this by the market's price-earnings ratio of 11 gives 1.15 as the comparable "what you get for what you pay for it" result. So, by this reckoning Neff's whole portfolio was twice as attractive as the market as a whole.

Neff lays out or "arrays" these figures for specific stocks to compare their relative attractiveness. He does find that *his earnings estimates for the stocks he buys are usually more optimistic than those of Wall Street in general, or in his term, more "aggressive."**

For a long time Windsor Fund's income grew 17 percent compounded, probably because of Neff's practice of selling stocks that had gone up, and whose yields had therefore fallen, to buy lower-priced stocks with high yields.

In determining the price he is prepared to pay for a stock, Neff projects earnings over a number of years. Then he determines a reasonable price-earnings ratio that a normal market should put on those future earnings. This, in turn, gives him a target price several years out. He then calculates the current market's percentage discount from that price, from which he derives the indicated percentage-appreciation potential.

Of course, subjective factors have to enter in to some extent. For instance, if Neff has unusual confidence in the stability of the growth rate, or if he considers management to be exceptionally skillful, then all the figures are adjusted. In reverse, unfavorable factors may reduce the target price.

He calculates the similar consolidated figure for his existing portfolio, which he designates its "hurdle rate." If the indicated compound growth rate of a stock he wants to buy is not at least as high as the "hurdle rate" of the existing portfolio, then he defers purchase until the stock falls to where it does equal the hurdle rate.

There are, of course, times when he somewhat deforms this method. For instance, if he has raised cash in his portfolio and the market starts

---

*This is less likely to be true when the market is enamored of growth stocks. Then the brokers are prone to make optimistic estimates of their favorites.

up, then he will buy stocks below the hurdle rate in order to get the cash working fast. (This is another way of saying that he expects the hurdle rate to rise soon.)

Within a portfolio, Neff weights the holdings according to their calculated appreciation percentage. With seventy to eighty stocks in the portfolio, implying an average size of slightly over 1 percent, he will in practice put 5 percent into one stock if he develops a real conviction; indeed, he will buy several positions of that size within a single group. In other words, if he is confident he will act with force. And, given his careful analysis, he usually is confident.

Neff's method should, one would think, be highly suited to the use of computers, to screen the stocks of target companies and make value comparisons. In fact, however, he avoids computers. Nor does he believe in the dividend-discount models, and other mechanical devices that are favored by some institutional investors. In that way, Neff is surprisingly old-fashioned.

When it comes to actually executing a purchase, Neff is again extremely disciplined. He has his target price, and he waits for the market to come down to that level. He waits and waits, and if the stock doesn't get there, he simply won't buy it. Neff's traders are ordinarily able to buy stocks below their opening prices of the day. That is, in spite of the size in which he deals, he succeeds in buying on intraday weakness.

Neff's selling discipline has two parts: the market price at which he is willing to sell a stock, and the tactics of executing that trade.

As to the target selling price, again it is based on the "hurdle rate" of the whole portfolio. When the market thinks well enough of the prospects of any one of his companies so that it rises, in due course the company's further appreciation potential will fall below that of the rest of the portfolio. When it gets down to only 65 to 70 percent of the whole portfolio's appreciation potential, Neff starts to sell. He likes to make a substantial sale initially, and then let the rest of the stock go as it moves on up. If it falls back he will stop selling. If it falls enough, he becomes a buyer again.

When the time comes to execute an actual sale on an exchange, Neff moves carefully. He almost always wants to *sell into market strength that day*, and avoids accounting for more than a quarter of the trading in a given issue. Of course, if a stock starts running up, it makes less difference to him what proportion of the trading he is responsible for. Here again, Neff *can usually sell a stock higher than its opening price on the day of the trade.*

For the manager of a large portfolio, the largest element in trading costs is the impact that the transaction has on the market. Neff depends on the skill of his traders to minimize that.

Once his bets pay off, however, Neff will start selling without waiting for the top price. "That's simplistic, but essentially the way I operate. If you get a significant price move, you begin selling early and look for something else."

Neff holds that *one should sell a stock before it has achieved its full potential gain.* One must leave a sufficient incentive for the next buyer to take the merchandise off your hands.

Still, a feature of Neff's method is that he does not mind waiting almost forever if a stock he owns does not realize its potential. Here he differs from some other "value" buyers, who like to see something happen within a year or two; if it doesn't, they move on. Neff will hold a company for years, as long as its outlook remains satisfactory and it remains cheap relative to the rest of the portfolio.

Dull and Woebegone

Since the stock groups that Neff considers to be good value will virtually always be out of favor in the market and viewed with suspicion by investors, they generally partake of a common characteristic: *A stockbroker would have trouble selling them to a customer.*

For instance, when he made the huge bet in Ford that I have described, the industry was in deep disfavor among investors. Chrysler's virtual bankruptcy had shaken them, and the news of rising Japanese penetration sounded alarming. So the car companies fell to giveaway prices, and Neff moved in massively, as he also did in the oils, the financials, and, indeed, most of his other big themes.

This style of investing, major bets on a relatively small number of conceptions, served Neff well in the long run but was vulnerable to short-term downdrafts. Indeed, after doing well immediately after the crash of 1987, Neff fell into a slump. Windsor dropped a full 28 percent in fiscal year 1990, which ended October 31. "Dismal results," Neff told his shareholders. "The worst year we have ever experienced." A few months later, in February 1991, Neff was the subject of a *Forbes* article entitled "Tarnished Glory." "If Neff's 'value' approach—buying companies at low multiples of their earnings and dividends—is out of sync, is that a temporary phenomenon or a permanent loss?" True to form, Neff had a lot of money stacked behind a relatively small number of bets. The ten largest positions in Windsor accounted for 40 percent of its assets at that time. The dismal fiscal year ended with 14 percent of the fund invested in banks, 11.8 percent in autos, 8.5 percent in insurance, and 6 percent in thrifts. He had suffered serious losses, particularly in Chrysler and Ford, Bank of America and Citicorp, and Aetna and Cigna, each of which represented roughly a $200 million position. Those losses ranged from 36 to 62 percent. *Forbes* summed up: "All in all, Neff's portfolio . . . looks like a basket case in search of an infirmary."

Neff even got letters from his shareholders saying that he was "an idiot to own thrifts and banks and insurance companies because everyone in the news media said they would go down," as he explained to *Kiplinger's*.

Citicorp had been particularly painful. Having purchased the stock in the low 20s, Neff watched it fall as low as $10 in late 1990. Shortly afterward, Chairman John Reed slashed dividend payments by 44 percent. "I'm shattered," Neff said at the time. "It is foolish, inconceivable, and inconsistent with everything that went before it. As recently as two weeks ago, Reed in a public investment forum said that it was an inefficient thing to do." It is not unusual for Neff to be extremely vocal about his major investments. Indeed, when Chrysler stock fell dramatically some years before, he publicly called for Lee Iacocca to announce Robert Lutz as his heir apparent.

Neff weathered those down years with the same strategy he has held all along: stick with your plan and wait for the returns to come. He did not panic and move into more popular stocks. In fact, *of the fifty biggest stocks in the S&P, Windsor owned none.* And indeed Neff did recover. Citicorp was selling at below 13 in January 1991; by the time Neff retired at the end of 1995 it was over 67. Most of Windsor's other bank stocks took off in late 1991.

By 1994, Windsor had almost $11 billion in assets, invested in only sixty-nine stocks. Neff had found some big winners. He built up a position of just under 10 percent (SEC rules bar the fund from owning more than 9.9 percent of a company's market capitalization) in Seagate Technology, makers of disk drives. Prices of drives were falling 10 percent a quarter, and the manufacturers had to make up the difference through productivity. Seagate, almost alone among its peers, was managing to make a profit. Neff bought it at $16 per share; by the end of 1994 the stock had risen to $28 and become the darling of the industry.

Neff noticed that consumption of aluminum was growing at a rate of 3 to 5 percent worldwide without any new capacity in sight. Reasoning that the price would have to go up, he took large positions in Alcoa and Reynolds. Correct! The price of aluminum rose from 51 cents per pound in 1994 to 72 cents in early 1997.

I trust that these examples of Neff's strategy, plus the description of his extremely meticulous methodology offered earlier, explain why other professionals think so highly of him and like him to be *their* manager. It's slow and it's dull, but it's strictly based on value, and it almost always works.

The Future

Neff is worried about the future of equity mutual funds. "The boomers have been raised to count on 16 percent annual return on the S&P 500. You and I know that's not sustainable, particularly from the levels we've ascended to, and when the boomers discover they can't get instant gratification forever, they may have second thoughts about stocks and put their funds elsewhere."

He has high hopes for the emerging countries, which he feels will turn themselves around despite setbacks. He points out that these countries generally grow at three times the rate of the developed world. As a contrarian, he naturally likes the ones that have suffered the most: Thailand, India, and Korea. He adds Mexico to this mix, and South America in general.

Ten

JULIAN ROBERTSON
THE QUEEN BEE

JULIAN ROBERTSON, RUNNING THE PRODIGIOUSLY SUCCESSFUL Tiger Fund, is talking about Peter Lynch, who retired from running the Magellan Fund at the early age of forty-six: "Peter missed one thing: He wasn't having fun. He didn't get people to help him." It's quite true: Peter Lynch didn't have fun the way Julian Robertson does, and again unlike Robertson, Lynch is a loner. A fanatic worker, Lynch lived and breathed stocks, stocks, stocks morning, noon, and night. Almost all investment geniuses are born poor, and are haunted by the feeling that the wolf of evil times is overtaking them. They're anxious. Robertson certainly doesn't fit the poor-boy pattern. He is exuberant. His family was comfortably off, and to judge by his flamboyant manner, he has enjoyed almost every day of his career—while making a great deal of money at it.

Virtually all great investors—and Robertson is certainly one of the very greatest—are solitary souls who love pursuing stocks the way a Don Juan loves chasing women or a hunter loves stalking deer. It's not something they can bear to delegate. This can make them intolerable managers—they're too subjective and authoritative. Robertson doesn't quite fit that mold either. Now in his sixties, a tall, powerful, red-faced man, he loves coaching a competitive team. He always gives full credit to its members and exults in the collective result rather than his individual cunning.

He was born in 1932 in Salisbury, North Carolina, the son of a textile plant manager. After attending Salisbury School, he attended Episcopal High in Alexandria, Virginia, followed by a business degree from the University of North Carolina at Chapel Hill. Then came two years as an ensign on a Navy munitions ship. Finally, the big question: What to do with his life?

After the 1929 crash, the Erlanger family, which owned the plant that Robertson's father ran, had been convinced that the market would recover, and had lent him money to buy stocks. He became a keen investor, and he made a point of explaining to his son Julian how business functions—the essence of successful investing—and how to interpret financial statements. Robertson remembers being exposed to stocks when he was six! His father, who was ambitious for his son, urged him to head north to seek fame and fortune. "That's where the money is," he declared. Julian obeyed, moving to Wall Street, where he spent the next twenty-three years with Kidder, Peabody & Co., first as a broker, and thereafter, at the age of forty-two, as head of Kidder's investment advisory subsidiary, Webster Management. Thus far, a conventional success.

Withdrawal and Return

Then, a strange development. In 1978, at the age of forty-six, after four years running Webster Management, Robertson decided to quit, move off to a great distance, and think things out from the ground up. With his wife, Josephine, and their two sons he shifted base to Auckland, New Zealand. One can see several reasons for this decision. Brokerage commission rates were falling rapidly, putting tremendous pressure on the industry. Then, orthodox money management, whether by trust companies or investment counsel firms, is a typical gray-flannel-suit life, satisfying in its way—you help nice people—but with little excitement, or prospect of real wealth, or benefit to society at large.

Anyway, a year and a half went by in the pleasant city of Auckland. Meanwhile, things started popping back in New York. A different style of investment, the limited partnership or hedge fund, was making its managers a huge amount of money in a jazzy way, although at the price of much more work and imagination than required by conventional brokerage or advisory work. Some of Robertson's contemporaries, such as George Soros and Michael Steinhardt, were doing wonderful stunts in the market and being astonishingly well rewarded for it. However agreeable Auckland seemed to be, it was hard for as keen a competitor as Robertson to sit on the sidelines while the big game was being played at home.

So back he came, setting up his own hedge fund in May 1980 with $8.8 million. He and partner Thorpe McKenzie put up $1.5 million, all of their then available capital. The arrangement was that they got 20 percent of the profits, and the limited partners got the rest. He called the fund "Tiger" after his wife, Josephine, whom he had met in 1974 at a party. (He also calls other people "Tiger.") Josie, after receiving a fine arts degree from the University of Texas, had moved to New York and gone into the Christmas ornament business.

1980 was the year the Dow Jones Industrial Average finally broke out of the long trading range that had held it below 1000, marking the launching of the prodigious bull market following the Reagan transformation of America's feeling about itself from losing to winning. Thus, the timing of Tiger Fund's inception was extraordinarily favorable. In its first year the fund rose 70.4 percent. Net of management's 20 percent share of profits, the limited partners had a gain of 56.3 percent— almost 25 percentage points better than the S&P. The following year, 1981, the market declined by 5 percent, but the fund advanced 24.3 percent, which after management's 20 percent cut meant that the limiteds received 19.4 percent, or over 24 percentage points better than the S&P. In 1982 the limiteds got 42.4 percent compared to 22.3 percent for the S&P, again over 24 percentage points better. It was becoming clear that those wonderful results were no accident.

Although Tiger Management grew throughout the 1980s, it remained quite a small operation. Like almost all of his colleagues, Robertson was hit hard by the crash of 1987, but he rebounded quickly. He returned to his core strength of stock-picking and began laying the groundwork for international moves.

In the 1980s, Robertson was willing to put outside consultants on the payroll if required: insurance executives, aviation specialists, doctors. Later his internal research team grew sufficiently so that this was less necessary. He wanted each of his employees to be the best in his category, whether at analysis, trading, or administration.

Criteria

By 1989, Robertson became powerfully attracted to the idea of businesses that he called "monopolistic and oligopolistic." Companies, in other words, that *dominated their industries.** For example, he invested heavily in De Beers, which controlled 80 percent of the world's dia-

---

*My first book, *Dance of the Money Bees*, published in 1974, had a chapter titled "Investing in Oligopoly."

mond market while selling at only three and a half times earnings; also UAL and AMR, parent companies of United Airlines and American Airlines, respectively. He foresaw that they would dominate certain long-distance domestic routes well into the future. He began a love affair with Wal-Mart that would last for years. Wal-Mart had no monopoly, but its extremely low cost structures made it almost unassailable. As a part of this strategy, Robertson shorted Wal-Mart's smaller and higher-cost competitors—that is, its victims.

He also identified companies that he expected to succeed because of a favorable regulatory environment. One was Tosco, the only significant independent refiner in its market area. Because regulatory restrictions inhibited the competition, Tosco, he concluded, should hold its position.

In all these choices, Robertson was searching for little-noticed outperformers, strong companies, well positioned in their markets, likely to stay on top.

First of all comes a company's management. He wants dedication to the bottom line, like that exemplified by Stephen Wolf at USAir, Robert Crandall at American Airlines, and Martin Sorrell at WPP Group. He seeks managers with the resolution to make tough decisions and the ability to execute them. He becomes involved with management in almost a personal way. Ford underwent a period of mismanagement that he refers to as "one of the big disappointments of my investment life."

By the end of the 1980s, however, Robertson was focusing more and more on global developments—a timely change of vision, as it turned out. He started two new funds, Jaguar and Puma, to complement Tiger. He caught the rise of the German stock market in 1989 and 1990 following the collapse of the Berlin Wall, and also shorted the Japanese market in time to benefit from the crash there.

"Fame has not come to Julian Robertson," wrote *Business Week* in the autumn of 1990. "Fortune, yes. But not fame." That would change! His outstanding returns inevitably attracted attention, as did stories mentioning him as a money manager for celebrities like Paul Simon and Tom Wolfe, and such institutions as Princeton, which gave him a portion of its endowment to manage. He appeared at a Museum of Natural History gala with live tigers in tow, which did not go unremarked. He also began taking more frequent breaks—up to eight weeks a year. These were not real vacations, since he studied the countries he visited and their companies.

His success let him attract some of the cleverest younger people on Wall Street to work with him, often Southerners. (Besides his accent, he retains other Southern links, notably as a supporter of both his old school and Chapel Hill.) By 1991, Robertson reached $1 billion in assets under management, but in that year he was mentioned in the Salomon Brothers scandal, a scheme to corner the U.S. Treasury bill auctions in April and May, although no charge was brought. This was a most painful experience, since he sought to maintain the highest ethical standards in all he does: dealing with other firms, with his employees, and with the public.

In 1991 he drew David Gerstenhaber into the firm. A London-based economist, Gerstenhaber brought an international vision to supplement Robertson's knowledge of companies. By 1992, with Gerstenhaber's help, Tiger made two-thirds of its profits from "macro bets"—large speculations in currencies and derivatives—and in subsequent years this pattern continued. Gerstenhaber left in 1994 to set up his own shop, forcing Robertson to become his own macro analyst for a time before recruiting David Morrison and Jeremy Hale, who became his economic and bond strategists, respectively.

International Maneuvers

Robertson has given particular attention to Japan, Europe, and Mexico. He approaches foreign markets in much the same way as the U.S. market, seeking individual stocks or industries to buy long or to sell short, not whole countries to bet on. Of course, he doesn't always get things right. In 1993 he fared very poorly with a large short position in Japan, even though the country overall went into a downswing. In general, Robertson holds a negative view of foreign companies. He finds that most non-U.S. managers are not focused enough on the bottom line. "It is amazing how in the rest of the world no one really seems to care about profitability."

While he began to lay the groundwork for a global approach in the 1980s, it wasn't until the end of the decade that he made a concerted effort to develop a deep body of knowledge on what was happening abroad. In 1989 he set out to learn all he could about the European markets. "Can you really know the merits of Schering-Plough, Merck, or Johnson & Johnson without having a decent knowledge of Smith-Kline Beecham and Fisons?" he asked.

This study meant slogging through the accounting peculiarities of individual foreign companies. His first look at Germany, for example, almost dissuaded him from investing there at all. Management seemed to have little incentive to act primarily in the interests of shareholders. Managers rarely owned stock, trade unionists generally made up half of the boards of directors, and the comfortable old-boy network running much of industrial and financial Germany was well content with the status quo. Nevertheless, Germany offered cheap assets and strong technology skills, so if one could find the right companies, one ought to prosper. Robertson's team set about laboriously analyzing German companies one by one. When the Berlin Wall came down on November 9, 1989, he was ready, his homework done. Two days later, on November 11, he was buying German banks. German banks are, among other things, holding companies, and they were selling in the market very cheaply compared to the value of their own investment portfolios. Among industrials, Bayer was an easy call; it traded at nine times vastly understated earnings. The company made excellent products, sold them at fair prices, and was burdened with very little debt.

However, the murky accounting practices that had hidden German corporate assets were gradually phased out. By 1994, his discovery having become general knowledge, Robertson was somewhat unkindly referring to Germany as "a giant flab bag of inefficiency" whose managers tossed around expressions like "cost-cutting" and "restructuring" without knowing how these objectives were to be achieved. So he sold down in the German market, and indeed acquired a small short position.

For a long time Japan occupied center stage in Robertson's global strategy: Solid fundamental analysis of Japanese stocks barely existed. So the best companies usually sold at price-earnings multiples perhaps one-third of the multiples of U.S. companies. He began investing in Japan in 1970. Then, in 1987, he developed a charming strategy. He found that one could buy three-year puts on the Nikkei average for roughly $1\frac{1}{2}$ percent per year, a small fraction of their U.S. cost, or of their arithmetic value. By 1991 he had 12 percent of the portfolio in Nikkei puts, which he held for years. He referred to them as his insurance policy—reasoning that they would rescue him in any catastrophic market plunge.

He developed a view of the Japanese economy in a world context, and following startling events could act swiftly. For instance, following the Iraqi invasion of Kuwait, he sold over $100 million in Japanese currency and bonds that he had purchased only days before, reasoning that Japan's oil supply was threatened.

He has been correctly bearish on Japanese banks for many years. They have had the largest market capitalizations and the lowest measures of profitability of any banks in the world. Citibank, for example, had barely over half the assets of Mitsubishi—Japan's *best* bank—but almost four times the return on average assets. Robertson's repeated interviews with Japanese bank managers revealed almost no evidence that they were coping with their bad-debt problems. They lent to shaky customers for fear that if they didn't, someone else would. Robertson's bank play took time to pay off, but it finally did, handsomely, in 1997. (For his colleague Tim Shilt's statement of the bear case against Japanese banks, see Appendix III.)

He decided that the fall of communism lifted a shadow and made investing in developing countries much more interesting, and he started looking closely at Brazil, Chile, and Argentina. By 1991 an instructor was coming to the Tiger office three times a week to offer Spanish lessons!

He is intrigued by India. The high national level of education gives Indian enterprises an important advantage. A substantial number of many companies' managements there hold doctorates or M.A. degrees. A solid business environment, an understandable legal framework, and a well-established stock market also impressed him. He built up a long position of 3 percent in Indian stocks.

The notorious problems of Russia discouraged Robertson for many years; then he took a token 1 percent long position there by 1995.

In Mexico, he built up an 11 percent short position by 1994. As he watched hordes of novices going south of the border, sharing expectations of a continuing boom, he decided he needed to be on the opposite side.

An example of Robertson's international approach was in retailing. At home, he had, as mentioned, been keen on Wal-Mart. He then switched his enthusiasm to Penn Traffic, an up-and-coming owner of several grocery chains. Groceries seemed like an excellent opportunity. But then he and his team found a surprising opportunity in British retailing. He realized that the two biggest supermarket chains in Britain, Sainsbury and Tesco, had something that their American competitors lacked: They owned popular brands that they also sold in their stores. So they benefited from two levels of profit—both in manufacturing and in selling—and better control of their business. He invested heavily in the pair.

However, Tiger had become unwieldy, along with many of the other very large hedge funds.* The back office needed overhauling. In 1992, the Jaguar Fund substantially overstated its July–November performance and had to send out an embarrassing letter of apology. The problem was corrected by installing more advanced computer systems.

In the spring of 1992, Robertson started the Panther Fund. Being SEC-registered, it was more limited than the others in what it could do, and by its first year-end it was lagging. Robertson waived Panther's performance fee—15 percent of profits—through 1994.

Panther aside, Robertson was in top form. He made several hundred million shorting Japanese banks in 1992, and in 1993 cashed in on European fixed-income instruments—bonds and currencies—using European interest-rate options, which he employed increasingly thereafter. At home he took large positions in Time Warner, Comcast, and TCI. He also continued his enthusiasm for retailing and sought out particularly well-managed medium-sized companies, such as Harley-Davison.

But despite having a more conservative technique than some other hedge funds, Robertson's fund could not fully escape the jagged pattern that bedevils investment programs with highly leveraged positions. Thus, Robertson saw a spectacular gain of 63 percent in 1993 wither into two bleak years thereafter. The fund declined 9 percent in 1994, and rose less than the average in 1995. A number of investors withdrew. Other managers were caught in the same downdraft. Michael Steinhardt's fund, for example, fell by over 30 percent in 1994 before recovering.

A nasty *Business Week* cover story in the summer of 1996 entitled "The Fall of the Wizard" accused Robertson of alienating his associates and losing control of his operation. He filed a libel suit, which he later dropped after the magazine admitted it had overstated his problems. After earning $300 million in 1996—making him the second-highest-compensated financier on Wall Street—he was reported by *Forbes* to be a billionaire.

---

*As Professor Parkinson proclaimed, "Growth brings complexity, and complexity decay." Few escape!

In October 1997, Robertson finally, after many years, closed out some of his short positions in Asian stocks. Unfortunately, before he could complete that operation, the Japanese market rallied, costing him $400 million. Still, it was an outstanding year, in which Tiger Management reached $16 billion in assets. The Tiger Fund's average annual gain since its inception in 1980 stood at 36 percent, making it the most successful large fund of all time in its category.

Robertson's Technique

Robertson ran a classic hedge fund. One might even call it virtually the only true large hedge fund, meaning one that takes aggressive long positions while maintaining short-side positions to counterbalance them and to define risk. He has no confidence in his ability to catch market swings. Indeed, in his basic system it is not of decisive importance whether the market is overvalued. The key is to bet *for* the good companies and *against* the lemons. Sometimes he hedges across borders—for example, long U.S. banks and short Japanese banks—which can, however, leave an exposure if both markets move against him. He would hedge one industry against another—long oil refiners and short airlines, for instance, where an expected event should benefit one and hurt the other.

To contain the risk arising from a particular event he held many, many positions. Still, he placed major bets when the situation warranted. Most of the time, eight to ten big positions gave him most of his profits. (See the listing in Appendix IV.) He uses a stress test, continually querying the effect of a 10 percent loss in every holding. What will be the liquidity then? Having determined that he has an adequate margin, he can relax a bit. (Failure to think in these worst-case terms killed Long Term Capital Management.) Soros speaks of moments when he was convinced he was having a heart attack from stress. Robertson does not want to approach that condition. He always seeks a steady flow of good ideas rather than home runs.

He is receptive to many sources and types of information on a company, but quickly determines the one, two, or (at most) three decisive variables—revenue growth, margin expansion, or whatever. Then he pursues every possible avenue to get at the truth, hiring specialized consultants if absolutely necessary. When he's convinced, he acts.

Even in a changing environment, Robertson maintains a fairly constant pattern. His net long exposure tends to fluctuate between 20 percent and 40 percent; the fund is usually leveraged between two to two and a half times its assets; and it balances its exposure fairly equally between U.S. and foreign stocks. Robertson remains a stock-picker above all. Except at particular moments, most of his gains have not come from massive currency and interest-rate gambles in the Soros style. "We have never felt compelled to be in macro," he reminded investors in a 1994 letter. "Stock selection has always been our stock in trade." In this he differs from George Soros, for whom macro bets are the essence and stocks a sideline.

Management by Walkabout

He likes to wander around his office asking questions. He wants to hear sharp, strong responses. I find this a common attribute of outstanding team managers.

Rules of the Game

Robertson is very quick to understand corporate strategy and a company's comparative advantages. He keeps this knowledge current through frequent company contacts. Key features he seeks in a company are *quality of management, a disciplined corporate strategy,* and *solid growth*—all at an attractive price, of course. He is wary of lack of management resolve, a threatening regulatory environment, and unexpected quality control problems.

Robertson is intent on seven main themes in picking stocks:

1. *Wonderful management.* Any company he invests in must be outstandingly well run. Management must be wedded to the bottom line, as against building sales. It must have both a long-term plan and the means to implement it. He is also alert to new managements about to clean house.

Robertson's heavy reliance on his own personal impression of management sometimes backfires. Once in the late 1980s, he had dinner with one Eddie Antar, and was so impressed that the next day he bought a large block of stock in the company. Alas, the company was Crazy Eddie, under which handle Antar became notorious when he had to take flight following accusations of fraud. The stock dove, and Robertson got burned.*

2. *Monopoly or oligopoly.* Robertson seeks companies enjoying competitive advantages by virtue of their market position. For example, the route structure of American Airlines and United Airlines made it almost impossible for competitors to break into their territories. Wal-Mart's sheer size meant that other companies would have to go through a long process of growth and consolidation before they could hope to compete by cutting their margins. Sainsbury and Tesco in Britain had dominance through their brand ownership.

3. *Great value, based on careful examination of the company books.* Robertson keenly scrutinizes foreign company accounts. In Japan, for example, he established the banks' true liabilities, and how much cash flow was available to retailers he was interested in. The *price/earnings multiple* of a stock is only somewhat less important. Citicorp was a good example; he was highly enthusiastic about when it was at just over eleven times earnings, while being an outstanding enterprise. But one must worry about what could go wrong to push earnings down and the P/E up.

4. *Regulation.* A company can benefit when the government is tying the hands of its competitors. He becomes extremely wary when a company faces liability for environmental or regulatory infringements.

5. *Upstream needs.* Once a growing industry has been identified, rather than seek out its leading companies, look for the companies that will supply the whole industry. In 1998, for example, Robertson invested heavily in palladium, used in cell phones and auto-emission-control devices. He is convinced that the Russian and South African mines will not be able to meet the world's demand for the metal.

6. *Growth.* It will bail you out of a bad market.

7. *Big core positions.* Robertson's portfolio is heavy in tried-and-true companies with solid track records, usually dominated by a dozen or so giants, recently including Intel and Citigroup.

---

*J. P. Morgan believed in character above all. When he interviewed the Van Sweringen brothers, Oris P. and Mantis J., he asked, "Do you work hard?" "Oh, yes, sir, like beavers." "Do you sleep well?" "Like a top, sir." Morgan liked these answers and responded, "Good. You shall have your money." He lost several hundred million (1930s) dollars.

The Queen Bee

"Management is like sailing," Robertson has said. "When the weather is nice, there is nothing more fun." He enjoys the process. His funds were run more or less as they were when they started. All the lines of communication in the firm led to Julian Robertson. He still oversaw selections as if he were atop a $250 million portfolio instead of one of over $10 billion. He is like the queen in a beehive colony: The workers around him are engaged in hundreds of tasks, but everything revolves around the central figure. He describes himself as the "trigger puller," while usually accepting the stock picks of his top analysts. Their compensation is linked to the success of their choices, including those that he has rejected. Once a stock has been bought, he "takes possession" of it, side by side with the analyst. No single worker is essential to the success of the hive, but without the queen, it would collapse. Similarly, while those around Robertson have profited greatly by their association with him, he has rarely lost heavily from the departure of one of his employees.

On the other hand, there has to be a limit to concentrated decision-making, and sooner or later the constraint in hedge fund management becomes the ability to attract top talent.

While the *Business Week* article that accused Robertson of having a personality that alienated many of his associates was a bit strong, he certainly likes to squeeze the best out of every employee, which means they are stretched to the limit, and thus tempted to depart. Indeed, the then president of Tiger Management, John Griffin, who was credited with expanding the firm's global role, deserted in early 1996, after ten years, to set up his own fund. Many others did the same. The article asked a reasonable question: Why do good people leave Tiger? One answer is because Robertson's enterprise actually worked as a school of hedge fund management for many of those who joined him. When they graduated, they were ready to undertake their own ventures.

Sources

In addition to all the obvious sources of information, Robertson liked to tap the limited partners in his fund for ideas on their industries. Talks with him in his office are interrupted by calls from CEOs. His Rolodex has thousands of names.

Robertson thrives on conflict. One technique is to put two of the most knowledgeable analysts with contrary opinions about a particular stock on the phone together to argue. He will then go long or short or stand aside depending upon who he thinks has won the debate.

Robertson's incessant travel gives him valuable insights. He may not have the access to foreign leaders of George Soros, but he comes close. He describes his trips in letters to his investors, mixing golf stories with news from bank managers and officials.

Recent Position

Robertson established a new fund in 1997 called Ocelot—once again a big cat, of course. He capped the fund at the end of the year, after reaching his goal of $1 billion in assets. The minimum amount for entry was set at $1 million, instead of the $10 million theoretically required to join Tiger. Investors commit to stay in for at least five years.

In mid-1998 Tiger was leveraged at about 200 percent of its assets, with net exposure hovering around 40 percent. Robertson believed that the United States still had the strongest stock market in the world, thanks in large part to the fundamental concern of American CEOs with profitability. The standard whales of Europe and Japan should, he says, be regarded with a skeptical eye.

Just seven positions accounted for $3.5 billion of Tiger Management's holdings. As usual, Robertson was enthusiastic about the airline industry, and is one of the largest shareholders of AMR and USAir, which account for nearly $1 billion of his portfolio. He remained enchanted with the tenacious Robert Crandall at AMR and with Stephen Wolf at USAir. The risk of competition on their routes is almost nil, he thinks. His major technology holding is Intel.

In 1998, Robertson unloaded many of his financial industry shares: 2.76 million shares of Citicorp, 2.57 million shares of Travelers Group, and 1.1 million shares of Merrill Lynch, and 40 percent of his Bank One holding. He retained large positions in Morgan Stanley, Dean Witter, and Discover.

In late 1998 and into 1999, Robertson's performance was weak. The big USAir position wasn't working out, and Robertson signaled that he wanted to move in and take corrective action. The overall market, he complained, was feeding on its own momentum, leaving his value stocks behind. He was horribly punished by an unimagined dollar-yen divergence on heavy leverage. His 1999 performance was dismal: down 19 percent, or 40 percentage points worse than the S&P 500. And there were massive withdrawals, which continued into the New Year. January alone saw redemptions of $1 billion, an eighth of the capital remaining. If this accelerating rate of withdrawal was not stemmed, Tiger risked a chaotic rout. Early 2000 brought continued performance decline.

Robertson had previously taken a highly prudent step, deleveraging his whole operation. At the beginning of 1999, his stock positions were margined up to 270 percent of their base value. By year's end, fortunately, the total stock positions were only about 35 percent over their base value.

So far so good, but the real problem was that his stock-picking failed, so that any leverage at all compounded problems. He had never taken the leap of faith required to buy high-technology companies, which had attracted most of investors' enthusiasm in the previous years, and had stuck to his "value" selections. Unfortunately, the market didn't accept his diagnosis of where value lay. He owned a quarter of USAir (called by the *New York Times* "the incredible shrinking airline"), which disobligingly fell by more than half from its high. Another major holding, Federal Mogul, had collapsed, and several others, such as Royal Bank of Scotland and Columbia/MCA, had been hammered.

So, basically, the jig was up. According to an article in *Business Week*, Robertson had periodically agreed to form sector funds concentrated in specific industries, which Fidelity and others had done with great success, but, according to a former Tiger employee, "When push comes to shove, he hasn't let go." The risk that such funds might outperform his own record, said the magazine's source, was "not something that, frankly, his ego can handle."

Thus, at the end of the first quarter of 2000 Julian Robertson decided to close up shop while he still could in an orderly way. The funds he ran had shriveled from over $22 to $6 billion, and above all the performance had been so weak that management's 20 percent profit participation, the chief incentive of the key partners, would only resume after a 50 percent gain—not something one could bet on in that environment.

Alan Abelson, in a typically acerbic *Barron's* editorial, differed from the conventional wisdom that Robertson's troubles arose from strictly following his "value" style; rather, said Abelson, it was from seeking the glamour of making huge macro bets à la George Soros. "Between bad guesses on Japanese currency and bad bets on emerging markets,

Julian dropped billions. . . . the hubris-driven macro strategy, meanwhile, also affected his micro, or stock-picking, tactics. . . . When you're
a megabuck hedge-fund investor and the stock you own too much of is
leveraged, the negative effect is vastly magnified."

A structural explanation is that with increasing size, the whole
machine became too complicated and fast-moving to be handled by one
queen bee. It was contrary to Robertson's nature to delegate ultimate
authority, and he himself didn't have the flexibility needed for the
"new economy" market.

So, in the end what did him in was the Parkinson principle: Growth
brings complexity and complexity decay.

The Icarus Syndrome

Curiously enough, though, Robertson may also illustrate the phenomenon I have named for the myth of Icarus, who crashed into the
sea when, flying too high, he approached the sun. The hot manager
sometimes accumulates more and more capital until his mechanism
breaks down, so he carries to ruin a much heavier load than when he
rose. As to Robertson specifically, he started very small, and by August
1998 was running over $22 billion. From that point, by quite rapid
stages, he declined 47%. Possibly, therefore, he lost his investors as a
class more in gross dollars than he made them; certainly, his later
investors.

To sum up, in his good times—indeed, overall—Robertson is one of
the great masters. An investment of $10,000 in 1980 had turned into
some $800,000 in twenty years, resulting in an amazing compound
growth rate of 25 percent per annum. For eighteen years it had been 31
percent compounded, a prodigious record. And he rises from the table
with $1.5 billion in his pocket personally—a handsome consolation
prize!

Eleven

JIM ROGERS
FAR OUT

JIM ROGERS MAKES BIG BETS ON UNPOPULAR COUNTRIES, such as Botswana, Peru, and Mozambique. He gets attractive bargains because he tries to be the first and only buyer at the time.* He has four tests of a good country to invest in:

1. It must now be doing much better than previously.
2. It must also be better off than is generally realized.
3. The currency must be convertible. If it is going to become convertible in a month, then he will wait a month. There is plenty of time to invest *after* the currency has become convertible.
4. There must be liquidity for the investor. "I always like to be able to get out of something if I'm wrong," he says.

Aside from anything else, it is useless to buy if no other foreigner can. So Rogers wants to enter a country through conventional channels, to see what the experience is going to be like for those who come after. People sometimes say that they are getting an introduction to the chairman of the board of the central bank, or whatever. However, that

---

*I offer a coda to Rogers's formula of being the very first in line when a valid country tentatively opens up for foreign investment, so that every later buyer puts your prices up. Another wonderful moment comes quite a long time later, if two things happen simultaneously:

1. First, the government significantly liberalizes investment conditions.
2. Second, local pension funds are partly privatized and allowed to buy stocks. The buying power thus unlocked should cause the equity market to soar.

dignitary may, in Rogers's words, be "foaming at the mouth" to attract investors. Other less well introduced investors may not receive the same welcome.

Take Portugal. After a takeover by the far left in 1974, the country had hovered close to civil war, like Chile under Salvador Allende. Both times the government imported professional activists to help prepare a far-left takeover: several thousand (armed) from Cuba to Chile, and many hundreds from the Soviet Union to Portugal. Capital fled and business slumped. Then the Portuguese anti-Communist faction fought its way back to power and displaced the radical left. The risk of a Communist takeover faded. The country began to breathe again. Gradually confidence returned. Tourism and business picked up, although not to anything approaching the previous level. Some substantial foreign industrial investments began to appear, but the stock market, a very modest affair in any event, remained closed to foreigners.

In 1984, Rogers felt that the time might be ripe. He approached the Portuguese financial authorities about investing there. In 1985, after six months, he received permission to reconvert into dollars the proceeds of transactions he might make on the local stock exchange. The leading investment firm in Lisbon told him that it was not recommending Portuguese equities. Rogers nevertheless instructed it to buy all twenty-four stocks on the Lisbon exchange, and thereafter to buy every new issue that came out. He eventually reached a total of thirty-five. Portugal has been looking better and better ever since; his bold stroke succeeded brilliantly.

Another Rogers coup was Austria. In 1984, the Austrian stock market had stagnated at barely over half its level of 1961, twenty-three years earlier. A number of European countries had passed investment incentives to encourage their capital markets, including the French, whose economy and currency had collapsed under the socialist government of President François Mitterrand. Rogers saw that the Austrian government was preparing to follow suit. He was sure that European money managers, looking around for whatever hadn't moved yet, would in due course fasten on Austria. He inquired at the New York branch of the principal Austrian bank how a foreigner could invest in Austrian stocks. The bank didn't know: There had been virtually no investment interest in this largely socialist, yet stable and successful, country. So little information was available outside Austria that Rogers went to Vienna to inquire. At the Ministry of Finance he asked what political factions or other interests were *against* the idea of liberalizing the stock market and encouraging foreign investment. When the answer came back that there were none, he felt he couldn't miss.

One problem did emerge: Morgan Stanley's International Index showed Austrian stocks selling at sixty-seven times earnings, an appallingly high figure. Upon investigation, though, Rogers discovered that this was a completely misleading statistic, since the index consisted of only nine companies, three of which were losing money. Morgan Stanley also said that the Austrian market had inadequate liquidity. That, however, turned out to be an illusion: Banks traded actively among one another, off the exchange. "Morgan Stanley should be shot" is Rogers's charitable judgment. On the other hand, thanks to Morgan Stanley's dismal figures and, probably, the intellectual laziness of foreign investors, there was almost no other interest in Austria from abroad. So Rogers bought, and in the very next year the Creditanstalt Share Index rose 145 percent.

Rogers is just as happy to be short a market as long—that is, to sell stocks he doesn't own, in the hope of repurchasing them more cheaply later. "It's a lot of fun finding a country nobody knows about," he says. "The only thing better is finding a country everybody's bullish on and shorting it." In the same year as his Austrian flier, he bet on a drop in the Swedish market, which had risen nearly sixfold in four years. The Swedish market only sagged 10 percent or so over the ensuing year, but the particular speculative favorites that Rogers shorted, including Ericsson, ASEA, Pharmacia, and Gambro, fell by 40 to 60 percent.

In 1986, he tried again on the short side, this time in Norway. As he explained, "They had enormous oil revenues and they thought things would go on forever. Since then, the price of oil collapsed. And earlier this year that market was at an all-time high. It seemed an obvious place to be short." The Norwegian market rose but fell in the 1987 crash. Rogers covered Norway, with all his other shorts, in November 1987.

In 1985, Rogers tried the Malay Peninsula. At that time Singapore had a 42 percent savings rate. Prime Minister Lee Kuan Yew ran an exceedingly tight ship, economically speaking. He required that both employers and employees contribute to a central retirement fund. Then he permitted some of that money to be used to buy blue-chip stocks. Then he also cut taxes on investment. This coiled the spring for a leap in demand for stocks, but did not actually trigger it, since the economy and the markets were still weak. Growth had plunged from 8.2 percent in 1984 to a negative 1.4 percent in the second quarter of 1985. The government thereupon introduced a number of emergency measures to stimulate the economy. But a major Singapore-based holding company, Pan Electric, which had dozens of subsidiaries in Hong Kong, Malaysia, Bermuda, Brunei, and Britain, went bankrupt. The government panicked, and on December 2 the Singapore and Kuala Lumpur stock exchanges were closed.

Rogers told friends in the government that this was a ghastly mistake, and indeed, when the two exchanges reopened a few days later, prices dropped by up to a quarter. However, for Rogers that was the bottom. He moved in. Malaysia barred new public issues of securities until order was restored in the market; Singapore passed a similar ban. This cutback of supply, coupled with the growth in demand from the tax cuts, finally propelled stocks upward. Both markets doubled in the next eighteen months. Rogers feels that because they are basically natural-resource economies, the countries should continue to do well, if one can assume that commodity prices will rise even slightly.

John Templeton once called him to say that things seemed extraordinarily cheap in a particular country. Rogers replied that he needed to know *why* things were cheap. There are lots of countries where things are cheap and will stay that way. So *he also wants to see reasons for change.* When he bought into Austria and Portugal, investors did not even know how to conduct the process of investing there. So when he learned that this information was going to become available, he could foresee a better investment outlook, based on rising demand from abroad.

How does one get a sense of the risks and opportunities in different countries? *Through travel, and by reading in history and philosophy—not in business school.* Rogers says his own success has come from discovering things that others haven't yet noticed. Rogers quotes Kipling: "What can he know of England who only England knows?" He says he got a perspective on England in the United States and on the United States in England.

A self-styled "poor boy from Alabama," Rogers was raised in Demopolis (population 7,800), where his family's telephone bore the easily remembered designation Number 5. The nearest big city, Selma, with a vast population of 19,000, was fifty miles away. His father, a member of an old Alabama family, managed a plant for the Borden Chemical Company, which produced Elmer's Glue and formaldehyde.

Rogers attended Yale, graduating in 1964. Confused about what he wanted to do in life, he applied to several graduate schools and had interviews on campus with company recruiters. One of the interviewers, from Dominick & Dominick, had grown up in Hell's Kitchen in New York City. Rogers and the interviewer liked each other, and a job offer resulted. By that time, Rogers explained, he had decided to go to Oxford in the fall; he asked his interviewer friend if he could work just for the summer. This was arranged. At the time Rogers did not know a stock from a bond. But he fell in love with the securities business almost at once.

"What I liked about it was not so much investing money, because at that time I didn't have any, but that if you were smart, used your wits, and paid attention to the world, it was all you had to do. At that time I was extremely interested in what was going on in the world and used to read voraciously. You didn't have to wear the right tie, you didn't have to join the country club, you didn't have to join the PTA. You could do what you wanted to do, and they would pay you to do it. I thought that was the most exciting thing I'd ever seen." That autumn he went to Oxford, where, being a small man, he earned a rowing blue as a cox. (John Templeton, curiously enough, also grew up in a small Southern town and went to both Yale and Oxford. He and Rogers were introduced by the master of Balliol.)

Rogers speaks in a quiet, almost shy way—but rapidly and exactly to the point. A small man with a wide, pleasant face, he invariably wears a sports jacket with a garish bow tie, nonmatching trousers, and no overcoat, even in New York's bitter winter weather. By the time he came home to the United States, he realized that his keenest interest was in international finance. He wanted to be a "gnome of Zurich," who invested everywhere and in everything. In the summer of 1965 he returned to Dominick & Dominick to work at the firm's over-the-counter trading desk. Then came two years in the Army, where he ran his commanding officer's portfolio and developed a growing determination to make money. "I wanted to make enough so that I would never have to worry about working again," he says.*

---

*That rarely happens. Stimulated by success, the tycoon goes on working harder than ever. Eventually, work becomes all he knows.

Right after the Army, Rogers worked at Bache, and then for Dick Gilder, where, as he puts it, he learned that "you'd better understand the numbers. So many people in the 1960s didn't know what they were doing. As far as that goes, lots of people right now are making money, but don't know why." Subsequently, he went to Neuberger & Berman and Arnhold and S. Bleichroeder. In 1970 he met George Soros. They formed the most successful twin-star investment team in the business. While they were together they never had a down year, and from December 31, 1969, to December 31, 1980, the Soros Fund chalked up a gain of 3,365 percent while the Standard & Poor's composite index advanced about 47 percent. At the outset, there were just the two of them and a secretary. Soros was the trader, and Rogers specialized in research.

The fund was characterized by independence of thought: *Neither Rogers nor Soros has much time for Wall Street research analysts, almost all of whom follow the herd. Nobody gets rich doing that, says Rogers. "It's a fast way to bankruptcy."* But Rogers does not think of himself as merely a contrarian, whom he defines as someone who would have bought U.S. Steel (now USX) every year since 1959 and lost money. You have to be *right* as well as different.

The fund's greatest successes came from an ability to foresee large and general change—secular, as opposed to cyclical. Rogers, who still follows this orientation in his own investing, explained at the time: "We aren't as much interested in what a company is going to earn next quarter or what aluminum shipments are going to be as we are in *how broad social, economic, and political factors will alter the destiny of an industry or stock group for some time to come.* If there is a wide difference between what we see and the market price of a stock, all the better, because then we can make money." This is what Wall Street calls the top-down approach.

A decade after inception, Soros and Rogers were still the only thinkers in the firm, although the staff had grown to thirteen. In the same period, starting with $12 million under management the fund had grown to $250 million. That was one of the factors that prompted Rogers to leave in 1980: He thinks large funds become unmanageable. His share of the profits on leaving came to $14 million.

Rogers describes himself as "very much a loner, a maverick, a misanthrope." He has a somewhat bohemian point of view, and says he doesn't like people in general, although he has been happy to teach security analysis at Columbia's Graduate School of Business. He traded the teaching fee for his first course for a lifetime membership at Columbia's gymnasium facilities.

He plans to leave most of his money to Oxford and Yale for travel fellowships, to give others the same broadening exposure that he had. Students will receive a stipend if they agree to spend 75 percent of the succeeding two years out of their own country. Other than that there will be no restrictions. To his Columbia students he says, "Study history and philosophy. Do anything in preference to going to business school—wait on tables, hitchhike in the Far East." Only thus, he emphasizes, can they develop a rounded perspective on life.

Rogers once considered getting an M.B.A. himself. However, a senior partner at Dominick & Dominick told him: "Go short some beans and you'll learn more in just one trade than you would in two years at B-school." Rogers didn't go, and indeed soon learned how to lose money. In January 1970 he felt that a bear market was coming, and with all his money bought puts on machine-tool companies. On May 26, 1970, he sold his puts: "I got it to the day," he says. Many of them had tripled in value in three or four months. Then the market rallied for a few months, and Rogers went short all over again. After that, the market advanced strongly for two years. Rogers lost all the money he had in the world. It wasn't much, but what he had, he lost. He feels that the Dominick partner was right: Although painful, it was a most useful experience, which he is glad to have undergone.

Now "retired" to run his own capital, Rogers says, "Everybody dreams of making a lot of money, but let me tell you, it isn't easy." He ascribes much of his success simply to industriousness. He says that when he was a full-time money manager, "the most important thing in my life was my work. I didn't do anything else until my work was done." When he joined George Soros he moved into a handsome beaux-arts house on Riverside Drive. He rode his bicycle every day to the office on Columbus Circle, where he worked nonstop—taking not a single vacation in a ten-year period. He still lives in the house, which he has furnished in what might be called club style, with an office staff in the basement. "At the time I worked most intensely," he says, "I really knew an enormous amount about what was going on in the world, just about everything that any single human could." He says he never felt anxiety about whether he was right when his views differed from everybody else's. "Other people can't sleep at night. I hit the pillow asleep."

Investing in Change

In domestic portfolio investment, Rogers bets on whole industries in the same way as, when investing abroad, he bets on countries. First he develops a massive investment concept. He then buys every stock available in an industry that he thinks is set for a turnaround, the way he buys every stock in a country. How does he select the industries? *He looks for a major secular change, ignoring fluctuating business conditions.* "The way you find things to buy low and sell high is to look for *unrecognized or undiscovered concepts or changes.* Whenever you see something, don't look at it and say, 'That's a brown rug': say, *'How can that rug change or is that rug going to change? What's happening in the world that may make it different now or three years from now?'* If you look at a company that's bankrupt, it is not necessarily always going to be bankrupt. If you look at a company that is growing by leaps and bounds, it is not necessarily always going to grow by leaps and bounds. So look for a change. And by change I mean *secular change, not just business cycle change.* I'm looking for companies that are going to have good performance even when the economy is going down, like the oil industry in the seventies. A major ten-year change took place in the oil industry."

Rogers looks for four principal types of changes:

1. *Disasters.* Examples include Lockheed and Chrysler. Company crises of this magnitude imply that the whole industry of which the company is a part is in a catastrophic situation. *Usually, when an entire industry is in a crisis, with two or three major companies bankrupt or on the verge of it, the whole industry is ready for a bounce, as long as there is something in the situation that should change the fundamentals.* As one instance of a sector in need of a catalyst for change, Rogers notes that the steel industry has been bankrupt for years, but nothing has yet happened to bail it out.

2. *Changes for the worse.* These usually fall into the "trees do not grow up to the sky" paradigm. *When an industry is so popular that investing institutions own 80 percent of the shares of its top companies, one can be reasonably confident that the stocks are overvalued in the market.* In this situation, Rogers will go short many of the stocks in the industry, not just one. Here one must be particularly careful. Just because something is high does not mean that it cannot go a lot higher. So he tries to chart precisely when the major change for the worse is about to take place.

3.   *New trends.* When in the seventies women began to turn away from overdone makeup, and indeed any makeup, Rogers studied Avon Products and decided that at over seventy times earnings, it was due for a fall. He shorted at $130, and covered a year later under $25.

Other new trends have included day-care centers, hospital chains, and the garbage business. Rogers attended a garbage convention in 1969, when new competition was taking the business out of the hands of the municipality/Mafia duopoly. The other delegates, some of whom were very rough characters indeed, were stunned: Someone from Wall Street had actually turned up at a garbage convention! However, many of these same rough characters now have houses in Palm Beach, and some of their companies are on the New York Stock Exchange. He sees growth in gardening supplies, nursery centers, and so on because of the increased number of retirees and their need for leisure activities.

Another example is the motorcycle. In the 1950s, "motorcycle" meant (as he says) "trashy," "low-rent." By the 1960s, however, Honda could advertise, "You meet the nicest people on a Honda," perhaps including Malcolm Forbes. Rogers didn't happen to spot this conception in time, but he says that if he had been smart enough he could have worked out that Honda was a buy.

Other major trend changes include hospitals, which a generation or two ago were run by municipalities and charitable foundations, and today are more and more run by profit-making companies; alcohol-treatment and mental-health centers; and mobile homes, which were considered an atrocity when Rogers was a boy—his mother didn't want him consorting with people who lived in them, whom she called "trailer trash."

Somewhat similar are hotel chains. Rogers pointed out once that Hilton had gone up one hundred times in the market in the last thirty years. In the old days hotels in different cities, even very fine hotels, were all separately owned and run. Then it was realized that running them as chains under the same banner offered high efficiencies of scale and improvements in quality control.

4.   *When the government decides to act.* It then throws money at a problem. Rogers became the largest outside shareholder of Lockheed in 1974, when the company was a rumored bankruptcy candidate. Rogers noticed that in the Arab-Israeli War of 1973 the Egyptian air force

enjoyed an extraordinarily high degree of success against the
Israelis, even though the Israelis had far superior aircraft and pilots.
Rogers discovered that the Egyptians had been supplied with Soviet
electronic devices that the United States was unable to provide to
the Israelis, because during the Vietnam War our defense effort had
concentrated on day-to-day supplies at the expense of long-range
technological development. On learning this, Rogers reasoned that
the United States would have to catch up with the Soviets in defense
electronics. Lockheed had some of the best. The stock went from $2
a share to $120, Loral went from $0.35 to $31, and E-Systems went
from $0.50 to $45. At that time E-Systems was little known, but
Rogers discovered it by asking Lockheed and Northrop who their
most effective competitors were, along with reading trade journals
and consulting defense experts. (When E-Systems had advanced to
$8, Rogers discussed it with a banker who liked the story but said he
couldn't buy it for his bank until it rose to at least $10, because that
was the cutoff point that the institution's policy imposed.)

Another industry changed by government intervention was nursing
homes. Until the 1960s young people used to look after their parents,
but then the government increased its involvement, with Medicaid,
Medicare, and nursing-home support. Nursing-home companies began
floating large public issues. When one of the largest, Four Seasons,
went bankrupt, it was found to have been using fraudulent accounting.
Many other companies proved to be overextended, not really making
money. Other scandals followed. So the whole industry collapsed in the
market. After a while, Rogers noticed that some of the companies had
tightened up their operations, were selling off marginal divisions and
money-losing operations, and were turning profitable. So he visited a
number of them and in due course realized that although very few
homes had been built in recent years because of the notorious problems of the industry, the American population was still inexorably
aging. So he invested.

Supply and Demand

This illustrates another central Rogers principle: the importance of
supply and demand. Rogers says *the trick to getting rich is correctly sizing up
supply and demand.* Neither the Communists, nor Washington, nor any-

body else has been able to repeal that law, he observes. It is one of his most important ideas.

As an instance of the principle he cites the oil industry. Why, Rogers asks, did the price of oil soar in the 1970s? The general perception is that OPEC did it. However, he replies, OPEC had tried every year since 1960 to lift the price of crude, but never successfully: The price always went down again. The real reason goes back much earlier. In the 1950s the Supreme Court determined that the U.S. government could regulate the price of natural gas. The government thereupon did so, at an extremely low rate; so low, in fact, that by degrees it became unprofitable to produce gas at all. It was often simply burned off—flared—when it was produced along with oil. So for the rest of the 1950s and through the 1960s there was very little drilling for gas. At the same time, though, consumers woke up to the excellence of gas as a fuel: It is cheaper and cleaner than oil or coal. Then householders increasingly converted to gas at the very time that exploration was winding down. So by the early 1970s many of the gas pipeline companies were running out of supply. Rogers remembers noticing that prospectuses for pipeline bonds had stopped promising that there would be a sufficient supply of gas to pay their interest. From an annual report of Helmerich & Payne, a drilling-rig supplier, he learned that the number of rigs in use in America was steadily declining, simply because people were not keeping up the exploration required to maintain the national oil and gas supply.

Rogers went to Tulsa and visited several drilling companies. All reported dreadful business conditions. He decided that it was unimaginable that the pipelines would be allowed to go bankrupt and thus cut off gas to stoves around the country. So starting with the onshore drilling companies, which were suffering the most, he bought oil drilling stocks, oil shale company stocks, everything in the industry. Not long after, OPEC's fourfold price hike and the oil embargo gave the market a tremendous boost. Yet in 1971, two years before OPEC finally succeeded in raising prices in 1973, Rogers had already determined that the gas industry *had* to undergo dramatic improvement. The fundamentals were in place, and OPEC merely provided what is called in physics the "exciting cause."

Then, however, came the "trees do not grow up to the sky" sequel. When oil rose from $2.80 to over $40 a barrel the whole country went on an energy-conservation binge: insulation for buildings, smaller cars, more efficient appliances. And at the same time there was an enormous step-up in oil exploration. As a result of these two factors the supply-demand equation reversed. Oil and gas prices—and stocks—plunged.

The Investing Process

What are Rogers's techniques in stock selection? One has been mentioned: *He never talks to brokers or security analysts.* The important thing, in his view, is to *"develop a way to think independently,"* as he and George Soros did so profitably. He says: "I have always found it much better just to sit and do your own reading. When I talked to people it would muddy up my thinking. I was much more successful just sitting back, reading, and figuring things out."

Rogers says that *he has never been able to make money from inside information,* even if legal and ethical. Nine times out of ten it is wrong, he says, because it is factually incorrect, or because it has been garbled en route. "If you get inside information from the president of the company, you will probably lose half your money. If you get it from the chairman of the board, you will lose all of your money. So stay away."

While working as a money manager full-time, he used to read newspapers from at least five different countries, some forty periodicals, and about eighty trade journals, including *Variety, Publishers Weekly, Iron Age,* and the like. Most of these are deadly dull, and indeed full of fluff provided by public relations agents. But sometimes there is a suggestive article or advertisement. He also read hundreds of annual reports and followed insider trading figures for lots of companies. He still reads a great deal, but less than before.

Many of Rogers's investment ideas come from observing the everyday world around us. A typical discovery was Bank One (formerly Banc One). His broker at Merrill Lynch urged Rogers to open a cash-management account. Rogers noticed that the checks for his CMA were drawn on Banc One, of which he had never heard. He looked into the company and found that it had a computer system that was primed to participate in the growth of check and credit-card processing for the rest of the big brokers. The more he studied the situation the more he liked it. In due course he became a shareholder. The stock went from 6 in mid-1980 to 30 in mid-1986.

One of his key ideas in buying a stock is to insist that it must be so cheap that even if everything goes wrong the worst that can happen is that your capital will be sterile for a while. "I look down before I look up," says Rogers. An example would be buying stock in a company that is actually in bankruptcy at the time. One can never be sure on the short side, though: However right you are, the market may move against you and cost you a great deal of money.

He makes no attempt to avoid taxes. As he says, when he came north he "aspired to a tax problem." He has never availed himself of tax shelters. Most of them are economically disastrous, he points out.

True to his principle of underlying supply and demand and trading anything that can make him money, Rogers is active in commodities. He has traded orange juice, rapeseed oil, and potatoes, and he even bought a seat on the Sugar Exchange as an indirect way of betting on higher sugar prices.

One of his primary rules is: *Don't lose money. If you don't know the facts, don't play.* Take your money, put it in Treasury bills or a money market fund. Just sit back, sit on the beach, go to the movies, play checkers, do whatever you want.

"Then something will come along where you know it's right. Take all your money out of the money market fund, put it in whatever it happens to be, and stay with it for three or four or five or ten years, whatever it is. You'll know when to sell it again, because you'll know more about it than everybody else. Take your money out, put it back in the money market fund, and wait for the next thing to come along."

Rogers loves accounting spreadsheets: They are his chief analytical tool. "Thousands of spreadsheets, lots of numbers." He does not use computers, but has the work done by hand. He used to have three people at this task and is now down to one. He does not have access to any computerized databases, because he cannot know whether their facts are reliable. He says that it is better to have no information than to have wrong information: If the basic facts are wrong, a geometric pileup of errors will follow, probably leading to a wrong conclusion. Specifically, one should avoid such secondhand figures as those in Standard & Poor's, Value Line, or brokerage-house reports. It is essential to go back to the annual reports and 10Ks—a more detailed version required by the SEC.

Rogers says that when he writes to a company he always asks it for *any* filings it has with *any* regulatory authorities. There are sometimes filings of which he is unaware. He points out that for foreign companies on American exchanges, notably the American depositary receipts, one can request the U.S. form 20K, corresponding to the 10K that an American company files in addition to its annual reports. It is particularly important to get the 20K, because the annual reports of foreign companies give little information.

Within a financial statement, Rogers says, the balance sheet is much more important than the income statement. He also gives great weight to the depreciation account. He likes to buy companies that are on the verge of bankruptcy. The cash available from depreciation may tell him if the company will survive in spite of reported losses. Depreciation and amortization are bookkeeping, not "cash going out the door."

He has developed his own spreadsheet format over the years. When he makes a serious mistake, he may add a line to his basic spreadsheet to reflect what he has overlooked before—the trend of a company's receivables, or whatever. He finds that it is essential to have very-long-term spreadsheets—ten to fifteen years—to provide the historical perspective necessary to understand a company. (For an example, see Appendix V.)

He looks, for instance, at profitability over the years: When the results were good, *why* were they good? When the results were bad, *why* were they bad? Rogers likes to buy when things are bad, but just about to get better—not when they already are getting better. So he needs to know how bad things *can* get, as well as how good things can get.

Some of the ratios he tracks with care are the following:

1.   Capital expenditures:
     a. In absolute terms,
     b. As a percentage of depreciation,
     c. As a percentage of gross plant and equipment, and
     d. As a percentage of net plant and equipment.

The ratio of capital expenditures to depreciation is not a scientific figure, but spread over many years it gives an instructive insight. When it is very high you are likely to be at a top; when it is very low—that is, when the industry is not spending money—the outlook is good, since the supply of what the industry produces will be drying up.

2.   Then he looks at the ratios of sales to receivables, debt to equity, and the others. *When there is almost no inventory, when receivables are low,*

when the profit margin is 20 percent and the pretax return on equity is 25 percent, when capital expenditures are growing at 40 percent to 50 percent a year, then *Rogers begins to smell a classic top,* a promising time to go short.

He notes that *everything has been considered a growth stock at one time or another.* Even aluminum was considered a growth industry in the 1940s and 1950s. Most former growth industries have had recoveries at some time. That does not truly turn them into growth stocks all over again. But when they are being *thought* of as growth stocks . . . *then* you have a shorting opportunity!

As an example of how an industry looks when it is ready to take a turn for the worse, Rogers cites financial services, such as investment bankers and stockbrokers. They hire huge staffs, expand their services, and raise money in the marketplace. You read that most graduates of the Harvard Business School have announced that they wish to become investment bankers. At that point, the end is near. Business school graduates crowding into an industry can also signal a top. For instance, one year Atari, a rapidly expanding video game producer, hired 5 percent of the graduates of the Harvard Business School. Three years later, the company was bust.

Rogers likes to look at his tried-and-true ratios to see how bad things can get; and *when they reach the lower limit, he assumes they will start going the other way.* For instance, *when three or four of the big companies in an industry are losing money, as the car companies were in the late 1970s, either there will be no auto industry at all—most unlikely!—or else conditions will improve.* And in fact, this industry, which was grossly overregulated in the 1960s,* had a relaxation of regulations in the 1970s, and its capital needs fell. So he bought Ford, General Motors, and American Motors (subsequently taken over by Chrysler, now part of DaimlerChrysler). A similar turn-around, as already mentioned, lay ahead for nuclear utilities. They have endless problems, and yet there has to be such an industry. So Rogers foresees a buying point. *When you see several major companies losing money, and capital expenditures coming to a stop, then look for an industry recovery!*

---

*I figured out during that period that the capital requirements of General Motors to cope with regulation and modernization exceeded the then market value of the corporation!

The Market Cycle

Here is how the turn comes in the market, he says: The situation of a company or an industry is a disaster, but the stock is still holding its own. Then a few people buy because their grandfathers worked in the plant, or some such reason. Then the Grahamites buy. About this time the supply of whatever the industry produces starts to dry up: supply and demand, a key tip-off! Then the outlook begins to lift, and a wider circle starts to buy. Then the stock goes up and up, and the Wall Street brokers turn positive, so their customers start to buy. Then, after a five-year recovery, the company is acclaimed as a growth stock (which it is not), and still more people buy.

Then the stock starts down, and the entire sequence operates in reverse.

In bear markets, things first decline to reasonable prices, then they fall to cheap prices, and then they reach unbelievable giveaway prices. After that, things get *really* bad, and everybody gets cleaned out.

The View from Abroad

On March 25, 1990, Rogers set forth on a two-year, 65,000-mile motorcycle trip around the world. He crossed Europe and Asia to Tokyo, returned through Siberia to Amsterdam, then headed south across Africa to Capetown. He flew to Australia, motored around the country, then crossed to Cape Horn at the bottom of South America and drove north across the continent, through the United States to Alaska. He ended in San Francisco and then flew back to New York. In his book *Investment Biker: Around the World with Jim Rogers,* he describes entering a board meeting after two years' absence:

> "I haven't seen you in a while," a guy asked. "What have you been up to?"
>
> "I've just been around the world on a motorcycle."
>
> He smiled and said that was nice.
>
> It takes a lot to impress a New Yorker.

Rogers liked the look of China. "Splits and recombinations of nations will be a historical theme of the next fifty years," he says. While Russia's clashing ethnic groups will lead the country to chaos, China can break into three smaller countries—north, south, and west—and still be a coherent unit.* "Many of the overseas Chinese have expertise and capital and want to go back and help, or invest in China and make lots of money," he explains. "The Chinese welcome them with open arms."

But he warns that since outsiders are regarded with suspicion, a prudent investor should not invest directly in China, but through an offshore Chinese-owned company. "For instance, if XYZ Cosmetics Corporation announced it was going to make a major effort to market directly in China, I'd be tempted to short it, but if instead it hooked up with an overseas Chinese-owned health-and-beauty company already marketing successfully in China . . . I might be an eager buyer of XYZ Corporation or the overseas Chinese company itself."

He evaluates Africa country by country. He expected Mobutu to fall and Zaire to collapse. He liked Cameroon, with its growing democracy, abundance of natural resources, and educated, outward-looking population. "At the right time," explains Rogers, "an investor here could put his money into agriculture, metals, lumber, and food production. He should buy into any company that is well financed and sells to its neighbors down south, such as South Africa and Botswana, or north into Europe."

Botswana is another country to which Rogers took an immediate liking. After months of wrestling with bureaucracies elsewhere in Africa, he was astonished to find a friendly welcome.

Rogers noticed surprising prosperity there—new cars, buildings under construction—and realized that as he moved south he was encountering solider economies. Before leaving, he decided to invest. "I had ascertained that Botswana had a sound economy and a sound social structure. I had ascertained that there was a new stock market† and that the government wanted it, and that the opposition also wanted to develop and encourage it. I had further ascertained that the stocks were cheap relative to dividends and other traditional stock-market valuations." But the last and perhaps most important reason

---

*China is well described as a civilization masquerading as a country.
†Botswana enjoyed a government revenue surplus and a positive balance of trade and investment. I well remember its stock market, a table in a room in the office of the only broker. Once a week he entered the room, laid out the buy and sell orders on the table, completed what trades he could, and closed the door until the following week. All this sounds a bit outré, but, looking at the chart (see Appendix VI), you could easily have doubled or tripled your money there!

Rogers chose Botswana is its proximity to South Africa. If South Africa were to grow dynamically, Rogers reasoned, he would do very well in Botswana, while avoiding South Africa's political, economic, and social dangers.

He liked what he saw in Latin America. "Its governments have tried exchange controls for decades and have now eliminated them. Latin Americans have gone through the complete cycle. They know. That's why they're ahead of the Africans. The Latin Americans have learned after seventy years that exchange controls don't work. The Africans are just now getting to the stage of 'Okay, we know exchange controls don't work, so now let's try something else.'"

Rogers observes that wherever there are exchange controls there is a black market in currency. That market can tell you a lot. "I find such markets, capitalism in the raw, fascinating, because if there's one quick and sure way for an investor or a traveler to find out what's going on in a country, this is it." The premium over the bank rate is his clue. "If I can buy five zlotys for a dollar at the bank, but I can get eight on the black market, it tells me the government is trying to foist its currency on its own people, that it's afraid to let it float on the world market."

A Sure Thing

"In all my years of investing, there's one rule I've prized beyond every other," Rogers explains. "*Always bet against central banks and with the real world.* Central banks and governments always try to maintain artificial levels, high or low, in a currency, a metal, wool, whatever. Usually these prices are absurd, and the market knows they're absurd. When a central bank is defending something—whether it's gold at $35 or the lira at 800 to the dollar—the smart investor always goes the other way. *It may take a while, but I promise you you'll come out ahead.*"

Upon his return, Rogers regularly discussed his ideas in the annual *Barron's* Roundtable and on a show he cohosted on the CNBC cable network, although he did not reveal the size and returns of his positions. Through these channels he announced his favorite countries. At the top, China. He proclaimed that the twenty-first century would be China's, just as the twentieth had belonged to the United States and the nineteenth to Britain. "Teach your children Chinese!" he urged. His reasoning was cultural and historical: The Chinese like to work very hard; they think entrepreneurially; they are extremely motivated; they are prepared to delay today's gratification for tomorrow's benefit. And they have before them the overseas Chinese as an example of how to prosper. China began embracing free markets as early as 1979, and unlike Russia, it retained a memory of prewar capitalism in the model of Hong Kong. He claims that it will be the world's richest nation in the next century.

Rogers is enthusiastic about India. It has the world's largest middle class, between 150 million and 300 million. Its economy is larger than that of France, Britain, Italy, or Brazil: fifth in the world, in fact, after the United States, China, Japan, and Germany. It has a legacy of democracy and the rule of law. The Indians are clever, and indeed subcontract writing software for Silicon Valley. "Twenty years from now, many Americans may have their taxes calculated over the Internet by a New Delhi accountant, their financial planning done by a firm in Calcutta, and routine legal work such as a will or divorce agreement in Bangalore," he writes.

More recently, he has continued to be enthusiastic about Africa. "Africa's fifty-plus countries have learned much from the mistakes of the past four decades. Very quietly, so quietly that the investment world has not noticed, Africa over the past few years has developed more than twenty-five public stock markets—several of which offer delicious opportunities." He also maintains that tribal wars are winding down, and dictators being replaced by multiparty systems. In fact, one of his recommendations for investment is in the tourist business in Africa. "It has the Sahara Desert and Arab culture in the north," he wrote in a 1998 *Worth*, "the Congo River and deep, mysterious jungles in the middle, and that California of the continent, South Africa, as its southern tip." In 1994 he also began investing in Ghana, which he called "a play on cocoa and gold," including Ghana Unilever, Ghana Mobil, Ghana Guinness, and Ghana Standard Charter Bank.

Another Rogers favorite has been tea. For fifteen years tea prices have been falling, and tea plantations have given way to palm-oil, rubber, and soybean production. As Asia gets richer, he holds, the vast populations of the East will consume ever more of it. After tea comes sugar, whose futures, Rogers noted in 1998, had fallen 85 percent from their all-time high. He has felt that a sugar estate in Latin America would be an attractive flier. On similar reasoning he recommended buying a seat on a foreign commodities exchange. The best locations would be Tokyo and Buenos Aires: "Buying such a seat is a cheap way to enter these markets. Regional commodities markets will continue to develop and integrate further into worldwide markets."

He summed up his global investment advice in a 1997 column: "Scout for nations that are living up to the ideals and principles that made our country great—namely, those with unshackled economies and free markets." To support this approach, he cites a study conducted by the Fraser Institute in Canada. Its researchers examined the performance of 103 nations in four major areas: money supply growth and inflation; government operations; taxation; and restrictions on international exchange. Their conclusion? "Nations that rate consistently high in economic and political openness have much better growth rates than those that are more statist or closed," says Rogers.* The study also showed that a sound economic system is far more important than any short-term windfall or jackpot. Both Nigeria and Indonesia ranked among the top ten nations in oil production in the 1960s, for example. But while Nigeria mismanaged its wealth horribly, Indonesia pursued a more open approach and prospered.

In late 1997, Rogers listed an investor's "countries for the next century." They included Ireland, Denmark, Botswana, Portugal, China, New Zealand, Australia, Chile, Canada, Peru, South Korea, Ethiopia, Uganda, Mozambique, and Eritrea.

In late 1999, having progressed from Western Europe to Central Asia in another trip around the world, he liked the international oil companies, but opined that the only country he had reached so far that showed real potential was Turkey, where, however, he was not yet ready to act. Russia would, he believed, fall apart, as well as the Central Asian former USSR republics. He didn't like what he saw in Western Europe, and Eastern Europe didn't have what it takes.

In late 1999 and early 2000, Rogers concluded that commodities in general were due for a major long-term advance, and to that end he has started a commodity index fund. It is based on a weighting of his own devising that seems to him to reflect the proper allocations between various commodities more appropriately than the existing indices.

"Learn to sell short," he says. "That's going to be of more value in the next few years, in many parts of the world."

---

*Undoubtedly true, although one must distinguish between cause and effect. Well-proportioned women often wear revealing dresses, but that's not why they're well proportioned.

Twelve

GEORGE SOROS
MACRO GAMES

Today George Soros is the world's best-known manager of capital, partly because of the performance record of his offshore funds—whose day-to-day transactions are largely delegated—but even more because of his Eastern Europe pro-democracy activities, to which he has so far committed some $1.5 billion, with more dedicated in the future.

He probably has the top performance of publicly held portfolio operators: about 33 percent per annum compounded for some twenty-nine years. He is a speculator, betting on short-term movements, not a true investor. Since like others, including Warren Buffett, who makes use of the leverage inherent in an insurance company, he makes heavy use of borrowed money and derivatives, his results are not comparable to those of a conventional fund manager. In any event, the Curaçao-based Quantum Fund, his main vehicle, has assets of some $9 billion. Ten thousand dollars invested when it began in 1969 was worth over $30 million in 1997. It was badly battered in 2000, losing some 30 percent—and several key managers—early in the year.

Soros's personal fortune is in the low billions. With his pretty and intelligent second wife, Susan, who now runs the Bard Graduate Center for Studies in the Decorative Arts, he lives on the Upper East Side in Manhattan. He also maintains residences in Bedford, New York—where he has set himself up as a country squire—in Washington, Connecticut, and in South Kensington, London. He had a clamorous squabble with a departing cook in the latter establishment, and another with the city fathers of Bedford over an outsized front gate that violated local zoning. He plays good tennis and has been an excellent skier. He spends little time with other financiers and generally avoids clubs and associations, although he frequents New York's Council on Foreign Relations.

George Soros (in Hungarian pronounced Shorosh; originally Schwartz) is an intense, squarely built man with a wrinkled brow, an angular chin, and a thin mouth. His hair is cut *en brosse*. He has a flat, somewhat harsh voice and retains his Hungarian accent. (He also speaks French and German.) Unlike most outstanding speculators, he is authentically cultured. His father, a wealthy Jewish lawyer, was captured by the Russians in World War I and escaped, thus experiencing the Bolshevik Revolution at first hand. George received his own lesson in survival as a boy in World War II. In German-occupied Hungary, his father is said to have administered Jewish assets for the then government, but at a later stage was often in flight, hiding out in friends' houses. Two years after the war, at the age of seventeen, George moved to England. After attending the London School of Economics, he became a stock arbitrageur at Singer & Friedlander, calculating the relative values of shares or bonds carrying warrants, and trading the separate elements.

He came to the United States in 1956 and worked at F. M. Mayer & Co. and Wertheim & Co., living in a small Greenwich Village apartment with his musically inclined German first wife, Annalise. He sold European securities, which the introduction of the Interest Equalization Tax brusquely stopped. He spent three years working on a book of philosophy but gave it up, although some of its ideas are embodied in his *The Alchemy of Finance*.* In 1963 he joined Arnhold and S. Bleichroeder as a securities analyst. The firm started an offshore fund called Double Eagle, which Soros was assigned to run in 1969. That year he wrote a research memorandum describing the attractions of a new vehicle, the real estate investment trust, or REIT. He correctly predicted that they were a good enough idea that they would boom, go much too far, and eventually collapse. He did buy them, and when they had become overblown in 1974 he went short, making a tidy profit. He put a quarter of the fund's portfolio into Japanese securities in 1971.

In 1969, aged thirty-nine, he finally decided to hang out his own shingle and joined with Jim Rogers to found Quantum Fund—one of the

---

*New York: Simon & Schuster, 1987.

most successful large funds in history. Not registered with the SEC, it cannot be sold in America, so the shareholders are virtually all foreigners, mostly European. It engages in multidirectional international speculation in commodities, currencies, stocks, and bonds, using massive margin. Soros says that the capital of the fund is kept basically in stocks, while its bets on commodities and currencies are done using futures and/or borrowed money. It went short the major institutional favorites, such as Disney, Polaroid, and Tropicana, and thus made money in both 1973 and 1974, which for most investors were horrible years. He went short Avon, the archetypal "one-decision" stock, at 120—a brilliant move.

Thanks to Rogers, the fund was one of the first to recognize the investment merits of defense stocks. It was also well ahead of the pack in high technology. In 1979 it owned 8 percent of M/A Com, and in 1980, 23 percent of Bolt Beranek & Newman; also 5.3 percent of Chem Nuclear Enterprises and 3.4 percent of Planning Research. It made money in oil service stocks, and lost it by going short the same issues. Quantum had a good run in Mortgage Guaranty Insurance Company, MAGIC, after it suffered in the collapse of the California residential market. Soros on that occasion formulated a rule that one should *avoid a stock that is facing a difficult test, and buy after it has survived the test.*

The fund grew rapidly, but Rogers, says Soros, did not want to hire more people, nor would he accept criticism from anyone except Soros himself. So the partnership blew up. Under the stress of rapid growth, Soros also separated from his wife. To cope with his anxiety, he underwent psychiatric treatment—which was beneficial, according to his friends.

I have a certain feeling for Soros, since my first employer (and indeed the only one, except for the Army) was also a London-trained Hungarian emigré economist, Imrie de Vegh, who turned to investing and became a master of that craft. The Hungarians are a hard, proud people, used to defending themselves against invasion from every quarter. Their language, Magyar, can be understood by no one else. They approach the world as strangers—if Jewish, the more so—and contemplate life without illusions. Like Soros, de Vegh sought to apply his economic savvy to a wider purpose; in addition to his investment firm he started a consultancy with Professor Wassily Leontief, the Nobel prize–winning father of input-output economics, to offer input-output analysis to very large companies, industries, and governments. It was not successful. (Leontief is also, as it happens, on the board of Soros's foundation.)

The Soros Foundations

From his earlier forays into philosophy, Soros developed the concept of an Open Society Fund, which he began in New York in 1979. The name came from philosopher Karl Popper's term for a society of free and open discourse, one that by its very nature repels dictatorship. From that base a network of philanthropic foundations has grown that now operates in thirty-one countries, employing thirteen hundred people. The hands-on manager of the whole bundle is Aryeh Neier, the former head of Human Rights Watch—but Soros remains the master.

The Soros Foundation–Hungary was the first to have a major impact. Established in 1984, it began by providing grants and scholarships, focusing on academic and social research. But by the late 1980s the foundation was backing the underground political forces that grew into the nation's democratic opposition parties. Often, the most critical supplies were photocopying machines and computers.

With the collapse of the Soviet Union, Soros saw a storm brewing. He recognized that without significant funding, the countries of Eastern Europe—and Russia itself—would never develop the basic institutions and structures essential to preserving an open society. As he frequently remarked, an open society is a far more complex creature than a closed society, the latter requiring only centralized forces of censorship and oppression. At a Potsdam conference in 1988, Soros advocated a vast Marshall Plan to support the emerging democratic nations. *Frankfurter Allgemeine Zeitung* reported on its front page that this idea met with derision. New Soros foundations began springing up in quick succession—in Poland, Rumania, Bulgaria, Latvia, and on and on—but Soros remained fearful that his own input would be inadequate. His greatest concern was the looming threat of a nationalist dictatorship emerging in Russia. In 1992, he proposed a "cold cash" plan in which Western nations would give $10 billion a year to Russia to create a social safety net. He was virtually ignored.

It is against the backdrop of this inaction by the West that Soros unveiled his boldest gifts: $230 million for educational programs in Russia and the former Soviet Union and $100 million for Russian scientists. (The latter gift is more tactical than it appears: The funds could help discourage the sale of nuclear technology to hostile nations.) In

1997, Soros would commit another $500 million to Russia, making him a larger donor than the U.S. government. Soros is also the founder of the thriving Central European University, headquartered in Budapest, which he has endowed with several hundred million dollars.

Keep It Simple

Soros does not spend a great deal of time on economic study, and does not read Wall Street research. He develops his opinions essentially by reading newspapers and dispatches from abroad, and particularly by talking to well-placed sources around the world. Through his participation in the Council on Foreign Relations, he has developed friendships with a number of high-ranking U.S. officials, such as Secretary of State Madeleine Albright and Assistant Secretary of State Peter Tarnoff. In most countries of significance to him, Soros has access to high levels of government.

He processes raw intelligence with exceeding rapidity, observes an employee, if he is confident that it has been processed accurately up to his level. He is also highly intuitive, but his intuition is based on a great deal of knowledge.

Jim Rogers, who had a 20 percent interest in Soros Management, was essential to the early success of Quantum Fund, those close to the situation say. Soros had the large and general ideas and was the trader, while Rogers did much of the country selection and was an extremely diligent stock analyst.

After being accused by the SEC of manipulating the price of Computer Sciences in 1979, Soros signed a consent decree; in 1986, accused of exceeding trading limits, he signed another. Neither is too significant: It is almost impossible to obey every regulation when running so complicated an operation.

On and off, Soros has had some bad dips. In 1981, for instance, the shares of his fund dropped 23 percent. Many of his investors were flighty European performance-chasers, and a number, fearing he might have lost his grip, dropped out, reducing his fund by exactly half. It would be understandable for the shareholders to get skittish. Soros's method is inordinately difficult for most investors to understand, let alone apply, and depends on consummately honed skill, applied every day with unremitting concentration. A typical Soros maneuver, such as going long on yen and short sterling on margin both ways, while immensely profitable if it works, can also have disastrous results if it doesn't. However, the next year, 1982, was one of his best, up 57 percent, and by the end of 1983 the fund was bigger than ever.

In 1987 a horrible downdraft came in a matter of days. During the weeks before the 500-point crash, Soros had declared that the Japanese market was wildly overpriced. So he shorted Japanese stocks. But Wall Street caved in first, catastrophically, on October 17. Two days later, Soros was said to have doubled his exposure to U.S. equities by buying over $1 billion worth of index futures. After a brief bounce, Wall Street crashed again, and in a panic he had to throw in his hand. But as his broker, Shearson, dumped his S&P futures contracts, the traders, like vultures circling over a staggering beast, refused to bid. The price plummeted from 230 to 200, a discount of 20 percent below the value of the underlying stocks. Finally he caved in and sold. After his block was out of the way, the S&P futures snapped back at once, to close at 244.50: a jolly treat for the vultures! Soros also had to sell stocks heavily in the cash market. In all, the turmoil cost him $840 million, or 28 percent of his fund. But despite this blow, his fund still ended the year up 14 percent.

In the fall of 1992, Soros made a notorious windfall $1.5 billion profit on the rapid decline of the British pound and the associated chaos in Europe. Then in early 1994, he bet that the yen would fall in the wake of U.S.–Japanese trade talks. This misjudgment cost him $600 million and became known as "the St. Valentine's Day Massacre." Suddenly, four of his eight Quantum Funds—Quantum Industrial, Asian Infrastructure, Quantum Realty, and Quantum UK Realty—were selling at a discount. Articles proclaimed that Midas had lost his touch.

Quantum continued to tumble in 1995 with mistaken bets on the dollar and the Japanese market. This time, surprisingly, not macro investing but stock-picking saved him. Identifying companies where a significant change in management changed the outlook—notably Scott Paper—he recovered, and at year's end was up 39 percent.

In 1997 came a harsh test. Quantum had gained 22 percent for the year, but it was caught overextended in Russian securities, among other problems, and took a pounding. In one day, the funds collectively lost $2 billion—almost 10 percent of assets under management. Nevertheless, Quantum emerged 17 percent ahead for the year.

Soros follows a method that permits no distractions. By 1987, however, he had found himself increasingly caught up with philanthropic projects, enough so that perhaps investors had reason to get wary from time to time. In 1988 and the first half of 1989, Quantum did worse than the Dow. And, indeed, Soros was wary himself. Being used to having partners in management, such as Jim Rogers and Victor Niederhoffer, he set about bringing in a new set of submanagers: He installed one team for risk arbitrage, one for options arbitrage, a man to work with him on macroeconomics, a team for U.S. investments, another for European investments, and another in Japan. Also a short-side group: an internal manager, and several others on a semi-independent basis. Each manager independently ran his own "book" (in Soros's terminology a "mini-account"); Soros increased the volume of any transaction if he liked the look of it. He was moving more to the position of a coach.

After Soros began bringing in his new stable of managers I mentioned to him that my former mentor Imrie de Vegh was brilliant but not a good leader, and had failed in his great ambition, which was to found an enduring institution. "We'll see if I do any better," Soros replied at the time. "It's not my forte either. Still, it's fun bringing in younger people."

But Soros's two most significant recruits, though younger, were anything but novices. For the Quantum Fund he found Stanley Druckenmiller, who has maintained its high returns in spite of massive growth, primarily through large-scale currency and bond bets. He makes good money for himself: $1 billion in 1999. He left in 2000.

A more elusive figure is Nick Roditi, brought in by Soros in 1992 from Rothschilds in London to run the Quota Fund. "Who is this guy?" *Financial World* asked in the summer of 1997 after it was reported that Roditi had earned $125 million in the previous year. He had only begun to emerge from the shadows in 1995, when he generated profits of 159 percent net of the 20 percent management fee, in the Quota Fund, which then had $1.5 billion in assets. The following year Quota made another 82 percent. Operating from a house in Hampstead, London, Roditi built Quota up to nearly $3 billion by 1997. That year, investors were willing to pay a 68 percent premium to get in, but the October plunge pushed the premium below 50 percent. (Premiums for Quantum have been much lower.) At 1997 year-end, Quota's size was $2.5 billion.

Roditi takes huge gambles with terrifying margin on equity indexes and currencies in six markets. In one complex bet on the dollar, he staked over $38 billion. Like Soros himself, he can turn on a dime. In the spring of 1997, Roditi bet $19 billion on European and U.S. government bonds. Three months later he had wiped off most of those positions, and

instead plunked down $13 billion on a bet against Japanese government
bonds. Publicity-shy Roditi escapes to a colonial homestead outside Cape
Town, South Africa. In 1998, after a bad start, he announced that he was
suffering from burnout, and retired from the Soros stable; after a time of
resting up he reappeared, only to withdraw definitively a year later.

Shaken by a billion-dollar losing bet on the Euro, Soros was apprehen-
sive about the excesses of the tech stock boom in 1999, as was Druckenmiller. "I don't like this market. I don't want to go out like Steinhardt,"
he said, and went short. But then the tech stocks soared. In midsummer,
Druckenmiller reversed field, bought them back heavily, and by year
end was well ahead.

Early in 2000 he declared that the tech stock rally was only in its
eighth inning, with another inning to go. Not so! A sharp drop in March
slaughtered both the funds and Druckenmiller, who, moreover, was troubled by constant squabbles with Soros. Deeply discouraged—although
consoled by a large personal fortune—he went out . . . like Steinhardt, as
did many of the funds' investors. Soros then consolidated Quantum with
another fund, and announced that the survivor, Quantum Endowment,
would shift to a much more conservative investment policy.

Soros's Trading Diary

One can get an idea of Soros's methods from the trading diary in his
book *The Alchemy of Finance*, which offers a highly detailed description of
his transactions between August 18, 1985, and November 7, 1986.

As we will see as we go along, Soros devises exotic terms for familiar
things: He calls this trading diary "The Real Time Experiment." It covers a successful period, during which his fund's net asset value per
share doubled.

The diary starts in August 1985. It will be recalled that the Reagan
election of 1984, followed by tax cuts and a defense buildup, had set off
a boom in both the dollar and the stock market. Foreign investors
liked what they saw—a United States resolved to stand firm against
Soviet pressure, and an expanding economy that welcomed foreign participation.

The influx of foreign money during the early Reagan period lifted
both the dollar and the capital markets and helped fuel a round of economic expansion that attracted even more money, putting the dollar up
farther, and so on. Soros baptizes this syndrome "Reagan's Imperial
Circle." (See Appendix VII for his wondrously complicated diagram of

this effect.) The usual metaphor would be a bubble, snowball, or band-wagon. A boom must by its nature collapse eventually, at the latest when mounting debt-service costs exceed its ability to attract new money. Even before that, however, many factors can prick the bubble, which must then burst, perhaps with a fall in the local currency and a rush of specu-lative capital out of that market. That, in turn, is likely to produce a decline in the economy, resulting in a general downward spiral.

Soros's trading diary opens on August 18, 1985, with his fund worth $647 million. Some readers will remember that at this period investors were worried that a rise in the money supply meant a boom, with higher interest rates, and subsequent bust; the economy was feared to be in for a "hard landing." Cyclical stocks, beneficiaries of the boom, were strong, and stocks whose fortunes depended on low interest rates were weak.

In his diary Soros declares that he doubts this conventional wisdom *in toto*. He thinks the "imperial circle" is faltering, and thus expects the dollar to weaken and interest rates to rise, provoking a recession. So instead of buying cyclical stocks that would benefit from a continued boom, he buys takeover candidates, together with shares of property-insurance companies, then enjoying one of their best years on record. As to currencies, Soros is playing the thesis of a weaker dollar by buy-ing D-marks and yen. In addition he thinks OPEC is breaking up, and so goes short oil. So the opening position on the board looks as shown in the first column, August 16, 1985, of the Quantum Fund table (see Appendix VIII).

Three weeks later, nothing has worked. The mark and yen have both declined, and since Soros had been long some $700 million in those two currencies—more than the value of the whole fund—he has lost money. By September 6 he has built up his D-mark and yen positions to just under $800 million, almost $100 million more than the value of the fund.

Now comes the so-called Plaza meeting of a group of five finance ministers with their central bankers, called on a Sunday by the U.S. Treasury. That night, Sunday in New York but already Monday morn-ing in Hong Kong, Soros plunges in and buys yen heavily. The yen rises strongly, and Soros makes 10 percent on his yen position, which he has built up to $458 million.

In his September 28 entry, Soros describes the Plaza accord coup as "the killing of a lifetime . . . the profits of the last week more than made up for the accumulated losses on currency trading in the last four years. . . ." Four years is a long time to be underwater! This statement certainly illustrates the difficulties of currency trading. If the reader looks at the entries for September 6, 1985, in the Quantum Fund table he will see that the exposure in D-marks is $491 million and in yen $308 million, or a total of $799 million, somewhat more than the value of the fund. By September 27 the D-mark has risen from 2.92 to the dollar to 2.68, or 9 percent, and the yen from 242 to 217, or 11.5 percent. The combination of profits and reinforcing the bet have pushed the combined holdings in these two currencies from $791 million up to $1 billion by September 27, but because of adverse movements in the stock market and oil the whole fund has advanced only—if that's the word—7.6 percent a share. In other words, the 8–10 percent currency profit has been diluted by other holdings.

Soros regards the stock market decline as reinforcing his bear position on the dollar: A poor stock market will discourage both consumer and business outlays. Also, a decline in the value of stocks reduces their value as collateral, a further depressant.

By the first week in November 1985, Soros has reached the peak of his speculation against the dollar: D-mark and yen positions total $1.46 billion, almost double the value of the fund. This implies increasing his commitment to a trend as the trend continues . . . also known as pyramiding. Pyramiding is a good way to sustain serious damage in margin speculation, since when the trend reverses, even temporarily, you risk being caught overexposed.

"The reason I am nevertheless willing to increase my exposure is that I believe the scope for a reversal has diminished. One of the generalizations I established about freely floating exchange rates is that *short-term volatility is greatest at turning points and diminishes as a trend becomes established*"—an important hint for the currency speculator.

Soros continues by observing that other speculators have not realized this new principle, which follows from floating rates, and indeed previously he hadn't himself, or he would have been able to build up to his full position sooner, and make even bigger profits on the fall of the dollar. He further reflects that *"by the time all the participants have adjusted, the rules of the game will change again.* If the authorities handle the situation well, the reward for speculating in currencies will become commensurate with the risks. Eventually, speculation will be discouraged by the lack of rewards, the authorities will have attained their goal, and it will be time for me to stop speculating."

I urge the reader to note this passage. This is the right way to approach market movements. The fatal weakness of almost all "systems" of speculation is that they are simplistic formulas, using partial data describing a particular slice of previous experience. If the slice does not entirely resemble what comes up next, or if different data are more applicable, then the approach won't work.

You can always come up with formulas covering past events that have little use in predicting future events, because they are fragmentary simplifications. Such formulas indicate what you should do to optimize your situation on the assumption that you are playing a game with fixed rules, but the essence of understanding markets is to understand how the rules are evolving.

Returning to Soros's diary, in the first week of November 1985 he notes that the collapse of the International Tin Council, a cartel, foreshadows the collapse of OPEC. He is now short in the oil market to the tune of over $180 million, and in addition buys shares of oil-refining companies, reasoning that if the price of oil—their principal cost—drops, then their profits will improve.

During November, Soros decides that the Gramm-Rudman amendment, which is intended to reduce government expenditures, together with the Reagan-Gorbachev summit meeting, which could force defense-expenditure cuts, may presage a strong market, so he buys stock market index futures.

In addition, the Japanese bond market has fallen, because of higher domestic interest rates. Soros thinks that since the Group of Five has agreed to stimulate worldwide economic activity, Japanese interest rates should be cut. Furthermore, he notes that *the best time to buy long-term bonds is when short-term rates are higher than long-term rates . . . when the yield curve is inverted,* as one says. He therefore buys $300 million in Japanese bond futures.

So now Soros, with a fund of about $859 million, holds $1.5 billion in yen and D-marks and is short $87 million in pounds; he is betting against the dollar by some $600 million more than the funds he is managing.

Also, he is long about $1 billion in stocks and futures plus almost $1.5 billion in bonds, and is short over $200 million worth of oil.

It's hard to add all this up, because of duplication, but, roughly speaking, in November 1985 Soros has almost $4 billion of action, long and short and in various markets, on the strength of his underlying capital of around $800 million, or about five to one.

On December 8 he says, "I have about as firm a conviction about the shape of things to come as I shall ever have, as witnessed by the level of exposure I am willing to assume." It certainly seems so! That conviction is, however, quite different from what he started with back in August. Then, he considered the "imperial circle" as a final round of credit expansion to stimulate the economy and finance the military buildup; when the waterspout collapsed, everything would collapse with it. By November, he realizes what has actually happened and is somewhat reassured: The government has organized an international campaign to moderate the fall of the dollar, which may thus be reasonably gentle. And the rise in the stock and bond markets helps, since stronger bond prices help the Fed to lower interest rates.

Thus, notes Soros, "We may be on the verge of a great stock market boom." Many companies have been taken over, reducing both excess capacity and shares outstanding. The companies that have not been taken over have cut costs. And the lower dollar has eased pricing pressures on American companies. Taking all this together with the emergence of a concerted international economic policy, he feels that conditions are good enough so that stocks may once again sell at a premium over their underlying assets. Still, it is not clear how the U.S. budget deficit can be reduced, or how the economies of the debtor countries can be stimulated. But the attempt to do all these things should itself be enough to improve the market's feelings.

As for OPEC, most producing countries operate with what Soros calls a perverse supply curve. That is, the lower prices fall, the more they produce, in order to attain a target level of income, forcing prices down more than ever. So he stays short in oil.

By early January 1986, Soros has made some large changes in the makeup of his portfolio. Reflecting his more bullish stance, he has increased the portion in U.S. stocks and stock-index futures by $643 million, plus an increase in the foreign stock position of $47 million to $318 million, or a total of about $2 billion. He has also added $207 million to his U.S. bond holdings. He has shrunk his bet against the dollar from half a billion to zero; that is, his net position in dollars is down to just the amount of the fund. He has also expanded his short position in oil to $224 million. Quite a month!

He notes that *the usual bull market successfully weathers a number of tests until it is considered invulnerable, whereupon it is ripe for a bust;* this will happen in due course, but that point is still a long way ahead.

In February he reduces his stock position to about $1.2 billion, but by March 26 he decides that his bullish thesis for stocks is right, after all, and is reinforced by the fall in oil; so he rebuilds his position in U.S. and foreign stocks to about $1.8 billion. His fund has increased since early January from $942 million to $1.3 billion.

By April 4 he has backed off again from his stock commitments by $831 million, but in the following week he has repurchased $709 million—very nice for the brokers! By May 20 he has once more sold $687 million. These maneuvers are conducted largely in index futures.

Forty percent of his stock positions, and two-thirds of his foreign stocks, are in three conceptions: the Finnish market, Japanese railroad and real estate stocks, and Hong Kong real estate stocks. Finland is a little-known and underpriced market, but it contains some outstanding companies, notably Nokia. The last two conceptions are really variations of the same idea: Excessive liquidity has created a land boom in both Japan and Hong Kong. As for the Japanese railroads specifically, they have not moved in the market for over a decade and are selling at a small fraction of their underlying value. Furthermore, they have discovered that they can invest in commercial real estate with borrowed money and make a profit, since the interest on the money they borrow is lower than the return on the real estate they buy.

By July, Soros is playing two contradictory theses: (1) We are still in a major bull market; (2) The fall of oil prices may after all engender a deflationary spiral, which will abort the boom.

It must seem odd that a speculator would operate on the basis of two opposed theories, but in fact it makes good sense in many situations involving human reactions. In military negotiations between countries it has come to be called a "two-track" position: If you don't take out your missiles I will install my own missiles; if you do take them out, I won't install mine.

I have often noticed that when there are two main pressures, one favorable and one unfavorable, the stock market, instead of neatly assuming a balanced middle position, will usually at different times discount both of them. So you have to keep both in mind and be prepared for both. For instance, war may ruin a country, and so is bad for the market. On the other hand, war means overspending, which is inflationary, so in wartime investors flee depreciating currencies and buy things, including things represented by stocks. A war threat thus often precedes a violent fluctuation down, and thereafter up, as first one possibility is discounted and then the other.

Anyway, in late July, Soros is once again intrigued by the bear argument. The fall in oil prices, he observes, has bad economic effects as well as good ones. It is inhibiting U.S. oil exploration, and other oil-producing states are hard hit. Then, the new tax-reform bill knocks out real estate tax shelters, undercutting the commercial real estate market. Agriculture is sick, and defense spending is tapering off.

Furthermore, the fall in the dollar makes it harder for the government to cut interest rates in order to stimulate business, since high interest rates are needed to hold volatile foreign money in the country.

So now within the "bull market of a lifetime" hypothesis Soros sees a case for the opposite. What to do? His answer is interesting: "As a general principle, I do not dismantle positions that are built on a thesis that remains valid; rather, I take additional positions in the opposite direction on the basis of the new thesis." This is also what happens if within a single fund two or more managers happen for a moment to find themselves going in opposite directions.

He gives an example, which to most investors would be puzzling. "If I start with a fully invested position and then sell short an equal amount, a 20 percent decline, even if it affects the longs and the shorts equally, leaves me only 80 percent invested on the long side. If I cover my shorts at the right time, I come out way ahead, but even if I cover my shorts with a loss I am better off than if I had sold my longs at the wrong time."

All this would be much more complicated in practice than in this example, because he would be operating simultaneously in several markets. For instance, here are his moves in mid-July: "On Monday, July 14, I actually bought some S&P futures on the argument that if we are dealing with a technical reaction, the market ought to close higher. The Dow had dropped 63 points the previous Monday, July 7, and the bears would expect another drop on the subsequent Monday to establish a cascadelike bear market. When the market did in fact close lower, I reversed myself on the following day, and by the end of the week I built up a short position that probably outweighs my long position. I also shorted some long bonds and went long some T-bill futures. Then I piled into the Japanese bond future market, and doubled up on my short position in U.S. government bonds. The idea behind these maneuvers is that eventually I expect concerted action to reduce interest rates but, with the dollar declining, U.S. bonds may react negatively while Japanese bonds would move up."

How many of us would have figured that out?

These extracts from Soros's trading diary should give the reader a fair impression of his method. The book itself, of course, provides considerably more.

Recent Moves

Soros is fond of railing against elephantine, unwieldy institutions, and even chafes at the notion that he is an "accumulator." But accumulating is indeed what he has been up to for decades, and the price he must pay is that his Quantum is no longer a $500 million frigate but rather a $9 billion battleship. Unavoidably, Soros has become somewhat more conventional. A large part of his U.S. equity positions are in blue-chip Dow stocks.

For many years Soros stuck to a self-imposed ban on investments in any of the countries where his foundations were active (with a few minor exceptions). By 1994, however, he determined that Russia was simply too vast and dynamic to be off-limits to his speculations. His initial forays were disastrous—the market plunged just after his arrival. But Soros always viewed Russia as a long-term proposition and, indeed, a learning process. In the summer of 1997, Soros took a bold step and teamed up with Oneximbank president Vladimir Potanin—one of the most powerful businessmen in Russia—to win a privatization auction for a 25 percent stake in the telecommunications giant Svyazinvest. Soros provided $980 million of the $1.8 billion bid. While he did express concerns over the slanted playing field of Russian privatization, Soros could not resist the opportunity. In late 1997, Quantum got caught overextended in Russian securities and took a fearful beating in the October turmoil. Soros wrote that (a) Russia should have a modest devaluation, (b) it should stabilize the ruble with a currency board, and (c) the IMF and G7 should infuse $15 billion. Alternatively, just the $15 billion, immediately. None of this happened, and Quantum fell over 10 percent in a day, losing $1 billion. He was immediately, and harshly, denounced—not an unusual occurrence, as we shall discuss later. In the following weeks, however, Quantum recouped some of the losses, and by mid-November emerged 15 percent ahead for the year.

Soros's greatest coup to date was set in motion by a speech by German Bundesbank president Schlesinger in the summer of 1992. A reference to possible instability in Europe was all Soros needed to hear to reaffirm his own belief that the British currency position in the Exchange Rate Mechanism was not sustainable. Soros quickly grasped the immensity of the opportunity before him and called upon Stanley Druckenmiller—in an early trial by fire—to leverage a $10 billion position, shorting British pounds and Italian lira and loading up on German marks. (Soros knew the mark would be the safe haven for investors in the midst of an ERM crisis.) The Italian lira was the first to tumble. As pressure mounted, the British central bank raised interest rates 5 percent and used almost half its foreign currency reserves in an effort to prop up the pound . . . to no avail. By the time the British and other central banks had thrown in the towel, Soros had reaped a 25 percent return for September and found himself dubbed in London headlines "the Man Who Broke the Bank of England." True to form, once Soros was convinced his position was correct, he had reinforced it from every angle. Part of the operation included selling British bonds short while attacking the pound: Since the Bank of England was forced to raise rates to defend its currency, bond prices would inevitably drop. As the climax approached, however, Soros reversed himself—once again with impeccable timing—and began buying up British bonds in anticipation of the coming surrender and ensuing decline in interest rates. "I was prepared for a regime change," Soros explains in his book *Soros on Soros*, "whereas other people were acting within a prevailing regime and this is where I think my awareness that conditions can undergo revolutionary change was useful."

Investment Techniques

Here are some of Soros's principles of speculation:

1. Start small. If things work out, build up a larger position. This ties in with his view that in a world of floating currencies, trends get steadier and more determinable as they develop.
2. The market is dumb, so don't try to be omniscient. "Investors operate with limited funds and limited intelligence: They do not need to

know everything. *As long as they understand something better than others, they have an edge.*" For example, when he was a European securities salesman for Wertheim, Soros discovered that the securities portfolios of the major German banks exceeded the banks' market value, so that if you bought stock in the banks you were in essence being paid to accept the operating businesses of these excellent institutions for nothing. That was all one needed to know to justify acting, and he acted. This thesis was powerful enough so that detailed information would just have been clutter. By the same token, however, Soros finds it difficult to invest in technology stocks, because there you do have to possess specialized knowledge. He thus missed most of the great technology boom.

3. A speculator has to *define from the first the level of risk that he dares assume.* This is a most difficult judgment.

Market Theories

There are three main theories of stock market behavior, Soros observes: the "efficient market" theory, the technical, and the fundamental.

1. He and many others have demonstrated the falsity of the efficient market theory through consistent superior performance—which, according to the theory, is virtually impossible. Determined professors have written that the Soros phenomenon can be explained by luck; but if so, Mozart can be explained by luck. No one in the business believes it. Soros notes sardonically, "The more the theory of efficient markets is believed, the less efficient the markets become."

2. Technical analysis has a feeble theoretical foundation and does not in fact work consistently.

3. Fundamental analysis holds that value, defined in terms of earning power and assets, determines stock prices. But stock prices also change fundamental values, by permitting the sale or repurchase of shares, or mergers and acquisitions, and the like.

My own comment is that value determines stock prices—eventually. The investor, unlike the speculator, does not have to worry too much about the short term. However, Soros concludes that "reflexivity" is a better approach than any of these.

The essence of Soros's theory of reflexivity is that *perception changes events, which in turn change perception.* The usual name for this effect is "feedback." In my own language, if when the princess kisses the frog the frog turns into a prince, she will kiss him some more, he will kiss her back, and . . . I know not what. If, on the other hand, you chain a good dog and kick it, saying "bad dog," the dog will indeed become vicious and bite, provoking more kicks, and more bites.

Switching to money, if speculators are convinced the dollar should rise, their purchases may well push it up. That, in turn, will produce lower interest rates and stimulate the economy, justifying a still higher dollar. Similarly, if many speculators become convinced that Microsoft or whatever is going to rise, then they will bid up the stock, and management can use it as a trading token to buy other companies on advantageous terms, thus justifying a still higher stock price. Soros calls this reciprocal sequence of facts to perceptions to facts to perceptions, and so on, a "shoelace" pattern, one lace consisting of facts and the other of opinion. Others call it the bandwagon effect.

Feedback, or reflexivity, works because the participants don't fully know what's objectively true. Their own actions *are* that truth. (This is the essence of the military decision-making problem: The "fog" of war—another competitive game—prevents you from having all the information you need; indeed, by the time you have it, the situation has changed, as the opponent is always moving against you.)

Edward N. Luttwak has written, "Uncomfortably aware that Berkeley and Heisenberg among many others have preceded him since antiquity, Soros alternates between *sotto voce* claims of originality and disclaimers of any such merit." *The Economist* wrote of "reflexivity," "Here is a challenge: Find anybody who ever denied it."

Soros once hoped to develop a broad theory of reflexivity that would explain his expected great bust of the 1980s, just as Keynes's *General Theory of Employment, Interest, and Money* explained the Great Depression of the 1930s. He now admits that he does not have a properly formed economic theory, although he considers the idea valid and interesting. Speculators, politicians, and strategists have always understood it, but not necessarily the public.*

---

*"It is distressing for an economist to hear it claimed that this idea has been ignored by economists. The simultaneous determination of market prices and investor expectations features in virtually every recent study of financial markets, including orthodox theories based on economic fundamentals or rational expectations, as well as those that challenge the orthodoxy." Jeffrey A. Frankel in *Foreign Affairs*, March–April 1999. Indeed, the present author has some claim to priority. (See Appendix IX.)

Soros is particularly interested in two financial areas where reflexivity operates: the relationships between lending and collateral, and between regulators and the economy.

The act of lending increases the value of the collateral the loan is based on, assuming the money earns more than the interest rate it's borrowed at. If, like the Japanese railroads, a company or a country can borrow money cheaply to buy productive assets at bargain prices, it will gain. Bringing in loan money usually stimulates economic activity in general, and a strong economy enhances the asset values and income streams that build creditworthiness.

Eventually, however, if debt rises beyond the point where it can be serviced, the collateral has to be sold, which depresses its value, throwing the process into reverse.

One of the keys to Soros's success has been his adroit large-scale use of derivatives, notably futures contracts. Not only do derivatives provide the leverage Soros needs to build up large positions but, skillfully handled, they can also be used to execute massive trades in a very short time without moving markets too significantly. This allows Soros to operate with at least some level of secrecy. But federal regulators have expressed concern over the volatility of derivatives. They particularly fear that the banks that lend money to Soros and other high-risk money managers may be getting in over their heads, as they did with Long Term Capital Management.

Equilibrium

The bandwagon effect of speculation is not explained by the equilibrium theory of classical economics, which holds that there is a natural price for most things at which transactions will occur and the market should clear. But this theory does not apply to markets with wide public participation, which fluctuate with the ebb and flow of group passions.

It would have been quite a stunt if Soros had been able to squeeze speculative market behavior into classical economics, and it's not surprising that he couldn't. Speculative markets and other conflict situations, such as war and poker, are analyzed by sociologists—and in mathematical terms by newer disciplines, such as game theory and complexity theory: Soros admits to being unfamiliar with them. Rather, Soros prefers to cite the uncertainty principle. He feels he can gain an edge in the game by constantly questioning his own analyses. His awareness of his own fallibility—and that of markets—is his advantage.

Soros accepts that the concept of equilibrium in classical economics is a myth, along with a number of other assumptions of economic theory, such as perfect competition, perfect knowledge, homogeneous products, and smooth supply-and-demand curves. In reality, he says, decisions to buy and sell are based on *expectations*. If a producer expects the price of his product to decline, then like a commodity speculator he will sell more rather than less as it begins to fall. (Also, like the Japanese, he may start up an oversized production line to bring unit prices down in order to capture his prospective market.) In reverse, if prices rise, one would expect supply to mount and demand to fall, tending to put a brake on the upward movement. However, in some cases the reverse occurs: A currency rises, and because of the dampening impact on inflation and for other reasons the rise can become self-validating. Thus, since the supply-and-demand curves are in considerable measure determined by market influences, you have trends instead of equilibrium.

Soros sees the prime mover of stock prices as a combination of the underlying trend and the prevailing "bias"—usually called the standard forecast—both of which are influenced by stock prices, which influence may be either self-reinforcing or self-correcting.

Every cycle is unique, but one can make a few generalizations:

1. The importance of speculative transactions increases as the trend continues.
2. Bias (i.e., the standard forecast) follows the trend; the longer the trend persists, the stronger the bias.
3. Once a trend is fixed it will run its course.

Currencies, particularly, tend to move in great waves. So adding the three generalizations together, he finds that speculation progressively destabilizes currencies. This is part of the reason for Soros's opposition to freely fluctuating exchange rates.

For Soros, the main features of a typical boom/bust sequence are:

1. A little-recognized trend
2. The beginning of the self-reinforcing process just described
3. A successful test of the market's direction
4. A growing conviction
5. A resulting divergence between reality and perception

6.   The climax

7.   Then, the start of a mirror-image self-reinforcing sequence in the opposite direction

The first time Soros used the boom/bust-sequence concept was in the conglomerate boom; another was his play in real estate investment trusts (REITs). Both times their attraction lay in the companies' "reflexive" access to capital gains by selling stock at a premium over book value.

Further, he says, things can go wrong even if foreseen: Events can only reverse prevailing opinions at reversal points, which are hard to spot. In other words, you can know that something will happen, but unless you also know when, it may not do you much good. Particularly when you are on the short side, it's essential to catch the moment of the reversal quite exactly.

Now, this is Soros, a trader, speaking. Suppose you are sure the yen will fall and you have $1 billion of borrowed money riding on it. Next quarter or next year it may indeed decline, but you may have been wiped out in the meantime. So for today and tomorrow what governs will be the immediate supply-demand factors, influenced by current news, moves by the authorities, and, above all, momentum. That's what is meant by the old trader's axiom "The trend is your friend." To buck it, particularly on margin, is terribly risky, since you probably won't catch the exact moment of the turn.

For the patient long-term investor, on the other hand, who really understands the underlying values and is working with only part of his assets, the important thing is value. If you can buy $1 of value for 50 cents, or if you can pay 50 cents today for what will grow to $1 of value in a couple of years, you needn't worry about pinpoint timing. And one of the ways you know you're probably getting good value is that there are almost no other buyers.

So contrarianism is the hallmark of the good investor, although it can be very dangerous indeed for the margin trader.

A Flexible Theoretical Framework

Soros welcomes the discovery that he has been wrong, and acts accordingly, without fighting it.

By maintaining a flexible theoretical framework, he hopes to cope with whatever comes up. For instance, at the time his trading diary or "real-time experiment" begins, he considers the "imperial circle" vulnerable: The weakness of both the dollar and the U.S. economy will, he feels, lead to high interest rates, which in turn will provoke a decline in the economy. But then the U.S. monetary authorities changed to a "dirty float," cushioning the dollar's fall. That kept interest rates down. The resulting boom in the financial markets prevented the economy from slipping into recession and led to a prolongation of the boom.

As we see from his trading maneuvers, one of Soros's most important traits—as with every successful trader—his willingness to reverse field instantly when he realizes he has made a mistake. For example, he went short Resorts International in the midst of the vast enthusiasm for gambling stocks in 1978 and 1979. So did Robert Wilson, in a widely discussed disastrous short-side transaction. But Wilson, having announced his position to all and sundry, then went off on an extensive vacation to the Orient. Resorts soared from 5 to 60, where he was forced to cover, costing him a fortune. Soros, on the contrary, seeing that things were going wrong, simply changed sides: He closed out his shorts, bought the stock (thus helping squeeze Wilson), and ended up modestly ahead.

Highly intelligent investors, like people in general, would sometimes rather die than admit error. Not Soros. "My approach works not by making valid predictions but by allowing me to correct false ones," he says.

He observes that "the outstanding feature of my predictions is that I keep on expecting developments that do not materialize.... In part because markets can influence the events that they anticipate ... reflexive processes do not have a predetermined outcome: The outcome is determined in the course of the process." (This, by the way, is a central idea of complexity theory.)

Soros is a contrarian in the sense that he thinks that most institutional money managers are usually wrong: "The more influential their position, the less I consider them capable of making the right decisions." And markets shape events; looking out from the bow, so to speak, they may give off loud warning cries when the ship seems to be going on the rocks. "So we live in an age of self-defeating prophecies," he says. Perhaps, he adds, this explains the joke that the stock market predicted five of the last two business collapses: *The market did indeed anticipate them, and frightened the authorities into taking action to prevent them.*

That is what Soros means by the "alchemy" of the market, since unlike science, which tries to understand,* alchemy tries to change.

One of Soros's pleasant foibles is his fondness for grandiose names for his ideas, some of which are quite familiar under their usual designations. This eventually becomes quite good fun. I have mentioned "reflexivity" for feedback, "bias" for standard forecast, the "imperial circle" for bubble, and "cooperative" for a club of leading banks, and "real-time experiment" for trading diary. In his trading diary entry of December 8, 1985, he decides that perhaps the world is not coming to an end right away, that instead things may be all right for a while. This he describes not as a reprieve but as the "Golden Age of Capitalism," which occurs four times in six paragraphs; he also announces "the bull market of a lifetime." At this point the S&P 500 stock average is about 2,000. Nine months later, on September 29, 1986, he writes, "It is better to declare the phase I have called the 'Golden Age of Capitalism' as complete and try to identify the next phase." This is the last we hear of the "Golden Age of Capitalism." The S&P is now about 2,300, so the Golden Age of Capitalism is "declared" to be at an end after nine months and a 15 percent move in the averages—probably the shortest golden age on record!

Soros rightly observes that just as you have to live *somewhere*, you have to keep your money in some currency. Most investors, and indeed most money managers, never consciously decide where they want to be; they stay put. That's fine if you're in Zurich: less so if you're in Port-au-Prince.† Consciously choosing between countries other than your own comes hard to the patriot, and particularly to an American, for whom Morgan's dictum never to be a bear on the United States has been excellent counsel. But short-term, neither the dollar nor dollar stocks have always been the best choice. So, says Soros, you have to take a stand: Not to decide is itself a decision. "Sometimes I envy my more ignorant fund-managing colleagues," he modestly reveals, "who do not know that they face an existential choice."

---

*This refers to good science. Bad science is often harnessed to politics, e.g., the Marxists' "scientific" view of history and the Nazis, "scientific" racial theories. In our own days, "political science" and indeed "concerned scientists" have often been more political than scientific. "By calling politics science," Soros observes cynically, "you can influence events more."

†I once had a charming friend who was the ambassador from an African country to both the UN and to Haiti. He used to go to Haiti once a year to participate in celebrating its national day. His family fortune consisted of some rental houses back in Africa. He used to ask me wistfully whether, in the interest of diversification, in case there was trouble at home, he should not buy a rental house or two in Haiti.

In the 1980s, Soros reached the stage that all intelligent money managers—and, indeed, human beings—come to in time of wanting to do something useful for mankind with the rest of his life. Many assemble art collections and look for someone to give them to, or go on museum or charitable boards, or enter public service and consort with big shots. In the best cases, they give useful donations to universities or well-established charities. Soros has taken a quite different route and developed an innovative—indeed, unprecedented—network of foundations that are easing Central Europe through the birth pangs of democracy.

Montaigne drew a noteworthy distinction between his position as mayor of Bordeaux and himself as a thinker. The mayor is supposed to set an example and make uplifting pronouncements; the thinker may—indeed must—have his own ideas: "You can put powder on your face, but not on your heart also." Similarly, Soros preaches regulation of currencies and denounces greenmailers, but while things continue as they are, speculates both in currencies and takeovers, since that is what is allowed. "My defense is that I operate within the rules," Soros has written. "If there is a breakdown in the rules, that is not my fault as a lawful participant but the fault of those who set the rules." Soros chose not to downplay his triumph in England but rather to publicize his success in order to draw more attention to himself and his ideas. It was, he had decided, his lack of a larger platform that had frustrated his proposals for the future of Europe. So from 1992 on, a deluge of articles on Soros appeared, most with the willing participation of the subject. He developed a PR operation, which distributed bound copies of his speeches, and put out a newsletter describing the doings of the foundations. This fomented some revival of interest in his books *The Alchemy of Finance* (1987), *Opening the Soviet System* (1990), and *Underwriting Democracy* (1991). In due course he wrote a fourth book, *Soros on Soros: Staying Ahead of the Curve* (1995),* and a fifth, *The Crisis of Global Capitalism* (1998). These later works are of interest, but are not important for understanding his investment technique, so I will not dwell on them here.

Critics

Not all critics take Soros the politico-economic philosopher as seriously as might be hoped. *The Economist*, for instance, observed of his last

---

* One of the few book covers on which the author's name appears three times.

work, "These remarkable distinctions do not satisfy him. He craves recognition as a great thinker. . . . None of this alters the fact that his books are no good." As to his proposal on how to prevent global collapse, the magazine asks, "Is this a joke?"

Starting on page 156 of *The Crisis of Global Capitalism,* Soros devotes ten quite interesting pages to his attempt to be useful in the ruble crisis of August 1998. Again he calls it a "Real-Time Experiment," but this time there is no investment action. It describes his telephone calls to influential persons in Washington and Moscow, and his letter to the *Financial Times* suggesting a "modest devaluation of 15 to 25 percent," followed by the introduction of a currency board. The financial markets noticed the devaluation recommendation. Soros's concern was justified: In the event, the ruble was allowed to collapse, and there were serious repercussions in the developing markets worldwide, quite aside from the misery in Russia itself.

Jeffrey A. Frankel of the Brookings Institution and the President's Council of Economic Advisers wrote in *Foreign Affairs* of Soros's quite public and generally misunderstood efforts to stabilize Russia: "To his horror, he has precipitated the very crisis he set out to prevent. . . . His funds reportedly lost $2 billion in Russia in August. . . . One only wishes he had recorded in the book the conversation with the fund manager following the Russian default."

Ever since he hammered the pound in 1992 (not alone—banks and institutional investors were on the same side), Soros has attracted criticisms of the casino aspect of his activities in the international currency market. Many central banks are afraid of being overwhelmed by speculators if flaws in their economic policies are exposed. Prime Minister Mahathir Mohamad of Malaysia, facing excessive eternal debt and budget deficits, devalued the currency, as, in the summer of 1997, did Thailand, Indonesia, and the Philippines. Mohamad singled out Soros as a villain and hinted at his involvement in a Jewish conspiracy. (The same charge has been leveled by nationalists in Eastern Europe who resent his influence.) However, while Soros had indeed been shorting the Malaysian ringgit in the spring, he had reversed himself, guessing that it would not collapse like the Thai baht, and repurchased his position—at that point, in effect, supporting the currency.

Ironically, Malaysia's own central bank was on the opposite side from Soros in the British pound gamble of 1992, wrongly betting that it could hold its own in the ERM. That flutter cost the bank almost $4 billion—more than its capital. (Malaysia's government has wisely barred it from further currency speculation!)

There have also been many attacks upon Soros's foundations. In China, one of his staff members was arrested on a spying charge, which led to the closing of the foundation there. Some Russian newspapers claimed in 1995 that Soros's foundation was a front for the CIA, as they claim of many American endeavors there. In Hungary his foundation has been accused of a left-wing bias. In Albania, Kyrgyzstan, Serbia, and Croatia the employees have been assaulted and threatened with fines or imprisonment. The deplorable president of Belarus simply seized the bank account of the local Soros foundation and announced a multimillion-dollar fine for supposed tax violations.

These vexations increase his merit, to my mind. Difficult undertakings are more worthy than easy ones. And from time to time, he has embarrassed the Western world into action, as he did with his sudden proposal to provide $50 million for humanitarian aid to Bosnia, and his plan to commit another $500 million to Russia. On that occasion he observed that most Western governments had lagged behind him in their support. His backing for education in newly independent Europe has been particularly beneficial.*

Soros has also developed a philanthropic presence in the United States. When President Clinton signed the welfare reform bill, Soros felt that aliens were being short-changed, and he created the $50 million Emma Lazarus Fund. After the difficult death of his father, Soros was affected by the comfort his mother received in her final hours in the family home. Most Americans die badly, since the health establishment regards the dying person as a failure and wants to shove him out of sight. He created a Project on Death in America and committed $20 million to it. He has created a drug policy reform center to examine the issues of decriminalization of marijuana and providing clean needles for drug users. He holds that drug abuse should be handled as a public health problem. "No politician can speak about such things," says Soros. "It is like the third rail—instant electrocution." His financial power gives Soros that liberty.

. "Rockefeller established his foundation when he was accused of making monopoly profits," Soros has said. "He hoped to improve his

---

*To declare an interest, I should note that I am a trustee of the American University in Bulgaria, an admirable institution to which Soros has made a much-valued contribution.

public image with his foundation. Many large firms have set up foundations for similar reasons. It was different in my case. . . ."* In fact, though, Rockefeller's philanthropy began very early. To quote from my own review in the *New York Observer* of Chernow's *Titan*, "From the first he [Rockefeller] gave generously to charity, even when he had very little money himself. At twenty, he gave away more than 10 percent of his income, including a gift to a black man in Cincinnati to buy his wife out of slavery. When he joined the Erie Street Baptist Mission Church in Cleveland, he helped sweep out the halls . . . and wash the windows."

Conclusions

Soros is unique among our subjects in having first created a substantial fortune for himself and then put it to work in a way that in a small degree changed our world for the good. It is not yet clear that he can establish a permanent operation to run his fund complex, though. His writings are of uncertain value and contain understandable elements of self-justification. While his philanthropies deserve great credit, one must remember that he is giving back to Paul what he extracted from Peter—Peter being the people on the wrong side of his winning bets. Unlike a manufacturer or a farmer or an artist who creates new value, the speculator moves existing wealth around. Still, very few successful speculators do that as usefully as has Soros. On balance, he is a great figure.

Soros on Soros.

Thirteen

PHILIP CARRET
THINK SMALL

I VISITED PHILIP CARRET (PRONOUNCED "CARRAY") IN AN OLD art-deco office building on New York's Forty-second Street, just across from the south entrance of Grand Central Station. On the front of his desk stood a sign saying "A cluttered desk is a sign of genius." "Look at this!" he said, grinning fondly. "My wife gave it to me." The desks of all investment managers (as distinct from investment administrators) are covered by dunes of paper, from which they always hope to absorb facts and still more facts, until an incoming tide of new papers washes over them.

Another large sign on the wall quotes Shakespeare: "The first thing we do, let's kill all the lawyers. . . ." Carret, nevertheless, is the son of a Boston real estate lawyer—what used to be called a conveyancer. "My first Harvard ancestor was the Reverend Daniel Gookin in 1669," he announced with satisfaction. I told him that my father and grandfather had also been lawyers, both born in Boston, and that my great-grandfather, a clergyman, had been in the class of 1805. Carret manifestly felt that this was a seemly ordering of things.

"Did you go to the Harvard-Yale game this year?" he asked in his slight New England twang. I said I hadn't. "Very interesting game: fourteen to ten. I was on the thirty-yard line . . . almost froze to death. I'll bet I was the only one in the Yale Bowl who was there when it was christened, at the Harvard-Yale game of 1913. That was another very interesting game: Harvard won thirty-six to nothing."

Carret must be the most experienced investment man around: Having entered the field in the early 1920s, he can boast three-quarters of a century's immersion in the hurly-burly of the market. At ninety, he still arrived at his office early every morning, and he seemed perfectly unimpaired in faculties.* He has a large, generous face with deep lines. He chuckles often and radiates benevolence.

Carret started the Pioneer Fund in May 1928. It had about twenty-five stockholders: members of his family and a few friends. He ran it for over half a century, until he retired as its manager. During that fifty-five-year period, Pioneer's compound annual total return was 13 percent. (Fifteen percent if you start at the Depression bottom.) That means that an original shareholder who had put in $10,000 and reinvested all his income would have been able to withdraw over $8 million when Carret left. (He would have been jarred by a 50 percent drop in the early 1930s.) Thirteen percent is not a remarkable performance figure today, but it meant a great deal when inflation was low or even negative, in the Depression. In any event, the lesson is that over long periods compound interest works miracles.

"Nobody can be expected to pinpoint a depression," said Carret. "When I was in my first job at Blyth & Company, Dr. Wesley C. Mitchell, a professor of economics at Columbia, who invented the term 'business cycle,' came to lunch. Two partners asked him about his opinion of the outlook for the economy. Dr. Mitchell may have been annoyed at being asked for free advice, which he would have been glad to receive a fee for giving, but anyway he answered that he had been working on a book and hadn't had time to think about the economy overall. That was exactly one month before the Crash!"

I mentioned that the Harvard Economic Society announced in 1929 that there was no chance of a repetition of the economic downturn of 1920–21. "The Harvard Economic Society never should have been started," said Carret. "It was an embarrassment to the university. In 1929, just after Thanksgiving, it held a meeting in Boston. A friend of mine had a cup of coffee with Colonel Leonard P. Ayres of the Cleveland Trust, who was regarded as the number one business economist in the country, and Jimmy Hughes, one of the great students of the stock market. Everybody agreed that the Crash had only 'blown the froth off the boom' and wouldn't affect their or anybody's lifestyle. Here were some very brilliant individuals, as well informed as anybody could be, who, all the same, were absolutely

---

*At the age of a hundred he cut down to three days a week.

wrong."* "So instinct is the best guide?" I asked. "Instinct—the sub-
conscious—is much more reliable than statistics.† One should follow
one's own convictions," he replied.

"In a business, debt is quite reasonable. *But margin debt—stock market
debt—is terribly dangerous, because it's so easy to get.* You can just pick up the
telephone and generate debt in the stock market. A businessman has
to go to his banker and explain everything: what his assets are, where
his cash flow comes from, how the business works, what he wants the
money for, and how the loan he wants will generate the cash to repay
the bank."

I explained that in studying the careers and methods of great
investors, increasingly I had come to the conclusion that they often
actually invented a way of investing, or at least revived one: thus
T. Rowe Price, who exploited the idea of stocks with perennially rising
earnings; thus Benjamin Graham, who reduced the investment art to
a quasi-science with a series of formulas that worked for fifty years,
until they became too popular; and thus Templeton, who made the
whole world his investment backyard. Could Carret identify his own
contribution?

"I like over-the-counter stocks. And yet I'm more conservative than most
people. Most people think that 'conservative' means General Motors,
IBM, et cetera. But I've always been in offbeat stuff. They're less subject to manipulation than New York Stock Exchange companies, and
are less affected by crowd psychology. For instance, I remember the
popularity of Winnebago, Coachman Industries, and all the other 'rec
vehicle' outfits. To justify their peak prices you would have needed to
have half the population abandon their houses and ride around continuously. I avoid fads like the plague. When I invest, I gamble with a certain amount of my capital, buying dogs. The usual way I lose is by
buying concept stocks. They rarely work."

He continued, "Ralph Coleman had a fund called the Over-the-
Counter Securities Fund. It had about three hundred stocks in it.

---

*In 1929, the society announced, *after* the Crash, that "a severe depression like that
of 1920–21 is outside the range of possibility. We are not facing protracted liquidation of inventories, worldwide demoralization in commodity markets, and rising
money rates." Later that year, the society proclaimed that "the easing of money is
itself evidence of the soundness of the present business situation."
†Freud correctly urges us to be rational about minor decisions, but to follow our deep-
est instincts about the great ones.

When one of them got listed, he would sell it. The fund did extremely well. In my own managed portfolios, I have about half of the equity money in over-the-counter stocks."

I asked Carret if he could prove that over-the-counter stocks were an inherently better value than listed stocks. "No," said Carret. "All sorts of junk is sold over the counter, but also some crown jewels. Berkshire Hathaway, for instance"—which later got a New York Stock Exchange listing. He said he knew Warren Buffett, who runs it.* "He's a friend of mine. He's smarter than I am. He proved that in General Foods. It was a stodgy company, mostly coffee. When Berkshire Hathaway bought the stock, I said to myself, 'Well, Warren's made a mistake this time.' It was about $60 when I noticed the transaction. In a matter of months it went to $120 . . . ha, ha!" (Carret has a deep, throaty chuckle when he tells stories of this sort. He particularly enjoys tales describing common opinions that are completely mistaken.)

For that matter, Carret is in a way an older version of Warren Buffett. They are quite similar in appearance: round-headed men with wide grins. Both have a completely contrarian mentality: They seek what nobody wants. When Buffett was still a "value" investor, both liked dull stocks, such as waterworks or bridge companies, and did not mind if they sat dead in the water for long periods. Especially, both have the patient temperament of the successful value investor. They exchanged ideas regularly for many years.

"For instance, one of my favorite stocks is Magma Power. I've had it in the family for years. Magma has a great advantage, which is that under California law a neighboring utility is obliged to buy any power Magma generates at the highest 'avoided cost.' So it has an absolutely guaranteed market. That's a pretty good thing to have in a depression. It's not what everybody would call a conservative holding. They might never have heard of it. But to me it's very conservative."

Since one of my own rules is that, when appropriate, we should examine the actual physical facilities of a company we are interested in, I asked Carret if he had been to see Magma. He said he had. "The original property was north of San Francisco—'The Geysers.' It's fascinating to approach it. You can see the steam coming out of the ground."

---

*Buffett has said of Carret: "He should be studied by every investor." He has also called Carret "a man who knows an extraordinary amount about business itself as well as the markets. If there ever was a hall of fame for investment advisers, he'd be among the first ten in it."

He continued, "I'm a collector of odd little outfits. I have a few shares of something called Natural Bridge Company of Virginia. The highway goes right over the Natural Bridge, so if you want to see the bridge itself you have to go down into the valley, from where you can look up at it. The company owns the land under the bridge. They have a restaurant and a motel. People go and stay for a day or two. Someday the state of Virginia will have a profligate administration that will buy the company for more than its market price. In the meantime, I don't mind waiting."

Carret likes to see growth of earnings but adds that "if a company has increased earnings for fifteen years, it is probably just about to have a bad year.

"I do like very good balance sheets. I get floods of annual reports. I look at them all, at least briefly. *If I see that the equity ratio is low, or the current ratio is low, I don't go any further. I want no term debt, and a better than two-to-one current ratio.* If it's a utility, I want reasonable financial ratios, a good territory, and a favorable regulatory climate.

"Another important criterion for me is that I always want to see management own a significant amount of stock. Once I had some correspondence with the chairman of National Gypsum. I noticed that the president only had five hundred shares, so I wrote the chairman. I was flabbergasted by his reply: 'How much stock Mr. Brown owns is his business and nobody else's.'" I don't agree with that at all. It may have been true before the SEC required making the officers' and directors' shareholdings available to everybody, but it certainly isn't true today. An officer should have at least a year's salary invested in the business. If he doesn't have that much faith in the company, he shouldn't be a key executive of it. If they don't own a lot of stock why should I own any?" asks Carret, adding that he always looks for large insider shareholdings in proxy statements.

That, I observed, seemed like a perennial principle of good business. Had Carret found that business principles had changed during his life?

"No: Business principles are just that, principles. One deviates from sound principles at his peril. Some people are smart enough to do it— to dart in and out, for instance—but they are few and far between. I saw a study that set forth the average life of a margin-account trader. It turned out to be two to three years. One customer had lasted for thirteen years before he lost all his money, but he'd started with several million."

Carret's Principles

Here are Carret's twelve investment precepts:*

1. Never hold fewer than ten different securities covering five different fields of business.
2. At least once in six months reappraise every security held.
3. Keep at least half the total fund in income-producing securities.
4. Consider yield the least important factor in analyzing any stock.
5. Be quick to take losses, reluctant to take profits.
6. Never put more than 25 percent of a given fund into securities about which detailed information is not readily and regularly available.
7. Avoid "inside information" as you would the plague.
8. Seek facts diligently; advice never.
9. Ignore mechanical formulas for valuing securities.
10. When stocks are high, money rates rising, and business prosperous, at least half a given fund should be placed in short-term bonds.
11. Borrow money sparingly and only when stocks are low, money rates low or falling, and business depressed.
12. Set aside a moderate proportion of available funds for the purchase of long-term options on stocks of promising companies whenever available.

Did Carret always get to know management personally? "It's desirable. But there are only so many hours in the day and so many days in the year. I have too many stocks to know everybody concerned. I might say that *I'm always turned off by an overly optimistic letter from the president in the annual report.* If his letter is mildly pessimistic, to me that's a good sign. I like a point I once heard made by a corporate chief executive, that he was less interested in hearing good news from subordinates than bad news. The good news takes care of itself. 'If I get the bad news early,' he said, 'I can do something about it.' Norman Vincent Peale once met a man who said that he was tormented by problems: problems, problems, problems. Peale replied that he had just come from a place where there were sixty thousand people with no problems. The man was excited: 'I'd like to be there!' 'I don't think you would,' Peale answered. 'It's called Woodlawn Cemetery.'"

---

*From *The Art of Speculation* (New York: *Barron's* Revised Edition, 1930; Burlington, Vermont: Fraser Publishing Company, 1979).

"Doctors usually make poor investors," said Carret. I asked him why. "A doctor has to be as close as possible to infallible with his patients. He can't be right two-thirds of the time. If he were only right that often, he ought to be thrown out of the profession. But in investing, it's fine to be right two-thirds of the time. So when doctors start to invest and discover how things really are, they get nervous and bothered." When *his* stocks go down, on the contrary, Carret remains completely unruffled.

He invests partially on the basis of fundamentals. In 1939, for instance, raw sugar sold for less than a cent a pound. Then came the war. Carret knew that in wartime the price of sugar always rises. He sought out a Cuban sugar company and bought stock at $1.75, a lot more at $7 to $8. He sold most of it at $60, and the last little bit at $200.

Carret viewed every total eclipse for many years, and went to any lengths, including one trip up the Amazon, to see one. But other than this distraction, which does not take much time, he admits to no outside interests or hobbies.

"Every individual human being is unique," says Carret, smiling. "I guess I'm more unique than most."

A person of evident frankness and honesty, Carret does not hesitate to express and act on his opinions, which are often strongly held. Some people do not care for this traditional New England downright manner; others find it praiseworthy. A friend described him as being at peace with himself: a strong, solid character, with no inner misgivings.

He was born in Lynn, Massachusetts, ten miles north of Boston. His family moved to Lexington, where he attended high school, and later to Cambridge. He attended Harvard College (Class of '17) and had a year of business school. On being discharged as an Army aviator in 1919, he went to work for a little firm in Boston, long since defunct, at $15 a week. After five months he got a raise to $20. Feeling that so small an advance was insulting, he quit. He then decided to wander around the United States and by November of 1920 found a job selling bonds in Seattle, where he met his future wife, Elisabeth Osgood. She had done social work in New York but, suffering like Carret himself from a certain wanderlust, had gone to Seattle and continued in social work.

Elisabeth was a perfect wife, according to her husband. "I used to tell her that she was 99.99 percent perfect, but actually I think she was 100 percent perfect," he says. A graduate of Wellesley, she became president of her alumnae class. She was also active in their church in Scarsdale. When the Carrets' daughter was eight years old, she was asked in school what she would like to be when she grew up. "A peaceful woman, like my mother," she replied.

They returned together to Boston, and he rejoined his old firm—in sales. He quit all over again after four or five months, since he didn't like selling, and joined *Barron's*. He stayed until 1927, when he decided to come to New York "to make my fortune." He joined Blyth & Company, and he and Elisabeth rented a house in Scarsdale. In due course they bought it, and lived there for the next forty-nine years. In 1975, their children being grown, they moved into a cooperative apartment in Scarsdale.

When Blyth let Carret go in 1932, during the Depression, Carret hung out his own shingle—the best thing that ever happened to him, he now thinks, although he didn't like it at the time. At the outset he had two partners: one was his own former assistant at Blyth, the other was a salesman. His salesman-partner brought along a clientele, but, as Carret says, "the rest of us rang doorbells, literally." Carret obtained the stockholders' list of Amerada, which he considered the best of the oil companies. He reasoned that the shareholders of Amerada would be persons of good judgment who would understand what he had to say. He started down the list of shareholders, beginning with *A*, and called on those within a few blocks of his office at 120 Broadway. He came fairly soon to a shareholder whose name started with *B*, with whom he struck up a cordial relationship. He became a customer, and they remained friends for many years.

The Money Mind

Carret has a name for what he says is the particular mentality of the keen investor: the money mind. To illustrate, he cites a story. "Years ago, New York went through one of its periodic droughts. You had to ask for a glass of water in a restaurant." Then one day Carret remembered an area in Queens he had learned about, where the city collected its water charges on the basis not of consumption but of the front footage of each residence. He reflected that the city would eventually have to install water meters there, so that a distinction could be made between households that consumed a lot of water—doubtless wasting a good deal of it—and those that consumed less. He studied the subject and found that the likely candidate for the business would be Neptune

Meter. He looked up the company and saw that one of the directors, an officer of Bankers Trust, held two thousand shares—an encouraging sign. The company's figures were favorable. So Carret bought the stock for his clients and over the years was well rewarded.

"The money mind," he says, "is just a quirk, like the mathematical mind." Apropos of that, he described a friend of his who at church, instead of listening to sermons, would let his thoughts wander over the numbers of the hymns that were posted where the congregation could see them. He could not prevent himself from playing arithmetical games with these numbers and eventually had to plead with the minister to take them down, so that he could concentrate on the sermon.

I mentioned a story in G. H. Hardy's book on the Indian mathematical genius Srinivasa Ramanujan. Hardy was visiting Ramanujan in the hospital and mentioned that he had arrived in a cab numbered 1729 . . . a dull number. Ramanujan instantly expostulated, "No, Hardy, it is a very interesting number! It is the smallest number expressible as the sum of two cubes in two different ways."* It's hard for the layman to conceive of a brilliant mathematical—or investment—mind.

Looking at his desk, which had three or four inches of annual reports, letters, and papers on it, I said it certainly conveyed an impression of industry.

"I'm not sure that desk has ever actually been bare," said Carret. "When I was back at Blyth, the department I was in was called Economic Research. They discontinued Economic Research when they fired me. They didn't need their furniture, so I was able to buy the desk for a dollar. It's served me very well for sixty years."

---

*12^3 plus 1^3 and 10^3 plus 9^3.

Fourteen

MICHAEL STEINHARDT
STRATEGIC TRADER

MICHAEL STEINHARDT HAD ONE OF THE GREATEST TWENTY-year runs in investment history. If you'd put $10,000 into his hedge fund, Steinhardt Partners, at its inception in July 1967, twenty years later you would have had over $1 million, thanks to its annual compound growth rate, net of his own fees, of 27 percent. How did he do it?

One answer is that Steinhardt paid tens of millions of dollars a year in commissions to Wall Street brokers. That kind of money can buy masses of research, if that's what you want: hundred-page analyses of companies, economic projections, studies of the outlook for foreign countries. In fact, though, heavy Wall Street research is one thing that Michael Steinhardt had almost no interest in. If you look around his office you see scarcely a scrap of paper. So what did the millions buy? The answer is, a little edge in each of innumerable profit-making transactions.

Thanks to his commission dollars, he gets* incessant calls that suggest profitable trades. "We're lowering our estimate on General Electric's earnings next quarter!" "The Citi is putting Brazil on a cash basis!" Some Wall Street houses have so much influence that when they change an opinion they can move the market by themselves. Steinhardt wants to get the "first call" when the key analyst of such a firm changes his mind. Not because the analyst is necessarily right; rather, because the people he calls after Steinhardt will *think* he'll be right. So if you read in the papers that some wizard believes that prospects are improving for Texas Instruments, don't be surprised if the stock has

---

*I use the present tense, even though he eventually wound up Steinhardt Partners.

already moved up: Steinhardt (and the other Steinhardts) probably got the word first.

On the other hand, these small gains alone do not explain his overwhelming success. He has gained more from betting on "directional moves." As he says, "If we get involved in bonds, it's because we expect interest rates to go in a certain direction. . . . I look first at the big picture of where the market is going and then try to find stocks to fit a portfolio that reflects my generalized view of things. That contrasts with focusing first on companies that have terrific value regardless of the market." Steinhardt could thus be called a strategic trader. First, he forms large and general conceptions like those that we all derive from reading the papers. Having them, he looks for the specific.

From the broker's standpoint, a great advantage in dealing with Steinhardt is that he will give you an immediate yes if he trusts you, without referring the idea to a committee or waiting to think about it. For one urgent telephone call, you can get a 100,000-share order. For that, you give your very best attention! Steinhardt could also help a broker by purchasing an unusually large position in some stock he's interested in if the broker is stuck with it . . . at a price concession, to be sure. In return, if Steinhardt gets a piece of news that he thinks will knock a stock down, he may be able to twist a broker's arm to take it off his hands before the word gets out widely.

For Steinhardt, as for a racetrack bettor, the short term, the here and now, is reality. The long term, and Wall Street research that tells you about the long term, is for him the hereafter—a world of dreams. As a trader, Steinhardt feels much more comfortable carving out little gains—5 percent, 10 percent, 15 percent—over and over again, than he would buying a stock and salting it away to await distant events that, as far as he is concerned, may never materialize. In 1983, for example, he bought IBM at $117. The stock had a modest move, advancing 15 points. Most investors would look in the paper, note the advance, give a little grunt, and leave it at that. Then the stock dropped back to $120, giving up most of its gain. Oh, well! The difference is that Steinhardt had *borrowed $100 million* to buy his stock at $117, and sold out at approximately $132—making over $10 million! Then, to top it off, he went *short*, covering as the price dropped back toward $120: more millions.

"I do an enormous amount of trading," says Steinhardt, who would whirl his portfolio around every month or two in a good year, "not necessarily just for the profit, but also because it opens up other opportunities. I get a chance to smell a lot of things. Trading is a catalyst. How I envy the multiyear, long-term investor who fixes on a distant objective and can just wait and wait! No successful investor in the history of the universe can have had fewer doubles and triples than me. I'm always just making small moves. But still, most of the money I make is in holdings that I keep for more than a year." That is also about the length of time Steinhardt allows for his "directional" bets, which can be somewhat longer-term than the bulk of his trading.

Steinhardt is also prepared to speculate temporarily on the direction of the general market. He would go long on leverage, and, on occasion, move to a net short position. "I have five or six security analysts, three to four traders, and one economist. They look for what sectors of the economy are going to undergo important changes. What I hope that I can find using the economist's ideas is the difference between the consensus perception and a variant perception."

In 1981, he became convinced that medium-term Treasury notes would have a big move. Steinhardt's economist-partner, George Henry, who had previously been a Federal Reserve Bank official, agreed that interest rates, then in the 14 percent area, had to decline. So Steinhardt invested $50 million of his fund's cash and borrowed $200 million more to buy $250 million worth of five-year U.S. Treasury Bonds. Then he had to endure an agonizing wait for rates to drop, during which, at one point, the fund sank by $10 million. He lost some clients in that period, but eventually the gamble paid off: On his bond investment of $250 million, of which the fund had put up only $50 million in equity, he made a profit of $40 million. Steinhardt Partners was able to post a 10 percent gain in fiscal 1981, compared with a decline of 3.4 percent for the S&P 500. The following year, his leveraged investment in intermediate government paper pulled the partnership up to a gain of 97 percent.

Three years later, Steinhardt took a $400 million position, largely with borrowed money, in intermediate government bonds, again betting that interest rates would decline. And once more the bet was spectacularly successful. Rates were then near their record high: The prime was around 15 percent, and longer rates were about 13 percent. In July 1985, he let the bonds go, for a $25 million profit.

Steinhardt's command post is a big wooden console shaped like a ship's bow, full of screens, buttons, and blinking lights. He feels that he isn't being paid to wear a particular uniform, so a typical getup might be a black shirt open at the neck, with dark trousers. He is plump; his round, mustached head with a thinning cover rises like a seal's from a cylindrical abdomen. In repose, he has a soft, husky voice and an amiable, gentle manner. He talks in a clever and literate way, closer to one's image of a book editor than of a Wall Street trader.

Like most great investors, Steinhardt started poor. He was born in Brooklyn, the son of a jeweler. Steinhardt's parents were divorced when he was a year old. For his bar mitzvah, instead of cash, his father gave him a hundred shares of Penn Dixie Cement and a hundred shares of Columbia Gas System. He took to studying brokers' reports and following the prices of his stocks in the *World Telegram*. He started frequenting a Merrill Lynch office, with "the old men smoking their cigars and watching the tape. It became a fascination for me." Soon he himself was buying and selling.

An exceptional IQ let him finish high school at sixteen. Then came the University of Pennsylvania's Wharton School of Finance, from which he graduated at nineteen. He had no doubts as to his choice of career and in 1960 went to work doing research for the Calvin Bullock mutual fund organization. He was not a success. He then served in the U.S. Army Reserves, before a stint writing for *Financial World*. He was bored answering subscriber queries like "What is your view of General Motors?" and in due course was fired. "It was awful," he says. "I thought my career on Wall Street was over."

Next, Steinhardt worked as a research analyst at Loeb, Rhoades, where he became known as a top special-situations analyst. He also began exchanging information with another researcher, Howard Berkowitz, at A. G. Becker, who introduced Steinhardt to a fraternity brother, Jerrold Fine, then managing the partners' capital at Dominick & Dominick. All three had attended the Wharton School at the same time. On July 10, 1967, Steinhardt, Fine, and Berkowitz opened its doors, with an initial capital of about $7.7 million. The firm scored a 30 percent gain in its first year and 84 percent in its second, compared with 6.5 percent and 9.3 percent for the S&P 500. They were off to the races.

"It was a euphoric period," Steinhardt recalls. By the end of fiscal 1969, the firm had almost $30 million in capital, making all three of its under-thirty founders millionaires.

Steinhardt was chief trader, while Fine and Berkowitz concentrated on research. The firm added staff in the 1970s. The pace was always frenetic. It meant "not going to lunch, and making trades that involved fourteen conversations," says Steinhardt. The decade of intense, almost monomaniacal dedication to investing left Steinhardt feeling that his outlook was too narrow. He yearned for a break.

"I've always focused on the question of purpose. Am I doing the best for my family? What are we doing in the world? Is this the best thing to do in this life?" Puzzled by such questions, and exhausted by ten years in the investment business, Steinhardt took a sabbatical in 1978. He left $4 million of his $6 million net worth in the care of Steinhardt Partners, which at that time was running $110 million, and retired. As he said, he was smoking too much, was overweight (at 210 pounds), and felt that he "had quit for good. I didn't want to come back." Few of his circle, knowing his obsessive dedication to his work, believed he could keep away.

He did not get in touch with the office. Nor, he claims, did he keep up with newspapers or the stock market. He spent more time with his family in their Fifth Avenue duplex overlooking Central Park and their comfortable retreat in Mount Kisco, north of New York City. There he grew raspberries, made jam, took piano and tennis lessons, read the Old Testament with a rabbi, studied horticulture and yoga, tried jogging and gave it up, and restored a house. He also visited Israel several times.

He thought it would be useful to engage in a business activity in Israel, which at the time had an abominable environment for enterprise—high inflation, a grossly excessive and meddlesome bureaucracy, and a wily business mentality. So, with an Israeli partner he started a real estate and construction business in the so-called development towns. He was defeated by Israel's wretched business atmosphere, but he didn't give up completely. He bought an interest in the country's largest box manufacturer and introduced Merrill Lynch to Israel. After a year of "sabbatical," though, he returned to "this glorious business of ours." The problem was that he could not find any other occupation that was uplifting and rewarding. "I was trying to learn to deal with my life without the discipline imposed by a career," he says. "The sabbatical allowed me to come back and do largely the same thing that I had done before, but with a broader perspective and fewer questions about the purpose of my work." In any event, it was no longer money that kept him on the job.

His partner Fine left in 1976 to start his own private investment partnership, and Berkowitz followed in 1979. Thereafter, Steinhardt managed the firm alone.

The Mount Kisco mini-estate where Steinhardt and his wife, Judy, spend weekends includes an artificial pond, a tennis court, and a swimming pool. On one of the days we talked, Steinhardt was wearing a blue sweatsuit with blue-and-gray Nike sneakers and white socks. The architecture is contemporary throughout. Two horses browsed in a new paddock. There is a modern house for the caretaker and a cottage originally built as a cabana for the pool, where guests would change their clothes for swimming. They rarely used it for its original purpose, so Steinhardt converted the cottage into an office for himself. It now contains computers, telephones, and a fax machine. Sometimes Steinhardt would announce that he was taking a day off and invite friends to stop by. Invariably, however, he would remain in the cabana-office, glued to his computer screens and telephones, without returning to the house even for a moment to see his guests.

He is fascinated by the Holocaust and has read many books on the subject. Keenly interested in the history of the Jewish people, he has visited Israel dozens of times and has business interests there. He observes that his attachment to the place is for him a substitute for adherence to its religion. He has a ladder of values, he says, in which money management, where he is now, is by no means the top rung. He likes to think that he might someday be able to take the next step up. I asked him how he proposed to save the next generation from the perils of excessive wealth. Steinhardt thought a moment, and then said that he hoped to accomplish this by transmitting the traditional values of his people—not his religion, but his *people*—to his children.

Trading Techniques

When he thinks about a market, Steinhardt asks himself, *"What will change?"*

"I have no positions in my partnerships that I don't understand myself," Steinhardt has said. "If the analyst comes in and makes a case, I'll study it for five minutes and then do it. He'll have a story about better quarterly earnings, a management change, or whatever. I tend to manage passively—giving a good deal of latitude to the analysts whose ideas are working out. But if things *aren't* working out, I go over the story again and again. My principal role is general guidance, determining our overall exposure, and deciding what level of risk we can accept."

A *Wall Street Journal* article quoted some of his former employees: "It's a productive experience. It's just incredibly painful while you're there." Steinhardt "watches every stock you own like a hawk," the analyst added. "He wants answers. He won't let you slide by without answering his questions about each stock. It's a good way to run money. It's just a little too intense for some people." You wouldn't guess this talking to him privately. He has a smiling, amiable, pleasantly subtle manner.

"I see my rôle," Steinhardt says, "as trying to achieve the best possible return on capital, using the full range of techniques that will allow me to attain that goal, without commitment to any particular style. Every day I ask myself where the risk-reward ratio seems right. Our first concern is long-term investment positions. Second, new issues, when they are attractive: We demand and receive large allotments. Third, we lend stocks to brokers to cover short sales, on which we demand the maximum interest. The brokers used to keep all the income, but in recent years one has been able to keep 40 to 90 percent of it. Fourth, we have people doing arbitrage, including buying into bankrupt companies and buying trade claims. Fifth, we avail ourselves of the full range of modern gimmickry: index futures and the rest of it. I have four or five traders who deal with eighty or ninety brokers, in large measure to open doors. I couldn't achieve these results with long-term investing alone."

Wasn't this like the theory of A. W. Jones, I asked—recruit a stable of whizzes, give them their heads, and hang on? (The A. W. Jones partnership crashed and burned in 1974.)

"No," replied Steinhardt. "I devote a great deal of time to market analysis." The original A. W. Jones idea was that he wasn't able to analyze markets, but that he was able to determine relative values, so he could be long the good stocks and short the bad stocks. It didn't work out that way. His managers, who had a piece of Jones's share of capital gains, egged each other on to take more and more aggressive positions. "It's very rare, but I actually have been net short in my funds, to the tune of about 30 to 40 percent of their capital," says Steinhardt.

We talked about notable speculator Robert Wilson. "He doesn't do any research," said Steinhardt, shaking his head in disbelief. "He relies on brokers and reads company reports. He's one of a kind." He plays the images, I observed.

"Most of my long positions are chosen on the basis of their long-term fundamental prospects—not that I necessarily actually do hold them for very long. I often say to my people, *make your choices on a long-term basis, even though what you're betting on probably won't happen.* I figure out how the market will respond to a long-term conception, at least for a minimum period."

Among several stocks in the same category, Steinhardt *greatly prefers to invest in one that has a repurchase program in its own shares.* Such a program gives an additional boost to its upward movement and also gives the investor a better chance to sell when the time comes.

Looking at his portfolio, one found no intellectual or philosophical thread, although in most years two or three holdings made most of the money. By being very active in the market, he is exposed to endless opportunities and focuses on whatever areas of the markets are moving at the time. He is, in a word, eclectic.

"I started as a securities analyst myself—visited managements, studied the relative attractiveness of different industries, and so forth. That was in 1967. People were comfortable thinking in a long-term way. The best minds looked for companies which had the most promising secular growth characteristics. That, of course, led to the 'nifty fifty' heresy: People were willing to pay much too much for stocks that met those criteria. The search was on for baby-blue chips, in mariculture, or whatever, often ending in '-onics.' Everyone was looking for the new concept, the new service. They became insensitive to value, to the price-earnings multiples. The idea was to find the prospect of ten- or fifteen-year compound growth. The entrance fee didn't matter, when justified by projections of extraordinary growth forever. All that led to the debacle of 1973–74.

"Then the emphasis became overwhelmingly short-term, on trading techniques and computerization. We became equally exaggerated in that direction." He correctly predicted that investors would go back to long-term thinking in due course.

"More and more money managers now believe they need a variety of skills: They have to be able to handle Japan, the outlook for gold, fixed-income securities. For instance, suppose the market has a sudden movement. Why? It usually turns out that it's a breakout in a computerized index fund. So you have to understand how those programs work."

The S&P Futures Index

"I'm fascinated with the S&P futures," he has said. "They are a good measure of the essence of the market. There is an arithmetically correct price, called the premium, for an index future: the price that exactly expresses the value you are giving up in not owning the stocks, minus what you are saving by being able to use your capital for something else—the opportunity value. *An excessive premium during the period from 11:00 to 11:15 A.M. is bullish,* since it means that there is a powerful current of optimism out there. *But if the overvaluation of the premium lasts for days and weeks, that is a more and more bearish sign.* The number of programs that are carried out when the premiums are over fair valuation continues to rise, so at the end there are no new bettors left.

"Very few market participants understand the motivation for program trading. The chief one is that tens of billions of dollars in institutional hands have to remain liquid for weeks and months, since the institutions are going to have demands on the money—for working capital, or to pay insurance claims, or whatever. In other words, it's really short-term money. So if a broker offers the institution a higher riskless return over a short period than it could get in cash equivalents, that's attractive.

"Here's how it's done: When the S&P futures premium reaches a certain level, the computer says to sell the future and buy the underlying stocks. One doesn't need to buy all five hundred stocks. It has been figured out that one can do it with fewer than four hundred of them. So you have these sudden, very large-scale trades. It's been simply astonishing how much this technique has added to the business of some of the big firms."

Short Side Tactics

Steinhardt has commented that for most people, himself included, selling short requires a psychological adjustment to overcome the idea that one is against America, motherhood, and apple pie, and instead on the side of evil; also, it is hard to adjust to the idea that on the short side one can have infinite losses, compared with going long, where one can lose only 100 percent of one's own capital.

However, Steinhardt's own investment principle is that *"you never make big money in the market without getting in the way of danger."** He went out on a limb in 1972 by shorting big-name growth stocks or "vestal virgins"—Polaroid, Xerox, Avon Products, and the like—at thirty to

---

*Not necessarily, for a determined bargain-hunting investor. The Benjamin Graham technique minimizes risk.

thirty-five times earnings, and with dismay then watched the same stocks hit forty to forty-five times earnings before they topped out and produced a sharp gain when the market collapsed in 1973. There was also the black January of 1976, when the firm had one of its biggest short positions ever and the market soared. Fortunately, such losses have been the exception. In 1973, Steinhardt sold short over 100,000 shares of Kaufman & Broad, the nation's largest homebuilder, in the high 40s. The Steinhardt group made a bundle when the stock collapsed in response to spiraling interest rates and inflation—first to the low 20s, where the group covered its shorts, and later down to 4.

I asked what sorts of stocks he went short, observing that most good speculators' experience was that one did not make money on the short side, but used the shorts as a balance against a larger long position.

"On the long side, I'm looking for lower-multiple dull stocks, laggards, with a recovery potential. *On the short side, I want to be in the best-known companies in America, the areas of speculative focus. I'm usually short the Who's Who of the market,* stocks in the institutional universe. The stocks I'm short tend to be the reverse of my longs. They're high-multiple, popular stocks with big institutional expectations built into the prices, which I think will be a disappointment. My perennial problem is the difficulty of timing the breakdown of those speculative expectations.

"Financial expectations of a speculative nature are a good thing to be against, but you need the patience to hang in there, to suffer."

Steinhardt goes over his portfolio many times each day. He tends to focus on problems, not on successes. If a stock is acting well that day, relative to the market, fine. If not, he starts asking questions. Something may be wrong. It may be a random movement, but he wants to concentrate on it until he can establish that it is merely random.

Sources

Are there any good brokers? Steinhardt says he gets massive amounts of information on a regular basis, but has virtually never found a brokerage house or subscription service consistently superior over a long period of time. *People whose first interest is in commissions, he observes, are rarely the great stock-pickers. If someone is really great, it will make no sense for him to sell his ideas: The rate of return will be too low.* The less able may find it economically worthwhile. Most brokers "won't even come to bat, or hold an opinion for more than a few days if the tide goes against them," he says.

In his studies at the Wharton School of Finance, a course he found particularly worthwhile was on the philosophy of probability. It made him comfortable dealing with incomplete and inaccurate data. The probability course opened his eyes to a way of dealing with a variety of issues, even program trading; it enabled him to understand how much can be understood. Taking the probability approach to decision-making renders the whole process homogeneous, he says, and allows one to make judgments on matters relating to technology, for instance, while knowing little about the actual technology in question. If there's an important change in that industry he can ask the right questions in order to focus on the issue, perhaps better than someone who really knows all about the subject.

By "homogeneous" he means that different subjects can be handled similarly, such as the impact of a new computer on the other computers in a given market, or translating what he thinks the trade balance is going to look like into a view on inflation and its impact on the bond market—or, indeed, a view on when the Japanese are going to invest in the Dow stocks.

Steinhardt meets annually with a distinguished economist who each year is astounded that the world has not fallen apart since their last meeting. All the statistics—debt compared with savings, debt compared with GNP, debt compared with third-world earnings—are worse than ever. For his part, Steinhardt says. "One cannot help marveling at a system that has coped with so many shocks."

New Factors

"The historic inhibitors of volatility have been muted," Steinhardt has said. "Things like portfolio insurance, program trading, internationalization of markets, and the increasing of institutional investment have all made things worse. Specialists used to make markets, which is their role. Now they only *facilitate* markets."

So what about the stock market in the coming period?

Some time ago he told a Columbia Business School panel that the two main reasons for the rise in the stock market were lower interest rates and the leveraging of America—leveraging the whole industrial base of the country. The result was a supply of stocks sharply reduced through leveraged buyouts and corporate repurchase plans, and, on the demand side, a feeling among corporations that it was cheaper to buy than to build. This phenomenon became a dominant factor in the

American market. As long as it remained intact, neither corporate earnings nor anything else mattered.

The new dominant element is debt. It "will perhaps be the key to the economic future of the Western world," Steinhardt said, adding that debt is being used differently now: "The ethics surrounding debt are different. I doubt if anybody in this room could have imagined six or so years ago that a President with the conservative stripes of Ronald Reagan would have allowed and encouraged deficits and have run deficits for six years, doubling the national debt. The ethics with which he grew up were anathema to that, and yet he did it and it's been an important part of the economic scene. Debt questions related to quality, to the third world, municipal debt, consumer debt, which has grown to extraordinary proportions—all have changed so much as to put a different pattern in our life. The growth in stock prices since 1983 relates more than anything else to a new use of debt."

"There has been an enormous growth of debt in the world," Steinhardt once said, "as compared to earnings or assets or anything else. It amounts to an economic leaning tower that will eventually topple. It cannot be sustained. The debt will eventually be repudiated and turned to equity, resulting in inflation." (This in due course happened in Mexico, Russia, and Thailand among other places.)

Steinhardt rode a tumultuous roller-coaster in the 1990s. The strain contributed to his decision to retire from the market hurly-burly at only fifty-four. Having previously been well known mostly to specialists and Wall Street heavy hitters, in the 1990s he became the subject of dozens of articles.

He had expanded his repertoire of speculative investment techniques, adding currency trading. That complicated life. By May 1990, he was running $1.2 billion, making his hedge fund second in size only to Soros's Quantum Fund. In 1989, he lagged about 10 percent behind the S&P 500, returning just under 21 percent net of fees. Overall, he was 80 percent long and 50 percent short. His long positions included large stakes in Alcoa and Reynolds Metals, hoping for good growth in canning and cars. He held Intel and several oil service companies, such as Mesa and McDermott. As a balance, he shorted what he considered overpriced stocks that were too popular with other money managers: Coca-Cola, McDonald's, Merck, and AT&T.

At the same time he began making substantial purchases of U.S. Treasury notes. Since he ordinarily avoided fixed-income investments, this was an unusual step, but he felt that the slowing economy made it likely that inflation, and thus interest rates, would decline, putting up bond prices. Rates had indeed already started down; it appeared that the trend would continue. And the spread on borrowing money and reinvesting it immediately in Treasury securities was wonderfully alluring. (In November 1991, *Forbes* reported: "The Fed was practically begging the speculators to buy short-term Treasuries when it reduced the discount rate three times and the federal funds rate seven times so far this year. With that clear signal and the limited risk in Treasury notes, leverage did the rest." So in April 1991 Steinhardt invested heavily in two-year Treasury notes, and in May he bought another $6 billion in the when-issued market.

As he explained in his October 10, 1991, client letter: "This was based on our view that the economy was vulnerable and that the federal government would have little alternative other than to reduce short-term interest rates. . . . In early 1991, with the successful conclusion of Operation Desert Storm, there were frequent predictions of a vigorous emergence from the recession. We believed those predictions to be overly optimistic."

Unfortunately, he was losing heavily in his short-side stock positions, as were many of his peers. It was later reported that short-side money had fallen to roughly $1 billion from an estimated high of $4 billion in late 1990. The best-known short-side firm, the Feshbachs, was nearly wiped out: Steinhardt was rumored to have pulled out his stake by the spring of 1992—perhaps 15 percent of their $1 billion.

Fortunately, his Treasury profits more than offset that, so for the year the partnerships were up over 45 percent. His personal take was about $55 million.

The Salomon Crisis

In 1992, Steinhardt was embroiled in the Salomon Brothers Treasury note scandal. Salomon had made fraudulent bids, in the name of customers who had not been consulted, in the spring T-note auctions, hoping to corner the market and drive up prices. Steinhardt fell under investigation for possible collusion, along with George Soros and Julian Robertson. By the time the crisis was over, Salomon had been driven close to bankruptcy, its top management had been flushed out, and many reputations had been tarnished, as described in Chapter 2 on Buffett. The federal investigation dragged on for four years before a settlement was reached: Steinhardt paid over $75 million in fines and restitution.

Meanwhile, he had his hands full with a large investment in Sunbeam-Oster, a major household products company, formerly Allegheny International. Together with fellow fund manager Michael Price, Steinhardt had bought the bankrupt and scandal-ridden company in 1990. By mid-1992, their $125 million stake had risen to $1.2 billion.

During all this, Steinhardt made a huge profit in European bonds, as did many other hedge fund managers. The European currency crisis, along with a rally in U.S. bonds and his Sunbeam-Oster profits, gave his partnership a gain of 50 percent after fees for the year. In December 1992, when he announced he was taking in new money, $600 million was proffered within hours.

As a grace note, so to speak, he added a Picasso drawing to his growing art collection, *Boy with a Lollipop,* bought at Christie's for $986,000.

By 1993, Steinhardt had changed his U.S. bond strategy, having concluded that interest rates could well rise after all, given a strengthening domestic economy. He plunged more deeply into the foreign bond and currency markets. With all the money flowing into his funds, he needed a deep lake to fish in. The currency and foreign bond markets offered the volumes he needed. So he bet billions on Canadian, European, and Japanese bonds, while remaining bullish on the dollar.

By the time it was over, many on Wall Street were calling 1993 the year of the hedge fund managers. Three stood out in particular: Soros, Robertson, and Steinhardt. By January 1994, he had $4.8 billion in assets under management. He had also built up a $30 billion position in European bonds, using borrowed money. There he had some worries: Interest rates had jumped, meaning that bonds fell. Still, he was fairly sure that this amounted to no more than a temporary correction. In fact, though, Federal Reserve chairman Alan Greenspan was determined to put a brake on speculation by cranking up short-term interest rates. A hurricane struck the world bond markets in February and March. The hedge fund fraternity scrambled to cut back. By the time Steinhardt had been able to realign his portfolios they had lost $1 billion. His bet on the U.S. dollar had also gone the wrong way, and in the next quarter he was blackjacked when Canadian short-term rates rose from 4 to 6 percent and his $4 billion Canadian bond portfolio dropped $400 million. At home, he was doing no better. After being net short in the United States for some three years, he began covering his positions just before they would have finally paid off. With chagrin, he wrote investors on April 4, "Ironically, because of the recent portfolio liquidation, we did not benefit from this week's market decline."

By July 1994, Steinhardt was down 30 percent for the year. At the same time, he lost general partner Charles Davidson, who had masterminded the Sunbeam-Oster deal, which by then had earned Steinhardt's fund $500 million. But Davidson felt he could no longer work under such pressure. On July 19, Steinhardt wrote to his limited partners, "This has been, perhaps, my most difficult year." He fired some employees; others quit. At the end of the shakeup he had no right-hand man.

In September, *Forbes* reported that at age fifty-three, Steinhardt seemed to have lost his enthusiasm. His fund was down 32.8 percent in a market that was up 3.8 percent. His assets under management had fallen to $3.25 billion, and he was still oppressed by the Treasury scandal investigation, which seemed eternal. *Forbes* observed, "He has often spoken of how his self-image fluctuates with his performance—a potentially dangerous flaw in a career where taking risks often involves taking losses."

He also had to cope with the difficulties of running a very large fund. He had been down before, but had rebounded quickly. In those days, with only $1 billion-odd under management, he could move in and out of the market more easily. Gilbert de Botton, head of Global Asset Management in London, himself by no means free from error in all things, took this opportunity to sniff at the Steinhardt category of managers new to global investment: "While full-grown men in their own markets, they are boys in the global macro markets."

By the end of 1994, Steinhardt's fund had sunk 33 percent. "I made a vast amount of money in 1993 on the same bet," he told *Time* magazine. "Nevertheless, the pain in 1994 was far greater than the pleasure of 1993."

Still, he learned from his mistakes. He played his international hand more cautiously and staked more on the strength of U.S. equities. By June 1995, he had positioned 25 percent of his $2.5 billion portfolio in such standard U.S. blue chips as Sallie Mae and Chemical Bank. That move worked: The S&P advanced over 20 percent by the summer. The Chemical-Chase merger was perfect, since at the announcement on June 30, his Chemical holding of 2.5 million shares was his third-largest equity position.

"Morire in Gloria," Say the Italians

Nevertheless, in October 1995, Steinhardt announced that he would throw in his hand the following year. He thanked his investors for remaining with him through what he called "greatly varied circumstances." His decision, he declared murkily, was "irrevocable but not irreversible," reminding some of 1978, when he took a sabbatical from investing only to return a year later. This time, however, he really was leaving the game. He was up 18.5 percent for the year when he made the announcement. He had made 30.1 percent compounded for over twenty-eight years before fees, compared to the 10.8 percent annual return on U.S. stocks. After all fees, his investors had made 24.3 percent a year—off a bit from their twenty-year return of 27 percent, but still wonderful.

Steinhardt was certainly quitting while he was ahead. But he had been so buffeted by the financial tempests that many observers concluded that he was simply worn out. The Salomon bond scandal investigation had been humiliating, and managing a massive and extremely complex fund for demanding investors a constant struggle. He may have wanted to leave the global macro game. In any event, his personal fortune stood at $400 million.

Investor Richard Cooper, who had entrusted $500,000 to Steinhardt when he started up in 1967, was quoted in *Time* magazine in October 1995 after he saw his investment grow to $100 million over twenty-eight years as saying, "Thanks to him, I never had a sleepless night. I knew Steinhardt was always there, standing guard. Every investor loves him."

Next Moves

Steinhardt says he will now devote his time and energy to disseminating Jewish values. He is an atheist, so his concern is for secular, not religious, Jewish teachings. "The Jewish generation I'm part of was at the confluence of two great rivers: East European Jewish religious traditions and the openness of secular America," he explains. "That led to an extraordinary explosion of achievement. Just look at the number of Nobel prizes, academics, writers, and successful businessmen it produced. Not only that, this generation gives more philanthropically than any other group. And it has allowed itself to get kicked in the pants by the very minorities it feels so strongly about helping. But the present generation doesn't have the same commitment to Judaism and Jewish values."

He remains politically active, having served as chairman of the board of trustees of the Progressive Policy Institute, an emanation of the Democratic Leadership Council. He was originally a strong Clinton backer, but like many others soured. "He doesn't believe in very much. His promise has been a failed promise."

A patron of the arts, he has also donated several million dollars to the Brooklyn Botanic Garden, of which he became a valued trustee. In addition to his splendid apartment on New York's Fifth Avenue, he owns two uninhabited islands in the Falklands with a total area of 6,500 acres, which he bought for $375,000 in 1994 and may not feel impelled to visit right away, even to view the several rare species of wildlife, including the blackbrowed albatross. His fifty-four-acre estate north of Manhattan has its own zoo, including rheas—flightless South American birds—and capybaras, the world's largest rodents. A blue crane is said to follow him around the premises.

Fifteen

RALPH WANGER
ZEBRAS AND OTHER
SMALL METAPHORS

RALPH WANGER'S ACORN FUND REPORTS DISPENSE LESSONS
in history, psychology, and philosophy, as well as investing. Here is a
sample:

> Zebras have the same problem as institutional portfolio man-
> agers. First, both seek profits. For portfolio managers, above-
> average performance; for zebras, fresh grass.
>
> Secondly, both dislike risk. Portfolio managers can get fired;
> zebras can be eaten by lions.
>
> Third, both move in herds. They look alike, think alike and stick
> close together.
>
> If you are a zebra, and live in a herd, the key decision you have
> to make is where to stand in relation to the rest of the herd. When
> you think that conditions are safe, the outside of the herd is the
> best, for there the grass is fresh, while those in the middle see only
> grass which is half-eaten or trampled down. The aggressive zebras,
> on the outside of the herd, eat much better.
>
> On the other hand—or other hoof—there comes a time when
> lions approach. The outside zebras end up as lion lunch, and the
> skinny zebras in the middle of the pack may eat less well but they
> are still alive.
>
> A portfolio manager for an institution such as a bank trust
> department cannot afford to be an Outside Zebra. For him, the
> optimal strategy is simple: stay in the center of the herd at all
> times. As long as he continues to buy the popular stocks...he

cannot be faulted. To quote one portfolio manager, "It really doesn't matter a lot to me what happens to Johnson & Johnson as long as everyone has it and we all go down together." But on the other hand, he cannot afford to try for large gains on unfamiliar stocks which would leave him open to criticism if the idea fails.

Needless to say, this Inside Zebra philosophy doesn't appeal to us as long-term investors.

We have tried to be Outside Zebras most of the time, and there are plenty of claw marks on us.

So much for stock selection. Here is Wanger on market timing:

This time, the zebras are in a canyon, with the lions asleep at the far wall. Every zebra is going to munch grass right up to the lion's nose, then bolt down the trail just before the lion pounces. Unfortunately, it is a narrow trail, and in fact, the zebras will pile up into a helpless clot at the first narrow point and become instant steak tartare. Many large institutions claim that they can do a "market timing" quick switch from stocks to cash, or cash to stocks, for billion-dollar portfolios in a very illiquid market. No way. Any such strategy can only generate a highly volatile market, featuring lots of short but sizable swings as the chartists whipsaw themselves with bad guesses and high transaction costs.

Wanger even hypothesized a "Metaphor Committee," whose "ruthless and unsleeping members . . . can pounce at any time, crushing an overworked simile, dismembering a mixed metaphor, or deflating an unintelligible aphorism."

The "windfall profits" tax on oil suggested an arresting image:

This is a good example for the Metaphor Committee: the largest tax increase in history, an excise tax on petroleum, by being deceptively named, has lulled the American people into acceptance.* However, the zeal with which our elected representatives are burrowing into this enormous pile of money (roughly $140 billion—it

---

*The Chinese enjoy unique skills in this domain. The old government, fining farmers who didn't produce their quota of opium, called it a "Laziness Tax." When, fleeing the Japanese, the government vanished into the hinterland, this was styled "Long-Term Defense."

was certainly a windfall for them) reminded me of something I had read recently . . . "Ecology of the Dung Beetle." This fascinating article described in detail what happens when an elephant dumps its load on the African plain. Three different kinds of beetles show up in minutes. The little ones burrow into the pile, others bury little pieces on the spot, and the third kind, the big ones, scoop out big balls and roll them away. Once you read this fine article, the Senate Finance Committee will never look the same.

Wanger looks for metaphors in investing in order to grasp the sources of profit and growth in a company, the aims and thinking of the management, the competition and the dangers. "As long as the metaphor remains apt, the stock is a hold; if the reason to own a stock is no longer valid, the stock should be sold," he says.

"Most mutual-fund writers write an economic forecast of some sort which is both boring and wrong," Wanger says sardonically. "I'd rather be lively and wrong."

Wanger is a short man with a round face, which, since he loves little sardonic jokes, often bears a quizzical, humorous expression, although in repose it can be dour. He wears large glasses with thin, dark frames and is balding on top. The first time I met him, many years ago, he sat down in my office wearing a black Greek sailor's cap of the type worn by New Yorkers visiting Maine, which he kept on throughout our talk. He has a very quiet voice, approaching a whisper.

Born in Chicago, Wanger received a B.S. and M.S. in industrial management from the Massachusetts Institute of Technology. Management is not a science, says Wanger; instead, it is based on a knowledge of psychology, common sense, and a good disposition. "The principles of management don't change. You try to get other people to work in the same direction that you are, and you make sure that your direction is a sensible one. And you try to get someone else blamed if you fail!"

After a dismal job with Continental Casualty, now Continental Group, Wanger entered the investment business in 1960 at Chicago-based Harris Associates, which had begun two years earlier. He says he liked investing because the pay was good and "there's no heavy lifting." He worked as a securities analyst and portfolio manager until the firm formed the Acorn Fund. Wanger became portfolio manager, and in February 1977, president.

Wanger married his second wife, Leah Zell, a Harris security analyst, in June 1985. He has three children—Wanger calls them his "old children, i.e., with paychecks"—from his first marriage and two from his second.

Performance

A compound rate of return in the 12 to 15 percent area, Wanger feels, should be a reasonable objective for a good investor. Indeed, to my mind it's not worth it for most people to try hard to beat that figure, since even 12 percent compounded doubles every six years and will eventually make you rich, if you can avoid breaking the flow.

Wanger observes that Fidelity and some other fund management groups have in the past incubated infant funds, starting with modest capital. Hot stocks were fed in to generate an outstanding initial record. If the start-up was good enough, the fund was launched publicly. If not, it was put in the deep freeze or merged. So the records of existing funds sometimes bury less successful components, just as dozens of failed car companies went into General Motors.

Wanger's investing philosophy has two essential components:

1. Look for *good small companies,* which are more attractive investments than big ones.
2. Identify a major trend, then, unlike T. Rowe Price, who looked for the *leaders* in those industries, buy companies that will *benefit* from the trend: "downstream" beneficiaries.

Small Companies

In aggressively seeking smaller companies with superior potential, Wanger capitalizes on the "small firm" phenomenon that University of Chicago professor Rolf Banz documented in 1978. Professor Banz found that companies with low market capitalizations had above-average returns, even after adjusting for their higher risk.

Wanger wants "to buy the stocks of small companies below their economic value, let the companies grow, and resell them as proven successes at full economic value. Individuals often sell small companies below their economic value and buy mature companies at full value, thus providing the other side for our trades."

Even the armies of analysts employed by the large institutions neglect small companies. To provide this large inventory of potential holdings, Wanger collects ideas from a farm team of regional and smaller brokerage houses. He gives out annual awards, called the "Scarlet A" awards, to his best sources. "Most institutional money managers like to say that Wall Street research is useless," he says, "but then they take thirty calls a day from Wall Street."

Trends

"I see real change in people's lifestyles," said Wanger. "Twenty years ago at parties almost everybody had a cigarette in one hand and a martini in the other. The idea of getting up early and jogging would have seemed absurd. Middle age in those days was a safe harbor against such behavior. But we didn't know what was coming next. Had doctors known what the future held, they should have switched from cardiology to sports medicine. Look at me: Here I am, training for a ski race: Nutso!" (He is an avid skier.)

"This profoundly affects how people spend their time and their money. For instance, there are now lots more old people around with bad backs and bad knees—which require treatment and create an economic opportunity for someone."

"For Hillenbrand," I observed. Hillenbrand is a leading American manufacturer of hospital beds and of caskets.

"Hillenbrand gets you sooner or later," said Wanger wistfully. "Really, though, it's just a well-run company. It's like Worthington Industries. If the two of them swapped managements, after six months they'd be doing about the same. Both are below-average businesses run by above-average people. *Often you have businesses that are run by geniuses and don't do very well. The competitors are also geniuses, so nobody gains an advantage.* Take the semiconductor companies. The semiconductor transformed the world, but for years the whole industry probably lost money on balance. Only a tiny handful of companies did well. A far larger number didn't. It's like the oil business: It transformed the world, but many of the companies haven't done too well themselves. Or, indeed, the railroads in the nineteenth century.

"If you had bought all the stocks and all the bond issues put out by all the railroad companies, you would probably have lost money. The capitalization of the American railroads was an international wealth transfer—a Marshall Plan in reverse. It took the savings represented by the English and Scottish trusts and moved the wealth over here. It couldn't have been done more neatly if it had been planned. The net return to all those investors was probably close to zero."*

I pointed out that the theory of the railroads' rights of way had been to bind the country together, losing money on the carrying business if necessary, but offsetting the loss with the land grants that went with the concession.

"The land rights, of course, were where the money was," said Wanger, "not the carrying business. If you had put $1 million into railroads in 1880, you probably broke even. If you had put it into Chicago real estate, however, you would have made an infinite fortune in the next forty years. By 1910, Chicago, stimulated by rail transport, was the fastest-growing city in the world.

"In a transforming industry, the big money is made outside the core business. Going back to transistors, even though the transistor companies as a class didn't do very well, TV broadcasting, cable TV, computers, and data processing have been tremendous businesses."

I suggested that the investment business itself was experiencing a huge transformation because of the computer.

"It certainly is," agreed Wanger. "Index funds, databases: It's scary. Someday you'll be able to go to a computer store and pay $80 for a portfolio manager program. You'll put in everything that's known, and I'll be out of business myself. We're in the middle of a revolution that hasn't stopped revolving.

"There are programs now to automate supervisory processes—running a utility company, for instance. The hands-on manager of a utility plant needs to reset the dials constantly to optimize his results according to conditions, such as changes in the grade of coal the plant is using. Today, an 'expert system' can probably do it better. Aviation's another example: The autopilot can already land the plane in conditions where the pilot can't. Soon the human pilot will be a backup in case the autopilot breaks down.

"Chicago banks used to have substantial security-analysis staffs, and ended up performing consistently worse than the averages. Now they've laid off the big staffs and use computers instead. So they've moved up to achieve average results, and at much lower cost."

---

*As I mention elsewhere, the English got their revenge via Lloyd's.

Rising in the East

A big Wanger investment bet is the *future prosperity of the Pacific Rim*. The populations of some of those countries seem to work harder and to have more business sense than anyone else.

So how should the investor take advantage of this development? One way is to focus on what Wanger calls the *embourgeoisement* of, for instance, Singapore. Some years ago he took a cruise starting from there. On the boat was a Chinese family of nine. The grandmother had come to Singapore as a slave . . . yes, a slave! Her children, though, were already working in the government. Thanks to entrepreneurship, there is an explosive growth of the middle class in the Pacific. The newly rich go on trips. He has capitalized on this tendency by having three related vehicles in his fund: Cathay Pacific Airlines, based in Hong Kong, and thought by many to be the best airline in the world; Singapore Airlines; and Malaysian Airline Systems. "Cathay and Singapore Air hire teenage girls, very selectively," he notes. "Not being constrained by government regulations, they then lay them off again in their twenties and hire new ones." Aren't mature women more competent flight attendants than girls? "Yes, but they're not as interesting to look at on a six-hour flight," he answered, with a wry smile.

"To invest in an airline, one should seek a line with a very large route structure, short feeders, little discounting, and traffic growing at a high rate. Both Cathay's hub airport in Hong Kong and Singapore's in Singapore represent a substantial part of their territory. In other words, there's no feeder problem. The areas they serve include countries with real GNP growth of 8 to 10 percent, which is all the more extraordinary considering the large agricultural component of their economies.

"The Japanese have come to America en masse, the Taiwanese will be close behind, and after them will come the overseas Chinese in the Far East. Hotels in Hong Kong fill up as fast as they can be built, and the same will be true in Hawaii and then on our West Coast. One can also play the Pacific concept through tourist companies, such as Carnival Cruise Lines and Disney, and through luxury products, such as Waterford glass."

Cracks in the Crystal Ball

It isn't easy to spot the real trends in the world. In one report, Wanger analyzed twenty predictions made a number of decades ago by futurologists. Several had to do with cheap energy by 1985: drilling oil wells offshore in deep water, continued growth of nuclear power, the development of such low-grade fossil fuels as lignite, synthetic fuels, and solar power in a quarter of new homes. Of these, only deepwater drilling has come to pass to any significant degree. The moral that Wanger derives from this is simply that *technology is extremely hard to forecast*. The predictions were presented by wise and knowledgeable experts, but were wrong; even more important, they missed the important changes that *have* come about. He continues:

"In any environment, you're going to have some creatures that are better adapted than others, and those are the ones that will prosper and grow. We're in a world where the environment changes at an increasingly rapid rate. I think that by concentrating on smaller companies you improve your chances of catching the next wave. You could be one of the guys riding the crest instead of one of those just trying to hang on.

In watching trends you should be on the alert for negative as well as positive investment ideas, like the Sherlock Holmes story of the dog that *didn't* bark. For instance, in some winters there are no stories about shortages of gas, relatively few about oldsters shivering in their Bronx apartments, and so forth. This means that fuel is in plentiful supply. That's not front-page stuff: The news that's fit to print is the bad news. But cheap fuel is good for the airlines, for instance."

"And for motels, and for Disney," I added.

"Exactly," said Wanger. "Similarly, once a year or so one encounters the 'catastrophe in Bangladesh' paradigm: The monsoon comes on schedule, and the resulting floods temporarily push thousands of people out of their homes. However, all this usually means is that the monsoon has indeed arrived. The people return to their homes later. The real news would be if the monsoon *didn't* arrive."

In other words, Wanger suggests that when one doesn't read about "Catastrophe in Bangladesh—Thousands Homeless," it may well mean that the rains *haven't* come on schedule, and one should consider soybean futures.

Long Odds

Wanger asks the sensible question "Why don't people consider risk in proportion to its true statistical probability?" One answer, he says, may be that most people don't like to or can't do mathematical calculations to figure out the real odds. And of course the unusual makes a better media story than the commonplace. But, he says, there are sound companies with a small risk of trouble that are good buys because *the market is too fearful of unlikely disasters.* When something bad happens, a stock may go down much more than the news warrants. This has its own Wall Street name: "overdiscounting the bad news." So, as he points out, if you can find a good company when the market is cowering at inflated horror stories, there are profits to be made.

Some companies even do better as things get worse. H&R Block, for instance, makes money on tax complications and insurance brokers from difficult times. Wanger calls this category "misery stocks."

Criteria

Wanger has three tests of a good company—what he calls the "tripod" of *growth potential, financial strength,* and *fundamental value.*

1. Growth potential, in turn, lies in five areas: a *growing market* for the company's product, *good design, efficient manufacturing, sound marketing,* and *healthy profit margins.* High profitability is always the result of enjoying a special niche, such a technological skill. He likes companies with a dominant market share: "It's better to be the best company in the lightbulb industry than the third-best company in the tractor industry," he says. A television station, a regional shopping mall, or a newspaper can exploit a local monopoly.

    Then, Wanger looks for outstanding management, which understands its business, is skilled in marketing, and is dedicated to its customers. He prefers companies where managers own a large enough stake in the company for their interests to coincide with those of the other shareholders.

2. Wanger wants to be sure that the company enjoys a strong financial position: low debt, adequate working capital, and conservative accounting. A strong balance sheet will allow growth without the need to dilute the existing shareholders' equity capital.

3. Finally, the price must be attractive. Wanger points out that institutional investors go through periods when they confuse a company with its stock; you can have a good company and an unattractive stock.

To verify value in the marketplace, Wanger has devised an infallible touchstone—the *Quit Test*. "What you do is play a game in which you assume that one of your eccentric friends who runs a large bank has just offered to lend you a great deal of money at about 10 percent interest, with which you may tender for all the stock of the company you are studying at the current market price. If you study the company and say, 'Boy, this is terrific! Give me the loan and I'll do it. I'll quit my job and go run that company. It's a tremendous bargain,' then you probably have a good stock. And if you say, 'Gee, I think I'd rather stay where I am,' then there's not enough in that stock and perhaps you'd better look somewhere else."

To value a stock, Wanger has his analysts estimate a company's future earnings or, or for an asset play, its breakup potential, both about two years ahead. The computer then calculates what the price-earnings ratio should be at that time, based on a conventional dividend discount model, and thus produces a target price.

Next, it calculates the expected rate of return if the stock advances to that level from its current market price. Wanger then screens for the rate of return to determine where his analysts' expectations are different from those of the market.

The Rubinstein Rule

Wanger takes a "top-down" approach. He starts by determining the areas of the market that look particularly attractive. He limits his analytical labors by confining his portfolio to a few good stocks from those areas. He calls this the Rubinstein Rule: *Either they can play the piano or they cannot.* This comes, he explains, from a story of Artur Rubinstein judging a piano competition in London. Rubinstein was asked to score contestants on a scale between one and twenty. When the competition ended, the sponsors were dismayed to find that the maestro had graded most contestants zero, a few twenty, and none in between. They asked why he had scored in such an extreme manner. "Simple," replied Rubinstein. "Either they can play the piano or they cannot."

An attractive investment area must have favorable characteristics that should last five years or longer. Wanger's portfolio turnover is very low—historically, around 25 percent per annum. That is, he sells an eighth of the portfolio a year and buys other things. If a stock's central reason or "metaphor" for its purchase in the first place remains applicable, it stays. As a result of this limited turnover, Acorn has one of the lowest expense ratios among equity funds.

Some years ago a friend told Wanger that no institution ever invested in real estate. Another told him that his bank had no real estate stocks on its approved list. He thanked them for the tip and forthwith bought Koger Properties and Continental Illinois Properties. "After all," he explained, "my helpful friends had just explained why real estate stocks were cheap, and told me who would be willing to buy them from Acorn in a few years at higher prices." Wanger said that, first, most dwellings had at least doubled in the last ten years, as investors were well aware; second, American and foreign investors are bidding for good-quality real estate at ten to fourteen times cash flow, while real estate stocks could be bought at five to ten times cash flow. And third, institutions will eventually come back into real estate after the shakeout among REITs.

Shopping centers straddle three Wanger investing ideas: real estate, energy conservation, and the leisure trend. "For instance," he has written, "shopping centers are good investments because the big, covered-mall regional shopping center saves time and store-to-store driving energy by bringing dozens of stores into the same place. The most successful stores have been users of information, in most cases televised advertising, which builds national-brand identification and chain-store images."

Real and Unreal Banking

Wanger likes to describe a situation in *Sylvie and Bruno* by Lewis Carroll, the author of *Alice's Adventures in Wonderland*. In this story a professor runs up a modest bill with his tailor. When the tailor presses him for payment the professor offers to pay twice as much if he can have a year's grace. So a few years later the professor owes the tailor £2,000, but knows that since the tailor will always accept another year's delay in return for another double, the tailor will never get paid. The book was published in 1889, and Wanger has calculated that if the two characters were still around, the professor would owe the tailor about £1,000,000,000,000,000,000,000,000,000,000,000.

"When the borrower is an almost-real country like Argentina or Poland, and that country has no collateral and no intention of paying off its loan, when do banks figure that they have a deadbeat professor on their hands?" Wanger asks. "Every rollover of a weak bank credit just pushes the principal amount up a little higher into fantasyland." Precisely because of these fears, some banks are undervalued. Wanger especially likes small regional ones. "But we try to find the ones run by bankers, not by tailors," he says, adding that the term "aggressive banker" should be recognized as contradictory on its face, like "aggressive mistress."

Think Small

Still, Wanger's *idée de base* remains investing in small companies, simply because the returns are better. He cites a famous study published by Ibbotson Associates in 1995 on stock returns for the seventy years between 1925 and 1995. It found that large companies returned 10.5 percent on average per year, and small companies 12.5 percent. That is not a small difference. Over twenty years, $10,000 compounded at the lower rate runs to $73,662, but at the higher rate to $105,451—a 40 percent improvement!

Wanger admits that the experts still disagree as to the reasons for this difference. His own theory, which he calls Darwinism in the marketplace, is that *the managers of small companies respond better to change*. They also have more room to grow, and can make tactical moves more quickly than mature companies. In addition, large companies are better understood by the market, while *one can find out things about small companies that the market does not know*.

Unlike Peter Lynch, Wanger does not feel that individuals can usefully engage in stock-picking, least of all in foreign stocks. "Professionals traversing the globe to develop corporate and analyst relationships are able to dig up investments that a private investor couldn't hope to find," he explains. "How are you, on your own, going to match the diverse package of opportunities a mutual fund can uncover?" He lists some of his companies that an individual would not have found: a casino operator in Malaysia, a Dutch newspaper, a ceramic tile maker in Mexico, a cable TV operator in Switzerland, a French temporary-help company, a discount retailer in Japan, a German window manufacturer, a Chinese bicycle maker. "I can assure you that Southeast Asia and Latin America are not places in which the average individual should try to invest by calling up PaineWebber and placing an order. Buying stocks there is an invitation to a nightmare."

Timing

Wanger has little concern for timing and trends, and he subscribes to Peter Lynch's philosophy that fifteen minutes a year on economic analysis is quite enough. "Market levels have little to do with whether the economy is up 3 percent or down 1 percent," Wanger maintains. *"Every study shows that the stock market is a reliable indicator of where the economy is headed, but it's no help trying to look at events the other way around."*

To illustrate the point, he describes striding through New York's Central Park one day. A woman was walking her golden retriever. She walked through the park at an even pace from one entrance to another. The dog ran back and forth in all directions. At the end, however, the dog came back to her, and they left together. How difficult it would have been to try to predict and interpret the movements of the dog! But regardless of what the dog did, it was utterly predictable the animal would wind up next to the woman at the south entrance. Wanger maintains that following stocks day by day is like trying to chart the golden retriever.* "However," he concludes, "if you concentrate on the long-term basic trends that move smoothly and steadily over multiyear time spans, you know where the lady is going and therefore where the market dog will end up eventually."

Recent Themes

In 1997, Wanger had several concepts he hoped to profit from, including energy exploration, liberalization in Eastern Europe, social changes in developing countries, and radical progress in information technology.

Some of these themes pointed to obvious conclusions: Underdeveloped countries will invest in telephone systems, for example. Others were more original: The middle class emerging in developing countries will eventually want to travel to exotic locations. Thus, Wanger has put his money into the travel stocks of Genting International, a Singapore cruise line; H.I.S., a Japanese travel agency; and Burswood, an Australian casino. He is also sticking with cruise line Carnival Corporation, with a similar thought: If Castro finally goes and Cuba develops a favorable tourist climate, the island will again be a fine spot for American vacationers to visit.

Energy exploration excites Wanger. Much of our continental land area is already drilled up, and the major U.S. oil companies are turning their

---

*Dogs are supposed to be on a leash in Central Park, but no matter. I have published a similar comparison: country rambles with my Labrador, Daisy. She is with me when we set out, and likewise at the end, because she is going to be fed, but is all over creation in the middle.

sights offshore. This leaves room for small companies to profit by picking at the leftovers: redrilling or adding compressors. Acorn has bought several of these so-called exploitation companies: Benton Oil & Gas, Basin Exploration, and Snyder Oil, all small. It has also invested in Tesoro Petroleum, a San Antonio oil service business that has upgraded an Alaskan refinery and is buying another in Hawaii. Tesoro also does exploration and production in Bolivia and expects that gas production there will double after the completion of a pipeline to São Paulo, Brazil, in 1999.

When Russia and Eastern Europe opened up, Wanger saw that there would be a need for printing and packaging. He did quite well with a German firm, Krones, and a U.S. one, Nordson, both makers of packaging and labeling machines, and with Komori Printing Machinery of Japan. He also knew they would need safety equipment—goggles, masks, hard-toe shoes, and such. He bought into Mine Safety Appliances, the world's largest manufacturer of industrial safety equipment.

Even Wanger, though, warns against carrying a theme too far. One must be able to discern which situations are alike underneath as well as in appearance. He cites Robert Burns's "My love is like a red, red rose." "That doesn't exactly fit the reality," says Wanger. "Your girl is very beautiful, and you love to look at her, but you probably don't mean that she's short, thorny, and lives in your garden." He cites as one example the collapse of the Mexican economy in 1994. With the fall of the peso, investors paradoxically panicked and sold stocks in Argentina, causing a run on the Argentine peso. The strange logic? "They speak Spanish and use pesos as money; so they are the same. Never mind that Buenos Aires is 4,609 airline miles away from Mexico."

Investing Downstream

One of Wanger's fastest-growing areas has been what he calls "information," a theme repeated often in his reports. "I've practically built a career out of that one idea, since I've consistently built a large part of my portfolios around it," he writes. "It's a theme that never seems to give out." Often his key focus is on electronic information being processed more efficiently.

His advice for approaching information-related stocks is the following: *Recognize a transforming technology and then invest downstream from it.* In other words, invest in businesses that will *benefit* from new technology rather than in the technology companies themselves. Specifically, look for companies that gain by using computers and electronics.

His most successful example is International Game Technology. In fact, IGT fitted into not one but two Wanger themes: transforming technology, and a trend, the increasing enthusiasm for gambling. From a maker of routine mechanical slot machines, IGT positioned itself to create high-tech computerized electronic slots that allowed not only for different payoff arrangements but also for novel games and lottery components. Wanger bought IGT at $1 per share; it reached $40.

Wanger has rarely owned semiconductor companies. Motorola and Intel have never been in his portfolio. But he did well with LIN Broadcasting, Mobile Communications, and Telephone and Data Systems, all companies that *benefited* from the advances in semiconductors. Companies dealing in high-speed data processing also benefit from improvements in chip technology, so he has owned credit card issuers Advanta, First USA, MBNA, and People's Bank.

One of his favorite downstream companies in 1998 was ACT Manufacturing of Hudson, Massachusetts, which provides cable manufacturing and assembly services to the data networking, telecommunications, medical, and computer industries. It is a low-risk way to profit from the proliferation of electronics equipment.

Another Wanger idea, outsourcing, is growing 25 percent per year. He is playing it with Capita, a small English company that manages driver's license offices.

Wanger has a theory that could augur well for his fund. He believes that social programs such as Social Security, Medicare, and Medicaid have become essentially little better than Ponzi schemes. Since, he says, money is not there to fulfill their promises, the government is stuck. "Both politicians and would-be pensioners are worried they will wake up one day to a giant sucking sound coming from the benefits department of their national retirement administration," he has said.

One answer is to privatize the U.S. pension system. He cites a 1997 U.S. Advisory Council report recommending that Congress consider a degree of privatization of the system. Although it is still denounced by many in Congress, privatization has caught on in a number of countries abroad, including Chile, Argentina, Mexico, Australia, and Britain. Indeed, Wanger notes that 401(k) and 403(b) plans are really pilot programs for privatization.

He believes that as individually funded pension plans diversify, they will buy small-cap stocks. In a September 1997 report he notes that since May of that year, small-cap stocks made a turnaround and began outperforming the S&P 500. "This trend has not yet spread around the world, but it is likely to," he says. "If this unfolds as we hope, the Acorn Family of Funds will be rewarding investments over the next several years."

Media

Wanger has reduced his positions in cable television in favor of programmers. He believes that as channel capacity increases, video programmers will reap the benefits of increased subscriber fees and advertising revenues. His largest position is in Liberty Media, owner of such properties as the Discovery Channel, the Learning Channel, and the shopping channel, QVC.

Wanger has guessed right about some media companies. In 1994 he bought International Family Entertainment between $12 and $17 a share. After lagging for a time, the stock began to rise, culminating with Rupert Murdoch's announcement three years later that he would buy it at $35 a share. In 1997 he bought Gaylord Entertainment; eventually Westinghouse bought its country music and Grand Old Opry divisions.

Wanger notes that in recent years momentum investors have been bidding up the general market beyond reasonable value. As he explained in 1997, "You do get more efficient, but you also become more prejudiced, and at some point you end up knowing a lot of things that just aren't true anymore." To combat this, "It's not enough to have great investing insights, you have to evolve."

Sixteen

ROBERT WILSON
WITHOUT A ROPE

Robert Wilson is like the joker who wanders around a New Year's Eve party exploding balloons with the end of a lighted cigarette. Pop! Pop! Pop! His preferred activity is popping the stocks of mediocre "concept" companies that get wildly puffed up by hungry stockbrokers in need of something to sell to impressionable customers. There's always a new fad running around: crazily overpriced Net companies; hot new pharmaceuticals; something, with no numbers attached, that's going to change the world; a tree that will grow all the way up to the sky. As the speculators rush in, the stock rises from 5 to 10, let's say. The speculators, reinforced in their enthusiasm, buy more, putting the price still higher. New speculators rush in. Soon the whole self-confirming perpetual motion machine is grossly overinflated beyond any reasonable investment value. Robert Wilson, watching this fatally familiar process, sees the rubber beginning to stretch taut; more and more puffers don't seem able to blow up the concept any bigger. The stock hits 15. He sells it short in the market at 15, say, planning to repurchase at 10, 5, or even 2.

Thanks to the brokers' enthusiasm, the retail investors, with a final huge effort, run the stock up to 20. Wilson has lost a third of his investment. Does he panic? No. It's all routine. He sells short thousands of additional shares. The stock falters and staggers back to 15. Now Wilson scents victory: The enemy is in retreat! He explains to his friends, to brokers, to reporters, anybody who will listen, why the stock is absurdly overpriced, why the outlook is grim: the plant is antiquated, management insincere, competition intensifying. Costs are rising, the market is drying up, a better product is arriving from Japan, the company is in hock to the bankers, perhaps regulatory headaches are impending.

While the original brokers rally their troops and seek to enlist new recruits under the banner of "It's a bargain at 15, down from 20," and "It'll earn $5 for sure two years from now and go to 40," Wilson, his broker, and other short-side sharpshooters close in for the kill. That is, hundreds of thousands of shares sold short, brokers inventing explanations for the decline, sinister intimations circulating in the Wall Street lunch clubs, odd-lot sellers panicked, margin calls, the works. The stock goes into a free fall and Wilson meets his obligations by repurchasing all his borrowed stock between 7 and 10, ending up $500,000 to the good.

So for Wilson, the energetic brokers who puff up "concept" stocks are like the beaters in a European hunt, driving the pigeons toward him as he waits at his post. Bang! A hundred thousand dollars. Bang, bang! A hundred thousand more. As far as Wilson is concerned, the beaters—I mean the brokers—are not working for their customers, but for *him*.

Wilson is a slim man, with a trim brown beard and thinnish hair surrounding a slender face. He speaks in a bright and humorous way, in a slightly strangled Midwestern voice. Simply and neatly dressed, he has the figure of a man in his thirties and the face of one a little over forty. He is, in fact, in his fifties. He believes in keeping fit, and indeed in his line of work he has to be, like an air traffic controller.

Wilson sits with his sandaled feet on his desk in a large, clean Scandinavian-modern office in a commercial building on New York's West Side and buys and sells stocks. He spends* about two-thirds of his working day on the telephone (a tiny headset-and-mike gadget that he answers himself: "Wilson") and about one-third of it reading business magazines and telephone messages taken by his secretary. He also goes out a lot at night with stock market friends. The output of this information system is the investment ideas that have made Robert Wilson rich.

To keep this moneymaking apparatus in good order, Wilson gives much attention to his health. Things start with a big breakfast, which used to include eggs and bacon; he quit the bacon and cut down on the eggs when he discovered his cholesterol was too high.

---

*As usual, this is written in the present tense, although Wilson has cut back since.

He takes vitamins E and C, has a low-impact form of jogging that he likes, and practices yoga and other exercises. He goes around to the New York Athletic Club for calisthenics, but not to engage in sports . . . he dislikes the competitive side. He says he has always been weak and uncoordinated. His facial exercises, which he finds helpful in avoiding wrinkles and a baggy chin (he has neither), involve ominous grimaces, thrusting the corners of the mouth out sideways and down like an actor in a Japanese painting. When he started to go bald, he began grabbing his hair and pulling it about to stimulate the scalp, which has stabilized matters. He says that the blood flow of the body slows down with age, and one must keep it moving along. He drinks a great deal of water. Originally it was as a stool softener when he suffered from hemorrhoids, but he found it good for his complexion, which is, indeed, that of someone much younger, and he kept up the habit after he recovered.

In the mid-fifties, after two years in an Army clerical job, Wilson sought to join de Vegh & Co. The head of the firm, Imrie de Vegh, was an encyclopedia, and gave him a frightful grilling. At the end de Vegh mentioned that if Wilson wanted to work there he would have to give up the idea of speculating on his own. Wilson said he would never agree to that, and so the possibility foundered. (I got around the de Vegh house rule by paying the full fee for the firm to look after my own funds, which gave me the right to be treated as a client as well as a manager.) He did work for several other investment firms.

Now, though, his most important activity is managing his own money, which in recent years has been well along in the eight figures.

Wilson lives alone in a huge, bright apartment on Central Park West. He has been an important patron of several New York institutions, including the New York City Opera, the Brooklyn Botanic Garden, and the Whitney Museum, where his acumen has been much appreciated. He loves music, particularly Mahler, Wagner, Richard Strauss, Puccini, Mozart, and Beethoven, but walks out of two-thirds of the movies he attends. He has a keen practical sense and is interested in the problems of doing things right. His manner is simple, amused, sympathetic, and unostentatious.

What makes Wilson tick? He reiterates that more than anything else he wants to be rich, and yet he seems to like money as a token, not for what it can buy. He has simple tastes and no expensive hobbies. He doesn't want to have servants or a big, black car, which he feels would insulate him from life. Ostentatious spending "reduces vitality," he believes. He does like being in a position to make generous donations to cultural institutions and join their boards, and enjoys dining out in style a couple of times a week.

Life he describes as a process of enjoyment. "An up day in the market is as good as a performance of *Electra.*" He suffers when losing money, but not unbearably. A high tolerance for pain is necessary for success in his type of investment. "This business doesn't get to me too much—not fundamentally," he says.* He quotes Bernard Berenson: "In order to be comfortable, one should have a little more money and a little less time than one needs."

Wilson is highly intelligent and articulate, with a lively philosophical awareness about his many interests. When we came to discuss the disinclination of most outstanding investors to live ostentatiously, he pointed out that those lavish lifestyles tend to be for captains of industry and persons with high income but low net worth. Investors, we agreed, have a more philosophical bent, and thus less taste for outward display. Wilson has a curious dictum: "One of the dumbest things you can do with money is spend it."

Caught Short

In addition to following his exercise program, Wilson keeps refreshed by periods of inactivity, following J. P. Morgan's dictum "I can do a year's work in nine months, but not in twelve." One of his vacations did more harm than good. He set forth on a six-month trip to Europe, the Far East, and Australia, having moved his portfolio into what he thought was a satisfactory posture; the diversified list of stocks he held long were balanced by another list that he had sold short, and whether the market rose or fell (and he did not expect much activity) he felt he would be all right. Previously, he had usually been able to make more money by being simultaneously long and short than by simply being out of the market. He had enjoyed a "godlike" success in his short-side trading until then, he says.

Unfortunately, at that time one of his positions was a short commitment of over 200,000 shares of Resorts International, at an average price of $15. (It has since split.) The stock had moved up to about $20

---

*Alexander Pope was constantly subjected to merciless lampoons. One day a friend called and found him perusing a handful of them. "These things are my diversion," said Pope airily—but the friend noticed that his face was working.

before he left. "I'm getting crucified, but I may short more," Wilson announced in a widely noted interview. He predicted that Resorts International, which had just opened the first gambling casino in Atlantic City, would not do as well as the public believed, since Atlantic City's weather is not as favorable as that of Las Vegas. Also, Wilson explained, casino owners need the Mafia to help them collect debts; so if Jersey succeeded in its attempt to drive out the mob, then the casinos couldn't extend credit and wouldn't be attractive to the high rollers. On this confident note, Wilson set off on his planned junket around the world. As he meandered through Europe, Resorts International reported prodigious initial results from its new casino. Investors, fascinated, poured into the stock. Since Wilson had announced his huge short position publicly, brokers were well aware of it and told their customers that when the stock got high enough Wilson would have to buy all his shorts back, since his resources were not infinite; this, they said, gave the stock a measure of support.

Alas, as Wilson wandered between beautiful views, cathedrals, palaces, concerts, and fine repasts in famous restaurants, his destruction was slowly being engineered back home.

Resorts started to pick up momentum. From 20 when he left, it advanced to 30—double his cost. Then, as the hapless Wilson drifted from one attraction to the next, Resorts moved to 40, to 50, to 60—up four times! Now it had become one-third of his entire short position. He had lost millions. He remembers a grim evening in the Norwegian fjord country. He couldn't shake a dull couple he'd been drinking too much with, cables from Wall Street were accumulating in a sinister pile, and he began to have a sick feeling of things coming unstuck.

Writers in the financial press started speculating openly about his plight. Resorts continued to report brilliant earnings. The brokers urged their legions forward: Wilson's on the run!

He reached the Far East: Singapore, Hong Kong. Resorts crept up relentlessly: 5 points, 10 points. Even a minor percentage move now meant a loss of $100,000.

Squeezed

Wilson began to crack. The situation had been building up in his mind all summer. Deep down, he knew he was doomed; he was in an entirely new and different investment climate. Who could have conceived that from making "one phony million dollars a year" Resorts could jump to $50 million a year? It was one of the biggest success stories in business history. To this day Wilson can't think of another company that has ever gone from $1 million to $50 million in earnings in eighteen months.

Neuberger & Berman were telephoning regularly now. We gotta have more margin! What do you wanna sell? They gave him a dollar limit beyond which he couldn't go. They dared not risk what might be catastrophic financial damage to their own firm if Wilson collapsed. And they were right: Wilson admits that without that limit he would have been ruined.

"Cover some Resorts," Wilson ordered. Now he was in the position of squeezing himself. His own purchases helped force the stock up further, increasing the pressure.

Resorts reached 120. He had lost $10 million.

Wilson went to Taiwan. The catastrophe gathered speed. Taipei in September is a bright, steaming town, chaotic, gay, and vital, unlike beautiful, melancholy Hong Kong. Wilson settled into the Grand Hotel, a monument built by Chiang Kai-shek and the Kuomintang. He had a single room with high ceilings, like a pagoda. Every day he would sally forth in his rugby shirt, Adidas sneakers, pastel-colored pants, and sun hat to go through the noisy, colorful streets by taxi from one temple to another, from museum to museum. Chiang carried off the best of China's art when he left the mainland, so the Palace Museum in Taipei is stupendous.

And every day Resorts International surged forward. In a week and a half it rose from 120 to 180. Wilson was losing up to $500,000 on a bad day: $100,000 each hour the Stock Exchange was open.

Finally, he could stand it no longer. On September 4, he went to pick up his room key in the Grand and the clerk handed him the usual grim telex from New York. Up again! Wilson at last knew he was cooked. Rather than telex his reply (which would have been instantaneous) he decided to save a few dollars and went down to the communications desk to send Neuberger & Berman a cable: COVER ALL RESORTS. That was it.

But it wasn't. The next day Wilson had a substantial breakfast: a couple of eggs, porridge, and a banana (which he describes as a "cornucopia of nourishment").

He set forth, as usual, in a taxi—marveling, as always, at how little they cost in Taipei—for his scheduled rounds: temples, paintings, sculptures. At noon, he suspended operations to enjoy an excellent lunch, and then resumed.

Late in the day he returned to the hotel and went to his room to get ready for dinner downstairs.

At 7 P.M. the telephone rang. Wilson, still dressed in his rugby shirt, Adidas sneakers, and light blue pants, sat down on the bed to pick it up.

It was his broker at Neuberger & Berman.

"Resorts is 190," he said. "What do we do?"

Wilson knew that 190 had to be the top, or within a hairbreadth breadth of the top. The stock couldn't go any higher. It had no reason to be *that* high. It was a typical speculative blowoff—just froth. It would collapse in no time. But did he dare, even he, to sell everything else, his perfectly good long positions? If he was wrong, in another week like the one just passed he'd be finished. He *had* to close out Resorts, even if it was surely the wrong move. He was done, exhausted, beaten. All the invisible suckers out there were getting their own back.

"Didn't you get my cable?" Wilson asked.

"What cable?"

"I told you to close out Resorts."

"Is that what you want us to do?"

"Yes! Close it out!" After a few more words, he hung up.

Wilson's disaster came during the newspaper strike, but received lavish coverage in the financial press, including a major story in the *Wall Street Journal.* It may be remembered by Wall Street habitués as one of the most spectacular short plays ever, particularly since it was so elaborately telegraphed.*

Times Change

Wilson says that his mistake in Resorts was not an error of market judgment, but a misunderstanding of the fundamentals of the company. However, he also thinks that just at that moment America changed tack. In the 1960s nothing went right, politically or otherwise.

---

*Wilson may thus take a position alongside the never-to-be-forgotten Ahmed Abd el-Aziz, who farted in the Great Mosque during a silent moment in Friday prayer. Every head swung around to glare at the scarlet-faced Ahmed, who rose and crept out. All Damascus was soon buzzing. Finally, Ahmed decamped to Aleppo. Years later, with a gray beard, he returned, finding the city much changed: new shops, houses gone, others built, new faces. In the market he asked directions of a stranger, who complied, and then, looking at him keenly, said, "You are not from Damascus, then, brother?" "No, I live in Aleppo," said Ahmed, adding modestly, "I used to live here, though." "How long have you been away, brother?" "Twelve years." "Twelve years?" mused the stranger. "That is a long time." He smiled faintly. "Twelve years ago . . . that was the year that Ahmed farted in the Great Mosque."

In business, new ventures usually failed. But in 1978 a better era started. Who would have thought that New Yorkers would start picking up dog droppings? Perhaps Resorts and the dog droppings were both harbingers of profound change. Resorts International's Atlantic City venture, says Wilson, was the first thing in America that had gone right on a colossal scale in a long time. ("Right" depending, of course, on what you think of incorporated vice.)

Wilson chuckled on thinking of a *New Yorker* cartoon of some years earlier. A hippie couple with frizzy hair and shabby clothes are lounging in their pad. Junior, a well-brushed tyke nattily decked out in a three-piece suit and armed with an attaché case, is walking with stern purpose out the door. The freaked-out parents are moaning, "Where did we go wrong?"

This leads us to one of the most important of Wilson's Rules: *Any successful approach in investing is bound to fail in due course.* Things change. "Shorthand techniques are okay, but they finally blow up in your face. Then you have to do something different."

Robert Wilson's modus operandi would terrify conservative investors. It is, in fact, the same approach that costs the small investor so much money every year. The difference is that Robert Wilson does it better, and is financially fearless. He can't be shaken out of a good idea if things go wrong for a while. Mountain climbers are well advised to wear sturdy clothes, carry the appropriate equipment, not go out late in the day during avalanche periods, and to move carefully on the mountain face with competent companions, an experienced guide, and a strong rope. Nevertheless, a climber out to break records may well violate these rules: He may do away with the companions and the guide and thus not need the rope, may run up and down so fast that he needs only light equipment, and may even risk the avalanches.

Traveling light without protection is central to Wilson's technique: He virtually never visits companies or assesses their management firsthand. Almost all his ideas come to him from stockbrokers, and he essentially works with concepts and perceptions rather than the reality. When he buys a stock, he assesses what's going to make it go up, what will focus interest on the company, rather than worrying about the details of the underlying business.

That analysis he leaves to others. He's like the president of an advertising agency savoring a new slogan. "'*The Uncola.*' Interesting . . . interesting. But will they buy it in Pocatello? Why not?" Wilson's facility for imaginative synthesis, uncluttered by analytical baggage, lets him see the market outlook for a stock far more easily than a conventional analyst. He describes himself as a "long-term trader." If things are going his way he may stay with a stock for a year or more. If not—and many of his ideas don't work out—he moves on.

He hates to read long write-ups on stocks and rarely does more than glance at them. In fact, his entire information system consists of only three file drawers. If he owns a company, he files any information he receives about it; when he sells the stock, he throws the information away again. Instead, he gets his ideas from working the telephone: brokers, other investors.

Though Wilson never attends meetings with institutional securities analysts (who to him are "just bureaucrats"), he does go every year to the conference given by WEMA—formerly Western Electronics Manufacturers Association; now it includes manufacturers from many parts of the country.

He is indifferent to exact data. Once I ran through a list of the companies he was long or short and asked him the names of their presidents; he knew only about half of them. Doubtless Wilson would observe that with each new president a company changes no more, fundamentally, than Italy does with each new prime minister. The general position of the business is what Wilson wants to grasp, the key changes in its circumstances that the public does not yet understand—such as that a given company may go from $100 million in sales to $1 billion, and become a stock every institution will have to own. When the public finally does understand the business, realizes how good it is, and as a result wants to buy the stock, he will provide it—at a much higher price.

Risk

The major difference between Wilson's approach and that of most of the investors in this book is that a Graham, for instance, always sought situations where there is little risk of loss, the Margin of Safety. Wilson, on the other hand, says that he *insists on stocks in which there is a major risk,* because only such a stock is likely to go way up. *"Unless there is fear in a stock, it probably doesn't have a great capital gains potential,"* he says, adding, "I'd be scared shitless if my portfolio consisted of only ten out of my seventy stocks."

I find that to be the most useful single idea I have heard him express, and urge the reader to contemplate it carefully. What most enrages him, incidentally, is a broker asserting that "there's no down-side risk in this stock."

Something New

Wilson's cardinal principle is: *Buy companies that are doing something new and different, or doing it in a different way.*

He likes technology companies that could go up ten times in five to seven years. However, a special hazard of playing stocks of the hour with which the public is enchanted is that, not infrequently, unscrupulous brokers in league with management are pushing weak businesses so that insiders can sell the stocks to the public for more than they are worth, as happened with all the hot issues of the sixties that simply vanished. The speculator trying to stay just ahead of the public has to be nimble or he will be carried to ruin with them. So Wilson the speculator may well buy the same sort of merchandise that Wilson the balloon-pricker will attack when the time is right.

If you are betting on an election you don't necessarily bet on the best man, you bet on the man you think will win.* Wilson uses his flair and skill to bet on the stock *image* that he thinks will excite the public in a few months or a year, not necessarily three years from now. The market in a "T. Rowe Price company," clocking in its 20 percent earnings growth, quarter after quarter, probably reflects its prospects. You get a better move, says Wilson, "playing the surprises."

Pumping Up the Tulips

Wilson likes to see the brokerage fraternity get behind a stock and push. He knows that they are only wheeling his next target into position: the next tulip-bulb mania. In a pleasantly mixed metaphor he refers to the brokers as "pumping up the tulips." He likes to short into strength in a stock, not when it's already on the way down.

Colonial Commercial was one of his major shorts. Wilson describes it as a weak Long Island conglomerate. He started selling at $5 a share, beginning in early 1978. By October the stock had risen to about 20. The Wall Street fraternity, reasoning that Wilson would be unable to hold on in Resorts International, decided to force up Colonial

---

*John Maynard Keynes (who, incidentally, made most of his money speculating on commodities and currencies) compares speculation to a wager on the outcome of a beauty contest. You don't bet on the girl you find prettiest, but on the one you think others will prefer.

Commercial too, hoping that in order to cut his losses, he would be compelled to buy in his short position at higher prices. He was a big fish in that pool, and his own buying would have forced the stock up further—he would have squeezed himself. But the stock settled back down to 12, and Wilson shorted even more, closing out his position at a fine profit.

Wilson's short positions at one time or another have included Graphic Scanning, Astrex, Tom Brown, Tampax, and British Petroleum. Other stocks he has been short include the heavy chemicals, notably Dow, W. R. Grace, and Rohm & Haas, and also Air Products, National Presto, Applied Digital Data, Centronics, Advanced Micro Devices, and International Systems and Controls.

He shorted Bowmar Instruments at 20. This early producer of calculators had one great year, with booming earnings; then it borrowed to finance a major expansion just in time for the entry of Texas Instruments and National Semiconductor into the market. Wilson finally covered his stock at 2½ while watching it go from 20 to over 40 at a time when the general market was going down. ("That was a rough one!") When Technicare went against him, at least he was making money on the long side to offset his losses on the short side. Before shorting Bowmar, he talked to a lot of people, almost all of whom were wrong. Neither they nor he had any idea that the calculator market would get as big as it eventually did, or that Bowmar would do as well as it did. After all, says Wilson, a calculator is just a couple of semiconductors in a box with some buttons.

The Whites of Their Eyes

According to Wilson, the single rule that would have saved him the most money as an investor is this: *Don't try to anticipate how fast competition will undercut an established company.* There's no use theorizing how competition will unfold; it's best to wait and see what really happens. With Tampax, for instance, one could have started worrying about competition twenty-five years ago. However, one could have made a fortune in the stock before the problem became acute, as it finally has. Eastman Kodak's pounce on the instant camera industry alarmed followers of Polaroid, yet Polaroid did admirably *after* Kodak's appearance as a competitor. The wider availability of the product opened up the market. Still another example is hamburgers: Who could have dreamed that after McDonald's, Burger King, and all the others, the market could support still another major competitor? "How many hamburgers can America stuff in its face?" asks Wilson rhetorically. And yet a number of the competitors have enjoyed a prodigious success.

Companies are often destroyed not by the competition but by themselves. They get soft. How did imports take over so much of the U.S. car market? The foreign manufacturers were keen and efficient while the American manufacturers got complacent and sloppy.

Turning the Corner

In the late 1970s, Wilson says, Americans became disgusted with their lot as an "emerging second-class nation."

In the 1940s and 1950s, price-earnings multiples fell to single-digit levels. The Russians seemed to be gobbling up the world, and the investing public expected that there would be another great postwar depression. Instead, by 1953 it became apparent that there would not be one, and price-earnings multiples began rising. The reason that price-earnings multiples got so low all over again in the 1970s, Wilson reasoned, was that investors felt that the country was drifting into socialism. They began to demand incentives, not controls, for the economy. The capital gains tax was cut, an extraordinary turnabout. If it had been predicted before he went away on his great trip, he would have said it was simply inconceivable—as inconceivable as the prospect of Resorts going up 1,000 percent. Then, under Reagan, the creep toward socialism reversed. Wilson predicted that the market could rise from the depressed levels of the late 1970s to twenty times doubled earnings, or almost fivefold in five to seven years.* Wilson said he would be worth hundreds of millions of dollars by the time it was over.

After he had stopped speculating actively and instead had turned to philanthropy and living well, Wilson wrote down a number of investing principles he had learned from his experiences, which I published in my *Financial Times* (London) column. Here are my rephrasings of his key rules:

1. *Find intelligent brokers.* To succeed, you need brokers who are smart, honorable, and working for *you.* Even if you do not have lots of commissions to give them, you can gain their attention by providing them with facts and ideas they can use themselves.

---

*He was right.

2. *Look for the fundamental idea in a stock.* What two or three influences are going to make a stock move? If the answer is not clear and simple, stay away.

3. *Then, watch the script!* If the stock fails to conform to your scenario, act. If you can't beat the market, stay away. That is, unless you are ready, willing, and able to spend a great deal of time working intensely at beating the market, put your money in an appropriate mutual fund and stay out of individual stocks.

4. *Seek uncommon insights.* Successful investing depends less on knowing facts than on knowing whether other people recognize them too.

5. *Look forward to pleasant surprises.* Things may go much better and a stock may go much higher over time than anybody imagines.

6. *Kick a dog when it's down.* When a company is stumbling is generally the best time to go short in its stock. Never slip into the trap of thinking that because a stock has suffered more than had been expected or imagined, it is on its way back up. *Trends tend to go further and longer than anybody imagines they will.*

7. *Don't act too soon, even if you know you are right.* It can be expensive to anticipate the beginning of a move. Wait for it to start and *then* ride it.

8. *Beware of falling in love with a company.* Emotional attachment to a stock invites disastrous misjudgment. This happens most often when you have gotten too close to a company and its management. Keep your distance.

9. *Watch the forest. Beware of getting lost among the trees.* Profound studies of management staffing and attitudes, and exhaustive analysis of a company's products and processes, will often obscure the larger trend and lead to mistaken judgments.

10. *Beware heavily researched stocks.* In fact, often a good time to sell a stock is when elaborate research reports start appearing.

11. *Beware popular stocks.* Widespread enthusiasm can bloat values, mask weaknesses, and make management complacent. The more popular a stock, the more important it is to sell it promptly when the news really turns bad.

12. *Don't worry about a healthy company's competition.* Every good run will end, but don't anticipate. It's better to sell a winning stock too late than too soon.

13. *Neither good management nor market potential can by themselves create success.* A company without solid natural market potential cannot be managed into greatness. The illusion that it can is likely to be a trap. A company with great market potential but poor management will also fail to work out.

14. *Beware of management's encouraging comments.* Executives will not lie outright, which could send them to jail. But it is the nature of management to accept overly optimistic economic and industry assumptions. Usually, it will tell you the best and withhold the worst.

15. *Beware of windfall companies.* One-time gains from some novel development are unlikely to persist. Competitors will arrive, or the market for that product might turn out to be a fad.

16. *Accept taxes.* Never hold on to a stock just to delay paying a tax. Tax liabilities should have no bearing on the way you invest.

17. *In bad times, collect clues for good times.* How companies fare in adversity is very important. Weathering a recession well is a good indication that a company will do better in a coming boom than other companies in the same industry that were hurt more severely.

18. *Ignore advice based on institutional ownership of stock.* Concerns about the extent of institutional ownership tend to obscure the fundamentals of performance, and thus mislead you.

19. *Heed managerial motivation.* Proxy statements and annual reports show the extent of personal shareholdings by top management. *Rich executives like to get richer.*

Peter Lynch
Relentless Pursuit

Peter Lynch essentially created the Magellan Fund. After he took charge in 1977, it became the largest mutual fund in history, which it still was twenty years later. It had over a million shareholders, and during his tenure paid Fidelity, its managers, some $60 million a year in management fees and several hundred million in sales commissions. (The 3 percent sales commission goes straight into the pocket of the owners of the management company; there are no salesmen.) For that matter, Magellan's annual performance bonus, which it invariably earns, came to 0.2 percent of its capital, and thus alone to $20 to $25 million a year. Lynch received, and fully earned, his share of this bonanza: As the Biblical injunction goes, do not muzzle the ox as he treadeth out the corn.

Lynch is a bit over six feet tall, slim and athletic-looking, with silver hair over a pale, finely modeled, almost spiritual face that is faintly suggestive of a much handsomer (and healthier) Andy Warhol. He is pleasantly rather than elegantly turned out. A brown tweed suit rises from black wing-tipped shoes. A white button-down shirt is topped by a red knitted tie whose ends are a foot apart.

He speaks rapidly and profusely, making a colloquial, even somewhat adolescent, choice of words: "So I say to myself, gee, what'm I doin'?" In talking, he waves one or both of his hands, sometimes with his glasses in them, smiling faintly. His high tenor voice has a mild Massachusetts (not necessarily Boston) accent.

This investment prodigy is the son of a professor of mathematics at Boston College who later moved to the John Hancock Company. He got cancer when Peter was seven and died when he was ten, leaving the fam-

ily in straitened circumstances. His mother went to work for a manufacturing company, and Peter moved from a private school to a local public
school—a good one, to be sure. He attended high school in Newton, Massachusetts. Summers he worked as a caddy, which is where he began
hearing about the stock market. Businessmen out golfing exchange
investment ideas, and some businessmen are very well informed.

Young Peter sank $1,250 of his savings in one of the stocks he heard
about, Flying Tiger Line, a way of riding the explosive growth of the
Pacific countries as well as the development of air freight. He bought in
at 10. Flying Tiger went up and up. Peter sold some to get his money
back, and then sold more in dribbles all the way up. The last went in
1989 when the company was taken over by Federal Express. By the
time he had cashed in most of his stock he had made enough money to
pay for his graduate study at Philadelphia's Wharton School of
Finance. (Later he became much more skeptical about such tips.)

First, however, came college. Here another golf-derived bonanza came
his way: Boston College had a partial scholarship intended precisely for
caddies, which Peter won. And later the goddess of golf smiled upon him
yet again: In 1966, waiting to start in at Wharton, he got a summer job at
Fidelity. There were seventy-five applicants, but Peter was the one who
had caddied for D. George Sullivan, the president of the company.

He moved full-time to Fidelity, and after a few years in analytical
jobs became in 1974 director of research, while continuing to cover the
chemical packaging, steel, aluminum, and textile industries. Such a job
provides a marvelous chance to learn deeply about securities. One is
essentially running an active think tank that maintains constant, systematic coverage of all of industry, endlessly visiting companies, then
concentrating intensively on the most promising fish that turn up in
the net. One's task is to develop opinions that, over and over again, are
checked against actual results. Finally, one is constantly comparing
one's ideas with those of one's peers in the same department, honing
information and judgment.

In analyst meetings, *he would urge his colleagues not to tear down each
other's ideas*—"Don't rip up my Volvo idea," as he says—but rather to
explain why their own ideas are good ones. He adds that such meetings
are 90 percent heat and 10 percent light.* Lynch says that he has an

---

*This chapter often refers to Lynch's techniques in the present tense, although as
described later, his actual functions at Fidelity have evolved.

edge because *a lot of the people he competes with are looking for reasons NOT to buy:* The company is unionized; GE will come out with a competitive product that will kill them; or whatever. There is a whole list of biases that scare most investors away from studying the situation at all, so you miss a lot. *"To make money, you must find something that nobody else knows, or do something that others won't do because they have rigid mind-sets."* He also points out that it's all right to make mistakes as the price of catching huge winners: The stock that doubles from 10 to 20 pays twice over for the one that falls in half from 10 to 5.

In 1977, after eight years as a permanent employee, Lynch, by now thirty-three, was put in charge of a little fund that Fidelity had around, Magellan. When Lynch took over it had only $22 million in it, concentrated in relatively few holdings, and was an almost invisible part of the Fidelity empire. In 1981, Magellan, then about $50 million, absorbed Fidelity's unsuccessful Salem Fund, which was of similar size.

On May 31, 1990, thirteen years to the day after he took the job, Peter Lynch resigned as manager of Magellan. He had become so identified with the fund that his departure came as quite a shock to the financial community, to say nothing of Magellan's investors. Ten thousand dollars invested with Lynch's Magellan when he began would have grown to over $250,000 at his departure, for an average annual return of 29.2 percent. Although he had the best overall fund management record for the decade of the 1980s, he never ranked higher than sixteenth in any one year. He had bought over fifteen thousand stocks in all. Lynch points out that although under his management each share of the fund gained twentyfold, there were eight declines of between 10 percent and 30 percent. He has also observed that a great many investors lost money, because they held their shares for an average of only four to five years, often buying at peaks and selling in dips.

Lynch's reasons for leaving Fidelity were straightforward and personal. He wanted to spend more time with his wife and three children. He had taken almost no vacations while running the fund; indeed, demands on his time increased steadily. "It wasn't until 1982 that I came in on Saturdays," he observed. "The last eighteen months was the first time in my life I started working Sunday mornings." Also, at his forty-sixth birthday party he realized that at the same age his father had died of cancer, a sinister augury. "You remind yourself that nobody on his deathbed ever said, 'I wish I'd spent more time at the office,'" he writes in *Beating the Street*. In that book, he invokes a Tolstoy story about an ambitious farmer. A genie appears and offers him all the land he can circle on foot in a day. He tears off, and accumulates far more land than he can ever farm. Exhausted, he considers stopping, then sets off again. Finally, he drops dead from exhaustion.* "This was the ending I hoped to avoid," Lynch concludes.

There were other factors in his decision. Magellan was a mere $22 million when Lynch took over the fund in 1977. By 1990, however, it had grown to over $12 billion, with more than a million shareholders. "Peter was very smart," one Fidelity veteran told Diana Henriques, author of *Fidelity's World*. "He knew that his future reputation could not match his past. He'd actually had someone number-crunch the question of how much Magellan would have to go up to stay in the top slot in the fund standings. He decided to quit while he still held the title."

By 1990, he was probably the most famous mutual fund manager in America. Essentially, he became the face of Fidelity. His charm and offhand ease were a pleasant offset to Fidelity's ruthless aggressiveness. (See Appendix X.) This was intentional: From the moment Lynch took over Magellan, Rab Bertelsen, vice president of communications, had determined that Lynch would serve as an ambassador for Fidelity, and even worked with Lynch to develop his public speaking skill.

Lynch's cardinal advantage over the legion of his competitors, besides his basic talent, is simply the enormous dedication he brings to the task. Lynch tries harder. In twenty years of marriage he took two proper vacations. "I went to Japan and just saw companies for five days and met Carolyn in Hong Kong. So we had Friday, Saturday, and Sunday in Hong Kong. Then I saw companies Monday, Tuesday, and Wednesday in Hong Kong. Then we went up into China for two or three days. Then I saw companies in Bangkok. Then we saw a little bit of Bangkok. Then I flew to England and I saw companies for three, four days there. It was a fabulous time." Not every wife's conception of "a fabulous time"! A stockbroker who accompanied him on another trip for some days mentions that in a country where things barely get going at ten o'clock in the morning, Lynch insisted on starting to see companies at eight, and was quite grumpy that none could be found to talk to him at six! When at the end of the day the idea of dinner was raised,

---

*A similar Russian tale describes a man who hires a sledge for a journey. It gets fearfully cold, and the driver urges him to walk to warm up his feet. But no: Our man has paid to ride and ride he will. Result: He loses his feet to frostbite.

Lynch begged off: "I gotta read four annual reports by tomorrow." This broker said he had never seen someone so well prepared for company visits. Lynch estimated his mileage at 100,000 a year, implying 400 miles a working day, which would be impressive for someone who was on the road full-time, quite aside from someone based mainly in an office.

He set off to the office by car pool at 6:15 A.M.—reading all the way in—and was driven back by 7:15 P.M. in a Fidelity car (after eighteen years in the bus), still reading.*

Lynch finds that *there is no relationship between the length of a recommendation and its value.* Very often the most convincing idea will be encapsulated in a paragraph. That being so, the short, meaty reports are those he likes best. He is an indefatigable note-taker.

Catching the Turn

Knute Rockne had a pleasantly lame description of success: "If every man does his duty perfectly on every play, a touchdown will result." In a similar vein, Lynch has stated: "If you see enough companies and do enough work, you'll either be there when a company is doing poorly and is turning around, or you'll call them up a little later and they'll say things are better." This is a reminder that Lynch's basic objective is to *catch the turn in a company's fortunes,* which might be described as the time-efficient technique of deploying capital. *Often, there is a one-to-twelve-month interval between a material change in a company and the corresponding movement in its stock.* That's what Lynch wants to capitalize on.

Toward the end of 1991, Lynch declared that the most dreaded investment sectors were housing and real estate. The nightly news recounted one real estate horror story after another. Then one day he noticed an item in the papers from the National Association of Realtors: The price of the median house was actually going up! "I've found that on several occasions over the years, the quiet facts told a much different story than the ones being trumpeted. A technique that works repeatedly is to *wait until the prevailing opinion about a certain industry is*

---

*In his mid-forties he suddenly found that reading in the car on the way to and from his office was beginning to make him carsick. This is a widely noticed effect. However, he also found the cure. He asked an ophthalmologist friend of his who is a fellow trustee of the Massachusetts Eye and Ear Infirmary (which Lynch calls "Massaineer") what could be done, and his doctor friend offered a solution. If one reads using ambient light, the pupil of the eye expands, and in that state one can get sick reading. If, on the contrary, you focus on a spotlight on the page, then you don't.

that things have gone from bad to worse, and then buy shares in the strongest companies in that groups," he said, observing that the decline in interest rates had made houses more affordable than they had been in a decade.

Consulting his notes, Lynch dug out Toll Brothers, a building company. The stock had fallen from 12⅜ to 2⅜. But on examining the company's financial reports, he found that its debt had been reduced by $28 million, while cash had built up by $22 million. It had a two-year order backlog for new houses. He decided to recommend the stock to *Barron's*. Alas, before his recommendation was published, the stock quadrupled, to $12. "Here's a tip for the prospectors of year-end anomalies: Act quickly!" he said ruefully.

Ordinarily, Lynch doesn't accept calls directly. Callers have learned to leave concise messages with his secretary or one of his two traders. He may return one call for every ten he receives, but he will initiate calls on subjects of concern to him. Either way, he exhorts the person at the end of the line to compress his message to a minute and a half and actually starts a kitchen timer when the conversation begins. After ninety seconds, *brrringg!* Or he will just end the conversation: "Sorry, I got another call comin' in." Pretty soon the callers get the point about brevity. Even in that short time he will quite often ask some key questions several times, perhaps in different ways, like a cross-examiner.

Lynch's most solid investment information comes from company visits. After so many years, he has gotten to know hundreds upon hundreds of well-placed executives in the business world who desire nothing more than to be obliging to institutional stockholders, their most important owners. What's more, you learn how to interpret what you hear. Some company presidents promise more than they can deliver, some are always overcautious, some are honest and reliable. Knowing which is which gives the professional an inestimable advantage. And visit them he does, forty or fifty a month, five or six hundred a year. He groups them, of course. If he goes to see one company in Minneapolis, he wants to see several. One efficient method is to attend regional company conferences arranged by local brokerage houses. At these occasions, several dozen companies will field their best men to present their case in the most concise and informative way possible, and there is time for questions—an excellent way to stay up to date. And if Lynch is intrigued by what he hears, he might visit the plants afterward. Similarly, there are conferences on particular topics.

In reverse, Lynch himself is a first port of call for companies that want to tell their stories to the Boston investment community. At any time a score or so companies will be in town to deliver their pitch. Lynch could schedule four an hour if he wanted to.

A key element of Lynch's technique is his *insistence on firsthand contact with his sources.* Fidelity has dozens of in-house analysts, plus their assistants, and many other portfolio managers besides himself. Lynch could just rely on the information ingested and processed by this system. But he wants direct, regular contact with each company. *Investment managers who don't do this basic spadework, are, in Lynch's opinion, shirking their job.*

"When I actually see a company, I try to dig in: 'Your capital spending was $420 million last year; what is it this year? Depreciation was $288 million last year; what is it this year?' Management is much more on your side when you've done your homework."

Lynch's endless quest, his endless searching among companies, is directed above all toward the *obvious winner, based on changes in the key variable.* As he goes back repeatedly to a given company or industry he spots changes. Business has been dreadful for a year. Then it's not quite so bad. "Even when a company just moves up from doing mediocre business to doing fair business, you can make money," he says. Perhaps inventories are coming down. He learns of something afoot that will change things—a better regulatory climate, a new product or service. So he starts to buy, not just the leader in the group, as T. Rowe Price would, or what seems like the most attractive bargain, as Warren Buffett would, but, like James Rogers, the entire group, *in toto*: quite possibly dozens of companies. Then, as they start to move, he may winnow the list down to a favorite few.

I underline Lynch's emphasis on the *obvious* winner. Lynch claims that if other investors made as many calls as he did, they too would spot the changes in company fortunes that he does, and would almost always recognize the same buying opportunities. "You have to stay tuned," he often says.

There are, of course, a couple of differences between Lynch and most investors, or they would do as well at his game as he does. First, he has a sure enough grasp of the material to be able to act swiftly and smoothly, without troubling to get more facts than necessary . . . just enough to be right most of the time.

A second advantage is that since he can evaluate and develop buying and selling targets all across the range of his huge repertoire of actual and possible holdings, he perceives far more opportunities than most investors. Most fund managers reason that since knowing more than the competition is the key to superiority, they will focus on a limited area—"value" stocks, growth stocks, foreign stocks, resources companies, insurance companies, banks, or whatever—and rarely be outtraded in their chosen sector. But when that sector gets overpriced, as from time to time it surely will, what then? One is always tempted to carry on anyway, exposing the portfolio to the risk of a terrific header, or else branch out into some apparently different underpriced sector, where, however, one can easily make mistakes out of ignorance.

Lynch's technique of being prepared to deal in practically any stock whatever places the same sort of demands on a manager that a second-hand jewelry dealer would experience if he branched out into paintings, rare books, antique rugs, coins, furniture, manuscripts, etchings, and then commercial and residential real estate and wholesale vegetables. Auction galleries have a wide range of expertise, but they have considerable staffs to which specialized authority is delegated: a paintings department, a furniture department, and so on. Lynch had access to Fidelity's research, yet made all his own decisions.

Quite surprising, in my experience of notable investors, is Lynch's balanced, calm, modest, and unassuming approach to his profession and to life—except of course, for his phenomenally intense preoccupation with his work. Geniuses and obsessives usually have some burr under the saddle: poverty or family trouble in youth, or physical or social burdens, or some blow of fate later on that pushes them to pass their rivals. Lynch was presumably affected by the early death of his father and his family's suddenly reduced circumstances, which would have made him feel alone and responsible for his own destiny. Who knows? And one forgets today what it once was to be an Irish Catholic in establishment Boston. The inordinate drive of the Kennedys is a familiar example. Lynch mentions that when he joined Fidelity there were only one or two other employees who were not Ivy League graduates! He showed them. The same stimuli often lead hyperperformers to become self-centered, subjective, and tyrannical. Lynch shows no trace of that. Those around him all praise his relaxed and easygoing manner. Most have never heard him raise his voice or express irritation.

Lynch's office approaches the ultimate in clutter. Against a window run two yards of reports in a horizontal parade, and in front of them vertical stacks of the reports that have come in during the week,

arranged in categories. Manila files litter the floor. Inches of paper
blanket his desk, and I counted some sixty yellow legal pads peeking
out here and there from the debris. I asked him if placing the yellow
pads in a series of vertical racks across one wall above his desk would
make it easier for him to put his hand on them instantly. He seemed
puzzled. He scooped up a file off the floor, glanced at it, and said, "If
this guy calls me back—he's the CEO of a company—I want to be able
to talk to him right away about what I'm interested in, so I need to
have it right here." I suppose the point is that he can put his finger on
what he wants quickly enough, and he knows roughly where in the jum-
ble everything is lurking. Perhaps we have here the difference between
artificial order—the garden of a French chateau, for example—and
working order, such as a jungle, which looks chaotic to the passerby, but
makes sense to God or a naturalist.

A key Lynch technique is *fluency*, letting his portfolio flow easily from
one idea to another. He notices some apparent opportunity in the market and moves on it forthwith, without delaying for extensive analysis.
Of course, this requires both flair and a sure judgment based on a long
experience of the subject. One is reminded of superb generalship: At
Salamanca, Wellington watches Marmont marching parallel to him
across a valley. Suddenly he spots an advantage. "By God! That'll do,"
he announces, snapping shut his telescope and crisply issuing the orders
that will destroy his adversary. Or Nelson at the Battle of the Nile:
After months of chase, he sweeps around a headland to find the French
fleet anchored against the shore in a defensive position. It is close to
nightfall. Another commander would have reconnoitered, devised a
plan, and instructed his captains for an attack the next day. Nelson
does not hesitate an instant. In the failing light he daringly slices in
between the land and the enemy vessels on their unprepared side,
anchors his ships so two can pound each hapless Frenchman, and has
battered the French fleet to bits before it can even recover its foraging
parties from shore.

Similarly, Lynch, detecting a market inefficiency, will act immediately. The domestic car companies seem cheap: He buys Ford, Chrysler,
and GM. They go up: He adds a collection of foreign ones—Volvo, Subaru, Honda, Peugeot, and Fiat. The relative positions change again: He
calmly reverses field. Dreyfus, the mutual fund management company,
falls from 35 to 17 in the crash of October 1987. The market fears that
the fund business may be in trouble. But there is $15 a share in cash,

and Dreyfus has such a strong money-fund department that it should gain business on balance. So Lynch buys Dreyfus. He also usually takes small positions in stocks that *may* be interesting—what he calls his farm team—so that he will be reminded to follow them.

Since, like a racing skipper, he is constantly changing course to take advantage of small shifts in the wind, there is unending movement in Lynch's portfolio. Many holdings only last a month or two, and the entire list turns over at least once a year on average. Lynch feels that if he were doing his job perfectly the turnover would be even greater.

Mechanically, this creates interesting problems. In Magellan, Lynch often had about fourteen hundred holdings; the largest one hundred represented half the total capital, and two hundred represented two-thirds of it. On a typical working day he transacted some $50 million of purchases and $50 million of sales. To conduct this huge volume of business he had only three traders. One did the buying and another the selling. A third understudied both. Ordinarily there would be a hundred or so issues in each trader's book; that is, a hundred that Lynch wanted to buy, if he could get them cheaply enough, and a hundred that he wanted to sell, if they reached his price targets. His traders were extremely price-sensitive. Rather than bashing in and trading a block all at once, like many big traders, they would withhold their bids or offers if the stock moved away from them and wait until it came back. He would typically drop out of the market altogether if he learned of a large competitive order, reasoning that he was better off waiting for the other fellow to get out of the way and buy when the stock fell back again, if it ever did. Less than 5 percent of Lynch's trades were bigger than 10,000 shares. (Many institutional managers usually deal in 100,000-share blocks.)

Lynch likes to seek to profit from what many investors would consider minor price anomalies. In a huge list of holdings and prospective holdings there will at any moment be dozens that have gotten ahead of themselves, justifying some selling, and dozens of others experiencing some price weakness that are worth buying. Here his technique differs radically from that of most other investors and resembles that of a market maker, who, handling a dozen or two issues, has become so attuned to the rhythm of his stable of stocks and the factors that move them that he trades them back and forth, back and forth, year after year, making endless small profits over and over, getting slowly richer in the process. The big difference, though, is that most specialists work twenty or thirty stocks at the most, while at Magellan Lynch operated with a couple of thousand, and constantly changing ones at that.

Lynch believes in an old trader's rule: *If you buy a stock because you hope something will happen, and it doesn't happen, sell the stock.* Wall Street has a sardonic expression for this idea: "An investment is a speculation that didn't work out." You had an idea, based on an expectation; you were wrong. So now you really have no reason to hold on to the stock and should sell it cleanly and quickly. Lynch says he often sells too soon. "But *you don't get hurt by things that you don't own that go up.* It's what you *do* own that kills you.

"Of the stocks that I buy, three months later I am happy with less than a quarter of them. So if I like to look at ten stocks, it's better for me to buy all ten, and then go on studying and researching. Perhaps I won't like a number of them later on, but I can keep the ones that I do like, and increase those positions. And companies keep changing as you look: Competition may intensify; a problem plant may be sold off or closed; a competitive plant may burn down. So if you stay tuned, you can find that the fundamentals are changing.

"Or even if they don't change, the stock may go from 20 to 16. Perhaps I bought 10,000 at 20, and then I'll buy 100,000 at 16. If I look at ten companies, I may find one company that is interesting. If I look at twenty companies then I may find two. If I look at forty, I may find four. If I look at a hundred, I may find ten. If other people saw as many companies as I do, I think that nine out of ten of them, when they heard the same story, would say, 'Wow,' just the way I do, and be able to make the same buyin' decision. You have to be a good listener in this business. And of course you may not be able to decide on the first visit. It may happen a year later or two years later."

The Individual Investor's Advantage

Lynch often speaks of the value of watching for signs in the world of everyday life. He gleans information from the trends followed by his children. Whether with them or on his own, he visits a shopping mall as a place to spot rising consumer companies. "What sells in one town is almost guaranteed to sell in another," he writes. Thus, any mall roamer could have come across Taco Bell, Lands' End, The Gap, Wal-Mart, or Home Depot early enough to profit.

He paid a visit to Supercuts to get his hair cut. He received a dismal job, but was not discouraged. Hair care is a huge industry, and individual barbers are a vanishing breed. The average Supercuts franchise owner has invested $100,000 and is expected to generate a 50 percent pretax return on equity in two years. Lynch found that the company received 5 percent of gross revenues and 4 percent on sales of the Nexus products displayed at each location. Supercuts also had $5.4 million in annual free cash flow. So it was a solid 20 percent grower selling for sixteen times earnings.

The key was that each stylist was trained to cut briskly—just under three jobs an hour, the brochure stated. Thus, the cost could be kept low: $8.95 for a regular cut, $12 with shampoo. Lynch heard no raves from his family* about his new haircut—too bad! He reasoned that the average American just wanted to get a decent snip, and the low cost would outweigh other factors. So while he vowed never to get his own hair cut there again, Lynch felt confident recommending Supercuts.

When a consumer contemplates buying a major appliance, such as a stove, says Lynch, he researches it carefully. He asks his friends who own one and looks it up in *Consumer Reports*. Similarly, when he buys a house he will bring in a builder to look at the plumbing and wiring and will check whether the local school system is deteriorating. But when this same man buys a stock, he will often do it on the basis of a tip, without any research at all.

And yet the individual buyer *should* have "an unbelievable advantage over the professional. He can take his time, and concentrate, and can just stay put, the way he holds on to his house. If he had to buy and sell every month or every week he would go crazy.

Similarly, Lynch suggests that individual investors take careful note of retail products, services, and purveyors that they find outstanding. He gives examples from his own experience: Volvo, Apple Computer, Dunkin' Donuts, Pier 1 Imports, and (thanks to L'eggs) Hanes.

One of Lynch's preferred devices is favored by most good investors. It is to *ask the man you are interviewing about his rivals across the street. It isn't too significant when the competitors pan a company, but it is important when they say something nice about it.* For instance, the other steel companies praised

*My wife sometimes cut my hair on the porch in the summer until I reported that a White Russian woman in my office, after surveying the effect, had muttered, *"Quel massacre!"*

Nucor: a new formula, new people, doing the right things. Lynch looked into it and bought the stock. Nobody knows a company like the competitor who has to battle with it day after day in creating new products and struggling for market share. John Templeton has a standard formula: "If you weren't working for your present company, who would you most like to join instead?" Once when Lynch was visiting United Inns he was struck by the respect with which its management spoke of one of its competitors, La Quinta Inns. The very next day he telephoned La Quinta. After a while he called in person, and in a matter of weeks had sunk 3 percent of Magellan's capital in the company.

There is another by-product from asking executives about matters outside their own company: investment ideas about its suppliers or customers. News from a construction outfit that sales are much stronger than generally realized could start Lynch thinking about forest products, cement, gypsum, or roofing materials.

Visiting Sears, he may find that carpet sales are improving. While calling on a retailer, he may find that shoes are selling badly, but that sneakers are going very well. What then? Stride Rite, which makes leather shoes for children, bought the Sperry Division of Uniroyal, and thus got Top-Siders. But what really worked for Stride Rite was Keds, which it was almost *forced* to take as part of the deal, and which now constitutes over half of Stride Rite's earnings. Lynch says that he was feeling sick that he hadn't caught Reebok, but "then I said, 'Hey, I've got a person over here that's participating in all this.' Funny things happen along the way. You really have to keep your eyes open." So he bought Stride Rite and cleaned up.

In 1992, Body Shop caught Lynch's eye: He noticed it was one of the mall's three most crowded stores. He remembered that the Fidelity head librarian had resigned to start a Body Shop franchise of her own. Like Ben & Jerry, Body Shop gave its employees a day a week paid leave for community service activities. Despite the 1991 recession, Body Shop worldwide reported increased same-store sales—one of two or three key factors in evaluating a retail operation, Lynch says. Lynch believed Body Shop could dramatically expand internationally. Canada had ninety-two Body Shops, but there were only seventy in the United States. Logically, then, the United States could support at least over nine hundred. Body Shop, growing at 30 percent and selling at forty times earnings, thus seemed more favorably priced than Coca-Cola, a 15 percent grower at thirty times earnings.

The Insider Index

Lynch carefully watches when corporate insiders buy their own stocks. An insider, he notes, may *sell* his company's stock for many reasons. He may be buying a house or raising cash to exercise stock options. *But the insider only has one reason to buy: to make money.* It is safe to suppose that an insider will only buy if what he sees gives him good reason to be confident. *A company, Lynch observes, will rarely go bust in the face of heavy insider buying.* He particularly looks for a *depressed stock being scooped up by middle-level insiders,* even more than by CEOs.

Fidelity has a little team following insider trading. They receive and condense reports from the New York Stock Exchange and the SEC and put out charts showing where the insiders have bought in the past. Sales are significant if a number of executives are selling a large part of their position. If an officer has 10,000 shares and sells 1,000 to finance a house, that is not significant. If, however, he has 45,000 shares and sells 40,000 of them, and several other officers are making sales of comparable size, that is of the greatest significance and merits careful study and, probably, action.

Lynch finds one of the *worst traps to be buying exciting companies that do not have earnings.* He can remember buying dozens of companies where—had the story come true—he would have made 1,000 percent on his money, and losing every time. And yet, and yet . . . ! Wonderful new stories appear—"the sizzle, not the steak," as he says—and again he will bite, and again he will lose.

A useful investment concept that Peter Lynch has coined a name for is the "whisper stock." By this he means a company that his source—otherwise reliable—lowers his voice somewhat to describe, saying, "I have a great company that's a bit too small for a fund, but that you might want to consider for a personal account." The reliable source then describes some irresistible idea, which will be a huge winner if it succeeds. Lynch claims that he has invariably lost money on these conceptions.

Lynch distinguishes between companies that intelligently expand into related businesses where their knowledge and skill are applicable and those that make wild, unplanned purchases of companies that management hopes it can handle, but often can't. In general, Lynch feels that companies with excess cash are better advised to repurchase their own stock than to expand into business areas that may give them lots of trouble.

As some simple criteria of a desirable investment, Lynch suggests looking for *a company selling at a low price-earnings ratio that earns 15 to 20 percent on
equity, and 10 percent or so on revenues.* Also, it should have a strong and *understandable business franchise,* so that it does not need to be run by supermen.

Unlike many investors, Lynch loves *simple businesses that anybody could
run.* Other investors (notably Phil Fisher!) often prefer what might be
called the athletes, the top businesses with wonderful managements in
highly competitive areas—Procter & Gamble or 3M or Texas Instruments or Dow Chemical or Motorola—which, toughened by decades of
successful struggle, have developed lean, hard teams that make opportunities, scramble for markets, and constantly push growth by finding
new products. Sure, that's the company you'd want your grandfather to
have started. But for Lynch the crux is that you don't need to insist on
anything wonderful, just a good-enough company that's selling too low
and won't fall apart before the stock moves back up to where it belongs.
In his words, he wants a company that any fairly good group of new
managers could take over and run with reasonable confidence that
things would hold together for a few years.

It is not in the nature of business in general for a company to deliver
twenty years of consistently rising earnings. If one sees such a phenomenon, management should probably not get the credit, but rather the
business itself. Even if management is the essence, Lynch finds that he
has little chance of finding that out.

One characteristic a company may have that lessens worry about
management is that it enjoys what securities people call a niche and
Warren Buffett calls a moat: something unique or at least special. He
cites Service Corporation International, a chain of funeral homes that
is steadily buying the best existing homes in new locations; Dunkin'
Donuts, which seems to go on and on in its simple business; or Regis,
the largest independent beauty salon chain, specializing in shopping
malls; or Rockaway, which makes postage meters. His dream, he says,
somewhat surprisingly, is *the growth company in a slow-growth industry:* You
know something has to be profoundly right about the situation.

The same reasoning explains why Lynch is not comfortable with
high-tech companies: They may be just fine, but that doesn't do him
much good if he can't understand them. "How c'n I know if one outfit's
random-access memory is better'n some'n else's?" he asks. In reply, one
can only say that some analysts do try to know just that; however, they
are usually specialists.

Growth for Lynch is of course a cardinal virtue in a company, and growth stocks have always been the largest single category in his portfolios. Nevertheless, growth companies are for him by no means the only attractive category to hold. Anything may be underpriced or overpriced at some time, and thus a buy or a sale. However, in talking of growth, *Lynch looks particularly at unit growth,* even more than earnings growth. T. Rowe Price, the original apostle of growth-stock investing, looked for companies that reported higher earnings in each successive business cycle. However, higher earnings may derive from raising prices or from skillful acquisitions. Lynch looks for rising numbers of physical units sold, quarter by quarter and year by year.*

"The very best way to make money in a market is in *a small growth company that has been profitable for a couple of years and simply goes on growing,"* says Lynch, who further observes that it is easier to make big percentage gains in stocks of small companies than in those of big ones. It is much harder for a stock in the Dow Jones Industrial Average to triple than it is for a stock in a little NASDAQ company.

Nevertheless, he points out that if you get the facts right, you make more in a high-growth company selling at a high price-earnings ratio, assuming that the earnings justify the price. He cites as an example a company selling for twenty times $1 earnings per share, or $20, and growing 20 percent a year, and a company selling for ten times $1 earnings per share, or $10, and growing 10 percent a year. After a year, the first company will be earning $1.20 and the second company $1.10. In the tenth year, the first company will be earning $6.19, and if it is still selling at twenty times earnings, the market price will be $123.80. If, as often happens, the price-earnings ratio has declined, to 15, say, then the market price will be $92.85.

In the meantime, however, the company whose earnings growth is 10 percent will be earning $2.59, implying a market price of $25.90, a quarter or so of the price of the high-growth company.

---

*Annual reports may or may not state a company's unit sales. If not, securities analysts in the old days would sometimes go to the factory and count the number of tractors or whatever coming out the back door. Today this is generally impractical. My own firm, which is growth-oriented, tracks the approximate growth in unit sales from the reported figures by multiplying two ratios; the retained operating margin on sales and the turnover rate of gross operating assets . . . the latter being a measure of the capital required to produce $1 of sales.

Going Abroad

The inefficiencies of international investing can be astonishing. Lynch visited one of the major brokers in Sweden. No one from the firm had been to see Volvo, which was only two hundred miles away in Gothenburg. In Sweden, Volvo is the equivalent of IBM, General Motors, and General Electric. In England, five or six analysts will have visited any big company within a month. But this would not be true in Germany, France, Hong Kong, or Thailand.

Lynch's lack of inhibitions lets him invest abroad without qualms. He just compares the foreign company with its domestic counterpart and decides which he prefers: Ford, Subaru, or Volvo? Procter & Gamble or Unilever? Uniroyal or Michelin? AKZO or Du Pont? "You can arbitrage one against the other, depending on the price. Take depreciation. You determine what the gross plant account is, and then what AKZO's annual depreciation is as compared to Du Pont's, say. If AKZO has a 4 percent depreciation rate and Du Pont has 2 percent you know AKZO's profits are understated."

Lynch said at one time that he had enjoyed a far higher proportion of successes in Europe than in the United States. Three months after purchase he was happy with a good half of the companies he had bought in Europe, compared with only a quarter of his U.S. buys. "French brokers are terrible," he says. "You analyze a company division by division, and you find that it cannot possibly realize the projections made by the brokers. They've pulled the figures out of a hat."

Among countries, Lynch is likely to be most comfortable with the ones that other fund managers are uneasy about and thus don't have large holdings in. Take Italy, for instance: It has one of the highest savings rates in the world and some years ago introduced the concept of mutual funds, which would pull lots of money into stocks. When Lynch bought IFI on the Milan exchange, it was capitalized at only 40 percent of just the value of its holdings in Fiat and some other companies. SIP, a telephone company, was selling for 1.5 times its cash flow. In other words, Italian companies were extraordinarily cheap. When Lynch bought Del Haize Frères it was selling for much less than the value of just one of its holdings, an outstanding U.S. supermarket company called Food Lion.

Lynch is happiest buying foreign stocks abroad that American institutions are just beginning to accumulate. Some of them have huge market capitalizations and can absorb a heavy investment. After this process has gone on long enough, though, the stocks get over-owned by Americans and it's time to move on.

Theories

Lynch has a brusque, commonsense contempt for most of the formulas that are peddled as shortcuts to stock market success. He avoids the economic "overviews" and industrial-sector allocations that some institutions favor as a substitute for knowledge and flair; likewise, weighty punditry on economics and market analysis. Completing his repudiation of conventional trust company practice, which, based on an economic "overview," puts a portfolio into categories—cyclicals, utilities, and the like—and massages them by computer, *Lynch entirely avoids conscious "asset allocation," either between stocks and reserves or between industrial sectors.*

It follows from this that he doesn't believe in the antiquated approach quaintly called "modern portfolio theory," which essentially means that you don't understand the companies that you are buying, but instead fit them into categories and play with the categories.

Catching the turn is a maneuver that attracts Lynch strongly. He wants to make a partial investment a bit ahead of the turn in the fortunes of a company, and then build up his holding as the turn actually occurs.

Lynch gives little weight to a company's dividend policy. In his own language, "I can't say that dividends are something I feature."

A horrible fallacy, he says, is buying a stock simply because it has gone down, what is called bottom-fishing. If the market thought that Federated Fido was worth $50 six months ago, and it's $20 today, then it must be a bargain! But that was true when it was at $40 and then at $30, and it may well be true when the stock goes down to $10. You have to have a clear conception of the true value and base your decisions on that, not on the stock's recent performance history.

Lynch wants to be in the position of buying Company A at $20 a share rather than Company B at $30 a share, and then of selling A after it has moved to $30 in order to buy B at $20. He points out that several small gains make a very large one: "Three 30 percent moves equals a four-bagger," he says. His is a technique of relative values, not of majestic conceptions. "I never make any big decisions," he has said.

Heavy Thinking

"I spend about fifteen minutes a year on economic analysis," he says. "The way you lose money in the stock market is to start off with an economic picture. I also spend fifteen minutes a year on where the stock market is going. *All these great heavy-thinking deals kill you."*

He finds that worries based on economic predictions are particularly useless. "We don't make economic judgments," he has said. "Nobody called me to tell me about the recession in 1980 and 1981," he observes dourly.

Lynch notices that people always ask him about the outlook for the economy and the stock market and other such large and general questions. But nobody can give those answers. And even if anyone could, companies like Procter & Gamble and Colgate should be little affected by such fluctuations. If, instead, one buys a company that has inherent problems, one can lose one's money in the best of times.

In a way, what Lynch is really saying is that if a stock is cheap, that is a much higher degree of reality than some vague notion as to what the market will do next year. Quite the contrary: If a great many stocks are cheap in the eyes of an experienced appraiser, or indeed most stocks are cheap, then it follows that the whole market is cheap.

Market Timing

Starting in 1954, Lynch has written, an investor sticking with the S&P for the following forty years would have made an annual return on his investment of 11.4 percent. If he was out of stocks for the ten most profitable months, usually as the market bounced sharply from a bottom, the return fell to 8.3 percent. If he missed the forty most profitable months, his return collapsed to 2.7 percent.

He cites the remarkable statistic that $1,000 invested in the S&P on January 1 of every year since 1975 produced an 11 percent annual return. If the same $1,000 was invested at the peak of the market each year, the return was still 10.6 percent. Conversely, the same amount invested at the absolute low point each year produced an 11.7 percent return. *An insignificant difference!*

He points to the *Forbes* list of the richest people in America: "There's never been a market timer on it. If it were truly possible to predict corrections, you'd think somebody would have made billions by doing it." Indeed, he observes that Warren Buffett, always near the

top of the list in recent years, cares scarcely at all about market fluctuations.*

*Lynch is indignant about leveraged buyouts in general, because, he says, they
prevent the investing public from participating fully in a recovery following a
decline.* Here's the logic: A company is selling at 20, let us say. Then in a
market slide or because of bad news it declines to 8. A good company
reorganizes and bounces back. Along comes management or a takeover
artist and offers to buy out the shareholders at 12, which enough shareholders accept to enable the new owners to "freeze out" the remainder.
The insiders sell off assets to pay themselves back. But if that hadn't
happened, the stock might have gone to 40 or 50. So the public has suffered the loss and been done out of the recovery! Lynch also observes
sardonically that some investment banker or other will always, for a
huge fee, issue a "fairness opinion," to the effect that the bid of 12 for a
stock now selling at 8 is "fair." But if the buyers know it was 20 a while
back and fully expect it to be 20 or more again, two or three years
ahead, is 12 really fair?

Lynch observes that while you must of course master a company's
figures, balance-sheet analysis by itself is inadequate. " 'Very cheap statistically' can be a real trap," he says. "Book value can be hopelessly
misleading. There is nothing in the balance sheet of Coca-Cola for the
goodwill of the name and the logo, for instance. Then you can have a
company with $200 billion in assets and $100 million in debt: Fine,
except that sometimes the assets turn out to be worth only $50 million.
So even figures may in reality be very subjective.

"However," he says, "if a company has a good balance sheet when I
buy it, that gives me a big edge. If it doesn't turn around I can perhaps
lose a third of what I invest. But if it does turn around, then I can do
very well indeed."

Lynch notes that when he has lost almost all of an investment, it has
often been because he should have kept in better touch with what was
happening to the balance sheet.

He does, however, have an intellectual framework for his portfolio.
There are four conceptual categories. He had been running the Magellan

---

*To this I observe that from time to time there have been rich speculators, such as
Bernard Baruch; indeed there are today: George Soros, Stanley Druckenmiller, Bruce
Kovner, and others. On the other hand, it's an inordinately difficult way to prosper,
and can be a short route to bankruptcy.

Fund for three or four years before some outside shareholders who studied the portfolio pointed out to him what the different categories of holdings in fact were. He had not originally bought the holdings to fit into those categories, but agreed that they were valid.

1.   Growth companies on which he would hope to make two or three times his cost over time.
2.   Underpriced asset plays, "value" stocks, or smaller blue chips. He would be looking for a rapid gain of a third or so after which he would likely move on promptly.
3.   Special situations and depressed cyclicals.
4.   Defensive stocks, which he would hold in preference to cash. *"A market player has 50 percent of his portfolio in cash at the bottom of the market. When the market moves up, he can miss most of the move."*

Lynch never holds actual cash or cash equivalents. Rather, he holds conservative stocks with substantial yields, in stable industries. They should not be too much affected by economic downturns and should hold up well in market declines, although they lag during market rises. This category might include a hundred or two hundred stocks: food companies, advertising agencies, telephone and gas utilities, financial companies, and retailers. This group, since he is not looking for big gains, is also where his highest turnover occurs. "If a stock goes up, because it's had a road show or for some other reason, but the fundamentals are unchanged, then I'll sell it and add to the others in the category."

He has said, "You've got to go into places where other investors, and especially fund managers, fear to tread, or, more to the point, invest."

The Best of the Worst

Lynch makes a point of searching for "great companies in lousy industries." "As a place to invest, I'll take a lousy industry over a great industry any time." Why? Because in a lousy industry, "the weak drop out and the survivors get a bigger share of the market." In 1992 he selected a handful of survivors in odd industries, companies virtually ignored by Wall Street. One was Bandag, a company making retread tires in Muscatine, Iowa. Every year in America, twelve million worn-out truck and bus tires are replaced by retreads, five million of them made by Bandag. Despite this, and despite a stock rise from 2 to 60 in fifteen years, Lynch saw that only three Wall street analysts followed the company.

And carpets. "There hasn't been a worse business in contemporary America," says Lynch of that industry. But every time a company failed, Shaw Industries scooped up the business. He searched a database for articles on Shaw, a $1 billion enterprise, and found only two, even though it had captured 20 percent of the U.S. carpet business. Even in the worst of times, the company kept up a phenomenal 20 percent annual growth rate. Indeed, from 1980 to 1992 the stock rose fiftyfold.

The stock Lynch says *he most wants to avoid is the hottest stock in the hottest industry*—the one that gets the most favorable publicity, that every investor is told about by other investors . . . and that then collapses. He cites any number of formerly hot industries; digital watches, mobile homes, health-maintenance organizations, cheap wall-to-wall carpeting companies, disk drives, oil services—and, indeed, Xerox. In all cases, *the high growth is a honey pot for the competition,* which strikes the hot company just when it has spent huge sums to expand in order to hold on to market share. So its profit margin collapses, it gets into a financial bind, and since it is followed by every possible security analyst and speculator, its fall is precipitous.

In late 1992, Lynch was recycled by Fidelity. As described in Appendix X, the company had been racked by bad publicity following a scandal and SEC investigations.* Lynch's straight-arrow image seemed needed. He found himself in Fidelity's advertising and even "infomercials" on cable television. "They had to bring him back," said a Wall Street communications veteran. "He had become the Fidelity equivalent of the Merrill Lynch bull. He was their image." So today, in PR lingo, Peter Lynch "represents" Fidelity even though he no longer runs money there directly. (He does offer counsel to the analysts.) His relaxed, honest face and form appear in ads all over the country, including "Dear Friend" sweepstakes mailers from *Worth* magazine (which do not bother to mention that *Worth* is owned by Fidelity).†

The public is invited to think that Lynch is at the controls, but the image is very deceptive. Indeed, his stake in Fidelity is in nonvoting stock, and he has never been involved in day-to-day line management. On the contrary, he always made a point of avoiding such management responsibility. Anyway, absolute control is in the hands of the Johnson family.

---

*A January 27, 2000, article in the *Wall Street Journal* reveals that Fidelity demands that its IPO allocations from brokers be at least twice any other customer's.
†It's an interesting magazine, for which, to declare an interest, I've written columns.

Instead, he has been encouraged to write books and articles and appear in the annual *Barron's* Roundtables.

"My stock-picking method, which involves elements of art and science plus legwork, hasn't changed in twenty years," Lynch maintains in his book *Beating the Street*. He concedes, however, that sometimes his rules have been applied too strictly. His rule of only buying what he understood often meant ruling out technology. That was a mistake, he later admitted. "You didn't need a Ph.D. to figure out that Microsoft owned the rights to MS-DOS, the operating system used in the vast majority of the world's PCs." In a war, he suggested, don't back one or another combatant, buy the companies that sell them bullets.* Microsoft, as it were, sells the bullets. Similarly, one required little technical expertise to observe that most PCs seemed to have Intel chips inside them.

Another time, Lynch learned from his children. Visiting a college, he found himself stepping around crews installing campus-wide computer networks. Much of this work was being done by a single company called Cisco. A bit of research showed that the company's earnings were growing dramatically. And at that time only 10 to 20 percent of schools had been wired into networks—not to speak of offices, government agencies, and the like. Cisco was selling the bullets.

For years Lynch has been writing that wonderful bargains are to be found in savings and loan associations, or "thrifts." His attention was drawn to them initially by the same dismal pronouncements that held other investors at a distance. In 1992, by the key measure of equity to total assets, one hundred of the nation's S&Ls were stronger than J. P. Morgan. One of his favorites, People's Savings Financial in New Britain, Connecticut, had an equity-to-assets ratio of 12.5 percent, while J. P. Morgan's was less than 6 percent. Between 1991 and 1994, Lynch saw some three hundred new S&Ls issue shares that gained an average of 30 percent on the first day of trading and 60 percent within three months. Alas, in early 1994 regulators put a temporary stop to the bonanza.

When a thrift goes public—a "conversion," as it is called—anyone with a savings account at the institution is invited to buy shares at the initial low price. Despite Lynch's suggestions to small investors that they jump in, almost all these shares were bought by professional

---

*It is often observed that in the California gold rush, the big gainers weren't the poor prospectors out there in the wilds but the merchants who sold the jeans (led by Levi's), mining equipment, and alcoholic and feminine relaxation.

investors who opened savings accounts across the country to participate in as many conversions as possible.

In a May 1997 column he again recommended the thrifts, observing
that from 1992 to 1996 some 445 had gone public. Of those with prices
available, the average rise in value had been 98 percent. Only five were
trading below their IPO price. In fact, in 1995 and 1996, thrift IPOs
saw an average first-day gain of 14.2 percent. Lynch's favorites are the
Jimmy Stewart mom-and-pop thrifts, as in *It's a Wonderful Life:* low-cost
operators in small cities taking in deposits from neighbors and making
residential mortgage loans.

Lynch put together several principles for sizing up how to invest in a
thrift:

1. It should be profitable.
2. It should have a high equity-to-assets ratio and a solid balance sheet
    and not be saddled with problem loans.
3. You should see insiders buying the shares, and paying the same
    price you are. (Insider buying must be reported in the prospectus.)
4. The amount raised in the offering should roughly correspond to the
    company's value before the offering.

Lynch's long-term positive outlook on thrifts reflects a changing economic environment, as well as the inevitability of further takeovers and
mergers. He points out that Great Britain has a population of 58 million and only seven major banks, while the United States, five times as
populous, has some twenty thousand banks, including credit unions
and the like. In other words, there are many, many mergers still to
come. First and foremost, one should be on the lookout for thrift conversions taking place in one's own neighborhood.

At the top of Lynch's list of all-time financial industry favorites is still
Fannie Mae, the leader in the home mortgage business. Lynch has
owned Fannie Mae since the early eighties. He points out that in 1997 it
earned roughly $2.80 per share, while the stock had *sold* for $2.55 a share
(adjusted for splits) a decade previously. "That's what I call a remarkable
investment," he wrote, "when a company's per-share earnings in a single
year exceed the price you paid for the stock." Fannie Mae has posted
record earnings for ten consecutive years. *Forbes*, however, calculated how
well an investor would have done following his *Worth* recommendations.
"Probably not well at all," the magazine concluded.

Lynch has been bothered by the high price-earnings ratios of several popular companies. He believes that investors in McDonald's may be taking a risk if earnings do not accelerate quickly. Likewise, although he has always been enthusiastic about Johnson & Johnson, a great growth company with strong prospects, he is troubled by the high price-earnings ratio. Wal-Mart, conversely, had an excessive P/E ratio several years ago, but it has come down. He feels that Wal-Mart "has a decent shot at a decade of respectable growth."

To sum up the whole matter, Lynch is a fanatic about the stock market. His wife was quoted in an article as saying that on their first date, when he was at the Wharton School, his entire conversation was about stocks and the stock market. Well, dedication right from one's youth is what it takes for greatness in any field: to win an Olympic gold medal in gymnastics, to beat the Russians at chess, to star in the New York City Ballet. And Lynch is in that league. Great success, alas, usually requires obsession. Differently put, you won't get there if you don't love it so much that you'd rather do it than anything else, whether or not it's worth that dedication. As an ancient French saying has it, *La joie de l'esprit en fait la force*—loosely translated, "The spirit's joy gives it power." Delight in his craft is Lynch's secret.

Eighteen

LESSONS OF THE MASTERS

To THE READER WHO HAS REACHED THIS POINT, CONGRATULA-
tions! We have come a long way. Now, let us try to sum up what can be
learned from these studies. We can see in them several different basic
ways to do unusually well in the stock market:

1. Buy into well-managed companies that will grow and grow and grow,
   and stay on board for the ride as long as they keep growing. When
   they slow down, sell them and buy new ones. (For some examples of
   great growth stocks, see Appendix XI.)
2. Over and over, buy stocks that are priced in the market at less than
   their underlying assets are worth, and sell them when they are reasonably priced: value investing. Often such companies are badly
   managed and have poor growth prospects.
3. Discover a new investment area, or one that is seriously neglected,
   where the values are thus highly attractive.
4. Identify a really good specialist to do the job for you, directly or
   through a fund. This book should give some hints on how to go
   about finding such a person.

Stocks or sectors that are compelling buys will usually be under some
cloud at the time, or perhaps overlooked. The market exaggerates bad
news, so if the real prospects of a company decline by a quarter because
of an adverse development, the price of the share may fall by half. False
bad news is best, but true bad news—for example, a war scare—is fine.

The same works in reverse for good news, whence my maxim *"Nothing exceeds like success."*

At bottoms, almost everything is ridiculously cheap, and at the top almost everything is extravagantly overpriced. Thus, the great value investors often have a three- or four-year buy-sell cycle (sometimes based on the presidential election year stimulus phenomenon), while the top growth investors often hold their outstanding stocks as long as they stay outstanding—sometimes for decades.

Growth Investing

Is the growth or the value approach more valid today? A decade or so ago in a predecessor volume I wrote as follows:

> The price-earnings ratio of growth stocks in general oscillates from the same as the Dow stocks to twice that of the Dow.
>
> In mid-1989, therefore, while the Dow does not seem particularly attractive compared to either bonds or growth stocks, it also appears (as both Lynch and Neff observe) that growth stocks are good value compared to both bonds and the standard industrials. . . .
>
> It is not easy to calculate the rate of return of a growth stock. One method is to project its earnings for a reasonable number of years, and then assume that they will trail off to the level of the mass of all stocks—"regress to the mean." Then you calculate what discount rate will reduce that stream of earnings to the present market price. That gives the indicated rate of return. As I write, my own estimated rate of return on this basis for the growth stocks that I think I understand is over 20 percent, a far more attractive figure than either short Treasuries, long bonds, or the Dow stocks.

That's how it came out. Growth stocks were marvelous performers over the next decade.

So where are we in 2003? The growth stocks have had an enormous surge, but to my mind they still remain more attractive than either the Dow stocks or bonds as *long-term* investments. My estimated rate of total return on the growth stocks I think I understand is down to 12 to 14 percent per annum—less than before, but considering the fall in the inflation rate, acceptable.

For the substantial tax-paying investor I think the Buffett–Price approach the most practical, if he really can do it himself or can hire someone competent to do it for him, either directly or through a mutual fund. It requires less study and far fewer transactions.

It does, however, present the risk of losing money toward the end of a major bull market. Almost nobody—certainly not most fund managers—has the tough independence of spirit to get off the bandwagon to prune his portfolio of greatly overpriced holdings when it is in full gear: Even a professional manager working for a big cut of the realized profits can put a fortune in his pocket in one year toward the end of a bull market, without having to disgorge it when the collapse follows, so he's very tempted to overstay the party. Thus, the substantial investor dealing with an outside investment adviser must, in my opinion, impose some selling discipline on the operation, based on his own wisdom and common sense.

Equally, however, he can *make* exceptional profits by buying authentic growth stocks during market collapses. And once he has acquired a portfolio of such issues during a bear market washout, the investor can if he likes forget the vagaries of the market and stay aboard the growth escalator. He must, of course, make sure that the values are actually still building, by watching the profit margins, the growth of unit sales, the return on equity, and so on—all of which he can easily find in *Value Line.*

He should always keep enough liquid reserves to see him through any likely emergency and to provide ammunition for targets of opportunity. A comfortable reserve means that the investor needn't panic in bad times, and if he has reserves to spend during a first-class panic there is the possibility of acquiring some fantastic bargains, the foundation of a real fortune.

That brings us to the emotional demands made on the investor by the "growth" approach. It doesn't do much good to know all the rules if you do not know the specifics and therefore during a major decline become panicked into selling at the bottom.

So you must ask yourself when adopting the growth philosophy if you know enough about a company so that you can put up with the lack of yield and the quotational volatility that are the price of growth investing. If you don't know what you have, you're much more tempted to buy when a stock is popular—meaning when it is too high-priced—and then dump it if it falls: the opposite of the profitable strategy. So look at Fisher's tests of good management, for instance, and Buffett's main principles. If you feel comfortable with them, or your adviser does, you should have the confidence to hold on through bad times.

Value Investing

The Graham-Neff approach seems particularly appropriate to institutional portfolios, such as bank-managed pension funds. The method is obviously "prudent" and systematic—bankerly, in fact. It deals with the here and now. Banks are in an unusually good position to assess the business and financial situations of corporations—it's their daily business. And the capital gains tax penalties of the method won't bother a tax-free portfolio. A bank can execute such a program in-house, keeping costs down and preserving confidentiality, and it won't have to rationalize specific stocks, only the general method, to a client company's investment committee.

Further, if the simplified value criteria become too popular and the opportunities dry up, the bank can go back to full-scale analysis of the type set out in *Security Analysis*, which can readily be done by a computer. In this analysis the institution can make full use of its inherent advantages over the private investor: a much larger continuing research capability, and training and experience in dispassionate evaluation.

And the great merit of the Graham-Neff variation of the "value" strategy is that you can't lose any significant amount of money. Sooner or later objects selling well below their intrinsic value recover to their normal levels.

Spotting Change

Many investors, such as Jim Rogers, Ralph Wanger, T. Rowe Price, Richard Rainwater, and Robert Wilson, seek major trend reversals they can take advantage of—the "top-down" approach. Price called it, felicitously, seeking the "fertile fields for growth." He and the others mentioned look primarily to the world outside their door. Fiber optics? Pipeline companies exhausting their gas reserves? A new regulatory environment? Telecom? Microprocessors? HMOs? One then checks with industry sources and starts investigating particular companies.

The other method of catching trend changes is that of Peter Lynch and Julian Robertson, whose endless talks with the companies them-

selves reveal changes at the micro level—the "bottom-up" approach.*
Either way, though, *the investor hopes to notice change in time to take advantage of it ahead of his competitors.*

Novel Investment Areas

Surprisingly often the greatest investors, like an art collector who unearths and exploits an overlooked category, develop a new approach.

Here are some examples. In the mid-1930s, after the Crash, common stocks became most attractive, precisely because shell-shocked fiduciaries wouldn't hear about them as investments. A few practitioners, such as Paul Cabot, founded financial empires based on that simple conception. Then Benjamin Graham formulated and tested a series of rules for buying particular types of conventional stocks so cheaply you almost couldn't lose money. Decade after decade the Graham method worked admirably. He published his method and its results, but almost nobody followed his example. Then, some time after the period when I wrote about Graham in a 1980 predecessor volume to this book, a geometrically increasing number of neo-Grahamites piled in, and the field became overcrowded.

T. Rowe Price popularized the idea of "growth stocks" and devised a series of principles for buying them. By the late 1960s this approach had become excessively popular, and by 1972 that category became grossly overpriced. Later still, after growth stocks had crashed, they became wonderful values again, but investors were leery of the category.

Phil Carret and others concentrated on the over-the-counter world, and Ralph Wanger on very small companies—both areas often neglected by analysts, and thus often offering bargains.

After World War II a few hardy spirits, including John Templeton, realized that Japan was destined to be a great industrial power, and that some of its premier companies—the equivalents of our GE, Ford, and Prudential—were selling, adjusted for everything, at three or four times earnings. Fantastic killings were made by the handful of investors who knew that things really were what they seemed and dared to act on their knowledge. More recently, others noticed the Italian and German economic miracles. Mark Lightbown and James

---

*Lynch also suggests getting investment ideas from retail products and services you encounter, but that's deceptive for products facing intense competition.

Rogers dug out smaller new countries to invest in, or promising companies to buy there.

Mario Gabelli created an important firm by anticipating corporate buyouts, and the ill-famed Michael Milken made a fortune by developing a huge market for lower-grade corporate ("junk") bonds. In a way, Warren Buffett developed an unusual technique by redeploying insurance company reserves in equity equivalents, accepting the increased risk. However, this is a dangerous game; it sank Executive Life and other companies.

In other words, it has always been possible in the past to identify neglected techniques or neglected areas of investment: lots! The reader can reasonably ask if there are any today. Yes, I see several.

One that seems obvious is smaller companies. The popularity of micro-caps compared to big-caps moves in a long cycle, which should be ready for a turn. Think about Carret and Wanger!

Another is selling short, a disaster area in recent years. Some of the dot-com stocks are clearly in a speculative bubble, which should be deflated in due course. A similar swarming took the "one-decision" growth stocks into the stratosphere in 1972–73, followed by a horrible bust. It's best to wait until the collapse actually starts: What is too high can still go much higher. But, careful! A mistake in judgment can cost the short-seller a bundle as a large position goes heavily against him. To this, one counter is the Grahamite technique of wide diversification. Even then, short-selling is an extremely disquieting activity and should be undertaken only by professionals. In the future there may well be more limited partnerships pursuing this specialty.

Another category of perennial interest—again best conducted by professionals—is "distressed" securities of companies in reorganization, or bank loans to such companies (including Japanese bank loans to Japanese companies) that the banks need to get off their balance sheets. Richard Rainwater had great success in this sector. Not infrequently such opportunities arise as a result of misguided government intervention.

Companies in emerging countries that will make attractive takeover candidates for multinationals are a very interesting opportunity, as Mark Lightbown points out. Some skillful operators use guarantees from the Overseas Private Investment Corporation to insure their investments in odd countries against all risks except some opportunity cost.

A new category that could well be of interest is "shareholder activism"—buying enough stock in a troubled company to push management into making necessary changes, or to push the directors into changing management, or to push your fellow shareholders into changing the directors. This technique is being pursued by Lens Investment Management, Relational Investors, Greenway Partners, Trinity I Fund, Lawndale Capital, and (in London) Active Value. It makes great demands on its practitioners. You propose to break a bone in order to reset it, infallibly provoking howls of protest. The sluggish managers, the complacent directors, the indifferent trustees all must be shaken up and in many cases thrown out. Painful, costly lawsuits and personal vilification leaked to tame journalists are inevitable, even if the whistleblower is entirely right—perhaps even more if the whistleblower is right that management is corrupt. Not much fun! Still, if this useful function can be performed at a profit both for the shareholders of the target company and the reformers themselves, so much the better.*

What about investing internationally? You get excellent foreign exposure through the great U.S. multinationals, and the United States is more friendly to investors than almost any foreign country. So I see no need to invest in Europe, say, just for the sake of diversification. Still, if like Templeton, Rogers, and Lightbown you can plant yourself ahead of time in unpopular places where significant investment interest is just arriving, you should do well. A fund is the easiest way.

Relentless Pursuit

For a few of today's masters the investment cycle is as little as a few months, or whatever time it takes for a purchase to attain a previously calculated price level. This is an exceedingly hard discipline to follow, so in general, the retail investor should avoid it. Here is an analogy:

> Short Kwi was famous in his own right, famous as a hunter. . . . It was his technique of hunting to be relentless in his pursuit; therefore, if he shot an animal [with a small, weakly poisoned Bushman arrow] and suspected others to be in the vicinity he would let the wounded animal run where it would while he hunted on and shot another, and another, and when all were as good as dead he would

---

*This useful intervention must not be confused with buying out the shareholders of a company in a moment of market weakness. That's nice for you, but not for them.

rest, then return to pick up the trail of the one that he felt would die the soonest. He almost never lost an animal, for his eyes were sharp and he could follow a cold trail over hard ground and even over stones; he could tell from fallen leaves whether the wind or passing feet had disarranged them. .... *

So one new technique we find in this book is what might be called relentless pursuit: constantly scanning for new stocks to pick off for limited moves, rather than as long-term commitments. Here, for example, are some contrasts between these slalom artists, such as Peter Lynch, Michael Steinhardt, and Robert Wilson, and the traditional long-term style, as exemplified by Warren Buffett, Philip Fisher, T. Rowe Price, and Ralph Wanger.

Long-Term Investor	Relentless-Pursuit Trader
1. Trust to the magic of quiet long-term compounding.	Force the pace.
2. Stay with long-term trends.	Catch changes early.
3. Buy for the long term.	Buy and sell constantly.
4. Ride through minor setbacks.	Sell on possible adverse developments.
5. If the price becomes excessive, wait for the earnings to catch up.	Sell if the stock gets ahead of itself.
6. Give preference to existing holdings that you are familiar with.	Comparison-shop ruthlessly.
7. Put your eggs in one basket.	Diversify extensively.
8. Develop a congenial investment philosophy and stick to it.	Have no prejudices.
9. Know everything about a few big things.	Know about many things.
10. Develop helpful rules and formulas.	Avoid formulas.
11. Understand each company intimately.	Buy batches of companies that together represent a thesis.
12. Know management intimately.	Don't worry much about management.

---

*Elizabeth Marshall Thomas, *The Harmless People* (New York: Alfred A. Knopf, 1959).

13. Don't be too concerned about the exact price you pay or receive: Over a five- or ten-year holding period it should be unimportant.	Be very conscious of price in both buying and selling: Multiplied by many transactions it is critical.

In the relentless-pursuit technique, one tries to enter toward the bottom of a dip, at the same time setting a target for the later sale. This method can be practiced successfully only by authentic masters at the height of their powers, like Short Kwi. It also involves high turnover, meaning heavy transaction costs, unless the dealing side of the operation is conducted with the utmost skill. So one should follow the further discipline of always buying on weakness and selling into strength. That requires either a price-sensitive broker or putting in carefully set limit orders. The nonprofessional cannot aspire to this degree of skill, and supposing wrongly that he can will be expensive. This error is as I write being made on a vast scale by the horde of inexperienced computerized day traders.*

Investment Opportunity

Investment opportunity consists of the difference between the value and the perception. That is, if you can find something tradable that is seriously mispriced, you can profit from that anomaly.

So with any of these strategies, the cardinal rule is that *you must understand the values.* This starts, of course, with studying and fully grasping the basic figures ("numbers," in financial jargon) of any company that you invest in. All too many investors and, indeed, stockbrokers do not know the average age of the plants of a company they buy, or the depreciation rates, or the variations in its profit margin, or how its inventory turnover compares with that of its competitors. (It seems incredible, but most do not even master the prospectuses and 10Ks of their own companies.) Spreadsheets along the lines of James Rogers's (see Appendix V) are an excellent way to start, assuming that one carefully contemplates what emerges. (When I entered the business, one often spent years doing industry spreadsheets.) And of course you need a basic knowledge of accounting. In addition to knowing the figures, firsthand knowledge of the companies themselves is helpful. The

---

*One of them, furious at having lost all his money, recently irrupted into his broker's office and slaughtered the staff.

investor who can't spare the time for all this should hire someone who does possess those skills to invest for him.

Market Timing

What about trying to catch the overall market's ups and downs? The masters disagree. Buffett, Carret, Graham, Soros, Steinhardt, and, recently, Templeton move toward equities or defensive holdings according to whether the market seems a bargain or overpriced. On the other hand, Fisher, Lynch, Templeton, and Wanger believe that this maneuver usually doesn't pay.

So, manifestly, there is no rule.

For a *trader,* and particularly for a Soros-style margin or derivatives operator, who will be wiped out if he is caught for long on the wrong side of a move, there's no choice: You must be agile to survive. However, for a qualified stock-picker that's not true. If, based on thorough knowledge, one is convinced that a wonderful stock is going to grow five or ten or twenty times in twenty years, although from time to time it will drop a third or more, one can and probably should decide to ride through the bumps, rather than squeeze out any additional gains that periodic buying and selling might provide. Traders like Lynch or Steinhardt can buy and sell to advantage, but a long-term investor of the Price or Fisher school (and these days even Buffett, for his core holdings) would say that you'll probably outsmart yourself: You may execute a deft sale, but all too frequently fail to get back in before the stock bounces up sharply out of reach.

I find that most excellent stock analysts are poor market analysts and vice versa, like batters and pitchers, but a poor market analyst can still succeed entirely through stock analysis. Indeed, by far the best sign that the overall market is cheap is that there are a lot of obviously cheap stocks around.

The most powerful argument against attempting market timing is simply that if you are out of the market for even a few days at the bottom, your return is ruined. (See Appendix XII.) The market often explodes up from a major bottom or drops precipitously from a top, so that like Ralph Wanger's zebras, you don't have time to act.

Incidentally, *belief in market timing is itself a market indicator.* Well along in a great bull market, nobody wants to hear about timing, but at the bottom of a washout, when people wish desperately that they had sold, timing looks very attractive indeed!

Here are some more principles I observe that the best investors favor:

1. *Only buy a stock as a share in a good business that you know a lot about.* A stock is not a thing in itself, like a bird, that you hope will fly from 50 to 100. It should always be thought of as a specific share of a specific business, like owning a quarter-interest in a house.

Suppose, indeed, you contemplated buying a house and got a week's option on it. The silly way to spend that time would be to call the broker every hour or two and worry about what he said. The sensible approach would be to get an appraiser to check the house, find out how much the necessary repairs and improvements would cost, and perhaps go around to other similar properties in the neighborhood and elsewhere to compare values. You would want to talk to the neighbors, find out about zoning and contemplated changes, visit the school, the mayor, the police chief, and the bank. That would be a week well spent, and you would be infinitely more likely to make a sensible decision than would someone who sat at home badgering the broker.

So stated, it seems absurd to suppose that an investor would buy a stock without forming an accurate impression of what the underlying company was worth as a business: whether the management was competent and the research effective, whether these were competitive problems, how up-to-date the machinery was, whether the company was prosperous or strapped for cash, and so on. And yet in fact very few investors do know such things about the companies they own. It *is* absurd. And after they've bought, they look at the quotation in the paper rather than read the annual report. They often don't even bother to find out if the broker who sells them the stock really knows much about the company as a business, other than as a concept. Often he doesn't.

A good investor has a specific, detailed knowledge of the companies he is interested in, has an idea of what the entire concern is worth, and thus knows what he can reasonably pay for 1 percent of it or 1 percent of 1 percent.

2. *Try to buy when stocks have few friends—particularly the stock in question.* One way of avoiding competition when buying is to have knowledge and nerve enough to buy good value when it's being dumped.

Another is to know some class of company so well you're almost never outtraded.

3. *Be patient; don't be rattled by fluctuations.* They're to be expected, like rainy days. Particularly, don't sell just because a stock goes down from the price at which you bought it, or when it thereafter recovers to that price. Your cost is an accident. It's not as if the stock knows about it and wants to cross you up; nor does the quotation affect the company's outlook. Watch the business, not the ticker.

4. *Invest, don't guess.* Swinging for the fences with a series of plausible half-baked speculations is fearfully expensive, both in the turn-around costs (brokerage and the spread between bid and asked prices, plus buying high and selling low) and perhaps even more so in the opportunity cost. Trying, for instance, to catch the bounce off the bottom in a run-of-the-mill heavy industrial company without much intrinsic growth is fine for financial institutions that systematically cover every industry and know the values. But for the individual investor, even thinking about such things, let alone tying up money in them, prevents him from making the great buy of an outstanding company that is the best move most of us can hope for. Buffett's right: Only buy something that you'd be perfectly happy to hold if the market shut down for ten years.

5. *High yields may be a trap.* The perfect company to invest in has opportunities to put its cash to work at very high rates of return: 15 percent, 20 percent, or better. Leave your money in the company to grow at that rate, rather than taking it out in taxable dividends and then putting what's left to work in bonds or another investment at a much lower real rate of return.

And many high-yield companies are Ponzi schemes anyway. A company that is adding to long-term debt faster than it's paying out cash in taxable dividends is on a fatal treadmill that must stop sooner or later. When it does, the stock will take a beating.

6. *Only buy what's cheap right now, or almost sure to grow so fast that it very soon will have been cheap at today's price.* Sometimes, of course, you can get both. If, for instance, you buy a good bank stock at, say, two-thirds of hard book value and can determine that through reinvested earnings the value is growing at, say, 15 percent a year and paying a reasonable dividend, you're in fine shape. Someday, quite surely, the

market will appraise the stock at its then much higher book value. And of course the dividend should also double every five years or thereabouts, so whatever the market does you'll be all right. It sounds simple, and indeed it's not that complicated or difficult, if you confine yourself to realistic objectives, dealing with things you understand.

7. *If stocks in general don't seem cheap, stand aside.* The next bear market is rarely more than two or three years away.

8. *Be flexible.* The old order, as its principles become overexploited and overused, must always yield place to the new—not that the new is ever really new. That's a cardinal secret of master play in this business and the point of my epigraph, *tempora mutantur nos et mutamur in illis:* "Times change, and we change in them."

How About Mutual Funds?

One might conclude that while it is very difficult to do all this—to copy the techniques of, for instance, a Peter Lynch or a John Neff—one could well buy a piece of their action by investing (at the time they were in charge) in the Magellan Fund or the Windsor Fund; the same for Wanger's Acorn, Robertson's Tiger, Soros's Quantum, and so on. In other words, aren't selected funds a satisfactory solution? They can be. Fund management is one of the few areas in life where the good often costs no more than the bad, and sometimes less. Still, it does cost quite a lot. And there are so many funds! So how to go about choosing?

First, one must find an appropriate fund for the season. It's risky to buy a growth or high-tech fund just after there has been tremendous run-up in those stocks. Instead, one should put some money *in an investment sector that is out of favor* at the time, and add to the holding when it starts to move. The greatest peril for the fund investor is jumping aboard a "hot" fund just before everything collapses at the end of a bull market, and the fund, like Icarus, plunges into the drink. Very few funds indeed are superior over many successive time periods. The front-runners of one year often lag in a later one. Still, some funds really do offer consistently superior performance. You can extract them from the *Forbes* mutual funds issue. And a tiny handful even change their strategies as circumstances change.

In choosing a fund, shun excessive costs. Never buy a "load" fund— one sold with a commission. If you buy a closed-end fund, do so only at or below its historically usual discount. Beware of redemption and

12b-1 fees, and the costs of high turnover: 25 percent turnover a year is high enough, and yet many funds do three times that much, at your expense. Think of Mark Lightbown's 15 percent turnover! (See Appendix XIII.) Just this can easily consume 2 percent a year of the capital: better for the broker than the shareholder! Ordinarily, you shouldn't pay a hedge fund management fee—including a profit participation—for conventional portfolio management not hedged with leverage.

Third, a good smaller fund—a few hundred million dollars, say—will *ordinarily* do better for you than a big one. Superior performance will eventually attract too much money. For instance, Peter Lynch outperformed the market by a smaller and smaller margin as his fund grew to huge size. This margin was 26 percent a year for his first several years when the assets were in the low hundreds of millions; it dropped sharply during the five years after the assets passed $5 billion. So you must keep looking for new talent. Indeed, the probability of a good fund's getting too big means that as with a good stock, the investor should discover its excellence early, in order to be aboard during the best period. That's not easy. One should develop a list of candidates and then research the ones that seem appropriate in the light of conditions at the time.

How, beside its performance, should one size up the management of a fund? To speak of a "fund" can be misleading: There's usually an individual behind it all. Make sure that the key man is still at his post and doing what he has always done best. One good clue is the manager's own quarterly and annual statements. Usually they are gassy, but it would be hard to read Ralph Wanger's letters to the shareholders of the Acorn Fund, or Warren Buffett's to the shareholders of Berkshire Hathaway, without realizing that here are men who really understand what they are doing.

Funds are necessary for sectors one could not otherwise cover as a practical matter, such as emerging markets, smaller companies, and high technology. An ordinary investor will not ordinarily know how to invest on a remote continent, or in a business sector beyond his experience, such as at the frontier of scientific innovation. Most of the masters except for Philip Fisher profess to be mystified by high technology. So an interesting approach may be to conduct systematic growth and/or value investment on one's own, while using specialized funds for specialized purposes.

Remember Professor Parkinson's admirable rule: *Growth brings complexity, and complexity decay.* Specifically, Robertson, Soros, and Steinhardt are investment geniuses, but they got too big for their administrative skill, as distinct from their investment skill, and so got entangled. Make sure your fund or investing partnership hasn't reached that stage. If it has, lighten up!

Company or Fund?

Buying a fund in the hope that you won't have to think anymore is a seductive illusion. I find that on balance one can find a good company about as easily as a good fund. A good company *doesn't depend on a single individual* the way a fund does. It may not get fatally oversized as easily, may keep its superiority longer, and *saves that burdensome extra layer of overhead,* which impairs your odds.

The quasi-science of security analysis is, of course, no simple matter, but in one form it can be fairly straightforward: buying great growth stocks when they are attractively priced, and being prepared to sell them if they stop growing. Elsewhere in this book I present thumbnail sketches of a few. The wonderful company enjoys an immense advantage: It is a highly elaborated successful *system,* with depth of management, assets, and an understandable business franchise. You must stay on top of things to be sure the company isn't getting into trouble, but that's also true of a fund.

So, to my mind, the vogue for funds, which now outnumber listed stocks, has gone too far.

Performance

The search for superior performance is not quite as simple as it looks. Almost any manager will somehow produce a record superior to the market, thus apparently verifying the old poker joke "Let's all play carefully, boys, and maybe we can all win a little." It's not true, of course. *Most portfolios do worse than the averages over the long term.* Their collective performance is that of the averages, diminished by the transactional costs, which are considerable. What happens next, though, is that unsuccessful managers merge with successful ones, so the surviving entity displays its superior record. The failures disappear from the calculation. And the very early years, when the funds are tiny, have a huge weight in the look of things later on. Perhaps a comparable statistic is that although most restaurants you see appear to be doing quite well, most American (and New York) restaurants fail in their first year. The same location is often taken over repeatedly until someone finally succeeds. Thus, if you look at existing restaurants you may get an unrealistically favorable impression: "Survivorship bias." So too with investment managers. And as I've mentioned, funds can be reclassified: A lagging stock fund may claim it has become a superior balanced fund.

Also, many averages are highly unrepresentative of an actual portfolio, since they are dominated by a handful of stocks, which change. *The Dow is really a managed growth stock portfolio.*

Then, a paradox: *The average investor in superior funds has a substantially worse result than the fund's overall record.* The reason is that most fund shareholders hold their shares for only four or five years (the load fund investor stays in a bit longer than the no-load investor), ordinarily buying when the fund has been strong and then selling when it has gone down. So a volatile fund with outstanding long-term results may not be the best for you if you tend to sell on dips.

In any event, *bursts of superior performance are less important than consistent performance,* which has astonishing results. Consider a young person I'll call Pennysaver. He (or she) contributes $2,000 a year for eight years to a tax-free IRA or pension plan and then stops; the money grows 10 percent per year, a reasonable assumption. The table that follows shows what happens. At retirement age Pennysaver is in fine shape.

Even modest, steady growth eventually makes you prosperous. Any other tactic, particularly one that invites significant declines from time to time that may shake you out of your program can fatally interrupt the flow.

So search for superior performance, but treasure consistent performance. *There is nothing in the world like compound interest.*

Reverse Engineering

One technique that a reader who has gotten this far should find congenial, and that I strongly recommend, is to select stocks from among those favored by outstanding fund managers: Use the masters as a filter. They constantly scan one another's portfolios, so there's no reason not to do the same. Don't worry that it's somehow unsporting, like shooting quail on the ground. For instance, in recent years (and in this book), both Warren Buffett and Peter Lynch have publicly espoused Fannie Mae. One need only look at its chart to see that it seemed to be a wonderful opportunity. (See page 381.) Similarly, Warren Buffett's purchase of Coca-Cola was universally advertised before it quintupled. Why not take a tip from such a source?

Pennysaver's Progress

Age	Contribution	Year-End Value
19	$2,000	$2,200
20	2,000	4,620
21	2,000	7,282
22	2,000	10,210
23	2,000	13,431
24	2,000	16,974
25	2,000	20,872
26	2,000	25,159
27	—	27,675
28	—	30,442
29	—	33,487
30	—	36,835
31	—	40,519
32	—	44,571
33	—	49,028
34	—	53,930
35	—	59,323
36	—	65,256
37	—	71,781
38	—	78,960
39	—	86,856
40	—	95,541
41	—	105,095
42	—	115,605
43	—	127,165
44	—	139,882
45	—	153,870
46	—	169,257
47	—	186,183
48	—	204,801
49	—	225,281
50	—	247,809
51	—	272,590
52	—	299,849
53	—	329,834
54	—	362,817
55	—	399,099
56	—	439,009
57	—	482,910
58	—	531,201
59	—	584,321
60	—	642,753
61	—	707,028
62	—	777,731
63	—	855,504
64	—	941,054
65	—	1,035,160

Avoid the excessively popular, though. Look instead for stocks held by one or possibly two or three authentic masters, not by a large number of mediocrities. There are services that compile these holdings.* Ask a financial library or a bank or brokerage house, or look at the ads in investment publications. The information arrives a bit later that way, though, than if you get the fund reports directly.

You should observe a few obvious rules:

1. *Make sure they really are outstanding managers.*
2. *Establish that these are or could be long-term conceptions, not just trading maneuvers.* Julian Robertson, Ralph Wanger, and Warren Buffett (and his friend Bill Ruane in the Sequoia Fund), for instance, buy for the long term, while the "relentless pursuit" practitioners may be in for a trade. For starters, look at a stock's chart of earnings and dividends. A great long-term growth stock looks quite different from a depressed cyclical perhaps ready for a bounce.
3. *Make sure that the masters are adding to their holdings, or at least maintaining them.* Often a particular stock becomes a major holding of one or two masters, who can be expected to know it extremely well. A lot of other investors besides yourself will be watching the scene, so if one of these masters starts to sell it there will be repercussions.
4. *Only consider such a list a screen or "universe" from which you select a few candidates for further examination.* Then study those stocks fully. *Work through their reports line by line.* If possible, *talk to the company,* if you know what to ask, as well as to some of its competitors and customers, and to industry specialists.
5. *It's easier, if you are a nonprofessional, to specialize in one or two areas:* a *type* of stock (low-multiple, long-term growth, emerging growth, niche companies, or whatever) or an *industry* (pharmaceuticals, telecom, computer-related, media, consumer products, specialty chemicals, natural resources). Stock selection is a competitive game, and thus intrinsically difficult. Focusing makes the job easier, which increases the likelihood of success.

All in all, though, reverse engineering some choices of the masters is an excellent tool for most investors.

---

*E.g., Outstanding Investor, New York, N.Y.

Investment Don'ts

1. *Avoid popular stocks.* First must come the general class of anything that's too popular at the time, stocks that are on everybody's list. In 1928 the cry was "no price is too high for Radio"—RCA. Alas, in the next few years Radio declined 94 percent from its high. If you buy Highflyer.com when everybody feels it's sure to triple, you can be fairly sure that the stock is overvalued. It's not that the business won't do well or even that the stock will never rise; it's just that you will first have to work off that overvaluation, which takes time. IBM, then selling for 300, was a "religion stock" in the late 1960s, a certified member of the so-called Vestal Virgins. The company fulfilled all its owners' dreams: Earnings went up 700 percent over the next decade, and the dividend rose 1,000 percent. Still, for ten years the stock never advanced above 300. I sometimes save the lists of "consensus" stocks published in magazines and check the results a year or two later. One may safely expect that they'll do about 30 percent worse than the averages.

   That's the sinister meaning of the term *glamour stock.* A glamour stock is a good company overpriced because it's everybody's darling at the time. That's a hard way to make money.

   The same principle works for bursts of short-range enthusiasm. If a stock has run up wildly over a period of days or weeks, it's better to let it rest for a while. A highly favorable purchase is very likely to seem odd, uncomfortable, risky, dull, or obscure at the time you buy it. On the contrary, *a propitious reaction is, "I can't see it doing anything for the next six months."* Later, everybody gets the idea and feels comfortable with it. But, as the Wall Street saw goes, "By the time the smoke has lifted, the train has left the station."

2. *Avoid fad industries.* Fads and brokers' stories are variations on popular stocks. The number of them you can remember is limited only by how old you are: the atomic energy craze of the fifties; the computer mania, gambling stock, biotech, energy, emerging markets in the eighties; and the Net stocks in the nineties. There's an easy way to spot the terminal phase of these bubbles: If lots of mutual funds are formed to concentrate on the industry in question, or if companies'

stocks jump in the market because they announce that they *propose* to enter the field, then the buying is speculative and disappointment will probably follow. Remember that *companies can and will be fabricated without limit to satisfy any demand.* "When the ducks quack, feed 'em," they say.

The easiest way to be sure you aren't buying into a fad or popular stock is to consult the index of the *Wall Street Transcript* or ask your broker to check his research file. If little or nothing's been written about a company for a few years, you're probably safe. If I'm interested in a company, I usually contact its shareholder relations officer and ask him what the best brokerage house write-up is on his company. If there isn't any that really gets the point, then the discovery (or rediscovery) period is ahead of you.

A few years ago, for instance, H&R Block, the tax preparation company, seemed like a gift. It had a prodigious growth rate and no significant competition. The industry is imperishable, and the company was selling in the market for barely more than its cash in the bank. I asked Richard Bloch (that's how the family name is spelled), who didn't enjoy this state of affairs and was glad to be helpful, if there were any good current brokerage house studies around. He said that there was only one he knew of, by an obscure individual practitioner. I considered that very bullish, and in fact the stock eventually did extremely well.

Perhaps the archetype of this principle is the first great American oil strike, the fabulous Spindletop Dome. It attracted so many investors that at its height one was said to be able to walk across the field stepping from one drilling platform to the next. Result: More money went into the ground at Spindletop than ever came out of the ground. Warren Buffett points out that until recently investors lost more than they had ever made in both the automobile and the airline industries.

3. *Avoid new ventures.* Venture capital is for pros, not passive portfolio investors. By far the majority of new ventures—probably nine out of ten—go bust. As Buffett observes, the odds are poor when you buy a gamble, of uncertain prospects and management, with the promoters getting a big free cut, and the likelihood of financial asphyxiation in the future. If you wait a few years for the next bear market,

you know you'll be able to buy some of the greatest companies in the world, with superb managements already in place, for little more than their net quick assets, and with the company itself free—the plants, the patents, the goodwill.

4. *Question "official" growth stocks.* Stocks that have the growth label—and corresponding price tag—often are no longer growing rapidly enough to justify their prices. You might call them the "old champs." Many famous companies that have "Growth Stock" printed on the back of their robe and still wear the championship belt and buckle are really over the hill.

5. *Watch out for heavy industry.* A similar disappointment is likely to come from buying cyclical heavy-industry "blue chips." They may sell for too high a price because of their "security." But they are squeezed by union demands, regulations, foreign and domestic competition, and obsolescence.

6. *Avoid gimmicks.* Gimmicky investment "products" with high transaction costs and no intrinsic growth of value, such as option programs and commodity flyers, aren't investments at all. They're casinos. Forget about them. The economic role of real investment is to provide the capital needed for industry, for a good return. The role of the casino customer is to be fleeced.

7. *Don't expect bonds to preserve capital.* A final bad deal for the investor generally, is bonds, unless he reinvests all the income. The notion that they're "conservative" is usually unrealistic. Franz Pick, in his sardonic way, used to call them "certificates of guaranteed expropriation." After tax, bonds often yield less than the inflation rate.

8. *Forget about technical analysis.* One "system" of stock market investing not represented in this book is so-called technical analysis. The reason is that I have been unable to find any successful practitioners.

Twenty years ago in *Dance of the Money Bees* I had this to say on the subject of technical analysis:

> *Technical analysis of stocks.* The study of value is the basis of stock investment. There are no shortcuts. The "technician," however, tries to predict stock movement through the shapes on a stock's chart, without reference to value.

It is not knowable from what a stock did last month or last year how it will do next month or next year. Brokers' pronouncements on this subject are tea-leaf reading, fakery. A broker should establish facts and values, so the customer can decide if he wants to buy what has been described. This involves legwork, study, interviews with a company and its competition, consultation with industry experts, and the like, the whole then to be presented in a form which permits an investment valuation, but also where errors will stand out.

How much easier and what tripe to say that stock at 50 "seems to be poised for a breakthrough to the 54–56 area, although a stop-loss order should be placed at 47." One reader-adviser can issue pronouncements on hundreds of stocks on this basis, instead of clearly revealing his competence (or incompetence) on one.

I have a naughty bet that I offer any "technician" I meet and that none has accepted. It goes like this. He is asking his readers to accept his word for it that if they do what he says they will make money; that is, if he says Fido.com is "technically" a buy, and they buy a thousand shares, then they will come out ahead reasonably soon, after round-trip commissions and taxes. That is no joke. If the stock costs $20, they are supposed to put $20,000 at risk, equal to the down payment on a small house, on the strength of the wizards' reading of the wiggly lines.

Why not let him take a chance too?

So my bet goes like this: Somebody digs out some charts done on a daily basis from a few years back. He removes any identification and cuts each chart in the middle. He gives the first half to the technician.

All that worthy has to do is tell me, on a $1,000 bet, whether those stocks were higher or lower at any specified point in the second period than at the end of the fist. Since he claims the ability to prophesy, and is wiling to have the rest of us take a substantial risk on his say-so—paying brokerage and tax whether we win or lose—he should be confident enough of his powers to give modest odds. Three to two seems fair enough.

So far, as I say, no "technician" has ever accepted the offer. Particularly, I do not think a trustee should act on the basis of technical analysis, any more than astrology. I consider it unprofessional.

Brokerage firms that I know have spent millions of dollars (literally) on computer programs for technical stock analysis and then quietly scuttled them.*

Investment Is the Art of the Specific

None of the masters in this book relies on the tools so beloved of the pundits and institutions: regression analysis, modern portfolio theory, industry overweightings and underweightings, or higher math. Buffett has said he doesn't have a computer. Except for Soros and Steinhardt, whose methods are inimitable, they focus on the *specific*, rather than on "overviews" and big ideas, which essentially attempt to render general, simple, and easy what is intrinsically specific, complicated, and hard. Those formulas and abstractions do not yield superior results in the real world. Successful investing means knowing all about the companies you own. So look to the particular; let others be distracted by the generalities, the formulas, the simplifications. And don't spend too much time fretting about the Fed's intentions, or next year's GNP. As Peter Lynch says, "How is the sneaker business doing? That's *real* economics."

Alfonso the Learned modestly observed that had he been present at the creation he would have given God some useful hints for the better ordering of the universe. My own offering would be that our species is much too easily seduced by vast conceptions, particularly in politics, the opiate of the people, but also in the stock market, the encephalogram of the human race: Our hopes and fears for the future are reflected in those wiggly lines. Most of the time, however, grand, unknowable generalizations distract us from the specific, knowable, and useful. So leave them to befuddle your competitors.

---

*Andrew Tobias offers a pleasant "technical analysis" story. There was an $800 seminar on such matters in New York's Waldorf-Astoria Hotel on December 6–7, 1986. One of the most promising gurus was Norman Winski, described thus in the invitation: "In 1975, he became a member and market maker on the floor of the Chicago Board of Options Exchange. During an eighteen-month period, 1976–1977, he successfully parlayed $500 into nearly $1,000,000." (Tobias observes that one could scarcely do that unsuccessfully.) The invitation forgot to mention a little tiny trifling problem: In September 1977—*still ten years before the famous seminar*—Winski went bust.

Envoi: Midas

This book is a guide to investment success. But my last message to the reader is this: Understand the process, the way you should understand medicine and government, but don't try too hard yourself. The people who suffer the worst losses are usually those who overreach. And it's not necessary: Steady, moderate gains will get you where you want to go.

Furthermore, trying to achieve great wealth—far more than you need—is in fact irrational. You have to give up too much getting there, and having done it, you're often worse off than before. Midas is ruined by the gold he craves.

Our nature, says Shakespeare, is subdued to what it works in, like the dyer's hand, and in pursuing great wealth you become a money person. You see the world through dollar-sign binoculars.

Then, the exaggeration of any principle becomes its undoing, as the excess of a stimulant becomes a poison, and changing greed from a sin into a commandment dissolves the soul of a family. The children of excessive privilege are often purposeless and morose.

And great wealth spoils human contacts. Everybody wants something. Of the Rothschilds it was said that they had no friends, only clients. The hurly-burly of humanity, from which great wealth fences itself off—its joys and trials, the texture of everyday life—is what we're designed for.

Philanthropy, while meritorious, on a large scale becomes a political act: The tycoon who extracts a fortune from the public to build a museum in one place rather than another has not created new beauty, only imposed his priorities on society.

The rational and virtuous approach is to trust in a sufficiency of wealth as a by-product of a useful life. Happy are those who find fulfilment in their families, their work, and their civic duties, and hope for the best.

BUFFETT ON BONDS

To My Partners:

This letter will attempt to provide a very elementary education regarding tax-exempt bonds with emphasis on the types and maturities of bonds which we expect to help partners in purchasing next month. I have tried to boil this letter down as much as possible. Some of it will be a little weighty—some a little oversimplified. I apologize for the shortcomings in advance. I have a feeling I am trying to put all the meat of a 100-page book in 10 pages—and have it read like the funny papers.

Mechanics of Tax-Free Bonds

For those who wish our help, we will arrange the purchase of bonds directly from municipal bond dealers throughout the country and have them confirm sale of the bonds directly to you. The confirmation should be saved as a basic document for tax purposes. You should not send a check to the bond dealer since he will deliver the bonds to your bank, along with a draft which the bank will pay by charging your account with them. In the case of bonds purchased in the secondary market (issues already outstanding), this settlement date will usually be about a week after confirmation date whereas, on new issues, the settlement date may be as much as a month later. The settlement date is shown plainly on the confirmation ticket (in the case of new issues this will be the second and final ticket rather than the preliminary "when issued" ticket), and you should have the funds at your bank ready to pay for the bonds on the settlement date. If you presently own Treasury Bills, they can be sold on a couple of days' notice by your bank upon your instructions, so you should experience no problems in having the money available on time. Interest begins to accrue to you on the settlement date, even if the bond dealer is late in getting them delivered to your bank. Bonds will be delivered in negotiable form (so-called "bearer" form which makes them like currency) with coupons attached. Usually the bonds are in $5,000 denominations and frequently they can be exchanged for registered bonds (sometimes at considerable expense and sometimes free— it depends upon the terms). Bonds in registered form are nonnegotiable without assignment by you, since you are the registered owner on the Transfer Agent's books. Bonds trade almost exclusively on a bearer basis and it is virtually impossible to sell registered bonds without converting them back into bearer form. Thus, unless you are going to own great physical quantities of bonds, I recommend keeping bonds in bearer form. This means keeping them in a very safe place and clipping the coupons every six months. Such coupons, when clipped, can be deposited in your bank account just like checks. If you have $250,000 in bonds, this probably means about fifty separate pieces of paper ($5,000 denominations) and perhaps six or eight trips a year to the safe deposit section to cut and deposit coupons.

It is also possible to open a custody account with a bank where, for a fairly nominal cost, they will keep the bonds, collect the interest, and preserve your records for you. For example, a bank will probably perform the custodial service for you for about $200 a year on a $250,000 portfolio. If you are interested in a custodial account, you should talk to a trust officer at your commercial bank as to the nature of their services and cost. Otherwise, you should have a safe-deposit box.

Taxation

The interest received upon the deposit of coupons from tax-free bonds is, of course, free from federal income taxes. This means if you are at a 30% top federal income tax bracket, a 6% return from tax-free bonds is equivalent to about $8\frac{1}{2}$% from taxable bonds. Thus, for most of our partners, excluding minors and some retired people, tax-free bonds will be more attractive than taxable bonds. For people with little or no income from wages or dividends, but with substantial capital, it is possible that a combination of taxable bonds (to bring taxable income up to about the 25% or 30% bracket) plus tax-free bonds will bring the highest total after-tax income. Where appropriate, we will work with you to achieve such a balance.

The situation in respect to state income taxes is more complicated. In Nebraska, where the state income tax is computed as a percentage of the federal income tax, the effect is that there is no state tax on interest from tax-free bonds. My understanding of both the New York and California law is that tax-free bonds of entities within the home state are not subject to state income tax, but tax-free bonds from other states are subject to the local state income tax. I also believe that the New York City income tax exempts tax-free bonds of entities based within the state of New York, but taxes those from other states. I am no expert on state income taxes and make no attempt to post myself on changes taking place within the various states or cities. Therefore, I defer to your local tax advisor, but simply mention these few general impressions so that you will be alert to the existence of a potential problem. In Nebraska there is no need to have any local considerations enter into the after-tax calculation. Where out-of-state issues are subject to local taxation, the effective cost of your state or municipal income tax is reduced by the benefit received from deducting it on your federal income tax return. This, of course, varies with the individual. Additionally, in some states there are various taxes on intangible property which may apply to all tax-free bonds or just those of out-of-state entities. There are none of these in Nebraska, but I cannot advise on the other states.

When bonds are bought at a discount from par and later are sold or mature (come due and get paid), the difference between the proceeds and cost is subject to capital gain or loss treatment. (There are minor exceptions to this statement as, unfortunately, there are to most general statements on investments and taxes but they will be pointed out to you should they affect any securities we recommend.) This reduces the net after-tax yield by a factor involving the general rate of future capital gains taxes and the specific future tax position of the individual. Later on, we will discuss the impact of such capital gains taxes in calculating the relative attractiveness of discount bonds versus "full coupon" bonds.

Finally, one most important point. Although the law is not completely clear, you should probably not contemplate owning tax-free bonds if you have, or expect to have, general purpose bank or other indebtedness. The law excludes the deductibility of interest on loans incurred or continued to purchase or carry tax-free bonds, and the interpretation of this statute will probably tend to be broadened as the years pass. For example, my impression is that you have no problem if you have a mortgage against real property (unless the debt was incurred in order to acquire municipal bonds) in deducting the mortgage interest on your federal tax return, even though you own tax-free bonds at the same time. However, I believe that if you have a general bank loan, even though the proceeds were directly used to purchase stocks, a handball court, etc. and the tax-free bonds are not used for security for the loan, you are asking for trouble if you deduct the interest and, at the same time, are the owner of tax-free bonds. Therefore, I would pay off bank loans before owning tax-free bonds, but I leave detailed examination of this question to you and your tax advisor. I merely mention it to make you aware of the potential problem.

Marketability

Tax-free bonds are materially different from common stocks or corporate bonds in that there are literally hundreds of thousands of issues with the great majority having very few holders. This substantially inhibits the development of close, active markets. Whenever the city of New York or Philadelphia wants to raise money it sells perhaps twenty, thirty, or forty nonidentical securities, since it will offer an issue with that many a different maturities. A 6% bond of New York coming due in 1980 is a different animal from a 6% bond of New York coming due in 1981. One cannot be exchanged for the other, and a seller has to find a buyer for the specific item he holds. When you consider that New York may offer bonds several times a year, it is easy to see why just this one city may have somewhere in the neighborhood of 1,000 issues outstanding. Grand Island, Nebraska, may have 75 issues outstanding. The average amount of each issue might be $100,000 and the average number of holders may be six or eight per issue. Thus, it is absolutely impossible to have quoted markets at all times for all issues and spreads between bids and offers may be very wide. You can't set forth in the morning to buy a specific Grand Island issue of your choosing. It may not be offered at any price, anywhere, and if you do find one seller, there is no reason why he has to be realistic compared to other offerings of similar quality. On the other hand, there are single issues such as those of the Ohio Turnpike, Illinois Turnpike, etc. that amount to $200 million or more and have thousands of bondholders owning a single entirely homogeneous and interchangeable issue. Obviously, here you get a high degree of marketability.

Marketability is generally a function of the following three items, in descending order of importance: (1) the size of the particular issue; (2) the size of the issuer (a \$100,000 issue of the state of Ohio will be more marketable than a \$100,000 issue of Podunk, Ohio); and (3) the quality of the issuer. By far the most sales effort goes into the selling of new issues of bonds. An average of over \$200 million per week of new issues comes up for sale, and the machinery of bond distribution is geared to get them sold, large or small. In my opinion, there is frequently insufficient differential in yield at time of issue for the marketability differences that will exist once the initial sales push is terminated. We have frequently run into markets in bonds where the spread between bid and asked prices may get to 15%. There is no need to buy bonds with the potential for such grotesque markets (although the profit spread to the dealer who originally offers them is frequently wider than on more marketable bonds) and we will not be buying them for you. The bonds we expect to buy will usually tend to have spreads (reflecting the difference between what you would pay net for such bonds on purchase and receive net on sale at the same point in time) of from 2% to 5%. Such a spread would be devastating if you attempted to trade in such bonds, but I don't believe it should be a deterrent for a long-term investor. The real necessity is to stay away from bonds of very limited marketability—which frequently are the type local bond dealers have the greatest monetary incentive to push.

Specific Areas of Purchase

We will probably concentrate our purchases in the following general areas:

1. Large revenue-producing public entities such as toll roads, electric power districts, water districts, etc. Many of these issues possess high marketability, are subject to quantitative analysis, and sometimes have favorable sinking funds or other factors which tend not to receive full valuation in the marketplace.

2. Industrial Development Authority bonds which arise when a public entity holds title to property leased to a private corporation. For example, Lorain, Ohio, holds title to an \$80 million project for U.S. Steel Corp. The development authority board issued bonds to pay for the project and has executed a net and absolute lease with U.S. Steel to cover the bond payments. The credit of the city or state is

not behind the bonds and they are only as good as the company that is on the lease. Many top-grade corporations stand behind an aggregate of several billion dollars of these obligations, although new ones are being issued only in small amounts ($5 million per project or less) because of changes in the tax laws. For a period of time there was a very substantial prejudice against such issues, causing them to sell at yields considerably higher than those commensurate with their inherent credit standing. This prejudice has tended to diminish, reducing the premium yields available, but I still consider it a most attractive field. Our insurance company owns a majority of its bonds in this category.

3. Public Housing Authority issues for those of you who wish the very highest grade of tax-free bonds. In effect, these bonds bear the guarantee of the U.S. Government, so they are all rated AAA. In states where local taxes put a premium on buying in-state issues, and I can't fill your needs from (1) and (2), my tendency would be to put you into Housing Authority issues rather than try to select from among credits that I don't understand. If you direct me to buy obligations of your home state, you should expect substantial quantities of Housing Authority issues. There is no need to diversify among such issues, as they all represent the top credit available.

4. State obligations of a direct or indirect nature.

You will notice I am not buying issues of large cities. I don't have the faintest idea how to analyze a New York City, Chicago, Philadelphia, etc. (a friend mentioned the other day when Newark was trying to sell bonds at a very fancy rate that the Mafia was getting very upset because Newark was giving them a bad name). Your analysis of a New York City—and I admit it is hard to imagine them not paying their bills for any extended period of time—would be as good as mine. My approach to bonds is pretty much like my approach to stocks. If I can't understand something, I tend to forget it. Passing an opportunity which I don't understand—even if someone else is perceptive enough to analyze it and get paid well for doing it—doesn't bother me. We will probably tend to purchase somewhere between five and ten issues for most of you. We will try not to buy in smaller than $25,000 pieces and will prefer larger amounts where appropriate. Smaller lots of bonds are usually penalized upon resale, sometimes substantially. The bond salesman doesn't usually explain this to you when you buy the $10,000 of bonds from him, but it gets explained when you later try to sell the $10,000 to him. We may make exceptions where we are buying secondary market issues in smaller pieces—but only if we are getting an especially good price on the buy side because of the small size of the offering.

Callable Bonds

We will not buy bonds where the issuer of the bonds has a right to call (retire) the bonds on a basis which substantially loads the contract in his favor. It is amazing to me to see people buy bonds which are due in forty years, but where the issuer has the right to call the bonds at a tiny premium in five or ten years. Such a contract essentially means that you have made a forty-year deal if it is advantageous to the issuer (and disadvantageous to you) and a five-year deal if the initial contract turns out to be advantageous to you (and disadvantageous to the issuer). Such contracts are really outrageous and exist because bond investors can't think through the implications of such a contract form and bond dealers don't insist on better terms for their customers. One extremely interesting fact is that bonds with very unattractive call features sell at virtually the same yield as otherwise identical bonds which are noncallable.

It should be pointed out that most Nebraska bonds carry highly unfair call provisions. Despite this severe contractual disadvantage, they do not offer higher yields than bonds with more equitable terms. One way to avoid this problem is to buy bonds which are totally noncallable. Another way is to buy discount bonds where the right of the issuer to call the bond is at a price so far above your cost as to render the possible call inconsequential. If you buy a bond at 60 which is callable at 103, the effective cost to you of granting the issuer the right to prematurely terminate the contract (which is a right you never have) is insignificant. But to buy a bond of the Los Angeles Department of Water and Power at 100 to come due at 100 in 1999 or to come due at 104 in 1974, depending on which is to the advantage of the issuer and to your disadvantage, is the height of foolishness when comparable yields are available on similar credits without such an unfair contract. Nevertheless, just such a bond was issued in October 1969 and similar bonds continue to be issued every day. I only write at such length about an obvious point since it is apparent from the continual sale of such bonds that many investors haven't the faintest notion how

this loads the dice against them and many bonds salesmen aren't about
to tell them.

Maturity and the Mathematics of Bonds

Many people, in buying bonds, select maturities based on how long
they think they are going to want to hold bonds, how long they are
going to live, etc. While this is not a silly approach, it is not necessarily
the most logical. The primary determinants in selection of maturity
should probably be (1) the shape of the yield curve; (2) your expectations regarding future levels of interest rates; and (3) the degree of
quotational fluctuation you are willing to endure or hope to possibly
profit from. Of course, (2) is the most important but by far the most
difficult upon which to comment intelligently.

Let's tackle the yield curve first. When other aspects of quality are
identical, there will be a difference in interest rates paid based upon
the length of the bond being offered. For example, a top-grade bond
being offered now might have a yield of 4.75% if it came due in six or
nine months, 5.00% in two years, 5.25% in five years, 5.50% in ten
years, and 6.25% in twenty years. When long rates are substantially
higher than short rates, the curve is said to be strongly positive. In the
U.S. Government bond market, rates recently have tended to produce
a negative yield curve; that is, a long-term Government bond over the
last year or so has consistently yielded less than a short-term one.
Sometimes the yield curve has been very flat, and sometimes it is positive out to a given point, such as ten years, and then flattens out. What
you should understand is that it varies, often very substantially, and
that on an historical basis the present slope tends to be in the high positive range. This doesn't mean that long bonds are going to be worth
more but it does mean that you are being paid more to extend maturity than in many periods. If yields remained constant for several years,
you would do better with longer bonds than shorter bonds, regardless
of how long you intended to hold them. The second factor in determining maturity selection is expectations regarding future rate levels.
Anyone who has done much predicting in this field has tended to look
very foolish very fast. I did not regard rates as unattractive one year
ago, and I was proved very wrong almost immediately. I believe present
rates are not unattractive and I may look foolish again. Nevertheless, a
decision has to be made and you can make just as great a mistake if you

buy short-term securities now and rates available on reinvestment in a few years are much lower.

The final factor involves your tolerance for quotational fluctuation. This involves the mathematics of bond investment and may be a little difficult for you to understand. Nevertheless, it is important that you get a general grasp of the principles. Let's assume for the moment a perfectly flat yield curve and a noncallable bond. Further assume present rates are 5% and that you buy two bonds, one due in two years and one due in twenty years. Now assume one year later that yields on new issues have gone to 3% and that you wish to sell your bonds. Forgetting about market spreads, commissions, etc. you will receive $1,019.60 for the original two-year $1,000 bond (now with one year to run) and $1,288.10 for the nineteen-year bond (originally twenty years). At these prices, a purchaser will get exactly 3% on his money after amortizing the premium he has paid and cashing the stream of 5% coupons attached to each bond. It is a matter of indifference to him whether to buy your nineteen-year 5% bond at $1,288.10 or a new 3% bond (which we have assumed is the rate current—one year later) at $1,000.00. On the other hand, let's assume rates went to 7%. Again we will ignore commissions, capital gains taxes on the discount, etc. Now the buyer will only pay $981 for the bond with one year remaining until maturity and $791.00 for the bond with nineteen years left. Since he can get 7% on new issues, he is only willing to buy your bond at a discount sufficient so that accrual of this discount will give him the same economic benefits from your 5% coupon that a 7% coupon at $1,000 would give him.

The principle is simple. The wider the swings in interest rates and the longer the bond, the more the value of a bond can go up or down on an interim basis before maturity. It should be pointed out in the first example where rates went to 3%, our long-term bond would only have appreciated to about $1,070 if it had been callable in five years at par, although it would have gone down just as much if 7% rates had occurred. This just illustrates the inherent unfairness of call provisions.

For over two decades, interest rates on tax-free bonds have almost continuously gone higher and buyers of long-term bonds have continuously suffered. This does not mean it is bad now to buy long-term bonds—it simply means that the illustration in the above paragraph has worked in only one direction for a long period of time and people are much more conscious of the downside risks from higher rates than the upside potential from lower ones. If it is a fifty-fifty chance as to the future general level of interest rates and the yield curve is substantially positive, then the odds are better in buying long-term noncallable bonds than shorter-term ones. This reflects my current conclusion and, therefore, I intend to buy bonds within the ten-to-twenty-five-year range. If you decide to buy a twenty-year bond and hold the bond straight through, you are going to get the concentrated rate of interest, but if you sell earlier, you are going to be subject to the mathematical forces I have described, for better or for worse.

Bond prices also change because of changes in quality over the years but, in the tax-free area, this has tended to be—and probably will continue to be—a relatively minor factor compared to the impact of changes in the general structure of interest rates.

Discount Versus Full Coupon Bonds

You will have noticed in the above discussion that if you now wanted to buy a 7% return on a nineteen-year bond, you'd have a choice between buying a new nineteen-year bond with a 7% coupon rate or buying a bond with a 5% coupon at $791.60, which would pay you $1,000 in nineteen years. Either purchase would have yielded exactly 7% compounded semiannually to you. Mathematically, they are the same. In the case of tax-free bonds the equation is complicated, however, by the fact that the $70 coupon is entirely tax-free to you, whereas the bond purchased at a discount gives you tax-free income of $50 per year but a capital gain at the end of the nineteenth year of $208.40. Under the present tax law, you would owe anything from a nominal tax, if the gain from realization of the discount was your only taxable income in the nineteenth year, up to a tax of over $70 if it came on top of very large amounts of capital gain at that time (the new tax law provides for capital gain rates of 35%, and even slightly higher on an indirect basis in 1972 and thereafter for those realizing very large gains). In addition to this, you might have some state taxes to pay on the capital gain.

Obviously, under these circumstances you are not going to pay the $791.60 for the 5% coupon and feel you are equally as well off as with the 7% coupon at $1,000. Neither is anyone else. Therefore, identical quality securities with identical maturities sell at considerably higher gross yields when they have low coupons and are priced at discounts than if they bear current high coupons.

Interestingly enough, for most taxpayers, such higher gross yields over-compensate for the probable tax to be paid. This is due to several factors. First, no one knows what the tax law will be when the bonds mature and it is both natural and probably correct to assume the tax rate will be stiffer at that time than now. Second, even though a 5% coupon on a $1,000 bond purchased at $791.60 due in nineteen years is the equivalent of a 7% coupon on a $1,000 bond purchased at par with the same maturity, people prefer to get the higher current return in their pocket. The owner of the 5% coupon bond is only getting around 6.3% current yield on his $791.60 with the balance necessary to get him up to 7% coming from the extra $208.40 he picks up at the end. Finally, the most important factor affecting prices currently on discount bonds (and which will keep affecting them) is that banks have been taken out of the market as buyers of discount tax-free bonds by changes brought about in bank tax treatment through the 1969 Tax Reform Act. Banks have historically been the largest purchasers and owners of tax-free bonds and anything that precludes them from one segment of the market has dramatic effects on the supply-demand situation in that segment. This may tend to give some edge to individuals in the discount tax-free market, particularly those who are not likely to be in a high tax bracket when the bonds mature or are sold.

If I can get a significantly higher effective after-tax yield (allowing for sensible estimates of your particular future tax-rate possibilities), I intend to purchase discount bonds for you.

You should realize that because of the enormous diversity of issues mentioned earlier, it is impossible to say just what will be bought. Sometimes the tax-free bond market has more similarities to real estate than to stocks. There are hundreds of thousands of items of varying comparability, some with no sellers, and some with reluctant sellers and some with eager sellers. Which may be the best buy depends on the quality of what is being offered, how well it fits your needs, and the eagerness of the seller. The standard of comparison is always new issues where an average of several hundred million dollars' worth have to be sold each week—however, specific secondary market opportunities (issues already outstanding) may be more attractive than new issues and we can only find out how attractive they are when we are ready to make bids.

WELCOME TO BUFFETT WATCH

Berkshire Hathaway's Holdings
Value of Buffett's Berkshire Holdings: $36,993,812,973

December 3, 1999	TICKER	PRICE	UNITS HELD	MARKET VALUE	VALUE PER A-SHARE	% OF BRK's MARKET CAP.
HOLDINGS REPORTED OWNED AS OF 12/31/98						
Cola-Cola	KO	68 3/16	200,000,000	$13,637,500,000	$8,973	15.9%
American Express	AXP	157 1/4	50,536,900	$7,946,927,525	$5,229	9.3%
Gillette	G	43 15/16	96,000,000	$4,218,000,000	$2,775	4.9%
Wells Fargo	WFC	47 3/16	63,595,180	$3,000,897,556	$1,975	3.5%
Fed. Home Loan Mtg.	FRE	48 7/8	60,298,000	$2,947,064,750	$1,939	3.4%
Walt Disney	DIS	27 7/8	51,202,242	$1,427,262,496	$939	1.7%
Washington Post	WPO	565 3/16	1,727,765	$976,511,181	$643	1.1%
OTHER HOLDINGS OWNED AS OF 6/30/98*						
General Dynamics	GD	52 1/16	7,693,637	$400,549,976	$264	0.5%
Fannie Mae	FNM	67 1/2	5,868,000	$396,090,000	$261	0.5%
NIKE	NKE	46 3/8	7,788,911	$361,210,748	$238	0.4%
Gannett	GCI	75 13/16	3,963,900	$300,513,169	$198	0.4%
U.S. Bancorp	USB	35 1/8	7,237,638	$254,222,035	$167	0.3%
American International Group	AIG	104	1,906,298	$198,254,992	$130	0.2%

DECEMBER 3, 1999	TICKER	PRICE	UNITS HELD	MARKET VALUE	VALUE PER A-SHARE	% OF BRK's MARKET CAP.
OTHER HOLDINGS OWNED AS OF 6/30/98*						
Great Lakes Chemical	GLK	37 1/4	4,000,000	$149,000,000	$98	0.2%
Manpower	MAN	37 3/4	3,654,800	$137,968,700	$91	0.2%
First Data Corp.	FDC	44 1/16	3,000,000	$132,187,500	$87	0.2%
Allied Domecq	ALLD	5.0026	22,800,000	$114,059,025	$75	0.1%
Nucor	NUE	53 15/16	1,868,600	$100,787,613	$66	0.1%
Arrow Electronics	ARW	23 3/16	3,400,000	$78,837,500	$52	0.09%
Wal-Mart	WMT	58 7/8	1,340,600	$78,927,825	$52	0.09%
Costco	COST	98 11/16	555,000	$54,771,563	$36	0.06%
UST	UST	27 1/4	796,700	$21,710,075	$14	0.03%
Torchmark	TMK	31 7/8	662,562	$21,119,164	$14	0.02%
Zenith National Insurance	ZNT	20 1/16	853,655	$17,126,453	$11	0.02%
PS Group Holdings	PSG	10 7/8	1,208,032	$13,137,348	$9	0.02%
Morgan Stanley Dean Witter	MWD	128 3/16	56,100	$7,191,319	$5	0.01%
Omega Worldwide	OWWI	5.125	208,378	$1,067,937	$1	0.00%
Omega Healthcare Investors	OHI	15 1/4	60,100	$916,525	$1	0.00%
Total Stock Holdings				**$36,993,812,973**		43.1%
plus balance sheet cash and bonds				$35,966,000,000		41.9%
plus other investments				$1,755,000,000		2.0%

DECEMBER 3, 1999	TICKER	PRICE	UNITS HELD	MARKET VALUE	VALUE PER A-SHARE	% OF BRK'S MARKET CAP.
including silver		5.0900	129,700,000	$660,173,000		0.8%
plus implied value of wholly-owned businesses				$11,058,493,747		12.9%
equals stock value (Class-A and Class-B)				$85,773,306,720		
Warren Buffett's Holdings (514,146 Class-A shares)			514,146	$29,100,663,600		

*Based on financial filings revealed as late as one year after the fact.

Actual shares held may vary greatly due to sales and purchases.

Shares may have been purchased by Buffett or portfolio managers at Berkshire's insurance subsidiaries.

BUFFETT'S OTHER

RECENT INVESTMENTS	TICKER	PRICE	UNITS HELD	MARKET VALUE
Baker Fentress	BKF	13 13/16	2,831,390	$39,108,574
MGI Properties	MGI	5 1/2	1,800,000	$9,900,000
Town & Country Trust	TCT	17 11/16	797,200	$14,100,475
Tanger Factory Outlet Stores	SKT	25 3/4	417,100	$10,740,325
Consolidated-Tomoka Land	CTO	12 5/8	362,729	$4,579,454

TIGER—JAPANESE BANKS

TIGER

Tiger Management Corporation

101 Park Avenue, New York, N.Y. 10178 • (212) 984-2500

To: Tigers
From: Tim Schilt
Date: August 21, 1995
Re: The Japanese Banks

This report provides statistical data on the Japanese banks that we are short, as well as comments on the following important issues involved in these investments. This piece is an updated version of similar reports I wrote in August 1993 and November 1994.

Market Capitalization

The twenty-one major banks have an aggregate market capitalization of $610 billion, and have an 18.3% weighting in the Tokyo Stock Exchange First Section Index. There continues to be an anomaly at work here, as the Japanese banks have the largest market capitalizations and lowest measures of profitability of any banks in the world.

To appreciate the premiums being placed on Japanese banks, consider the following comparisons between the 1994 results of Japan's best bank, Mitsubishi Bank, and Citicorp:

	Mitsubishi Bank	Citicorp
Assets	$469 bvn	$251bvn
Return on Average Earnings Assets	1.1%	4.2%
Pre-Tax--Pre-Reserve Earnings	$2.3 byn	$6.5 byn
Shareholders' Equity	$18.8 byn	$17.7 byn
Market Capitalization	$62.9 byn	$33.1 byn
Market Capitalization/Pre-Tax--Pre-Reserve Earnings	27.3x	5.1x

Reported EPS-Core EPS

The banks have historically distorted their earnings via non-operating items. The difference between the reported and my own core EPS figures tries to get to the issue of the basic level of profitability generated from the banking business in any given year. In the years from 3/89 - 3/92 the core EPS figures on the attached sheets have two non-operating items deducted from them: gains on sale of shares and extraordinary profits; and three non-operating items added to them: losses on sale of shares, share revaluation losses, and extraordinary losses.

Two additional adjustments have been made in the 3/93–3/95 years as credit-related expenses have mounted. The estimated cost of funding the bad debt has been added back to pre-tax earnings, and credit provisioning expenses have been brought down to .20% of loans. In the case of the long-term credit banks, an adjustment for the estimated interest cost savings from the maturation of high-cost debt starting in September of 1995 has also been made.

The 3/95 results of Mitsubishi Bank are illustrated to show how the adjustment process works.

Reported 3/95 Pre-Tax Earnings - ¥43.8 billion
Unusual items within this figure:
Positive --
    Net gains on sale of stock and extraordinaries ¥198.1 billion

Negative --

Estimated funding cost of bad debt	¥27.1 billion
Credit costs (1.14%) of loans)	¥349.5 billion

Core 3/95 Pre-Tax Earnings - ¥161.2 billion
Adjustments to get to this figure:
Positive --

Estimated funding cost of bad debt	¥27.1
Credit costs at .20% of loans, not 1.14%	¥288.4
	¥315.5 billion

Negative --

Net gains on sale of stock and extraordinaries	¥198.1 billion
Total	¥117.4 billion

Normalizing credit costs at only .20% of loans may significantly overstate the banks' current core earnings levels. I used this figure to show assumptions under an optimistic framework. Credit provisioning expenses at the average U.S. bank last year ran at .40%. This occurred at a time when the ratio of non-performing assets to loans was at its lowest level in at least six years. The following table illustrates the difference in core EPS figures and subsequent P/E's with credit costs figured at .20% and then .40% of loans.

	Core EPS with Credit Costs as a % of Loans at:	
	.20% - P/E	.40% - P/E
City Banks		
Dai-Ichi Kangyo	¥17.78 - 98x	¥8.20 - 213x
Fuji	29.82 - 72	20.40 - 106
Mitsubishi Bank	25.18 - 84	15.63 - 138
Sakura	7.90 - 134	(3.42)
Sanwa	29.34 - 69	19.13 - 106
Sumitomo Bank	16.65 - 112	7.13 - 261
Tokai	14.30 - 75	12.90 - 83
Long-Term Credit Banks		
Industrial Bank of Japan	26.58 - 107	17.77 - 160
LTCB	8.11 - 112	(7.36)
Nippon Credit	3.03 - 140	(4.89)
Trust Banks		
Chuo Trust	43.20 - 31	20.01 - 67
Mitsubishi Trust	43.60 - 37	35.19 - 46
Mitsui Trust	16.35 - 65	6.36 - 168
Sumitomo Trust	43.20 - 34	34.69 - 42
Yasuda Trust	24.63 - 27	17.78 - 37

Core earnings for the City and Long-Term Credit Banks declined last year for the following reasons:

1. Return on average earnings assets declined, while total assets shrank modestly and general and administrative expenses were unchanged. Margins contracted because loan rates fell more rapidly than deposit and funding costs. Furthermore, the banks' practice of taking profits on long-term shareholdings to offset credit-related expenses, and then subsequently repurchasing about 80% of the former holdings is coming back to haunt them. In aggregate, the cost basis of financing their huge stock holdings increased by 12%.

2. Net gains on the sale of bonds declined 58% from an historically high level in fiscal 1993. Last year's figure is still way above trend.

The trust banks, on the other hand, registered continued improvement in core profitability last year, largely because fee income in the loan trust account side improved. Funding costs for the loan trust product declined in a falling short-term interest rate environment. As loan trust rates are reset only twice a year, the time lag contributed to a widening in spreads. Of course, the opposite will occur in a rising short-rate environment.

Looking ahead, continued huge credit-related costs will keep reported results at very low levels for all three classifications of banks for many years. From a core earnings standpoint, it is difficult to envision any meaningful improvement in net interest income for the City and Long-Term Credit Banks in an environment of modestly eroding assets and extremely competitive loan pricing. A major swing factor in core earnings will continue to be net gains on sale of bonds, which is impossible to predict. However, even when bond profits equaled an historically high 10% of net interest income, as was the case in fiscal 1993, the City and Long-Term Credit Banks still sold at huge multiples of core earnings.

The multiples of core earnings for the Trust Banks look more reasonable because of the aforementioned improvement in trust fee income in the loan trust account. However, loan trust assets are declining at a 6% annualized rate as their pricing terms have become less attractive. Fiscal 1994 probably represented peak profitability for this product, although predicting future profit levels is extremely difficult.

Return on Average Earning Assets

The following table shows the five-year trend of this basic measure of bank profitability (net interest income on the loan and investment portfolio before bad debt provisioning/average loans and investments) for the twenty-one major banks.

Return on Average Earning Assets

March 1991 yr.	March 1992 yr.	March 1993 yr.	March 1994 yr.	March 1995 yr.
.57%	.82%	.95%	.92%	.90%

At .90% last year, the margin was only 21% of that of Citicorp's, which in turn is about average for American banks. Returns for Japanese banks are very low by world standards for four basic reasons:

1. Higher yielding consumer loans account for a low proportion of total loans by world standards, a factor unlikely to change to any meaningful extent.

2. Competition for commercial loans is intense and spreads are very tight.

3. There is an inherent funding mismatch involved in maintaining a huge, low-yielding common stock portfolio.

4. Finally, and most importantly, banks are simply more concerned with absolute size and relative market share than in return on investment.

When Tiger first got involved with the banks many years ago, the major risk that we perceived was that loan pricing would improve in response to the deteriorating trend in credit quality. Aside from an unwillingness to grow their domestic loan portfolio, we find little evidence that banks have learned a lesson from their bad-debt-related problems, and will emerge as more profitable institutions. While most credit departments have gone back and scored loans from a perceived risk standpoint, the next logical step, namely repricing based on risk, has not taken place. If anything, there continues to be too much capital chasing too few loans, and there is no evidence that a structural improvement in spreads is taking place. In interview after interview with bank managements, the stock answer as to why credit continues to be available at such narrow spreads is pretty much the same -- "If we don't make the loan at this rate, there are any number of other banks that will."

Stated Book Value P/S - Adjusted Book Value P/S

The adjusted book value per share includes 45% of the unrealized gain on the securities portfolio. A figure of 45% is counted in tier II capital under BIS standards, and is used because total corporate taxes in Japan average around 55%. The following table traces aggregate unrealized gains on securities as a percentage of the loan portfolio for the twenty-one major banks from the March 1989 fiscal year onward. It graphically demonstrates how the market's decline, in combination with a continual averaging up of cost bases as stocks are sold at a profit and then repurchased, has decimated what was once, in essence, an incredible loan loss reserve.

Unrealized Gains on Securities/Total Loans

March '89yr.	March '90yr.	March '91yr.	March '92yr.	March '93yr.	March '94yr.	March '95yr.
18.5%	13.0%	9.9%	4.8%	5.0%	5.8%	2.6%

Non-Performing Loans

The twenty-one major banks reported aggregate non-performing loans (NPL) of ¥12.6 trillion as of March 1994, or 3.6% of total loans. Importantly, the banks disclosed non-performing loans include just two categories. The first is loans to either bankrupt companies or firms who are no longer permitted by the MOF to deal with banks. The second is loans where there has been no payment of interest and principal for over six months.

Excluded from the NPL category are loans to the housing loan companies where at least ¥5 trillion is in serious arrears. Also excluded are the restructured loans, where companies are being supported by reduced interest rate and principal payment terms.

Finally, loans that have been sold to the Co-operative Credit Purchasing Company (CCPC), the major avenue by which banks are taking bad-debt-related charge-offs, are no longer included in NPL's, a questionable practice, in my opinion. Since its inception in March of 1993 through July of this year, the banks have sold ¥8.8 trillion face amount in loans to the CCPC for ¥3.9 trillion, a 56% aggregate charge-off level. The banks provide the financing for the CCPC to purchase the loans from them, and then, believe it or not, start accruing interest and paying taxes on this interest as if the loans are current at the contractual rate.

The reasons why I question the validity of removing loans sold to the CCPC from the NPL category are twofold. Firstly, the ultimate charge-off to the bank is determined when the loan (in virtually all cases a real estate property) is actually sold by the CCPC, and, secondly, the CCPC has disposed of only ¥204 billion (5.2%) of the properties to date, a telling reflection that bid and asked prices are still way apart. The ultimate clearing value for these properties, which are the "best" of the banks NPL's, will not be known for a while, and is undoubtedly lower than the CCPC's purchase price.

While reported NPL's declined by ¥1 trillion last year and the loan loss reserve increased from ¥4.5 trillion to ¥5.5 trillion, total charge-off and reserving costs of ¥4.9 trillion indicate that loans are still going bad at an alarming rate. Brian Waterhouse, James Capel's outstanding Japanese bank analyst, estimates that the twenty-one major banks have ¥45 trillion in NPL's, a staggering 12.9% of their loan books. Brian's figures are on the high end of estimates. My estimate of ¥30.5 trillion (8.8% of loans) is more toward the lower end. Either figure is huge when measured against total shareholders' equity of ¥21.4 trillion, loan loss reserves of ¥5.5 trillion, and unrealized securities gains of ¥9.0 trillion, a total of ¥35.9 trillion.

I believe the banks will continue to use virtually all of their core earnings for quite some time to reserve against and charge-off NPL's. Line item (9) on the attached individual bank sheets is an attempt to show just how long that may take. The assumptions behind the indicated number of years for each bank are as follows:

1. Reserves, which in aggregate account for only 1.6% of total loans, will not be drawn down.

2. Fifty percent of the estimated NPL's will be charged off, a conservative assumption given the experience to date of the CCPC.

3. All of the banks' pre-tax, pre-reserve earnings (¥2.6 trillion last year) will be devoted to credit-related expenses. This, again, is a conservative assumption in that the banks are unlikely to leave no earnings to cover dividend payments.

Under these assumptions, and using Brian's ¥45 trillion in estimated NPL's, it would take the banks in aggregate 8.7 years to clear their books. Using my estimate of ¥30.5 trillion in NPL's works out to 5.9 years. Both figures are way beyond analyst consensus estimates of only another two to three years of heavy credit-related expenses.

Conclusion

If the banks are so mismanaged, have such low margins, are saddled with such enormous credit quality problems, and sell at such huge multiples, why then haven't their share prices collapsed? Bank share prices did not decline as much as the market did in the January-June period, and have surged in the recent six week rally.

I don't know the answer to that question but suspect it has to do with their huge weighting in the market, and a largely foreign-held view that the government is going to "bail out" the banking system and that will be great news for bank stocks. Eventually, taxpayers' money will have to be used to help the depositor-owned agricultural cooperatives, who have lent so heavily to the housing loan companies. However, the only relief the shareholder-owned banks will receive, in my opinion, is the ability to take pre-tax charge-offs against their housing loan commitments.

The Japanese banks have been a frustrating investment experience for Tiger. They continue to offer huge profit potential, and I am convinced that patience will eventually win out for us.

Appendix IV

TIGER FUNDS
EXPOSURE REPORT

(EXPRESSED AS % OF CAPITAL;

COMPOSITE OF ALL FUNDS)

AS OF DECEMBER 31, 1999

AGGREGATE EQUITY EXPOSURE

LONG	SHORT	NET		NET		GROSS LEVERAGE		GROSS LEVERAGE	
12/13/1999		12/31/1999	09/30/1999	LAST 12 MONTHS		12/31/1999	09/30/1999	LAST 12 MONTHS	
				MINIMUM	MAXIMUM			MINIMUM	MAXIMUM
88%	47%	41%	35%	60%	21%	135%	141%	281%	135%

EQUITY EXPOSURE BY GEOGRAPHIC SECTOR

REGION	LONG	SHORT	NET		GROSS LEVERAGE	
	12/31/1999		12/31/1999	09/30/1999	12/31/1999	09/30/1999
United States	60%	31%	29%	33%	91%	85%
Europe	15%	8%	7%	3%	23%	29%
Asia	10%	9%	2%	–6%	19%	22%
Other	3%	0%	3%	5%	3%	5%
TOTAL	88%	47%	41%	35%	135%	141%

TOP TEN LONG EQUITY HOLDINGS
LISTED ALPHABETICALLY (DOES NOT INCLUDE PUMA AND OCELOT HEDGE PORTFOLIOS)

Bear Stearns Co.
Bowater Inc.
Columbia/HCA Healthcare Group
GTECH Holdings Corporation

National Westminster Bank
Royal Bank of Scotland
Samsung Electronics

San Paolo IMI
Sealed Air Corp.
US Airways Group, Inc.

EQUITY EXPOSURE BY INDUSTRY SECTOR

REGION	LONG	SHORT	NET		GROSS LEVERAGE	
	12/31/1999		12/31/1999	09/30/1999	12/31/1999	09/30/1999
Automotive	6%	0%	5%	4%	6%	6%
Commodities	3%	1%	2%	1%	5%	6%
Consumer Goods	3%	3%	0%	5%	5%	8%
Energy	0%	0%	0%	0%	0%	0%
Financials	24%	2%	23%	21%	26%	29%
Healthcare	7%	4%	3%	−1%	12%	9%
Industrials	11%	1%	10%	10%	12%	14%
Non allocated	0%	1%	−1%	−2%	1%	2%
Technology	9%	2%	7%	4%	12%	16%
Transportation	12%	2%	10%	9%	14%	13%
Telecom/Media	10%	3%	6%	4%	13%	17%
Hedging Positions*	3%	27%	−24%	−20%	30%	23%
TOTAL	88%	47%	41%	35%	135%	141%

Tiger Management Leverage
January 1, 1999 - December 31, 1999

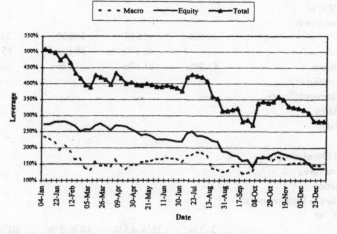

Notes:
1. Equity exposure includes futures and hedge-portfolio exposure.
2. Fixed Income exposure is expressed as 10-year equivalent exposure.
3. Foreign Exchange exposure nets cross-currency exposure.
4. Commodity exposure is expresed as spot-equivalent market value.
5. Values may not add due to rounding.
6. Data based on capital as of month-end and does not include pending contributions or withdrawals.
*Includes hedge-related tracking, cost of carry and other L.P. investments

JAMES ROGERS'S
INVESTMENT WORKSHEET

Redman Industries, Inc. (RE-NYSE)

(APRIL 1; 12/31 FOR '73 '74) ($000s)	4/1968	1969	1970	1971
Sales	74798	109814	117352	107065
Depreciation	1017	1075	1083	946
Operating Income				
Operating Margin				
Other Income				
Other Expenses				
Pretax Income	3353	10079	11536	8369
Pretax Margin	4.5%	9.2%	9.8%	7.8%
Taxes	1606	5082	5500	3911
Tax Rate	47.9%	50.4%	47.7%	46.7%
Earnings After Tax	1747	4997	6036	4458
Equity	—	—	—	—
Minority Interest	—	—	—	—
Net Income	1747	4997	6036	4458
Earnings Per Share	0.25	0.71	0.80	0.59
Dividend	—	—	—	—
Outstanding Shares				
Book Value Per Share				
Equity	10364	15546	29005	33544
Net/Equity, 1st		48.2%	38.8%	15.4%
Debt/Equity Ratio	43.8%	21.1%	11.7%	10.8%
Pension Arrears/Equity	—	—	—	—
Lease Commitments/Equity	—	—	—	—
Receivables/Sales				
Inventories/Sales				
Advertising				
Research and Development				
Capital Expenditures				
C-E/Depreciation				
C-E/Gross Plant & Equipment, 1st				
C-E/Net P&E, 1st				
Range	3–3¾	28⅝–15¾	18½–5⅛	30⅞–12¾
Backlog				
Backlog/Sales				
Number of Stores				
Sales/Store				

1972	4/1973	12/1973	12/1974	3 MOS. 4/1975	1976
159502	243806	276255	173249	18786	114288
1072	1683	1562	1742	—	1449
	23344	22804	3441	(2941)	(1045)
	9.6%	8.3%	2.0%	—	—
	—	—	—	—	—
	435	2262	4014	787	2122
14246	22909	20542	(573)	(3728)	(3167)
8.9%	9.4%	7.4%	—	—	—
6532	10752	9731	(230)	0	0
45.9%	46.9%	47.4%	—	—	—
7714	12157	10811	(343)	(3728)	(3167)
—	—	—	—	—	—
—	—	—	—	—	—
7714	12157	10811	(343)	(3728)	(3167)
0.99	1.54	1.37	(.04)	(.47)	(.36)
—	—	—	—	—	—
					9052
					1.01
39940	50797	34906	10161		9158
23.0%	30.4%	15.5%	—	—	—
13.5%	10.6%	85.1%	195.1%	—	237.2%
—	—	—	—	—	—
—	—	—	—	—	—
					9.2%
					8.1%
					531
					36.6
					—
37¾–20¼		23¼–3½	7⅛–1½		4½–1⅜

Redman Industries, Inc. (RE-NYSE) (continued)

(APRIL 1; 12/31 FOR '73 '74) ($000s)	1977	1978	1979	1980	1981
Sales	132835	183950	237794	279375	241879
Depreciation	1388	1385	3042	2159	2616
Operating Income	(874)	9593	17198	22001	8754
Operating Margin	—	5.2%	7.2%	7.9%	3.6%
Other Income	—	—	627	2363	4786
Other Expenses	1475	1291	800	739%	775
Pretax Income	(2349)	8302	17025	23625	12765
Pretax Margin	—	4.5%	7.2%	8.5%	5.3%
Taxes	0	3985	7683	11275	5570
Tax Rate	—	48.0%	45.1%	47.7	43.6%
Earnings After Tax	(2349)	4317	9342	12350	7195
Equity	—	—	—	—	—
Minority Interest	—	—	—	—	—
Net Income	(2349)	4317	9342	12350	7195
Earnings Per Share	(.26)	0.47	1.0	1.3	0.76
Dividend	—	—	0.06	0.1	0.20
Outstanding Shares	9115	9138	9196	9295	9511
Book Value Per Share	1.55	2.46	3.85	4.80	5.49
Equity	14149	22488	35369	44631	52823
Net/Equity, 1st	—	30.5%	41.5%	34.9%	16.1%
Debt/Equity Ratio	127.0%	68.7%	21.7%	16.2%	15.3%
Pension Arrears/Equity	—	—	—	—	—
Lease Commitments/Equity	16.5%	8.4%	15.1%	10.0%	9.3%
Receivables/Sales	8.1%	8.4%	6.9%	6.3%	7.8%
Inventories/Sales	7.9%	7.2%	5.3%	5.3%	5.1%
Advertising					
Research and Development					
Capital Expenditures	546	1262	1517	5631	7512
C-E/Depreciation	39.3%	91.1%	49.9%	260.8%	287.2%
C-E/Gross Plant & Equipment, 1st	2.0%	4.9%	4.0%	15.2%	17.6%
C-E/Net P&E, 1st	2.8%	7.2%	5.9%	24.0%	27.9%
Range	5¾–2½	4⅞–2⅜	7⅝–3½	9⅜–4⅛	11¾–6⅛
Backlog					4900
Backlog/Sales					6.2%
Number of Stores					
Sales/Store					

1982	1983	1984	1985	1986	1987
248735	262782	345391	339283	341531	372727
3127	3602	3642	3799	3886	3904
7286	5488	10731	8351	6435	7124
2.9%	2.1%	3.1%	2.5%	1.9%	1.9%
6327	4432	5048	3162	4390	4077
1042	3152	2751	2387	2124	2443
12571	6768	13028	9126	8701	8758
5.1%	2.6%	3.8%	2.7%	2.5%	2.4%
5364	(749)	5434	4075	3959	3937
42.7%	—	41.7%	44.7%	45.5%	45.0%
7207	7517	7594	5051	4742	4821
—	—	—	—	—	—
—	—	—	—	—	—
7207	7517	7594	5051	4742	4821
0.74	0.77	0.78	0.52	.49	.49
0.30	0.30	0.30	0.30	.31	.32
9737	9743	9752	9755	9755	9755
5.86	6.32	6.81	7.05	7.22	7.39
57027	61735	66541	68724	70443	72142
13.6%	13.2%	12.3%	7.6%	6.9%	6.8%
24.3%	20.7%	14.6%	16.5%	13.4%	12.5%
—	—	—	(7.4)	(7.8)	(9.3%)
6.4%	3.9%	2.5%	3.9%	2.7%	2.2%
6.6%	8.9%	7.8%	8.0%	8.4%	8.6%
4.9%	7.3%	7.2%	5.7%	9.0%	8.0%
10051	4234	7652	3935	5346	6361
321.4%	120.9%	210.1%	103.6%	137.6%	162.9%
22.4%	7.8%	13.9%	6.4%	8.5%	9.7%
37.1%	12.8%	23.1%	10.6%	14.6%	17.0%
14¾–9	25½–11	27½–11½	12⅜–8	12⅝–7	11⅛–6⅞
9600	20000	18300	11100	13200	11600
3.9%	7.6%	5.3%	3.3%	3.9%	3.1%

Redman Industries, Inc.

Period	Sales	Pre-Tax	Margin	Taxes	T.R.
6-76	38366	620	1.6%	298	48.1%
9-76	36435	(419)	—	(201)	—
12-76	29721	(394)	—	(97)	—
3-77	28313	(2157)	—	—	—
6-77	42037	1651	3.9%	792	50.0%
9-77	46338	2249	4.9%	1080	48.0%
12-77	47229	2375	5.0%	1140	48.0%
3-78	48346	2027	4.2%	973	48.0%
6-78	60908	3980	6.5%	1910	48.0%
9-78	61557	4201	6.8%	2017	48.0%
12-78	58710	4662	7.7%	1852	39.7%
3-79	56619	4182	7.4%	1904	45.5%
6-79	72504	6343	8.7%	2918	46.0%
9-79	73868	7148	9.7%	3288	46.0%
12-79	70070	5955	8.5%	2739	46.0%
3-80	62933	4179	6.6%	2330	55.8%
6-80	54752	2003	3.7%	952	47.5%
6-80	61160	3099	5.1%	1489	48.0%
12-80	64669	4242	6.6%	1858	43.8%
3-81	61298	3421	5.6%	1271	37.2%
6-81	70322	5565	7.9%	2244	40.3%
9-81	67710	3341	4.9%	1432	42.9%
12-81	52879	(112)	—	(29)	—
3-82	57824	3777	6.5%	1717	45.5%
6-82	66326	2459	3.7%	1032	42.0%
9-82	64930	1747	2.7%	740	42.4%
12-82	59306	1312	2.2%	561	42.8%
3-83	72220	1250	1.7%	361	28.9%
6-83	89050	5239	5.9%	2237	42.7%
9-83	94562	4286	4.5%	1834	42.8%
12-83	82128	3652	4.4%	1576	43.2%
3-84	79651	(149)	—	(213)	—
6-84	98120	4073	4.2%	1820	44.7%
9-84	92159	4057	4.4%	1798	44.2%
12-84	75628	686	0.9%	310	45.2%
3-85	73376	310	0.4%	147	46.9%
6-85	90965	4155	4.6%	1859	44.7%
9-85	89919	4256	4.7%	1901	44.7%
12-85	85261	1139	1.3%	513	45.0%
3-86	75386	(849)	—	(314)	—
6-86	94273	1184	1.3%	547	46.2%
9-86	95776	3282	3.4%	1497	45.6%
12-86	94066	2456	2.6%	1155	47.0%
3-87	88672	1836	2.1%	738	40.2%
6-87	99539	3526	3.5%	1409	40.0%

EARNINGS	INTEREST	EQUITY	NET	E.P.S.
322	—	—	322	.04
(217)	—	—	(217)	(.02)
(297)	—	—	(297)	(.08)
(2157)	—	—	(2157)	(.24)
859	—	—	859	.09
1169	—	—	1169	.13
1235	—	—	1235	.13
1054	—	—	1054	.12
2070	—	—	2070	.23
2184	—	—	2184	.23
2810	—	—	2810	.30
2278	—	—	2278	.24
3425	—	—	3425	.37
3860	—	—	3860	.41
3216	—	—	3216	.34
1849	—	—	1849	.20
1044	—	—	1051	.11
1603	—	—	1610	.17
2376	—	—	2384	.25
2172	—	—	2150	.23
3321	—	—	3321	.34
1909	—	—	1909	.20
(83)	—	—	(83)	(.01)
2060	—	—	2060	.21
1427	—	—	1427	.15
1007	—	—	1007	.11
751	—	—	751	.08
889	—	—	889	.09
3002	—	—	3002	.31
2452	—	—	2452	.25
2076	—	—	2076	.21
64	—	—	64	.01
2253	—	—	2253	.23
2259	—	—	2259	.23
376	—	—	376	.04
163	—	—	163	.02
2296	—	—	2296	.24
2355	—	—	2355	.24
626	—	—	626	.06
(535)	—	—	(535)	(.05)
637	—	—	637	.07
1785	—	—	1785	.18
1301	—	—	1301	.13
1098	—	—	1098	.11
2117	—	—	2117	.22

Redman Industries, Inc.
Division Sheet

(APRIL 2) (000S)	1977	1978	1979	1980	1981
Manufactured Housing					
Sales	89442	124315	170690	209737	170673
Operating Income	(1833)	5351	13064	16067	7424
Margin	—	4.7%	7.7%	7.7%	4.3%
Building Products					
Sales	43393	59635	66354	68631	63605
Operating Income	2459	4787	5955	6720	2740
Margin	5.7%	8.0%	9.0%	9.8%	4.3%
Mobile Home Parks					
Sales			750		
Operating Income			(199)		
Margin			—		

Redman Industries, Inc.

		BUYS		
DATE	NAME	POSITION	QUANTITY	PRICE
5/31/83	Weatherford, William	D	1000	23.50

Redman Industries Inc.

DEBTS MATURE IN:	1979	1980	1981	1982	1983	1984
As of 4/78	1401	3375	5190	2927	3030	
As of 4/79		155	149	108	114	121
As of 4/80			200	200	200	200
As of 4/03/81				350	350	350
As of 4/02/82					523	925
As of 4/01/83						1010
As of 3/30/84						1800
As of 3/29/85						
As of 3/28/86						
As of 4/3/87						

1982	1983	1984	1985	1986	1987
183502	178845	234237	233516	239689	271542
9183	3262	6672	5628	5733	9872
5.0%	1.8%	2.8%	2.4%	2.4%	3.6%
65233	83937	111154	105767	101842	10185
(156)	4411	5718	4518	3189	(127)
—	5.3%	5.1%	4.36%	3.1%	—

		SELLS		
DATE	NAME	POSITION	QUANTITY	PRICE
12/31/82	Redman, James	CB	1100	20.5
1/7/83	Redman, James	CB	28,900	20.5
2/3/83	Redman, James	CB	50,000	20
	Friedling, Harry	O,D	48,370	20.38

1985	1986	1987	1988	1989	1990	1991	1992
200							
350	350						
899	921	710					
991	1023	822	863				
1400	1219	1040	993				
1359	1301	1076	1017	942			
		1911	855	858	793	801	
			858	975	793	801	1236

BOTSWANA
STOCK EXCHANGE INDEX

1989–1999 (U.S. Dollars)

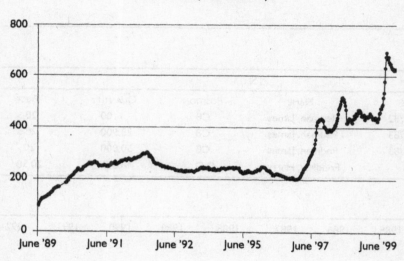

Source: Stockbrokers Botswana

SOROS'S IMPERIAL CIRCLE

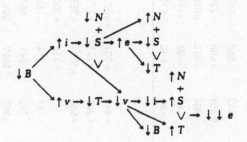

e nominal exchange rate (number of foreign currency units for one
   domestic currency unit; ↑e = strengthening)

i nominal interest rate

p domestic versus foreign price level (↑p = increase in domestic
   prices faster than in foreign prices and vice versa)

v level of economic activity

N nonspeculative capital flow ⎫ ↑ = increased outflow
S speculative capital flow   ⎭ ↓ = increased inflow
T trade balance   ⎫ ↑ = surplus
B government budget   ⎭ ↓ = deficit

Appendix VIII

QUANTUM FUND

($ millions) 1985

	Aug. 16	Sept. 6	Sept. 27	Oct. 18	Nov. 8	Nov. 22	Dec. 6
Currency Exposure							
$U.S.*	-73	-182	-289	-433	-592	-567	-569
D-Marks	+467	+491	+550	+680	+654	+668	+729
Yen	+244	+308	+458	+546	+806	+827	+826
£	+9	+10	-44	-72	-86	-87	-119
Other	+50	+45	+16	+34	+42	+40	+33
Holdings							
U.S. Stocks & Index Futures	+604	+588	+445	+253	+442	+707	+1020
Foreign Stocks	+183	+163	+142	+152	+206	+251	+271
U.S. Bonds	-113	0	-77	0	+580	+1074	+751
Japanese Bonds						+354	+300
Oil	-121	-145	-176	-37	-187	-214	-150
Size of Fund	647	627	675	721	782	841	867
Share Price ($)	4379	4238	4561	4868	5267	5669	5841

*A position in dollars indicates the amount by which exposure in the major currencies (which are as shown) exceeds the capital of the fund.

($ millions) 1986

	JAN. 10	FEB. 21	MAR. 26	APR. 4	APR. 8	MAY 20	JUL. 21	AUG. 8	SEP. 12	OCT. 31	NOV. 7
CURRENCY EXPOSURE											
$U.S.*	−1	+39	+81	+63	+153	+744	+159	+1192	+221	+1141	+1076
D-Marks	+609	+783	+1108	+1094	+816	+485	+795	+164	+905	+1280	+1334
Yen	+612	+726	+492	+474	+504	+159	+549	+141	+335	−955	−956
£	−278	−343	−389	−80	+177	−21	−25	−25	+3	+3	+7
Other	+21	+81	+63	+50	+57	+148	+202	+177	+221	+201	+201
HOLDINGS											
U.S. Stocks & Index Futures	+1663	+787	+1226	+432	+1062	+380	+53	+955	+1122	+589	+407
Foreign Stocks	+318	+426	+536	+499	+578	+573	+604	+563	+629	+460	+436
U.S. Bonds	+958	+215	+326	+652	+656	+313	−541	−503		+1073	+427
Japanese Bonds	+259						+1334	+2385	+2348	+1232	+983
Oil	−224	−55	−28	−29	−12	−75	−43	+85	+97	−127	+28
Size of Fund	942	1205	1292	1251	1290	1367	1478	1472	1484	1469	1461
Share Price ($)	6350	8122	8703	8421	8684	9202	9885	9628	9610	9296	9320

*A short position in dollars indicates the amount by which exposure in the major currencies (which are as shown) exceeds the capital of the fund.

SURVEY OF NONLINEAR THINKING IN FINANCIAL ECONOMICS

> The threatened wreckage is the greater part of economic theory.
> —John Hicks, *in 1939 on surveying the possibility*
> *of nonequilibrium in economics*

In looking at nonlinear financial economics it is informative to survey the developments that are taking place. In keeping with the information age's ability to absorb ideas democratically, do not look for financial economics ideas *only* from people with the financial economics label on their degrees or business cards. As financial economics begins to be modeled on principles that have been articulated in physics, computer networks, and ultimately biology, the list of people with insight becomes eclectic. We will see some academics, a practitioner, a computer scientist, and an editor.

Train

John Train is a cerebral, patrician, and eminently successful money manager who has also become noted for his many books on Wall Street and finance over the years.

In 1975, Train wrote *Dance of the Money Bees,* a title difficult to find today. It is the first book ever, to my knowledge, to use a biological example to describe financial phenomena. Bees forage for food, and when they return, the state of agitation of their dance before the hive indicates the status of the find. The larger the agitation the better the

From Christopher T. May, *Nonlinear Pricing: Theory & Applications*, New York: John Wiley, 1999.

find. Train used this phenomenon as an analogy to describe money managers when they are excited by a stock. Of course, fellow money managers and investors follow—they swarm like the hive. It is a wholly accurate, if unflattering, portrayal of how the real world works. Of course, it is now called swarm theory and modeled in computers.

Train's insight was more prescient than even he could have imagined. The same year *Dance of the Money Bees* was published, John Holland at the University of Michigan was siring genetic algorithm, the mathematical technique and formalism that mimics biological adaptation and which would in time give rigor to Train's intuition. Train effectively preceded the entire field of financial economics by over 20 years in using biology as a paradigm.

Train, in his investing style, is a no-nonsense sort that does not care for academic theory, derivatives, or exotica. In writing *Dance of the Money Bees,* one of the most conservative men in investing has penciled a sketch that many others, including myself, are trying to complete in color and with technologically appropriate terms. It will be interesting to note Train's reaction to the maturation of his thought. It may resemble Bohr's when he sired quantum mechanics. Bohr said, "Anyone who is not shocked by it has not understood it." The conclusion I would like to draw is that even if Train's peers do not explicitly embrace nonlinear pricing because they find the terminology offputting, implicitly they do because nonlinearity describes the state of the world that embraces them every trading day of the year.

Appendix X

Insider Information on the Investment King

John Train

Quiet, retiring Abigail Johnson, now 33 years old, should become one of the most powerful—and perhaps controversial—people in America. She is the granddaughter of Edward C. ("Ed") Johnson Jr., the founder of the Fidelity Fund management group, and the heir and eventual successor of Edward C. ("Ned") Johnson III, who controls it today. That means she stands to inherit control over $400 billion of other people's money, not to speak of her father's personal $4 billion. By the time Abby, now an officer of the firm, comes into her own, Fidelity may have a trillion dollars under management.

Fidelity is already the AT&T of the mutual-fund business. In two generations it has attained power over more portfolio assets—and thus influence over many companies—than have been gathered since the beginning of time in most countries. (As we learned last week, Fidelity owns more Chrysler than even the Kerkorian-Iacocca group!) Inevitably, as Fidelity grows ever larger, it will face more scandals, SEC problems and shareholder suits. There will be calls to provide independent trustees for each fund, to hold funds to their original objectives, and to cut fees. Abby can expect to be put on the griddle by Congress, which may want Fidelity split up. When those things happen, Diana B. Henriques's "Fidelity's World" (Scribner, 416 pages, $26)—her portrait of Fidelity's phenomenal success and sometimes troubling methods of doing business—will be the text that most people refer to.

As Fidelity has entered the junk-bond and leveraged-buyout worlds, it has become embroiled in proxy battles and other passionate disputes, to which Ms. Henriques devotes much space—more, perhaps, than some readers require. Still, it is interesting to be exposed to an area of financial activity so far from one's image of the good, gray Boston fiduciary.

"For much of its life," Ms. Henriques writes, "Fidelity has managed to glide smoothly across the cracks between its public image and its internal reality: Its image as a sagacious money-manager and its compelling determination to sell funds no matter how risky or ill-conceived they may be . . . and its frequent role as the sometimes clumsy 800-pound gorilla of an industry where rules were designed for lapdogs." In the shadows behind genial wise man Peter Lynch—the longtime head of Fidelity's spectacularly successful Magellan Fund and now a part-time executive at the firm—lurk management-shakeup tough guys Dorsey Gardner and John Kountz and super-hardball negotiator Joshua Berman. ("Go ahead and file for bankruptcy—I don't care.")

But "Fidelity's World" is less about the way the firm's managers achieve their impressive results than about the corporation and its environment, which was created by a handful of Harvard Brahmins who elaborated the theory and practice of the open-end mutual fund. They were sober fiduciaries who thought of their investors as shareholders and themselves as trustees. Something quite different is true today: The big fund groups think of themselves as consumer companies manufacturing a variety of "products" devised to satisfy every taste, including speculative whims. By having funds for every objective, Fidelity will have a few funds well forward in the performance derby in any market. This means that the sales side of the business always has alluring wares to push. But switching from one fund to another may not serve the best interests of the investor: Sitting still is in general a far more profitable strategy.

Why has Fidelity done so well? A key to success is, of course, attracting outstanding investment talent. Ed Johnson was himself an astute investor who recognized that stock-picking is an art, requiring flair. So the company is willing to take chances on young managers, often eccentrics rather than scientists. Its research department deserves credit, too. (The managers used to look down on the analysts until finally a compensation approach was devised that achieved sharing and collegiality.) The firm's public-relations department is a gigantic pipe organ that claims credit for a thousand newspaper and magazine articles a month, almost all favorable. One marketing device that has proved especially powerful is to spoon-feed a tiny fund to privileged investors. Once the fund establishes a superb record, it is opened to the general public, which is allowed to blow it up to enormous size. (This orchestration is not always made clear in fund-performance presentations—and should be.)

In two generations Fidelity has attracted 20% of the assets that the entire Swiss banking system has sucked from Europe over centuries. Even so, it has endured only a tiny fraction of the scandals and problems that have vexed the Swiss in recent decades. Ms. Henriques is tough—she tends to focus on Fidelity's problems—but in the end she is also fair. Ned Johnson will not like her book. Abby Johnson should study it intently.

FOUR GROWTH STOCKS

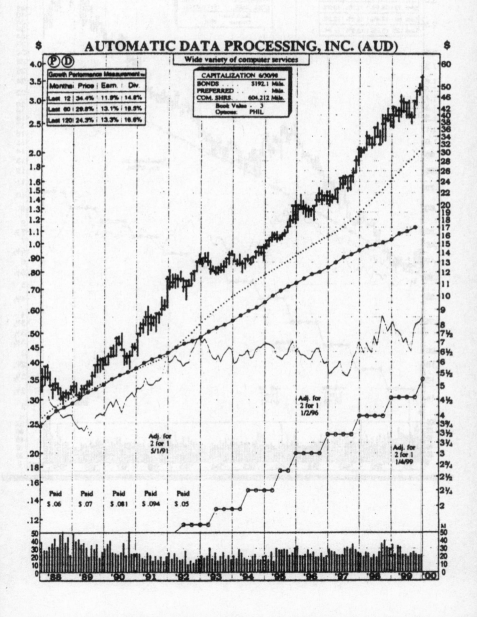

AUTOMATIC DATA PROCESSING, INC. (AUD)

Wide variety of computer services

Growth Performance Measurement

Months:	Price	Earn.	Div.
Last 12	34.4%	11.9%	14.8%
Last 60	29.8%	13.1%	19.5%
Last 120	24.3%	13.3%	16.8%

CAPITALIZATION 6/30/96
BONDS . . . . $192.1 Mils.
PREFERRED . . . - Mils.
COM. SHRS. 604.212 Mils.
Book Value - 3
Options: PHIL

Adj. for 2 for 1 1/2/96

Adj. for 2 for 1 5/1/91

Adj. for 2 for 1 1/4/99

Paid $.06   Paid $.07   Paid $.081   Paid $.094   Paid $.05

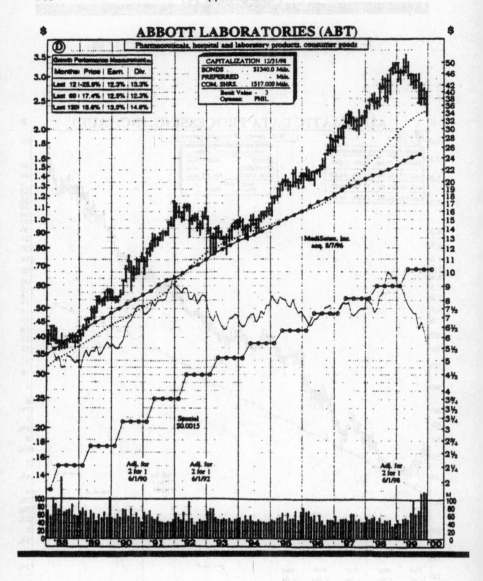

ABBOTT LABORATORIES (ABT)

Pharmaceuticals, hospital and laboratory products, consumer goods

CAPITALIZATION 12/31/98	
BONDS	$1340.0 Mils.
PREFERRED	Mils.
COM. SHRS.	1517.000 Mils.
Book Value · 3	
Options: PHIL	

Growth Performance Measurement

Months	Price	Earn.	Div.
Last 12	-25.9%	12.3%	13.3%
Last 60	17.4%	12.9%	12.3%
Last 120	18.6%	13.5%	14.6%

MediSense, Inc.
acq. 8/7/96

Special
$0.0015

Adj. for
2 for 1
6/1/90

Adj. for
2 for 1
6/1/92

Adj. for
2 for 1
6/1/98

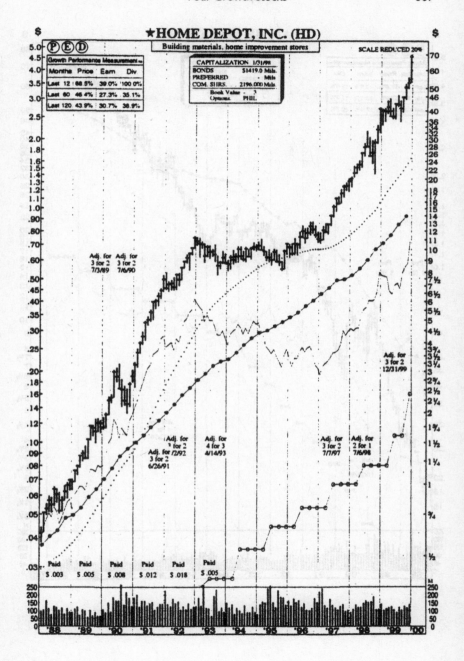

★**HOME DEPOT, INC. (HD)**

Building materials, home improvement stores

SCALE REDUCED 20%

Ⓟ Ⓔ Ⓓ

Growth Performance Measurement			
Months	Price	Earn	Div
Last 12	68.5%	39.0%	100.0%
Last 60	46.4%	27.3%	35.1%
Last 120	43.9%	30.7%	38.9%

CAPITALIZATION 1/31/98	
BONDS	$1419.0 Mils.
PREFERRED	- Mils.
COM. SHRS.	2196.000 Mils.
Book Value -	.3
Options:	PHIL.

Adj. for
3 for 2
7/3/89

Adj. for
3 for 2
7/6/90

Adj. for
3 for 2
12/31/99

Adj. for
2 for 1
7/6/98

Adj. for
3 for 2
7/7/97

Adj. for
4 for 3
4/14/93

Adj. for
2 for 1
12/92

Adj. for
3 for 2
6/26/91

Paid
$ .003

Paid
$ .005

Paid
$ .008

Paid
$ .012

Paid
$ .018

Paid
$ .005

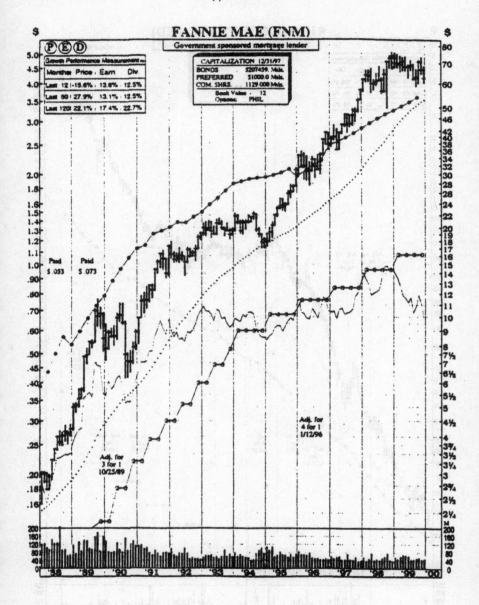

FANNIE MAE (FNM)
Government sponsored mortgage lender

MARKET RETURNS FOR THE DECADE OF THE 1980s

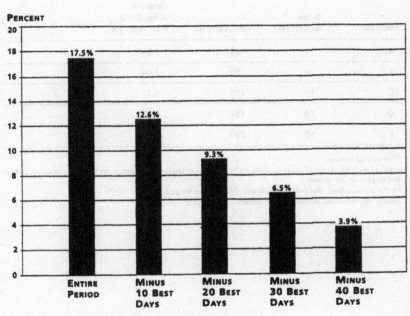

PERCENT

- 17.5% — Entire Period
- 12.6% — Minus 10 Best Days
- 9.3% — Minus 20 Best Days
- 6.5% — Minus 30 Best Days
- 3.9% — Minus 40 Best Days

Source: Reprinted with permission from U.S. Trust Corporation.

THE EFFECT OF TURNOVER

Manager	Gross Return (%)	Turnover (%)	Return* After Costs and Taxes (%)
A	10	25	7.37
B	10	50	7.06
C	10	100	6.21
D	10	150	5.55
E	10	200	4.70

*Twenty-year horizon.

Assumes that one-quarter of the gains taken at 100 percent turnover are short-term, as are half the gains at 150 percent and all gains at 200 percent.

Portfolio is liquidated after twenty years and all deferred taxes are paid.

Source: Reprinted with permission from Sanford C. Bernstein & Co., Inc.

Index